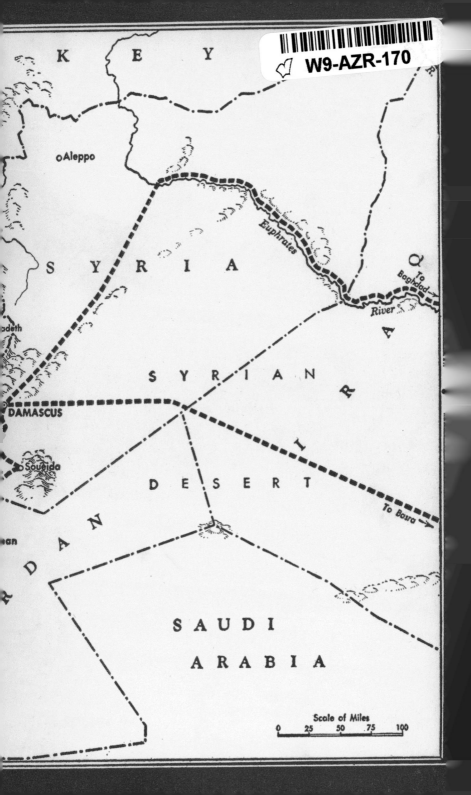

STRANGE LANDS
AND
FRIENDLY PEOPLE

Books by William O. Douglas

OF MEN AND MOUNTAINS
STRANGE LANDS AND FRIENDLY PEOPLE

WILLIAM O. DOUGLAS AND HIS SON, BILL

Strange Lands
and
Friendly People

by
William O. Douglas

HARPER & BROTHERS · PUBLISHERS
New York

Library of Congress catalog card number: 51-11901

To the memory of my mother
Julia Fisk Douglas
who once knew poverty in the
Middle East meaning of the word

CONTENTS

Foreword   xi

PART I   COMMUNISM SOUTH OF THE SOVIET BORDER   I

1. *Terror in Greece*   6
2. *Go Walking Man*   19
3. *A Picture Code*   30
4. *Azerbaijan*   38

PART II   THE TRIBES OF PERSIA   51

5. *Kurdish Nationalism*   56
6. *Once a Kurd Always a Kurd*   65
7. *Sons Are an Ornament*   72
8. *A New Deal for the Kurds*   84
9. *Independence Is Preferred*   87
10. *I Am a Lur*   95
11. *The Six Poorest of Us*   98
12. *Butcher of Luristan*   104
13. *Gun Play at Kuhdasht*   110
14. *The Bakhtiari Save the Constitution*   114
15. *A Goat Does Justice*   120
16. *An Audience at Oregon*   124
17. *Persian Hospitality*   130
18. *A Goatherd Sparks a Revolt*   133
19. *"By My Mother's Milk"*   138
20. *"Trust in God, but Tie Your Camel"*   142
21. *The Ghashghais on Horseback*   145
22. *The Ghashghais on the Move*   151
23. *It's an Old Ghashghai Custom*   154

Contents

PART III   RUMBLINGS IN THE ARAB WORLD   161

24. It's a Small World   166
25. The Poisonous Bite of the Goat   179
26. Cedars of Lebanon   185
27. The Agrarian Problem   188
28. Zayim   193
29. Jebel el Druze   196
30. Kemal Djumblatt   207
31. Siblene—the Magic of Ownership   212

PART IV   CROSS, STAR, AND CRESCENT   217

32. Hattin   219
33. Josef and Fouda   223
34. "Thy Faith Hath Made Thee Whole"   230
35. Moslem Women   236
36. Sukhneh's Arab Refugees   247
37. The Eternal City   256

PART V   ISRAEL   269

38. Into Israel from the East   269
39. Israel Experiments   273
40. "From Dan even to Beersheba"   280

PART VI   INDIA   291

41. A Girl and a Basket   291
42. India and Asia   294
43. Nehru's Welfare State   299
44. Jai Hind   310

PART VII   IN SUMMARY   315

INDEX   329

ILLUSTRATIONS

Feeling that readers of this volume would be particularly interested in the Iranian (Persian) scene, the publishers are including a special section of pictures of that area (taken by the author and his friend Elon Gilbert).

Frontispiece—William O. Douglas and his son, Bill Jr.

The following photographs will be found in a group facing page 112

Ghashghai mansion and gardens, Shiraz
Old home of Ilkhan of Debukri tribe of Kurds, Bukan
Nasser Khan, head of the Ghashghais, with the author on Namdam plain
Ghashghais on fall migration, 1950
Kurdish women, Debukri tribe, washing dishes in spring, Bukan
Ghashghais on fall migration, 1950
Amar Khan Sharifi, Ilkhan of the Shakkak tribe of the Kurds
Lurs sacrificing steer in honor of arrival of the author
A typical Kurd
Ziad Khan, winner of the Ghashghai shooting contest
Bakhtiari performing a stick dance
Thrashing floor, Azerbaijan
Bakhtiari women
Morteza Gholi Khan Samsam, Ilkhan of the Bakhtiaris, Shalamzar
Persian goats eat even the blossoms of thistles

Russian border, Azerbaijan, Persia
Persian girl gathering chips for winter fuel
A street in a typical Persian village
Typical tent and family of Bakhtiari goatherd
The author and Ahmad Khan, chief of the Papi tribe of
   the Lurs
The author interviewing Lurs of the Papi tribe
Maku, Azerbaijan

FOREWORD

REVOLUTIONS ARE sweeping Asia. These revolutions, though often encouraged and directed by intellectuals, spring from the peasants. These people—illiterate, with a life expectancy at birth of less than thirty years, and with a standard of living far below anything we in America know—are on the march. This is nothing new; it is part of a historic process that Wendell Willkie faithfully portrayed a decade ago.

These revolutions are important to the future of each of us.

Asia is the great staging ground for Russian imperialistic designs. Asia holds the bulk of the world's population. Asia has the great wealth of the world. That wealth is mostly in untapped natural resources—oil, rubber, iron, manganese, and other minerals. Asia is also rich in matters spiritual. The great religions of the world originated there. They supply today powerful fighting faiths among the peoples. While they are a cohesive force that holds large areas together, they occasionally pit one people against another in bloody combat. Asia is rich in literature and art; and it is steeped in mysticism and superstition. Asia is also filled with unrealized ambitions.

I wanted to see for myself the power and strength of Asia and to understand the forces that brew its revolutions. Therefore, I made two trips to that continent—one in 1949 and one in 1950. In 1949 my son, William O. Douglas, Jr., went with me. We visited Lebanon, Syria, Iraq, and Persia. Then we returned to Damascus and went south to Trans-Jordan and into Israel from the east. We saw all of the Arab world except Saudi Arabia and Egypt. On that trip we also stopped in Greece and in Cyprus. Those stops were merely layovers, going and returning to the Middle East. But we found Communist forces very active in each of those places; and what we discovered was so germane to the problem of communism in all of Asia that our observations in those countries have been included in this book.

In 1950, accompanied by Elon Gilbert of Yakima, Washington, I traveled again through Lebanon, Syria, Iraq, and Persia; and in addition into India. Most of the time was spent in Persia and India.

There was much forward planning necessary for each of these journeys—details with which I have not burdened the book. The assembly of equipment, the obtaining of permits, the approval of the routes we wanted to follow were time-consuming. The various governments were most co-operative and gave invaluable assistance. And so it was that even though most of our travel covered the back regions of these countries, our arrival in the remotest village was often heralded several days in advance. We were generally not restricted in where we could go, in what we could see, or even in the pictures we could take. So if there are deficiencies in the reporting, the fault is not that of our hosts.

The richness of the Persian material is due largely to the co-operation and help of my friend, the late Ali Razmara who was assassinated on March 7, 1951. He was Chief of Staff when I visited Persia in 1949 and Prime Minister in 1950; and it was he who opened closed doors for me, even those along the troublesome Soviet border.

I have not undertaken an analysis of the political forces in each of these countries. An American can easily miss the forest and see only the trees if he takes on that task. My undertaking was different and more limited. I have tried to present, through the medium of personal experiences, the main stresses and strains in the area.

The characters whom I present are real, not fictitious. I have occasionally changed the locale of an event and given a character a new name to respect a confidence or protect a life. But the events and conversations and other facts are true to the best of my knowledge.

I have detailed these episodes in an endeavor to take the reader with me on these journeys, so that he may see and hear what transpired. That is a difficult undertaking. Many of the experiences were for me almost beyond the reach of words. Some were filled with laughter and gaiety; others were crowded with tragedy and sorrow. Much of the material was highly charged with emotion. There were sometimes conflicting versions, compelling me to try to find out where the truth lay. The materials were so rich that I had to make selections. My purpose was to include those episodes which portray as fairly and objectively as possible the state of mind of the people whom I met, the extent of an evil, the nature and importance of a problem in a particular region.

Both the 1949 and the 1950 trips brought the Moscow radio to a high pitch of excitement. I was charged with being the Big Devil, my son (who accompanied me in 1949) with being the Little Devil. That pleased my son. I was charged with being a spy for the American Army, with landing guns in the Persian Gulf, with laying plans for guerrilla warfare in the Middle East, with living in the tradition of the famous Lawrence of Arabia and the fabulous Major Robert T. Lincoln of more recent years. These accusations were to me very flattering. But there was one Soviet charge that cut to the quick, that hurt deep-down inside. It was the charge that I was a decrepit mountaineer!

My trips included no mountaineering in the sense in which an alpinist would use the term. A few minor peaks were scaled; there was one walking trip; and there were several pack trips. By-products of these excursions were two collections of wild flowers—one in Lebanon and one in Persia—which I have presented to the Smithsonian Institution.

The trips were unconventional. For the most part I kept out of the lanes of tourist travel. While I saw some of the sights and visited the capitals, I spent practically all my time in the mountains and villages, traveling on foot, by horseback, or by jeep and stopping to talk with most of the goatherds and peasants I met along the way. I usually carried complete camping equipment with me, put my bedroll down in or near a village at night, and sat up late discussing problems with the villagers or a local khan or kalantar. In a word, I spent most of my time with the common people of these countries, rather than with officialdom.

Different people get different impressions of happenings and events. The best illustration comes out of the Middle East on the lips of Mullah Nasr-ed-Din, the twelfth-century legendary humorist of Persia whose yarns would have delighted Mark Twain, Irving Cobb, and Will Rogers. It seems that one day Mullah and his small son were walking down the road behind their donkey. The donkey, free of any pack, wandered lazily along nibbling as he went, while Mullah and his son sweated rather profusely under the hot sun. As they passed through a village, Mullah heard a man say, "Look how foolish that old man is—walking instead of riding this hot day."

Mullah thought about the criticism and in a little while both he and his son climbed aboard the donkey. At the next village, Mullah heard a village elder say, "That old man ought to be ashamed of himself—making the donkey carry the two of them this hot day."

That criticism stung, so in a short distance Mullah dismounted, leaving his son on the donkey. At the next village he overheard a villager say, "That little boy ought to be ashamed to let his poor old father walk while he rides."

Those words also stung, so after a turn in the road, Mullah lifted his son down and mounted the donkey himself. At the next village Mullah heard a woman shout, "Look at that mean old man riding, while the poor little boy has to walk."

This is the story the Persians tell when conflicting versions of events are discussed. They say that Mullah rubbed his beard, shook his head in wonderment over the misinterpretation of everything he did, and said, "You can't please any of the people any of the time."

Since people view events with different eyes, one who writes of this region owes his audience a statement of the prejudices behind his appraisal of the people he met and conditions he witnessed. The following are mine:

The Greece I saw was buoyant, courageous, idealistic. It was releasing energy in tremendous undertakings and showed the makings of a renaissance.

The Arab world I visited—Lebanon, Syria, Trans-Jordan, and Iraq—has a placid quality which makes for great charm and creates an intimate and friendly atmosphere where one finds relaxation and a reflective, contemplative mood. One learns courtesy there.

Persia has a fascination that is difficult to describe—an appeal that is as indefinable as the plaintive music in her spoken word or the elusive quality in the Persian personality. Persia shows the West the true art of hospitality. Persians are spiritually close kin to Americans.

Israel is an exciting place. A challenging experiment in social and economic organization is going on there.

And India—well, I fell in love with India. Partly for its Himalayas whose grandeur is not of this earth. Partly for its mysticism, its spiritual strength. Partly because India of today is an ancient civilization rising from the mire of poverty, illiteracy, and feudalism by the heroic efforts of a few men and women.

My impressions of the countries visited were largely obtained through the tribesmen, farmers, goatherds, villagers, woodcutters, shopkeepers who constitute the hard central core of each of these countries. These folks are worthy world citizens. They are hospitable, generous, honest, God-fearing folks.

Those are the prejudices with which I wrote.

I owe much to many who helped me along the way: to Saul Haas for his searching criticisms that enriched the manuscript; to Edith Allen, Gladys Giese, and Mercedes Davidson for carrying the burden of the mechanics of the volume; to my son Bill and to Elon Gilbert for their observations and their help in interpreting what we saw; to Maxine K. Jackson for painstaking field work in the Cyprus study; to General Reuben E. Jenkins of the American Army for assistance on the Greek project; to Clovis McSoud of Shweykat, Dr. S. B. L. Penrose and Professor William West of Beirut, Dr. Alford Carleton of Aleppo, and Josef Debbouss and Mary E. Nix of Damascus for help on the Arab world; to Nahum Astar of Tel Aviv and Jacob Ratner of Haifa on the Israeli project; to Gerald Dooher, M. Kazemi (assigned to me by the Shah), and Kurish Shahbaz of Tehran for the interpretation of the Persian material; and to Andrew V. Corry of New Delhi and Boshe Sen of Almora for help on India. Of these Kazemi and Shahbaz deserve a special word. One of them was usually with me on the Persian trips. They were patient with my interrogations and faithful in their translations. They have the insight, objectivity, intelligence, and tact rare in interpreters.

I traveled without portfolio and without official status. What I write expresses only my own views as a private citizen.

WILLIAM O. DOUGLAS

Lostine, Oregon
June 24, 1951

PART I

Communism South of the
Soviet Border

Soviet propaganda beamed to the Middle East exploits the news of the day. It emphasizes and exaggerates the weaknesses and frailties in existing regimes. It constantly reminds the natives of their grievances. It whispers suspicions about those in power. It charges America and England with having designs on every nation in the region, with planning to make each one a subservient colony in a large imperial system. It represents the Soviets as the forces of Good in the world, America and England and all non-Communist governments as the forces of Evil. It identifies the Soviets with every minority cause, with every nationalist ambition.

Soviet propaganda does not neglect the religious prejudices of the area. It reminds the Moslem population of their religious rivalries and conflicts, which in earlier days caused much bloodshed. It was a Pope who in the twelfth century summoned the Christian world to war against the infidel. Soviet propaganda today resurrects the specter of that bloody conflict and links the Vatican with Wall Street and Anglo-American "imperialists" in a conspiracy against the Middle East.

The word-of-mouth campaign is even more insidious. The Koran has a strong flavor of Christianity: care of the weak, feeding the hungry, the giving of alms. Those who preach communism by word of mouth relate it to the Koran. When Marx and Engels wrote the Communist Manifesto in 1848, they dipped their pens in the New Testament and in the Jeffersonian philosophy to make their document popular among Europeans. Today in the Middle East the Communists use the same technique in preaching Soviet communism to those

1

of the Islamic faith. They build elaborate syllogisms to show that their creed has support in the Koran. The Koran, they point out, was written in a different age and against the background of a different economy. If the Prophet were alive today, he would be against the "imperialistic" powers and the philosophy of the few who exploit the many. The Soviet apostles point to chapter and verse of the Koran; they construe and interpret; they give sly twists to dogma and make it communistic. The Koran is susceptible to this perversion, for the idea of equality is strong in it. The Communists are clever and astute in giving the Book their interpretations; it takes a scholar of the Koran to reveal their fallacies.

The political program which the Communists advance in this region is usually straight reform. They do not explain or describe the Communist system which they have designed for the world, but purport to stand only for honesty in government, land reform, rationing of food, elimination of unemployment, education for the masses, a rising standard of living. They use democratic slogans and propose democratic programs to gain favor with the peasants. They won several European countries by pretending to be strong in the democratic faith. They hope to win the Middle East the same way. Once they assumed control of a nation, the pretense would cease and the country would be saddled with a dictatorship. Meanwhile they exploit the democratic cause and pose as the true champions of the people. The technique is not secret or mysterious. Stalin made it as plain as day in Foundations of Leninism and The Problems of Leninism. The process of taking over existing governments is called the bourgeois revolution; the process of converting that government into a Communist dictatorship is called the proletarian revolution.

This strategy shows great astuteness, for the Soviets could not win many converts in this region by preaching the tenets of communism. They can whip up discontent, create social disorder, and give impetus to revolt. But the revolutionary feeling in these lands is basically incompatible with Soviet communism.

1. These people are mostly God-fearing folk, while communism is atheistic.

2. They want civil liberties—the right to vote as they choose, a free press, and free speech. Communism merely substitutes one group of armed political censors for another.

3. The peasants of this area (and they compose the great majority

of the population) want to be rid of their landlords; they want to own their own land. The Communists merely substitute one landlord (the state) for another.

4. The people of this region are increasingly nationalistic; they want to be free of all foreign domination. Soviet communism would make them subjects in the Kremlin's colonial empire.

The people know these facts. They do not always state them as precisely as I have done. But for these reasons they have a deep-seated and an almost instinctive reaction against Soviet communism. Soviet communism is a creed that is hard to sell in this region; it has few converts; the number of rock-bottom Communists between the Mediterranean and the Pacific is certainly less than one-tenth of 1 per cent. Today they are mostly underground. They meet secretly; there are three at a meeting and a meeting lasts perhaps ten minutes —just long enough to exchange confidences, bolster up courage, and decide on the party line. Being underground, they use the whispered word to stir discontent; at night they write messages on walls and distribute pamphlets. When I was in Tehran in 1950 Henry Grady had just arrived as American Ambassador, fresh from the successful project in Greece through which the Communist guerrillas had been liquidated and the economy restored. In the mornings I would see on the outside walls of the American compound in Tehran, "Butcher of Greece."

In 1951 after a religious fanatic assassinated Ali Razmara, Persia's Prime Minister, the Tudeh Party moved more and more in the open. Shortly before that time ten Tudeh leaders had escaped from Qasr state prison. Tudeh at once grew bolder and bolder, seeking to capitalize on the confusion that followed the assassination. It helped cause a mounting feeling against Britain and against America too. Britain had an unfair oil concession which it insisted the Persian government honor. In Persian eyes America stood behind the British and apparently supported that position. Sentiment for nationalization of the oil grew and grew. The Communists joined the Nationalists in sponsoring the program; they proclaimed themselves champions of Persian interests; they played on national heartstrings; their support among the masses increased. The Persian Parliament, resentful of British and American policy and propelled by mounting public opinion, quickly nationalized the oil. Yet in all of the Majlis there was not a single Communist. Tudeh thereupon used the prestige from that victory to

make more demands. It obtained the release from prison of more of
its leaders. On May 8, 1951 it made further demands on the government: freedom for all political parties; the end of martial law; release
of political prisoners; recognition of Communist China; the ejection
of the American military mission. Its demands ended by declaring
that Persia "will not allow its children to be sacrificed for the interests
of Britain and America."

Thus do Communists in the Middle East actively align themselves
with nationalist ambitions and exploit every advantage that chance
or political management offers them.

The bulk of Soviet propaganda in the Middle East is by radio—
popular programs, geared to the prejudices and interests of the people
of this area. The Russians do excellent intelligence and furnish
through their embassies and legations a wealth of current information.
Their diplomatic staff—at least in the lower echelons—mixes with
the people in the coffee shops and at the crossroads. They know the
pulse of these nations and the character of propaganda that will have
the best effect.

Radio propaganda is effective in the Middle East as it is here or in
Europe. Arabs and Persians alike have radios. In the town of Khoy
in northwest Persia (not far from the Russian border) there are
forty thousand people and close to ten thousand radios (American
made, run on batteries). There are in fact some radios in every village
I visited; I saw them even when I was in the mountains with the
tribes. The khans and kalantars (the chiefs and lesser chiefs) own most
of them. The hours when news is broadcast are known, and people
gather around to listen. Goatherds will even come off a mountain to
join the group. If they cannot leave their flocks, they will find out
later in the day what happened. No matter how far I was from the
nearest town, whether 50 miles or 250 miles, no matter how remote
I was in the mountains of the Middle East, I always heard before night
the important news in the capitals of the world. I discovered, contrary to my preconceptions, that the peasants of this area are well
informed on world events. They know their own complaints; and
they listen with an attentive ear to those who would remedy them.

Their suspicion of Soviet communism is so great that a real program of social reform would rob the Communists for all time of any
popular following. Soviet Communists can get substantial adherents
only with a democratic program and then only if they have no political

competition. Their great political success has resulted solely from those circumstances. They won in China against a corrupt and reactionary government which had liquidated the liberal movement. Those are the conditions under which Soviet communism threatens to win countries in the Middle East and southeast Asia. It is clear that it can win political victories in this region only when it operates in a political vacuum.

As long as the political contest continues, existing governments must keep a firm hand on their army and police. Communism in action practices terror with a religious fervor.

1. Terror in Greece

IN THE summer of 1949 the Greek guerrillas were keeping Greece in turmoil. They were under Communist leadership and were well organized. The Greeks called them *andartes* or bandits.

The core of the guerrilla army was the group of irregulars the Allies had armed during the German occupation. In December, 1944, a few months after the liberation of Greece the Communist party withdrew from the Greek government and tried to seize it. From that time on it used force and terror in an effort to gain control of the country.

In 1948 and the early part of 1949 the guerrillas held pockets throughout most of Greece—a village and a ridge here; a port, a highway, and a mountain there. The dots on the army maps which marked their positions gave Greece the scars of smallpox. They covered the whole country and practically encircled Athens.

The tactics of the guerrillas were terroristic. They burned and looted villages. They tortured prisoners, mutilating them and meting out a slow death. They abducted men, women, and children and forcibly recruited them into the guerrilla army. Over a period of two years they abducted close to thirty thousand people. They quartered themselves on the villages, forcing the peasants to feed and maintain them.

These practices caused a great exodus from the hills and the outlying regions. Early in 1949 one entire village of three thousand people (men, women, and children) fled before the guerrillas. These peasants traveled for days through snow to reach Athens. Half perished on the flight. In the summer of 1949 nearly 700,000 refugees (about one-tenth of the total population of Greece) were piled up in Athens, being fed by American funds while they waited for their home areas to be freed of guerrillas.

The guerrilla groups, though widely scattered, were closely knit together by a system of communication and intelligence. Word was passed along by men on burros. The man who ran the coffee shop listened to gossip by day and shouldered a gun in guerrilla duty at night. The old lady who hung out washing in the morning laid land mines at night. Hundreds of young girls in their teens patroled highways, watched over bridges, and stood guard at outposts. These girls carried guns and wore daggers on their belts.

When one saw these people, it was difficult to realize they constituted an army whose command went back through numerous links to Moscow. They had no uniforms, no hats, no insignia. They wore peasant costumes, like any one of ten thousand villagers or farmers.

The guerrilla army was a fluctuating group. Its size ebbed and flowed as a result of casualties, depletion through desertion, new recruitments. It was close to twenty-six thousand strong in 1948. When I visited Greece in 1949 it was down to about eighteen thousand.

By then, many nests of the guerrillas had been ferreted out and liquidated. Attica and the Peloponnesus had been largely cleared. So had Thessaly. But in the north large portions of Macedonia, where Albania, Yugoslavia, and Bulgaria border Greece, were still infested, with the guerrillas armed, trained, and supplied by their Communist neighbors. Russian boats were landing equipment for them at Albanian ports. The arms and munitions which the Russians furnished were mostly of German, Italian, and Czech origin.

The proximity of Albania, Yugoslavia, and Bulgaria to Greece had other military consequences. When the guerrillas were under hot pursuit, they often melted over the border of these neighboring states and thus eluded their pursuers. If the Greek Army were to cross the border, it would be an invader, and a serious international incident might result. Hence the problem of the Greek Army was complicated. The enemy became somewhat of a ghost army, melting away when going became difficult and reappearing from across the border with renewed strength a few days later.

By the summer of 1949, Tito had eased the problem somewhat by closing the Yugoslavia border to the guerrillas. But Albania and Bulgaria remained as their base.

The conditions of Greece had improved in other ways too.

General Alexander Papagos (later to come into conflict with King Paul) had been put in charge of the Greek Army. He had rid it of inefficient officers and the contamination of political influence. When I was there his new policy was having an electric effect. The son of a prominent Greek had hired a tubercular boy to take his Army physical examination for him. The new conscript was of course rejected. But a reviewing officer detected the fraud and Papagos ordered the boy shot. That was the end of special privilege in the Army. Papagos and the American military mission, headed by General James A. Van Fleet and General Reuben E. Jenkins, whipped the Greek Army into one of the finest. Henry Grady, the American Ambassador, bolstered the political front. By the summer of 1949 the tide had turned and the end of the guerrillas was in sight.

I said that by the summer of 1949 the Greek guerrillas had been largely liquidated in southern and central Greece. That is true so far as organized and armed resistance to the central government was concerned. There were many, however, who aided the guerrillas without bearing arms. How many Communists were in this civilian group no one knows, but the number was well over 150,000. Though the Greek Army swept on to victory after victory and cornered the guerrillas in the mountains of Macedonia, a great many Communists remained behind to become whisperers of rumors and purveyors of intelligence to the guerrilla forces up north.

One incident will illustrate the method by which the Communist underground in and around Athens operated during this period.

I was invited to a dinner at the home of the then Foreign Minister, Constantin Tsaldaris. The dinner was at 9 P.M. That afternoon I went on a motor trip with Mr. and Mrs. Robert G. Miner of the American Embassy to Sounion on the southeast tip of Attica. We were due back at 8 P.M. But this was Saturday; and a series of events delayed us.

The Greeks are enthusiastic vacationists. They exploit a holiday as eagerly and thoroughly as the British. When a week end arrives they pile into trucks, buses, and carts and head for the beach or the mountains. The traffic was thick the afternoon we crossed Attica. Dozens of buses were headed for the beaches. They were packed to capacity and the people were singing plaintive Greek folk songs with beautiful harmony.

This traffic slowed us. So did the pockmarks pounded in the black asphalt highway by German trucks during the occupation. So did the pedestrians. Attica is dotted with vineyards and olive orchards. The roads were filled with farmers, donkeys, and carts coming in from the fields. Geese, ducks, and goats, unconcerned with the honking of our horn, cluttered the village streets. The lead mines at Lavrion—first started by the Romans—were spewing traffic on the highway. Thus it took us nearly two hours to drive the forty miles.

We reached the ruins of an ancient temple of Poseidon shortly before sunset. There on limestone pillars Byron and other distinguished visitors had carved their names. Far below at the foot of a sheer cliff the Mediterranean pounded on rocks and filled the ruins of the ancient temple with a roar.

A sirocco was blowing in from Africa; sand high in the heavens gave a haze to the sky. We sat at a table, brought out by a nearby innkeeper, and sipped the light resinous wine of Attica and ate canapés of rice and meat wrapped in spiced grape leaves. We talked mostly of Elijah, who, according to legend, built the temples that dot the hills of Attica. That venerable man, tiring of the sea and all sailors, put an oar over his shoulder, and started inland. Whenever he came to a place where someone asked him what the oar was, he knew there were no seafaring people in the vicinity. In celebration, he stopped and erected a temple at each such spot. That is why all the temples are on peaks.

As we talked the sun set, turning the Mediterranean from aquamarine to deep purple. Clouds that had drifted up from Africa were streaked with rose, green, and orange as the sun touched the horizon. Now in the dusk they stood like a dark hulk of land against the southern skyline.

We tried to race back to Athens but our return was even slower than our trip down. In each village the highways were crowded. The coffee shops that line every village street were packed. People strolled in the middle of the road; children played ball in our path; young folks gathered at a corner listening to a radio; at the edge of one square a peasant had struck up a lively tune on his flute while a lad danced to the music. Even though our driver was a demon at the wheel and loved to make people, goats, and ducks fly out of his way, he was slowed to a snail's pace.

As a result I arrived at the dinner at 10:30 P.M.—an hour and a half late. As I walked into the Tsaldaris' home, first Mrs. Tsaldaris and then several other women—all strangers to me—rushed forward, with tears in their eyes, embraced me, and kissed me, uttering motherly words which, though Greek, were understandable. Surprised and puzzled by this affectionate greeting, I worked my way across the room to Mrs. Henry Grady, wife of our Ambassador to Greece, and asked her to enlighten me on the meaning of my welcome, adding, "It was most pleasant; but it has never happened before in all my life."

She told me that an hour or so before dinnertime an unknown lady, who seemed to be quite hysterical, had telephoned Mrs. Tsaldaris. She spoke in Greek and her conversation was broken by sobs.

"I have bad news, Mrs. Tsaldaris."

"What is it?"

"It's about Justice Douglas."

"What's wrong?"

"He's terribly ill as a result of the accident."

"What accident?"

"He can't attend your dinner."

"What happened?"

After much sobbing the answer came, "Oh, it's just too awful to talk about." And the mysterious caller hung up.

There were no state police to make an investigation along the highways of Attica. I could not be reached by telephone. When I did not appear by 9 o'clock, 9:30, or 10, the telephone report loomed larger and larger and began to assume the stature of the truth. Official Athens was on edge and under great suspense. When I at last walked into the drawing room alive and intact, it was as if the dead had returned.

Thus did the Communist underground in Athens harass and worry officialdom. The cold war, the war of nerves, was carried even to the insignificance of my visit to Greece.

I toured the front lines of the Greek Army in the Vitsi and Grammos areas of West Macedonia. This is high, rough country— sheer granite cliffs and hills studded with pine and juniper and reminiscent of the Wallowas of Oregon. There are mountain goats on the ridges and spotted trout in the streams. I reviewed Greek Army battalions just before they moved across the valleys and skirted the cliffs in the valiant military operation that was to liquidate all the remaining guerrilla strongholds in Greece. I watched artillery duels from an outpost near the Bulgarian border, and heard the roar of the recoilless 75's echo from the disk-shaped ridge and steep cliffs of Mount Kamen.

The hardest, most valiant unit in Papagos' army was composed of eighteen thousand soldiers who two years before had been youngsters with pro-Communist leanings. The Greek government had sent all such young men to Macronisos Island off Athens for a democratic indoctrination course. Here they had learned the glories of Greece, its history, its potential. They had been taught the relationship between religion and the dignity of man. In this school they had come to know the techniques of Soviet communism and the designs of Russian aggression.

Large numbers graduated as vigorous exponents of a new Greek nationalism. Less than 5 per cent turned out to be incorrigibles or confirmed Marxists.

The ones I met and talked with had seen the vision of a new Greece, the promise of a land of opportunity for all. They wanted to rededicate Greece to the ideals of political and religious freedom. Greece would be born anew. It would never be the tail to any kite—Russian, British, American. The problem was to find work and employment for the surplus population of 1,500,000 people. As soon as Macedonia was cleared of guerrillas, Greece, with American help, would introduce vast hydroelectric projects. New industries would be established. In time all of Greece's people would have employment, the specter of starvation would disappear, and Greeks would not be lured into the political slavery of a Russian satellite state. Soviet propaganda that only communism guaranteed work and bread for all would be disproved.

This was their dream of a new Greece.

Hundreds, however, had been converted to the Communist cause. I saw many of them (both men and women) in prison camps—camps for the guerrillas who had been captured by the Greek Army. I visited one camp at Kozani on the Florina Plain in north central Greece—a vast basin two thousand feet high, flat and fertile. The prison camp, fringed by a scattering of locust trees, housed at that time 401 men and boys and 97 women and girls.

Most of the women (77) had been drafted by the guerrillas. The other 20 had joined voluntarily. The most promising among them had been sent to Bulgaria for indoctrination courses in Marxism. After six months or more they were returned to Greece and assigned to military duty. Most of the women prisoners I met had carried guns and fought alongside men. Some with whom I talked had commanded troops. Others had worked on the supply lines of the guerrillas or had laid land mines for them or rendered other service. All of them had lived with troops.

That association with men was a circumstance that made their rehabilitation in Greek society difficult. In Greece a girl is held to high standards of chastity. She is closely chaperoned and knows few of the social liberties American girls enjoy. A girl who had camped and marched with troops was therefore beyond the pale. I was talking with the wife of a Greek officer about the problem. She said it was one of the most difficult in all of Greece's history. "A girl who has served with troops," she said, "becomes a social outcast. She cannot return to her village. She cannot return to another village, for every villager in Greece knows the private life of the great-grandmother of every other villager. We have no family secrets here."

If these girls were to have a future, it would have to be found in large centers where they could be trained for housework, clerical work, or industry. That problem early became a main concern of the Greek government, for a person who is an outcast from society is a ready recruit for the Communists. The problem was a considerable one since 35 per cent of the guerrilla army was made up of women. Accordingly rehabilitation homes and schools were established to care for these women and to train them for a new life.

The grant of equality to women by the Communists was a revolutionary measure. In Greece women do not vote, except in municipal elections. In Greece women do not even sit in the sidewalk cafes with their husbands, fathers, or brothers, or participate in the discussion of local and world affairs. They stay in the background, neither seen nor heard.

This grant of equality to women drew backhanded praise from some Greek officers. As one tough-minded general said to me, "The women guerrillas are the hardest of the lot to liquidate or to capture." With a knowing look he added, "The female *is* the deadlier of the species." This was a devilish twist which the Communists gave the internal problems of Greece. By using women in the guerrilla forces and granting them equality the Communists introduced a divisive force in the nation.

The women guerrilla prisoners were, indeed, proud of this recognition. The comment of an eighteen-year-old girl was typical. She was plump and stocky, her hair was light brown streaked with gold. Her brown cotton stockings were full of holes; her full black skirt was torn and soiled. She wore a boy's jacket too tight to button and frayed at the sleeves. She spoke slowly, telling how the guerrillas had raided her village, left her parents behind, but taken her and the other young people off to a camp in the mountains. She said she was forced to fight—that the guerrillas would have killed her if she had refused. (I later learned that 60 per cent of the women in the guerrilla army had been recruited the same way.) After she had finished I asked, "What do you think of the Communists now?"

As she looked up there was warmth in her brown eyes. "I like my country the best. But there is one thing the Communists did—they treated us girls the same as the men. They knew the things we could do."

I found the same theme running through the talk of the other women. There was no doubt that the Communists had launched an idea that would spread silently to every home along the Mediterranean. To these women there was one aspect of the Communist creed that was not evil.

So far as appearances went most of these women were teen-agers. They were all of peasant stock—strong and sturdy. But even the fifteen-year-old girls seemed middle-aged. They might have been women waiting at an employment office in Waterbury, Connecticut, or Schenectady, New York. The mark of poverty and hardship was on them. They stood dazed and bewildered. The weight of the world was on their shoulders. They were not only outcasts; they feared the prospect of trial for treason as well.

There were older women too, bent under the load of this worry. One had three babies from six months to three years old; another, a little girl of twelve and a boy of four. The husband of one and the father of the other were with the guerrillas. Some of the women were old and decrepit—seventy, seventy-five, eighty years old. I talked with one elderly, gray-haired lady who was as thin and gaunt as a scarecrow, and dressed in a coarse black dress with a black shawl over her head. Her teeth were gone, her mouth receded. Her profile was that of our Halloween witch. Her arms and hands were skin and bones, apparently too thin and fragile for any work. Yet when I asked, "What did you do for the guerrillas?" she proudly replied, "I laid land mines."

It was a long, rambling story. She was a widow and penniless. Her sons had been killed by the Germans. Some guerrillas offered to pay her for board and room if she would cook for them by day and lay mines for them at night. The mines were laid in the roads leading up from a strategic valley. Her eyes lit up as she told how expert she had become at the task. This unknown, penniless person had been swept up in a movement and given recognition. I do not believe she had the slightest idea what being a Marxist entailed. She only knew that there were people to be fed, work to be found for the unemployed, needs of the peasants demanding attention—and the guerrillas promised remedies for the ills. This was a cause she could serve; at last she felt a sense of belonging, of participating, of having a share in the life of her country.

"Do you think I did wrong?" she asked with an imploring look in her gray eyes. "Will the judges order me to be shot?"*

One nineteen-year-old girl represented the solid Marxist core of the female guerrillas. Like the aged widow she had been attracted to the guerrillas by the Communist propaganda of work for all. Neither she nor her family had had employment for months. There was no bread in the house. The central government was corrupt— it didn't care what happened to the peasants. She and her family could starve so far as it was concerned. The Communists, she thought, had the answers to the problems of Greece. These were the ideas that poured out of her like a torrent.

"I joined the guerrillas because they were on the side of the people," she said in a haughty voice.

The guerrillas shipped her off to Bulgaria where she went to a

---

* Through the year 1949 many thousand guerrillas were arrested or surrendered. Of these the Greek court-martials tried 43,419 men and 6,525 women. 15,573 men and 2,144 women were convicted, 5,466 men and 513 women being sentenced to death. Those executed by the end of 1949 numbered 2,618 men and 162 women.

Communist school for six months. When I interviewed her she had been with the guerrillas for three years and was a thoroughgoing Marxist. She knew all the answers; and they came from her lips in machine-gun fashion. She had a square face and as she talked of communism her jaw was set. Her fingers were blunt and coarse, her nails dirty, her hands hardened with toil. She stood with her legs apart, her hands on her hips. She defied the world. Her eyes blazed like those of a cougar at bay. She was proud of her creed; she stood ready to die for Soviet communism.

"What position in the army did you hold?" I asked.

"I was a captain."

"How many troops did you command?"

"Two hundred fifty men."

"Did any of your men ever try to desert?"

"Yes—a few rats."

"What did you do then?"

"I would bring the deserter before my company. I would walk up to him and say 'You attempted to desert.' Then before all my troops I would shoot him dead with my revolver."

"Without a trial?"

"That kind doesn't deserve a trial," she snapped.

She was a tigress who would spit in the face of her firing squad.

At Larissa on the plain of Thessaly, I visited a prison camp of 1,932 prisoners, most of whom were men. The Thessaly plain lies at sea level and runs flat for miles. It is the bread basket of Greece; and this day it looked as neat as a garden. The prison camp was also neat-looking. The buildings in the camp had open sides—like those in some of our county fairs—and housed several hundred men each. The prisoners apparently expected an inspection, for their bedding and extra clothes were in neat piles and each prisoner stood stiffly. Some were men with criminal records who had sought new adventure with the guerrillas. Sixty per cent were youngsters who had been drafted by the Communists and whose faces were still bright and fresh. Some had enlisted to find work, to share in an exciting cause. Some of the older ones had joined to protect a son or a wife. And others of course were pure Marxists. These were the incorrigibles—perhaps 10 per cent who were kept in a separate building and heavily guarded. Their faces were hard, sometimes cruel.

They reflected bitterness and despair. With one of these I had a long talk.

Dimitros was his name, and he came from Athens. He had had university training in economics. He was tall, thin, scholarly looking. Thoughtful eyes were set deep under a massive forehead. All of his characteristics—his sensitive face, his long thin fingers, little mannerisms that had an effeminate touch—marked him as an introspective person. He had studied Marxism at length. There was at first much of it with which he did not agree. He long had some lingering doubts. Those doubts centered on the loss of the great democratic traditions of Greece, should Greece become a Russian satellite. He talked with pride of Aristotle and Plato, how their ideas had enlightened the minds of men and eventually worked to free Europe from medievalism. He mentioned that Greece, though ancient, is relatively young. America had enjoyed its independence for fifty years before Greece freed herself from four hundred years of Turkish rule. He spoke eloquently of the great social reforms of the elder Venizelos (perhaps the greatest Greek statesman since Pericles) who, among other things, over thirty years ago rid Greece of sharecroppers and tenants, turned the peasants into landowners, and freed Greece from the scourge of feudal tenures.

Then he dwelt at length on the institution of the coffee shop in Greece. These sidewalk cafes are the center of the intellectual life of each village. They are frequented by men only, as custom does not allow women to sit there. A man, however, may for a few cents buy a demitasse of coffee and a glass of water and sit at a table for hours on end—arguing, listening, debating. Here all the news of the world is discussed and digested. Politics are bandied about. The problems of Greece are analyzed and solved. Public officials are denounced and defended. Freedom of speech reigns supreme in these sidewalk cafes.

"All that would be lost with communism," I said. "You could no longer criticize your government; you would have to cease denouncing its programs and the activities of its officials. You surely must know that the Kremlin sanctions no dissenting opinions."

He nodded assent. "That is what worried me," he added. "But I finally decided that those freedoms must be sacrificed."

"Why?"

There was a long silence as if he were steeling himself for the answer. In a few minutes he stood up and drawing from some deep reserve of energy which set his eyes ablaze, he shouted:

"Greece has run her course. She is decadent. She no longer has it within her to solve her problems. Her officials are self-centered and corrupt. They all have yachts waiting at the docks so that they may flee if real trouble comes. Our people talk aimlessly. Nothing is done. There is no work. Tens of thousands are unemployed. There is no bread. Severe steps are necessary. A powerful outside force—one with a thundering voice and an iron will—is needed to direct the people, to still dissension, to tell them what to do."

"And to destroy the present democratic traditions of Greece?" I asked.

"Yes, to destroy them," he said in a hoarse whisper.

"What you advocate is suicide—national suicide; suicide on a grand scale; a cataclysm that sweeps to destruction the best in your civilization."

There was now a fanatical look in his eyes, as if at last the man had transferred his own psychosis to all his people and made a grand compact with death. Beads of perspiration stood on his forehead and his voice had an exultant lilt as he cried:

"Yes, that is it! Suicide! Greece will die through suicide. A torrent of death will pour in from the north. It will overrun us, and destroy us. We will sacrifice ourselves in a great cause. We will die so that communism may reach the Mediterranean. We will find glory in death. Greece by dying will make its final glorious contribution to mankind."

Dimitros was trembling as he finished. He sat down, his head in his hands. I turned without saying good-by and walked through rows of silent prisoners to a high barbed wire gate that marked the entrance to the huge stockade. Suddenly something happened which proved that Dimitros, the psychopath, was a small minority among the guerrillas.

As I reached the gate of the prison camp, a great chorus of male voices rose from the barracks. It picked up volume as hundreds of men joined in the singing. Soon it was louder than a dozen organs. The music welled up from the hearts of these guerrillas. It came in a tremendous crescendo. It rose higher and higher, then broke almost to a whisper. Then it came again like a torrent—this time with a deafening roar. There was pride and confidence and challenge in it —the exultant voices of men marching to some glorious victory.

When the singing had started, my interpreter—a Greek Army officer—and I had stopped in our tracks. We both stood as if transfixed. As the singing ended with a sharp thundering clap, I turned to him and asked, "What was the song?"

There was a note of pride in his voice and a visible straightening of his shoulders as he replied, "The song is entitled 'Greece Will Never Die.'"

2. Go Walking Man

CYPRUS LIES like a deerskin on the Mediterranean, its tail pointing toward Asia. It is 240 miles north of Egypt, 60 miles west of Lebanon, 40 miles south of Turkey. One hundred forty miles long and 60 miles wide, it has a population of over 450,000 people. Of these not over 5,000 were Communists in 1946. Yet in that year their party carried 55 per cent of the votes in the municipal elections, electing mayors in four of the six cities and in five of the most important towns. By 1949 the Communists had dropped to around 3,000 in number. But they controlled about 40 per cent of the vote, electing mayors in three of the six cities and in two of the most important towns.

We learned in Cyprus how so few could control so many. Our research project bore cloak-and-dagger aspects; we ended interviewing Communists in dingy rooms over perfume shops.

Cyprus has been under British rule since 1878. England rules it as a colony today. The people have a voice in municipal elections; but they have none in the central government. England is in control of the police force.

England got Cyprus in a curious way. She made a convention with Turkey to oppose a Russian advance into Asia Minor. By that convention she was given the right to govern Cyprus. It remained, however, Turkish territory until England annexed it when Turkey joined the Central Powers in World War I.

I had remembered Cyprus as the home of Aphrodite, goddess of love; the place where Paul converted Paulus to Christianity; the scene of Shakespeare's *Othello*; the place where Richard the Lion-Hearted married his betrothed in 1191 on his way to the Crusades; the island long ruled by the Templars. But I was to learn that Cyprus was also a pawn in the politics of the Mediterranean.

Cyprus, populated by Greece in 400 B.C., has long shown the balance of world power. Egyptians, Phoenicians, Assyrians, Romans, Greeks, Franks, Venetians, Turks all held it. It has always been sought by contesting powers and won by the strongest. If Russia held Cyprus, she would cover Turkey on both sides and have a staging ground for operations along the whole Mediterranean littoral including Africa.

Mountains rim two sides of the island, rising to 7,000 feet. High on these ranges are numerous summer resorts—Troodos, Prodromos, Platres—that have throughout history been favorite retreats for refugees from the heat of the Middle East. The lower slopes are heavily terraced with olives, almonds, and grapes.

Some villages, with square limestone houses, streak like a glacier down the mountainsides. Others made of mud with flat thatched roofs cling precariously to cliffs. Usually there is a Greek Orthodox church or a mosque. Cyprus produces large quantities of oranges, lemons, and grapefruit—citrus fruit as juicy as any I know. Great orchards of carobs—the locust bean of John the Baptist, used for food by man and beast—fill the coastal plains. Apples, walnuts, caishas, cherries, figs, and plums also flourish in parts of the island. The hot, rolling central plain, the Messoria, grows most of the cereals—wheat and barley.

The goat has been the cow of Cyprus from time immemorial. It has furnished milk for cheese, wool for clothing, leather for shoes. It and the pig have long furnished the meat of the island. The damage caused Cyprus by the goat has been severe. It has mutilated olive orchards, dwarfed pine forests, and caused large acreages of trees to disappear.

The ancient wooden plow is still used—pulled by oxen or donkeys. A whole family goes to the fields in the morning—the men in blue or white shirts, black, loose trousers, and high leather boots; women in black dresses with tight bodices and shawls; girls in close-fitting colored dresses of linen. Wheat or barley is still harvested with the hand sickle. The sheaves are tied on donkeys and taken to the ancient thrashing floor. There has been very little mechanization in any branch of agriculture. The reasons are simple.

Ottoman law foisted on the island a crazy quilt of tenures. On death of the owner the land went to the heirs. As the heirs died and their heirs took over, ownership became more and more pulverized until in some cases several persons might own one olive tree. Holdings of a single peasant are often scattered. The average plot is only a little more than one acre.

Moreover the total holding of land of one peasant is small. About 25 per cent have three acres or less; 52 per cent ten acres or less. Yet about twenty acres are necessary for the support of a family of five persons. "Carob kings" and "olive kings" built big estates by making loans at ruinous interest rates and then foreclosing. The churches—both Greek Orthodox and Moslem—are perhaps the largest landowners. They own the most fertile acreage of the island; they and a few rich individuals own a ninth of the arable land.

For years the hand of the British lay as heavily on the island as had that of the Turks. Nothing was done to improve the lot of the peasant. About thirty years ago the British changed their attitude. They made rural surveys and looked into the living condition of the peasants. Since then, they have done a good job in Cyprus, apart from their traditional strategy of divisive politics.

Malaria was a scourge and ravaged whole villages. Today it has been practically wiped out—its incidence having been reduced from 42 per cent in 1937 to 1.3 per cent in 1949. The island has also been cleared of rabies.

The death rate in Cyprus is now one of the lowest in the world —8.5 per thousand people, lower than in the United States.

A health program has put hospitals in the main towns.

Reforestation and restricted grazing of goats have built the state forests—which comprise one-sixth of the area of the island—into model units.

Elementary schools have been extended to the remotest and smallest villages. More than an eighth of the budget goes to education.

Marketing co-operatives have been formed with about one hundred co-operative retail outlets.

Credit co-operatives have been formed—about six hundred of them—to help farmers finance their operations at reasonable interest rates.

An excellent asphalt road system connects the main cities and villages.

The supply of water has been increased with numerous wells,

reservoirs, and irrigation projects. Over 40 per cent of the villages now have piped water.

An ambitious electrification program is under way.

But these reforms bring the British little credit in the political agitation that sweeps the country. One finds complaint in every coffee shop and on every roadside. The Cypriot is a politically conscious, politically active person. He knows his grievances and is loud in proclaiming them.

The main political grievances are three: (1) concentration of land ownership; (2) overabundance of citrus fruits, potatoes, cereals, and grapes—the money crops grown for export; and (3) the desire for Enosis, that is, Union with Greece.

Enosis is an old and passionate cause with Cypriots. Cyprus was never a part of Greece. Yet no Greek province is more fervidly loyal. Eighty-five per cent of the population is Greek; 15 per cent Turkish. At least 90 per cent of the Greek population of Cyprus considers Enosis a sacred cause. At the same time it is anathema to the Turkish minority.

The depth of the feeling of the great majority of Cypriots was best expressed to us by an old Stroumbi villager. He was disconsolate. Wine exports had dropped 50 per cent, a disastrous blow to the economy of his village. With great sadness he said, "Now look at Greece. She has surplus. But she finds markets for her wines and grapes." There is always the faith that Greece can solve the problems of surplus. Behind that faith is a blind, passionate nationalism.

The Communists have vied with the Greek Orthodox church in making Enosis their cause. Their power has remained great, even though the late Archbishop of the Greek Orthodox church in Cyprus took militant measures against them. Beginning in 1947 he removed from the pulpit priests with "leftist" tendencies. He refused to admit known Communists to services. He had sermons delivered from every pulpit on the island about the menace of communism.

In Cyprus as elsewhere Communist propaganda seeks to harass the "imperialists." It promises markets for plentiful wines, factories to process abundant carobs, and full employment. It denounces the carob kings and the olive kings. It promises that workers will own not only the land but the large copper and asbestos mines as well. It speaks of the "unexploited mineral wealth" of the island as though some Michurian of Mines could succeed where the Cyprus Mining Corporation has during thirty-four years of intensive prospecting failed to find another deposit to compare with the copper deposit at Skouridiossa.

There are aspects of the Communist propaganda which have a more romantic touch.

One of the problems of a father is marrying off his daughters. As I have said, girls in the Greek world are carefully guarded and protected. They do not appear in public places unescorted; they live in seclusion or under close guard. Most coffee shops, like the voting booths, are for men only. But in these days a girl has to have more than a reputation of chastity in order to marry. Dowries are important because of the increase of women over men. A dowry of five goats is fair; a dowry of land is better.

And so—believe it or not—Moscow has promised to collectivize dowries in Cyprus.

The Cypriot father thinks he would have reached utopia if the state assumed the cost of marrying off his daughters. An Ayios Epiktetos villager expressed the local attitude toward large families. After proudly showing us pictures of his six children, he sadly apologized: "I have only the six. I am now thirty. But if I was not in Army for six years, I have twelve!"

Moscow also promises that workers will retire early and live out their days in the fashionable hill resorts. The Cypriot's hope has long been to join his cousins or brothers in England or America. But these dreams are now being replaced by visions of living in the hilltop palaces among the firs, pines, oaks, and cedars. Here he will escape the heat of the valleys and live in a land where gorgeous anemones and iris grow wild, where springs of cold water gush from the rocks, where the big-horn sheep is sometimes seen.

The Communists got a strong hold on Cyprus during the war. Cyprus had a Mule Pack Transport Regiment in the British Army. In 1943 the Communist party sent eight hundred trained agitators to enlist in the regiment. Four hundred, including a majority of the Party Central Committee, were accepted. They spread their theology among the troops. When these servicemen returned home they were well indoctrinated.

We talked with two—Nicolas, a city boy, and Dimitros, a rural boy—who were fairly representative.

Nicolas, a former lieutenant in the regiment, is educated and calls himself an anti-Communist. Like other Cypriots, he found Italy a land of similar interests.

"Italy was all Communist then. We all were too, or pretended to be when we talked to the people. We saw a lot during the war we never knew about in Cyprus. I suppose we all came back wanting to do something to improve conditions here and modernize the industry and agriculture. A lot of us quit going to church because we could see the church in Cyprus was more concerned with politics than with God. If the church would give up some of its extensive landholdings, there would be more Christianity for everyone."

But Nicolas has learned a lot about the Communists in recent years. He said to us: "You know communism in Italy has decreased. It has here too. We just didn't realize then that communism is a form of foreign domination, and didn't stop to think that we have to be free to work out our own welfare."

Dimitros is a rural agricultural worker. He lives in a small and attractive village between the Mediterranean and the mountains. He speaks perfect English, which he learned in the Army. He joined the Cyprus Regiment at the age of sixteen, spent three years in Africa, and the rest of the war in Italy, Greece, and Syria. He has great personal admiration for the British officers he chauffeured and not much use for the Russians.

After his wartime adventures he returned to his charming but backward village to find his mother still drawing water from one of the community wells. (That has been done in arid Cyprus since Biblical times, with the only difference that picturesque pottery jugs have today been largely replaced by square kerosene tins.) There is no electricity in his village. The majority of the population work on other people's farms, sometimes miles away. They start on foot or with their donkeys long before sun-up to sow or harvest spring wheat, summer fruit, autumn olives, winter oranges. They are among the hundred thousand seasonal rural workers who are to be seen on Cyprus roads late in the evening walking home from a long day's work.

"Look," said Dimitros, pointing out a group of barefoot women walking down the road at sunset, "those are my villagers. The sun will be down when they get home—it is still nine miles away. That woman carrying her shoes is my aunt. She carries them even though her feet get sore on brambles. She has only one pair. They must last a long time. Don't you think it's awful to have to walk so far and work so hard for so little?

"We used to own our own farm. But the landlords—we call them the olive kings and carob kings—got it in payment for a loan one year when we had a bad crop. If the landlords and the church did not own so much land, we could live on our own land like we used to and work and live much easier."

The Communist leaders are Cypriots and for the most part trade unionists. Many have been trained abroad. Their paraphernalia of political activities is familiar—front organizations, purges, infiltration of trade unions, indoctrination courses in Marxism for select students, scholarships behind the Iron Curtain, general strikes, the party line.

There is a robust, earthy quality in Cyprus politics. An incident in the 1949 election illustrates it. One Communist candidate for mayor had created a local scandal in Kyrenia by bringing his Hungarian cabaret girl friend to his hotel. During one of his political speeches someone in the crowd shouted: "What about the Hungarian girl?"

The candidate shouted back, "Would you have me molest a nice Cypriot girl instead? Would you like to have me take out your sister? Are you so fond of Hungarians?"

During the election the Communists brought busloads of peasants and workers from faraway villages to Nicosia. They came to the capital perhaps to give a helping hand to the leftist campaign, perhaps to make a show of strength. Almost as soon as the buses started for Nicosia, rumor spread like wildfire over the entire island that men with clubs in hand and fire in their eyes were en route to secure victory for the leftists.

One group of rightists, who were barricaded in their club, were picketed by workers. They retaliated by throwing bottles and squirting "gaseos" (a drink like Coca-Cola). Many a head was sore the next day, but the newspapers reported only one death—a traffic casualty.

The lengths to which the Communists go in conforming to the Soviet ideological pattern is illustrated by Costas Partassides, forty-one years old and mayor of Limassol. He is an amiable man and a popular one. His father was a grocer—a real bourgeois. But Partassides—striving to be truer to the Communist ideology—refashioned his ancestry for us. He told us his father was a "skilled worker."

The founder of the Communist party in Cyprus has a large popular following. He is a large man with silver hair, who might easily be taken for a banker or industrialist. His name is Ploutis Servas.

He has a strong hold on the electorate. In the 1946 election campaign, he appeared for a scheduled lecture in one village with a very sore throat, and hoarsely said, "Ladies and gentlemen, everyone who believes in something and fights for something must sacrifice something for the cause. I have sacrificed my voice."

This is still remembered in Cyprus as a stirring speech which continued amid dead silence as Servas whispered on.

The peasant has had no democratic leader of that popularity. Come election time, his choice has been between the extreme right (Nationalist party) and the Communists. He has had no other place to go, and since the Communists have espoused his causes he has given them his vote.

Nicosia was hot. It had the burning summer heat of our own Southwest. It was 80 degrees shortly after the sun rose. Before noon the temperature was marching toward 110 degrees or more. There was a noisy hum in the market place. Professional beggars lolled under eucalyptus trees, calling in cracked voices to passersby. Women swarmed over pomegranates, dates, lemons, onions, asparagus, artichokes, and tubs of snails, buzzing with the gossip of the town as they bargained with the stall holders. Strings of goat meat attracted flies. Chickens tied in bundles squawked at our feet. Occasional caravans of camels appeared, their high heads sneering, their masters shouting inexplicable commands. Burros loaded with produce trotted by. There was the pungent smell of fresh fruit and vegetables, the strong odor of fish and ripe meat, the smell of mules and camels, the odor of freshly dampened dirt.

By midafternoon the noise of the market had dropped to a low hum. Nicosia lay in shade almost asleep. The pulse of the city slowed. The scarlet rhododendrons and gladioli that decorated the stalls in the market began to wilt.

By 5 o'clock there was a new stirring of life. A light wind came up, cooling the hot plain. The cries of the stall holders increased. Automobiles—mostly British with right-hand drives—honked their way through the crowds that forsook the sidewalks for the streets. The coffee shops began to fill up. Then a thousand tongues picked up the news and gossip of the day and passed it from house to house. Street vendors worked through the crowds, selling toys and fruit juices. And high above the crowds were camels, walking saucily and with dignity, headed for some pasture on the city's outskirts.

We joined a group on the veranda of the Atlanta Hotel. It was now cool; the wind swept off the Troodos, refreshing the valley. It and the night gave us a reprieve from the sun. We reveled in the coolness as a fugitive from the searing heat of a treeless plain would relax in the shade of an oasis.

We sat in quiet conversation, sipping cool drinks. Our conversation was mostly about the ebb and flow of communism in Cyprus. One of the group was the charming Militza Stavrinides, a Greek girl in her twenties. It was an event to have a Greek girl in such a public place. She was one of the few females in Cyprus who had been freed from the ancient Greek customs that keep women subdued and subservient. Her family had given her the freedom of American women.

She sat for a few minutes talking freely about politics, the recent election, and the project for union with Greece. Suddenly she froze and refused to continue. I asked her what the trouble was. She whispered that a waiter whom she feared was a Communist was eavesdropping and that she should say no more. I told her that we were leaving in the morning and that this evening was my last opportunity to gather information about Cyprus.

She left abruptly saying she wanted to telephone her father. She returned in a few minutes and whispered, "Father will see you."

So I took a taxi downtown. The streets and sidewalks were packed with people. They were sauntering about town, getting a feel of the cool fresh air on their faces. The taxi slowly pushed through this sea of humanity as a boat pushes through water. And as we moved ahead the mass closed in around us. It was a gay, happy crowd that paid practically no attention to the horn which my driver used as a siren.

Finally he stopped in front of a darkened building in the business district. This was the office of the right-wing paper, *Freedom*, of which Demosthenes Stavrinides is editor. There was not a sign of life in the streets. I felt again the heat of the day on my face, for the stone faces of the buildings were as hot as ovens.

I went up a flight of stairs and was met by a young, swarthy man who spoke no English. He took me into a hot office. Militza's father was waiting. He rose to greet me, and as he came up out of his chair I thought his head would touch the ceiling. For he is a big man—tall, broad, rangy. His skin, eyes, and hair are typically Greek. He has massive features and a deep, guttural voice. He speaks English in a halting, unsure way. And his English vocabulary is quite limited.

He was a most gracious host—interested in my research project on communism and eager to help. So we reviewed much of what I have already related.

Finally I asked the questions designed to separate the true Communists from the others. I went through the lists, city by city. Finally I came to John Clerides, prominent lawyer and former mayor of Nicosia.

"Is he a Communist?"

"No."

"Many people say he is."

"They are quite wrong."

"What would you call him?"

He puckered his brow and looked at the ceiling, searching for the word. He was silent for a minute or so. Then with the puzzled look still on his face he said, "I think you in America would call him a Go Walking Man."

"A Go Walking Man," I said to myself. "What in the world is that?"

Finally his meaning dawned on me: "You mean fellow traveler."

"Yes, yes, yes, that's it," he said with a smile. "Americans would call him a fellow traveler."

The Cypriots have too great a love for independence, too much fondness for freedom of expression and discussion, too great an interest in the politics of parties, too deep a passion for land ownership to embrace communism as a matter of choice.

That is also true throughout the East. The Communist party with its Marxist ideology has attracted only a few in each country south of Russia's border. But a party controlled by Communists often garners most of the independent vote. The independent, the liberal is the fellow traveler. He is not a fellow traveler in the invidious sense in which we use the words. He is not a Communist in disguise. He does not embrace Communist doctrine. He uses the Communist-sponsored party to gain his immediate objectives. He has to go left and the Communists offer him the only effective, political machinery for expression of his views.

In Asia as well as in Cyprus he has needed his own liberal party organization, one that is free of Communist domination. The role of fellow traveler is thrust upon him. The fate of the peasant from the Mediterranean to the Pacific depends in no small measure on the degree of true independence of this Go Walking Man.

As this is written, word comes from Cyprus that John Clerides has taken the lead in forming a new party—the Socialist party of Cyprus. It is a new liberal party under non-Communist leadership.

3. A Picture Code

IN THE Middle East, Soviet propaganda has taken several quirks. In the first place, the Soviets, while deprecating nationalism in Europe, adopt it as a dominant theme for the Middle East. They profess to want every minority to have its own nation—under Soviet auspices, of course. In the second place, the Soviets do not denounce the church in the Middle East as they do in most places. Rather they use the church as a medium to reach the people.

Lenin preached freedom for the Mohammedans and protection of their mosques and religious ceremonies. The Soviet propaganda at an early date made a special play for the Russian Orthodox church, an ancient Russian institution. Soviet ministers and attachés in this region—particularly in the Arab world—made quite a point of visiting monasteries and convents of the Russian Orthodox church and even of attending church services. Clovis McSoud, a young Arab lawyer whom I first met at Soueida in southern Syria, has made a study of the impact of communism on the Arab mind during the 40's when Soviet influence in this region was at its peak. McSoud said, "Many a Greek Orthodox in Syria and Lebanon joined the Communist party incidentally to their religious attachment. Those who did not join sympathized with the Soviet Union and felt in her the protector of their faith."

That was also true of the Armenians who had special historic reasons for considering Russia as their protector.

Armenia is at the southwest corner of Russia. Ancient Armenia stretched from the Black Sea to the Caspian and embraced the rich valleys of the upper Euphrates. Today it is a small nation of less than four thousand square miles with no seaport.

Its neighbor on the south is Persian Azerbaijan, on the west Turkey. Its borders, like all Soviet frontiers, are for all practical matters closed to the outside world. Armenia's channels of commerce are to the north and east through two other Soviet states—Georgia and Russian Azerbaijan. From 1921 to 1936 these three states were one; their name, Trans-Caucasian S. S. Federative Republic. In 1936 Armenia became a separate state. Since that time she has been governed by a thousand or more members of the Communist party. Her population today is well over 1,250,000 people.

Armenia has suffered from its geographical location. It is a segment of a great crossroads from the Mediterranean to the Pacific. The Medes and Persians conquered it. So did the Greeks. Persia and Rome divided it. In the fourth century Christianity became the religion of Armenia and a holy war against Zoroastrian Persia was launched. Later the Arabs subdued Armenia. The Seljuk Turks took it. Then came the Tartars from Mongolia. The Ottoman Turks and Persia divided the nation in the seventeenth century. On the turn of the nineteenth century Russia invaded Georgia. Then came the war of 1828 between Russia and Persia with Russia taking much of the present Armenia. Both Turkey and Russia then held parts of Armenia. The Armenians were persecuted and massacred by both those powers. The British used the Armenians as a buffer between Russia and Asia Minor. Both Britain and Russia wooed them. The British did nothing to protect them. Turkey, filled with suspicion of the great powers, took evil steps. In 1895, eighty thousand Armenians died at the hands of the Turks; in 1896 six thousand more.

As a result of many invasions and persecutions the population of Armenia was widely dispersed—north into Russia, west into Greece and Europe, south into the Arab world and Persia. As another consequence of being the highway for conquerors, Armenia developed the habit of looking to an outside power for succor. Thus when the Greeks conquered Armenia, the Armenians looked to the Arabs for help. When the Moslem rule became oppressive, the Armenians turned again to the Greeks. In later centuries England was looked to as the protector. So was Turkey; so was Russia. Armenia suffered much from each one, but perhaps it suffered less from Russia than from the others. At least Russia became the symbol of salvation to the Armenians. When Soviet Russia gave Armenia its separate state, Russia seemed to many to be Armenia's best friend. Thousands went there from the Middle

East. In 1946 alone it is estimated that forty thousand Armenians left the Middle East for their old homeland.

Armenia has high plateaus and rugged mountains. The climate is extreme—hot, dry summers and severe winters. Traditionally an agricultural country and a backward one at that, Armenia has in the last thirty years undergone a transformation. Electric power has been developed and with it a large degree of industrialization; minerals have been discovered and exploited; food-processing plants have been built; irrigation systems have been constructed; modern machinery has been brought to the farms.

The Armenian language is in use. Many schools have been built. Theaters, opera houses, parks, museums, libraries have been constructed. A university, a musical academy, and many trade schools were established.

I learned in the Middle East (from non-Communist sources which I deem reliable) that there has been a substantial increase in the standard of living in Armenia S.S.R. during the last thirty years. Special emphasis seems to have been placed on education and industrialization.

It seems that research in the physical sciences and in engineering has flourished in the schools, and that students and faculties are left alone—provided they "keep their noses out of public affairs." How there can be any real academic freedom under those circumstances is difficult to imagine. But the growth of institutions of learning and the opportunities for education which the people of this area never enjoyed before have made a great impact; and word of the so-called renaissance spreads on facile tongues of propagandists.

The Soviets have used the church in spreading Soviet gospel. To do this they have taken a hand in selecting the clergy and in exacting from them loyalty to the Soviet cause. The results are often apparent.

Some of the clergy in their public utterances take the Soviet line—whether it concerns British and American "imperialism" in the Middle East or the intervention of the United Nations in Korea. For example on August 25, 1950, the Supreme Patriarch Catholicos of the Armenian church in Russia, George VI, protested to the Security Council against "the American aggression in Korea," calling the United Nations' intervention a "man-hating anti-Christian act." George VI also supported the resolution of the Stockholm session of the Permanent Committee of the Soviet-sponsored World Peace Congress.

Soviet propaganda saturates the Middle East with glowing stories of Armenia's progress. It is not used precisely to attract the remaining Armenians into the Soviet zone; rather the purpose seems to be to instill dissatisfaction among all peasants and to fire nationalist ambitions.

A classic example of Soviet propaganda is a radio broadcast of what purports to be a travelogue of a noted Russian author.

The author tells of the arrival in Armenia S.S.R. of Armenians repatriated from Persia. He describes how forlorn, dejected, gaunt, and impoverished they were—"a spectacle of great misery." He tells how Persia was the "jungle of feudalism," Russia the "land of socialism" where "the happy tunes of work and effort can be heard." He talks of the "derelict land and dilapidated villages and hovels" of Persia where primitive agricultural methods are still used. And he contrasts it with Armenia S.S.R. where "the roar of cars and tractors" can be heard.

Illiteracy in Armenia S.S.R. is wiped out, he claims; in Persia 85 per cent of the people are illiterate. Armenia, he boasts, is rich in schools—14 high schools and 43 research centers for 1,300,000 people, while Persia has only 5 high schools for 16 million people. He stresses the lack of medical facilities in Persia and relates how a hospital in one village in Armenia S.S.R. offers greater medical services than all those in Persia. He describes the beauties of the model villages and the model homes in Armenia S.S.R. He tells how well paid their workers are, what good food they enjoy, what luxuries are available to them. He ends his travelogue as follows:

The Persians who live in our neighborhood know full well what sort of country lies across the Aras River, and it is for this reason that the task of the Persian government and their so-called U. S. advisers is becoming more and more difficult. It is for this reason that they have savagely suppressed and are suppressing the national liberation movement.

It is for this reason that they have drawn an iron curtain between the peoples of the Soviet Transcaucasian Republics and the Persian nation, which suffers colonizing enslavement. The River Aras separates the Soviet Armenia and Persia—that is, the today and the yesterday of mankind. The Aras is one of the slowest-flowing rivers in Armenia, but happily history is otherwise.

This is the glowing story the Soviet radios tell. One gets quite different versions south of the border.

There are many Armenians in southern Persia. I visited among them and found them to be friendly, warm-hearted, industrious people. One day I stopped at an Armenian village between Shalamzar and Oregon in the Bakhtiari country of southwest Persia. I was met by the village elders, a dozen or more tall dark men with high broad foreheads and prominent noses who stood with dignity awaiting me. They were dressed in black—long trousers, looking like pantaloons, loose coats, and high felt hats without brims. In their midst stood another man, also in his Sunday-best clothes, holding a ewe. The ewe had been washed and scrubbed; it was as white as snow—a fluffy bundle in the arms of this swarthy Armenian. This was a sheep for the sacrifice—a ritual celebrating my arrival. I halted the sacrifice; and the pure white sheep scampered away.

The gesture of friendship established a bond and I became fond of these Armenians. For several centuries they have lived in this alien land where the great majority of the people are Moslems. They have nevertheless maintained their own customs, kept alive their religion and language, and preserved a racial solidarity that still thrives. Their Moslem neighbors think well of them; the Moslem landowners, for whom many of these Armenians worked, have only praise for them.

The Armenians in Persia do not know quite what to think of Armenia S.S.R. The reports sent them through Armenian sources about the economic conditions, the standard of living, the absence of unemployment, the modernization of farms are often glowing.

"Just how free are the Armenians in Russia?" I would ask.

This was the question that bothers these Armenians. They do not know what new kind of slavery may have been substituted in Soviet Armenia for the tenancy that held their ancestors in subjugation. They do not know what new persecutions may hold their people in terror. They know that men do not live by bread alone. And so the remaining ones are torn: they have a yearning to share in the glories of their new nationalism; they have doubts and fears about intolerance and oppression inside Russia.

Down in southern Persia I learned that all is not well in Soviet Armenia.

A few Armenians who migrated from Persia to Soviet Armenia have escaped to tell their story. Here is one tale from the lips of Hartoun, an Armenian peasant, who three years ago escaped with Khachik, another peasant and now lives not far from Isfahan.

Q. What happened when you arrived in Russia?

A. When we crossed the Iranian border in Azerbaijan we arrived in a Russian village in which we had a four-day rest. In the morning of the fifth a man who seemed to be the alderman delivered a short speech saying that the Russian government does not consider any right of ownership nor permit any commercial activities. "You must work as simple laborers and earn your living. We need no peasants," he said.

Q. What was your job?

A. Our job was to trim off the trees of an orchard. We had to work for ten hours per day beginning from 8 A.M. Our other friends did similar things. Some others were engaged in different constructions.

Q. What was your food?

A. All our food for twenty-four hours consisted of five hundred grams of black bread with one ladleful of a liquid called borsch which was by no means sufficient. This was the most important reason for our flight from Russia. That is HUNGER.

Q. Were you free to do anything and to go anywhere?

A. Most of the time they watched over us. We could not go anywhere without having a written permission from the alderman. I remember one day a friend of mine had a two-day leave. He left his home disregarding the necessity of having the written permission. He, after a couple of hours, was arrested. But we, to some extent, were free in our private affairs. Nobody interfered in our private affairs. Only in official affairs, viz. working, the same alderman of the village interfered, having four foremen at his disposal.

Q. Where were you living?

A. It was a village having buildings like barracks. Population nearly three thousand heads. We do not remember how many men and women.

Q. Did you have movies and theaters?

A. We frequently visited pictures and theaters.

Q. What were your wages?

A. The furniture for living was composed of a wooden bed, a mattress, a blanket and a drinking cup. Three hundred rials (six dollars) in cash was paid monthly together with one kilogram of sugar and one hundred grams of tea, the price of which was deducted from the three hundred rials. The furniture and the amount of cash paid monthly was hardly sufficient for a simple living. As a rule, to workers—as we were—

they give just enough to keep them alive. About other categories we do not know. But to me this rule has no exception.

Q. How did government officials behave to the people?

A. Very rudely and hard.

Q. Did the police have any contact with you?

A. No, unless they had to find a criminal or someone under suspicion.

Q. What about your vacations?

A. A month per year with written permission but we never got any.

Q. Can you tell me what feelings the people in your village had about their government? Did anyone venture to express any criticism?

A. On the whole people are discontented, but no one dares to express a thought against the government. We can say those whom we have seen in Russia are not living; they are existing. In spite of all that, these people love their country, i.e., the land which is called Russia. We can assure you that their feelings toward their country are quite different from those they have for their government.

Q. What happened when you were ill?

A. In case of illness, a doctor and a sufficient quantity of drugs were kept ready and the patient was treated without paying. When surgical operations were needed, the patient was sent to town. Wages were paid as usual.

Q. Why did you escape?

A. Migration to us meant repatriation; thus we expected to have a far better life; but when we got there, they told us they needed no peasants. We in Iran used to till the soil and grow crops, we were not hired men. So we had to be engaged in work of which we had no experience. In the first few weeks we found out that we were losing our time. We were not laborers. We were separated from our families.* We were not given enough to eat. We did not have anything. We were suffering from poverty and hunger.

Q. Do your other friends in Russia want to escape?

A. Beyond the slightest shadow of doubt. Their situation could never be worse than that. They are suffering now. But you shall not underestimate the risk of escaping.

Q. Tell me how you managed to escape.

A. We were four who planned to escape. We set off in the evening, we moved on all night southward. The next morning about dawn we took shelter in woods. One was on guard while the other three were asleep. Next evening we set out again. In the morning we reached the

---

* In Armenia S.S.R. women, as well as men, are assigned to work. When Hartoun and his group arrived there, the women were given work assignments in one village, the men in another; the children were sent to state schools; family life was broken up.

border. There was a mountain overhanging the border and the river Araxes (Aras). All day we took cover in the mountain. It was then we learned they are tracking us. Once the pursuers came close to our hiding place, we could clearly hear them talking but they never found us. The third evening came and the most dangerous part of our flight was to begin; we had to cross the border. There was a trail alongside the river. When we reached that trail it was 10 o'clock. We came across barbed wire, between the track and the river. It seemed that the wire was attached to an alarm, because when we were working our way out of it, we suddenly saw the sparkling light of a car coming toward us. Two of our friends fled back to the mountain; but we two managed to get through the wires in time and submerged into the water. We heard some shooting but we were not hit. Soon we reached the side of the river which was Turkish territory. From that side of the river, we in rays of the searchlight saw our two timid friends, who were found and caught by the Russians. After three months of internment in Turkey we were handed over to Iranian authorities in Azerbaijan again.

I also learned that the Armenians going to Russia have adopted a code to communicate with their relatives and friends whom they have left behind. If the family wants to get word back home that all is well in Soviet Armenia, that it is a desirable place to live, that the Armenians who are there like their new national home, and that the friends whom they left behind should join them, a picture of the group is sent in which the head of the family is standing. If, however, conditions inside Soviet Armenia are found to be oppressive or undesirable or disappointing, and those who are left behind are to be warned not to come, then a picture of the group is sent showing the head of the family seated.

I had first heard of this code in Damascus; and I thought it was a joke. But I learned in the Ali-Goudarz district of southern Persia that it is true. An Armenian family, filled with these doubts, had agreed to use the picture code when an uncle and his wife and sons left Persia a year or so earlier for Armenia S.S.R. In the winter of 1949-1950 a letter from the uncle arrived in Ali-Goudarz. With it came a photo showing the family group. Some were seated on chairs, others were standing. The uncle was flat on the floor in front of the group.

That decided the matter for the villagers in Ali-Goudarz. They remain in Persia.

4. *Azerbaijan*

AZERBAIJAN, the northwest province of Persia, lies snug against the Turkish and Russian borders. Mount Ararat—nearly seventeen thousand feet high, conelike and flecked with snow—looks down on it from the Turkish corner. The Araxes River which empties into the Caspian far to the north is the Persian-Russian border for two hundred miles or more. On the west is Lake Urmia, about the size of our own Great Salt Lake of Utah. Fish cannot live in it. It is indeed so salty that it clings like slime to one's skin. The Zagros Range—heading up in Turkey and the Russian Caucasus and running to the Persian Gulf—is a rough and rugged limestone rampart on the western border of Azerbaijan. Its passes are around eight thousand feet, its peaks as high as fifteen thousand. The Elburz Range on the east is both steeper and higher. Both are bare of trees on the slopes that face Azerbaijan.

Azerbaijan has the barren appearance of Nevada and Utah, though there are between twenty and thirty-five inches of rain a year. Most of the water comes in wintertime—snow that even in the valleys often lies eight or ten feet deep. And most of the water leaves in the spring in mad rushes that cut harsh gullies in the mountains, which long ago were studded with trees.

In the winter Azerbaijan is whipped by cold winds that sweep down from the north and whistle through mud-walled villages. In the summer it is parched and blistered. Whirlpools of dust dance across the basins, sending eerie-shaped funnels hundreds of feet into the sky. The flat mud roofs of the houses crack under a scorching sun; and dust as fine as flour sifts through one's clothing. This is the heyday of the lizards; this is when only thistles and licorice root seem to thrive.

But where there is water Azerbaijan is a garden. Valleys—such as Khoy—lie lush with crops at the foot of brown and burned hills.

Rezaieh, on the edge of the desolate salt sea, is a rich oasis deep in shade. In the north vast fields of golden grain ripple in the hot wind that sweeps up from the south. The climate of Azerbaijan is good for crops and for people. The days are warm; but the valleys which lie between four thousand and five thousand feet are cooled at night by breezes that come off the mountains.

Azerbaijan is a historic place. Here Zoroaster lived in the sixth century B.C. and taught the unending conflict between good and evil. This was the home of the Medes who, though they conquered Persia, were absorbed by it, losing themselves and their civilization in the process. The absorption was indeed so great that only one word of their language remains in the Persian vocabulary today— *sag*, the Medes' word for dog. The Arabs came in the seventh century, converting all of Persia to the Moslem religion at the point of the sword. In the middle thirteenth century the Mongols swept through Azerbaijan burning and slaying as they went. They made Maragheh their capital and later Tabriz and ruled two hundred years. Then came the Turks. Azerbaijan, the border province, was in the path of a host of invaders.

Azerbaijan was also the staging ground for revolt—and a buffer for the whole realm of Persia. Its character has not changed in the intervening centuries. Twice in the nineteenth century Russia invaded Azerbaijan; and in this century several times—the last time in 1941.

The location of Azerbaijan has had important commercial consequences as well. Tabriz linked Asia and Europe in trade. It was a key point on ancient caravan routes. Its trade tapped distant markets. Eight hundred years ago its bazaars sold spices from India and cloth from Flanders. History has not changed its strategic location. The Transcaucasian Railroad has its terminus at Tabriz. It is a broad-gauge road running north to Russia and then by various links into eastern Europe. Now it is closed at the Russian border and its rails in Azerbaijan are covered with rust. Russia permits traffic over it only when Russia's needs are served. Once was during the winter of 1949-1950 when people were starving in Azerbaijan. Russia made capital out of that event. She sent carloads of wheat by way of the railroad and dispensed it ostentatiously.

Azerbaijan, being from time out of mind an international highway, has seen the crossing of many races. The product is a people still Persian, but different from the rest. They speak a Turkish dialect which has absorbed many Persian words. They are a hardy lot—vigorous, aggressive, easily aroused, hearty and open-faced in their relations. And their hearts are warm and generous. An Azerbaijan friendship is a sturdy thing—robust and genuine—a commitment that carries through fair days and foul. The Azerbaijanis are friendly to the Russian people, for the two are neighbors and as individuals they get along well together. But the Azerbaijanis are not Communist nor Communist inclined. Not one-tenth of 1 per cent of them have been converted to Marxism or its Soviet brand.

Azerbaijan in size is only 7 per cent of Persia. In population it is only 18 per cent—three million out of sixteen million. Economically it is more important. It produces about a fourth of the wool, sheep, rugs, wheat, and barley of Persia; a third of the almonds, tobacco, and fats; a fifth of the raisins and sugar. Even in cotton its production is 15 per cent of the total. Azerbaijan is therefore important to Persia. It has long been coveted by Russia.

When England and Russia became allies in 1941 they invaded Persia. The purpose was twofold—to protect the Soviet rear from a German drive through the Caucasus; to provide a supply route to Russia. On August 26, 1941, British troops took over southern Persia; the Russian Army occupied Azerbaijan. During the occupation the Persian Gulf Command of the American Army managed the movement of some five million tons of war materials to Russia through this Persian corridor. At the end of the war the British and American troops departed. But Russia refused to withdraw. Her troops remained. It looked as if she was there to stay. Persia protested and carried the case to the Security Council of the United Nations. Public opinion forced Russia to retreat, and she at last withdrew her troops from Azerbaijan on May 9, 1946.

But before and after that event Russia put in motion a tide of events that still churns that ancient province.

Russian occupation armies are notoriously brutal. But the Russian Army that occupied Azerbaijan was a model of rectitude. Everyone told me the same story; even the most bitter critics of the Soviets conceded it. The Soviets put on an act which left a deep imprint on the people. Russian troops were dealt with summarily if they showed any discourtesy or offense to the civilian population. They toed the line of propriety in all respects. Discipline was severe. A Russian soldier would be shot for laying hands on a woman in Azerbaijan.

Russia had one unique opportunity to show its discipline of troops and the loyalty required of them. She exploited it to the limit. The Soviet Army of Occupation had one battalion composed of Moslems from the Caucasus. They were stationed at Khoy. One day they decided to desert. So at an opportune moment they left Khoy and headed for the Turkish border some twenty-five miles distant. Their secret was not kept. Soviet troops went in pursuit and captured the Moslems, brought them back to Khoy and killed them in a cruel way.

They chained them together and stacked them like sardines in the basement rooms of a garrison in Khoy. Then they flooded the floors with several inches of water and left the Moslems to die of cold and starvation. When a few weeks later the last man had died, they carried out the bodies. Thus did the Soviets publicize a lesson in discipline.

The Russians were equally severe on dissident elements among the native population. They did not molest or harm those who kept their thoughts to themselves. But occasionally a son of Azerbaijan— true to his tradition—would speak his mind and protest against some Russian policy. And once in a while he would raise his voice against the Russian occupation. Every such person was dealt with summarily. I talked with a man in Rezaieh who was a witness to what happened to one dissenter.

This man had made a speech in Rezaieh, objecting to the Russian occupation, pointing out how it subjugated Persia to a foreign rule, and asking for the liberation of Azerbaijan. He was at once arrested by Soviet soldiers and brought to the edge of town under military escort. He was given a shovel and ordered to dig a grave. When it was completed, the man was not shot; he was bound hand and foot and placed in the grave on his back. Then he was buried alive. As the shovels of dirt were thrown on him he prayed to Ali—son-in-law of Mohammed and first apostle of the Shiah faith. "Alee-Alee," he cried, "Alee, never fails." And soon there came from under the dirt the last muffled words, "Long live Azerbaijan." Then all was still, only the thump, thump, thump of dirt as shovels worked quickly

to fill the tomb with six feet of dirt and still forever the voice of
a lone dissenter.

The Soviets however used means much subtler than terror to win
over the masses. They sent through the province agents working
in pairs. One would be the spokesman; the other would purport to
be his secretary. They would come to a village and interview
peasants one at a time. A typical conversation ran as follows:

"What is your name?"

"Ahmad."

"How many in your family?"

"My wife and seven children."

"Which is your house?"

"This one here [pointing]."

"Look at the miserable place this good man has to live," the agent
said to his secretary. "Haven't we got something better for him?
Look at your list."

The secretary thumbed through a book and replied, "Yes, there
is the home of the deputy to the Prime Minister in Tehran. That
is unassigned."

"Put him down for that," the agent told his secretary. Turning
to the villager he said, "When the revolution comes and we take
Tehran, that will be your home."

Then he asked, "How many rugs do you have?"

Every Persian has a rug. It may be dirty and moth-eaten; but it
is always a cherished possession. This man ran to get his shabby
prayer rug—two feet wide and about four feet long. He held it up
to the agent, who turned to his secretary and said, "Put him down
for six rugs—the nicest that Kurish, the rug man, has in Tabriz."

And so the discussion went from houses to rugs, from rugs to
meat, from meat to schools for the children.

The campaign moved from peasant to peasant, from village to
village. This was pie-in-the-sky come to bedraggled, poverty-ridden
villagers. They received promises of rewards as tangible as any that
a precinct leader ever offered the faithful. Thus did the Communists go among the peasants, spreading discontent.

During this same period the Russians took more effective political
measures. They undertook to organize a government in Azerbaijan
which they could leave behind when their army withdrew.

Daniel Komisarov—Soviet press attaché—was the bottomrock of the Azerbaijan affair, the Soviet brain behind the various Communist parties in Iran. He had an excellent knowledge of the Persian language. He sat in the coffee shops and talked man-to-man with the Persians, who liked him for his seeming frankness and meekness. He molded political sentiment the Soviet way.

The man selected to head the government was a native of Azerbaijan, the son of a holy man—Jafar Pishevari. Pishevari is a Communist who was educated in Baku and who taught in Communist schools in Russia. He went back to Persia in the 30's, organizing a union and publishing newspapers—first at Resht and later at Tehran. His paper was closed by Reza Shah Pahlavi, father of the present Shah; and he was sent to jail. When Britain and Russia invaded Persia in 1941, Pishevari and all other political prisoners were released from jail. Tudeh party, the Persian Communist party that always meticulously avoided using the Communist label, was formed in 1942. Pishevari was one of its early members, promoting its causes through a new paper which he founded after his release from jail.

Late in 1945 Pishevari went to Tabriz and formed the Democrat party, the Azerbaijan counterpart of Tudeh. That party led a "revolt." Soviet troops immobilized the Persian Army stationed in Azerbaijan; and Pishevari came into power. A cabinet was formed, a parliament elected, and a political program put into effect. The Pishevari government lasted only from late 1945 to December, 1946. It and the central Persian government quarreled over the supervision of an election called by the Shah. Persian troops entered Azerbaijan, there were a few skirmishes, the government of Pishevari collapsed, and Pishevari left for Russia—forty-five minutes before the Persian Army reached Tabriz. The Russian Army, which had withdrawn from Persia six months earlier, did not come to the rescue.

I had assumed from press reports that Pishevari was not only a Soviet stooge but a bumbling and ineffective one as well. I learned from my travels in Azerbaijan in 1950 that Pishevari was an astute politician who forged a program for Azerbaijan that is still enormously popular.

What his long-range program would have been no one knows. Many suspect it would have followed the Russian pattern; others say it would have been tuned to Persian needs with a mild brand of socialism. But the bulk of the program which Pishevari actually imposed on Azerbaijan was purely straight reform.

1. The part of his program which most impressed the peasants was land reform. It had some communism in it. He confiscated the land of all absentee landlords and distributed it to the peasants. But he left untouched the land of resident landlords; a new law merely increased the tenants' share of the crop.

2. Pishevari also gave a socialistic flavor to his program. His government nationalized the larger banks.

3. Second only to land reform in popular appeal was the law that made it a capital offense for a public official to take a bribe. Two top officials and a few lesser ones were hanged for this offense. The law had an electrifying effect. Merchants told me that they could keep their stores unlocked all night and be safe from robbers. Natives told me that for the first time they could with safety keep their cars on the streets all night without losing wheels, headlights, or any other removable parts.

4. Health clinics were created, some being itinerant and serving the villages from Tabriz.

5. The prices of basic commodities were rigidly controlled, hoarding of food was severely punished, a rationing system was adopted whereby everyone received the minimum requirements for living. Pishevari promised that the cost of living would be reduced 40 per cent; and it was.

6. A minimum-wage and maximum-hours-of-work law was established and collective bargaining between employees and employers was introduced.

7. A public-works program was undertaken and many streets and roads were paved. The unemployed were put to work.

8. A broad educational program was launched, schools being planned for all the villages. The University of Tabriz was founded with two colleges—a medical school and a school of literature. (The University is still a going concern.) The cultural aspects of Azerbaijan were emphasized. Instruction in the primary schools was in the Azerbaijan language.

9. Pishevari sponsored autonomy for Azerbaijan, but not separation from Iran. He wanted at least half the taxes collected in Azerbaijan to be spent there. He wanted the province to have a

greater degree of self-government and a larger representation in the national parliament than it had ever enjoyed.

There were other parts to Pishevari's program; but these were the basic ones. Events intervening since the Pishevari government collapsed have made this program increasingly attractive to the people as they view it in retrospect.

When the Persian Army returned to Azerbaijan it came with a roar. Soldiers ran riot, looting and plundering, taking what they wanted. The Russian Army had been on its best behavior. The Persian Army—the army of emancipation—was a savage army of occupation. It left a brutal mark on the people. The beards of peasants were burned, their wives and daughters raped. Houses were plundered; livestock was stolen. The Army was out of control. Its mission had been liberation; but it preyed on the civilians, leaving death and destruction behind.

On the heels of the Army came the absentee landlords. They demanded not only the current rentals; they also laid claim to the rent which had not been paid while Pishevari was in power. These back payments were a severe drain on the food supply of the peasants. Moreover, the Pishevari crowd, when it left, took quite a few cattle and considerable grain out of the country. The combination of events made the winter of 1947-1948 a harsh one. The pinch on the peasants was acute. In order to survive the winter, they had to draw on their reserves of grain. As a result they had less seed for planting the following spring; and there was a skimpy crop that summer.

The winter of 1948-1949 was bitter cold. There was snow on the ground for seven months or more. Many livestock died, the shrinkage in many herds being as great as two-thirds. On the cold windswept Moghan steppe in northeast Azerbaijan close to 80 per cent of the livestock was lost; and ten thousand tribesmen were on the edge of famine and starvation before spring arrived. Grain and meat were scarce; prices soared.

The landlords of Azerbaijan—the most callous I have known— sold their grain at high prices on the market while their villagers starved. They even sold a lot of seed grain, cutting down the supply for planting in the spring. One hundred tons of wheat sent by the central government to Tabriz to relieve the hunger of the poor never reached them. The local officials sold it on the market and pocketed the proceeds.

The spring and summer were late; the crop of 1949 was slim. Peasants actually were eating grass and roots before the 1949 crop came in, and before the fall of 1949 had passed they were practically out of food. They were so impoverished that not more than 1 per cent of the people of Azerbaijan had enough warm clothes to face the cold of 1949-1950.

The winter of 1949-1950 was the severest of recent record. There were ten feet of snow or more in Azerbaijan. Villages without food were isolated. Peasants dipped into the feed they had for their livestock. Then the livestock died and they ate them. Then they themselves died. Thousands upon thousands died. In the village of Navaii near Khoy where I stopped, fifty out of three hundred people died of cold and starvation. In many villages every person in a household died. It was common to find whole families prostrate, none able even to stand. And yet the granaries of the landlords were often full, the grain being held for a higher price. An illiterate peasant in Navaii stopped his thrashing to tell me some of the lurid details.

The central government sent grain from the Persian Gulf. It is estimated that only half reached the people. The rest was diverted to the black market, much of it going to Iraq. Then came the Russians with their wheat train down the Transcaucasian Railroad, doling out food to the hungry people in an apparently efficient manner. "Russia was a true friend last winter," many a grizzled peasant told me.

But the tragedy of the situation, the pathos and suffering were best summarized for me by a blind beggar and his wife.

He was Karim and his wife was Fatima. Both were well over sixty.

I met them far below Tabriz on the western edge of Kurdistan not far from the village of Kamyaran. My party had had a sumptuous lunch and after eating lay down for the customary siesta. I walked outside to take pictures. Finally the glaring sun drove me to the shade of a senjid tree where the old couple were seated. There we talked for a half hour or so.

These people were beggars of low estate. The man was dressed in rags. His coat was not merely patched; it was made of patches, pieces cut from old blankets, gunny sacks, and canvas. I did not at first notice his finely chiseled features because of the heavy stubble of his gray beard and the streaks of dirt on his face. His hands were long, thin, and sensitive. A typical Azerbaijan felt hat without a brim sat on the back of his head. Gnarled toes stuck out from a pair of decrepit leather sandals.

He and his wife were Christians. She stood unveiled before me, a grimy tan-colored cotton shawl draped over her head. Her face was pinched and drawn, partly from a total absence of teeth, partly from hunger. Her skin was parched and dry like leather, her hands were as thin and skinny as talons. She talked in a shrill voice, nervously twirling the ends of her shawl.

This was their story:

They had been tenants of a landlord in a village which I will call Nourabad. There they had worked all their lives, paying as rent 60 per cent of the crop. Several years ago Karim had gradually lost his sight until now he was blind. He could tell when it was light or dark; but he could not see objects. The whole burden of the farm fell on Fatima.

The winter of 1948-1949 was long and cold. Running out of food, they bought grain from the local agent of the landlord. The legal rate of interest in Persia on agricultural loans is 12 per cent. Their landlord charged them 40 per cent. He collected in grain at the next harvesting.

"Listen," cried the old lady in a voice so shrill that it was almost a shriek. "He charged us eighty cents for grain, and when we repaid him the next year the grain was only forty cents. So we had to pay him back twice as much as we had borrowed. We had to pay the interest too. We paid him almost three times the grain we borrowed." Then looking me in the eye she cried, "Do you think that is just?"

After the landlord had been repaid there was only about a fifth of the crop left for the blind man and his wife. This included fodder and about two hundred pounds of wheat and barley. This couple had not only themselves to feed; they had two sheep, a goat, and a donkey.

Winter came in a rush. It was soon apparent that these people did not have food to carry them and their stock until spring. The landlord's granaries were full; but the agent wanted too high a price and 40 per cent interest. The loan would impoverish them. Further, Fatima's health was poor and she thought she no longer could do the farming alone. So they decided to sell their belongings, take what money they could raise, and go to Tabriz and find work and food. Apart from the livestock there was not much to sell—a small prayer rug, a few dishes, a picture of Christ in a wooden frame. All their belongings brought less than eighty dollars. But with this they could live the winter out in Tabriz. Or so they thought.

They left Nourabad on a bitter cold day, Karim carrying the blankets in a roll on his shoulder. Fatima put in her pockets their remaining food—the thin, unleavened bread which she had baked the night before with the last of their wheat, and a piece of goat-milk cheese about the size of an egg.

Two feet of snow covered the road. They broke a path for several miles and then came into a highway where sleds had passed. Until then Fatima had been guiding Karim by the arm. Now she set him in the broken path and he walked alone.

In this slow and plodding way they came to Tabriz at dusk. Their cheese was gone and most of their bread. They entered a bazaar to replenish their supply of food and inquire about work and lodging. As they stood before a stall where grain was sold a sergeant of the gendarmes stepped up and said, "Where is your home?"

"Nourabad," Fatima replied.

"What are you doing here?"

"We came to buy some grain."

Karim and Fatima did not know that it had been made a criminal offense to sell grain to a nonresident of Tabriz. Rationing had been decreed in all its rigors. Tabriz had enough food for its own population but no more.

"Now you will come to jail," said the gendarme. He hustled them off, Fatima shouting imprecations, Karim protesting. But their objections were of no avail. They spent that night and several more in jail.

"What happened?" I asked.

Fatima took time to answer. "One day the sergeant came in and said, 'How much money do you have?' I told him we had about four hundred tomans [eighty dollars]. He pulled out a book and wrote in it with a pencil. In a few minutes he looked up and said, 'Your fine is four hundred tomans. You can pay me now and I will let you go.'"

Karim spoke up, "I protested to the gendarme. Fatima also argued with him. The gendarme came over to me, took me by the throat, and shook me, saying 'Listen, you blind old devil. People are shot for doing what you did. Do you want to get shot or do you want to pay me that four hundred tomans?'"

"You paid?"

"Yes, we paid," Karim answered. "Now we were penniless, we had nothing. We were out on the streets in a blizzard, no work, no home."

"What did you do?" I asked.

Fatima opened wide her brown eyes now filled with tears and, spreading open her hands, said in a whisper, "See—we became beggars." Then she broke down and sobbed.

Karim and Fatima lived on the streets begging for rials, for food, for pieces of cloth to wrap up Karim's feet. They sought shelter at night behind walls, under packing boxes. Finally an old lady let them sleep on her floor. But she had no food for them. They could not find work. They lived on crusts of bread, on morsels of cast-off food. They and the dogs and other beggars competed for their very lives on the streets of Tabriz.

One night—a cold blustering night in January—something happened which shows how revolutions are sometimes brought to a boiling point.

Karim and Fatima were begging on a street corner of Tabriz when they saw a group of about a dozen peasants being herded along by gendarmes with drawn bayonets. They had committed the same crime that she and Karim had; they had come to Tabriz to find food. Fatima told Karim what was happening and whispered, "Come, let us go with the crowd."

She guided him to the middle of the street and the two of them followed behind the crowd. More joined the procession, all the ragamuffins and beggars of Tabriz. According to Fatima it was a big crowd of several hundred by the time they reached the jail. One of the peasants under arrest tried to escape and was laid low by the butt of a gun.

"We didn't like it," Fatima said. "We shouted at the gendarmes to stop. A big growl went through the crowd. The man who was knocked down was carried into the jail. The rest of the prisoners were shoved and herded like cattle. None of us liked what we saw. I shouted to the prisoners, 'Do not let the gendarmes rob you.' I was angry. Everyone was angry. When I told Karim what had happened, he swore. He was angry too."

Fatima stopped, looked me in the eye and said, "Karim and I are not Communists. Will you believe me? Will you believe my husband? You must believe me before I tell you what happened next."

"Yes, I believe you," I answered.

Fatima straightened up, put out her chin, and with all the pride of Azerbaijan on her face said, "It was awful what had happened to us and to the other peasants. Arrested for trying to buy food! Robbed of our money by the police who were supposed to protect us! Thrown out in the streets to die like dogs of cold and starvation!

"We could not stand it any longer. Everyone in the crowd felt the same way. We stood in front of the jail and shouted in the faces of the gendarmes, 'Pishevari! Pishevari! We want Pishevari!' "

This blind beggar and his wife are typical of those who today make Azerbaijan boil. Their story could be duplicated over and again throughout the length and breadth of that province. It explains why non-Communists flock to Communist leadership in this border area. Here communism gains merely by default, not by a swelling crowd of converts to its cause.

Soviet intelligence in this region is alert. At the time Karim and Fatima were starving in Tabriz the Moscow radio was speaking to Azerbaijan in Persian as follows: "Thousands of the starving people wander in the streets of Tabriz and no one helps them. They are all condemned to death by starvation."

Azerbaijan means the Place of the Keeping of the Fire. The Communists have fanned that fire to the point of blazing.

Pishevari's program was so popular—especially land reform, severe punishment of public officials who took bribes, and price control— that if there had been a free election in Azerbaijan during the summer of 1950, Pishevari would have been restored to power by the vote of 90 per cent of the people. And yet not a thousand people in Azerbaijan out of three million are Communists.

PART II

The Tribes of Persia

Persia, remote and mysterious, is increasingly important in our lives because of the critical frontier it and its oil occupy in world affairs. That is why we must understand it and know what makes it what it is. Persia is deep in our culture and traditions. We have vague recollections from our school days of a part of that influence:

Zoroaster, born about 660 B.C. in Azerbaijan, Persia's northwest province, who taught the unending conflict between good and evil, the dignity and worth of man, the immortality of the soul; the man who preached "Be like God"—

Cyrus, who, as Ezra relates, conquered Babylon from the Assyrians, returned the Jews from their captivity, and helped them rebuild the temple in Jerusalem—

Darius, who, bound by the law of the Medes and the Persians, caused Daniel to be cast into the lions' den and who, when Daniel came out unscathed, embraced Daniel's faith—

Xerxes, who married Esther the Jewess and saved the Jews from Haman's pogrom—

Persepolis, built by Darius about 500 B.C. and destroyed by Alexander the Great two hundred years later—

Sufism, that finds God in the stars and the wind, in the beauty of a countenance or flower, in the expression of love and tenderness—

Firdausi (who wrote the Shah Namah or the Epic of Kings), Omar Khayyám, Nizami, Hafiz, Saadi, Jami, and a long list of other poets whose songs have brought music to most of the earth—

The Bab and Baha'u'llah, who were founders of the Bahai faith—

These personages and events, plus Persian rugs, pictures of an attractive young man called the Shah, and news accounts relating to the assassination of cabinet officers and troubles over oil give a vague impression of the country known to us as Persia and now officially called Iran.

Persia needs to be known more intimately by the West. Though far away and remote, it occupies a strategic and important place in world affairs. It possesses about one-fifth of the known oil reserves in the world. Its ports along the Persian Gulf give access to India and Africa. Its northern neighbor is Russia, who either may need oil or may desire to shut off Europe's supply from the Middle East.

The pages which follow attempt to introduce the people of Persia, to describe their problems, and to analyze some of the major stresses and strains within the nation. I use as my main material the four chief tribes of Persia—the Kurds, the Lurs, the Bakhtiaris, and the Ghashghais who, I think, are a good mirror in which to see the soul and spirit of the nation. These tribes—with whom I have lived intimately—reside in the rough and broken Zagros Mountains that stretch from the Russian and Turkish borders on the north to the Persian Gulf on the south.

If we are to understand these people and see their problems in perspective, we must not only go to Persia; we must return to Persian history and reread it.

Persia, like Armenia, is the land of the invaders. The Greeks conquered it in 331 B.C.; the Arabs in the seventh century A.D. Then came repeated invasions from the east—the Mongols, Tartars, and Seljuk Turks—bringing destruction and devastation to the land, depredations still associated in Persia's villages with the name Genghis Khan. These Turanian invaders held sway for nearly one thousand years, the last dynasty being the Kajar, which ruled for nearly a century and a half until 1925, when Reza Shah, a pure Persian and father of the present Shah, seized power.

Thus the Persians have lived much of their history under foreign rulers. The foreigner has left a great imprint. The Arabs converted Persia to the Islamic faith at the point of the sword. Persians, however, did not accept the faith unconditionally. The orthodox Islamic creed is the Sunni, but the Persians mostly followed the Shiah sect.

This flair for the unorthodox is a distinctive quality of the Persian character. It is an important reason why Persians, though under foreign rule for much of their history, have survived as a race and kept pure the main stream of Persian culture. In fact, much of Persia's finest work in literature and the arts was done during the periods of the invaders. The invader was somehow a challenge; the Persian spirit of independence manifested itself in creative ways.

The invader had other effects on the Persian personality. The Persian is a master of subtle indirection. One hears in official circles that there are fifty-seven different ways of saying yes (bali) in Persian. That of course is a jest; but it has a kernel of truth in it.

Old-timers in Persia say that it is a place where one who comes with impatience learns patience and one who comes with patience acquires impatience. That jest also has a bit of substance to it.

A prominent physician in Persia told me that his greatest difficulty in diagnosis was to get from his patients a true and complete history of their ailments. The long centuries under the rule of the invaders quickened the instinct for survival: one avoided confessions and developed new values for secrecy and evasion.

Life under the invader also taught the art of circuity of thought and action. Indirection became the modus vivendi. One adopted the circuitous method not only for purposes of evasion but for important transactions involving life and honor. Thus if a Persian desired to pledge his loyalty and support to the Shah or the Governor, he never did it directly; he confided his promise to a third person, who by being a witness increased the value of the agreement.

These are minor facets of the complicated Persian personality; and in the main they do no more than add an intriguing flavor. In great measure Persians and Americans have a close spiritual affinity. The Persian is Aryan—the stock that gave most Europeans their culture and ethnic characteristics. The Aryans of Persia have a darker skin than we; but they are more Nordic than Mediterranean. Their heads are long, their foreheads high, their noses narrow. They have a tendency to sparseness. They are a quick-witted, friendly people with a yen for tall tales and dry humor. They know the art of hospitality; they thirst for discourse and argumentation. They love the outdoors— streams and mountains and the hunt. In the social sense they are as democratic as any people I have known. They have a reserve we associate with our New Englanders; but underneath they are close kin to our Westerners. These characteristics, most conspicuous among the tribes, tend to become diluted and modified in the cities.

These tribes of whom I write were from time out of mind principalities within Persia. The Ilkhan of each tribe was a king; the Shah of Persia was the king of kings. The Ilkhans constituted a council of nobles who governed with the Shah. The tribes paid taxes to the Shah and furnished soldiers for the Persian Army. But each tribe had a large degree of autonomy, greater in fact than the separate states of our nation. This system of government survived all invasions. It was somewhat modified by the Greeks, who introduced Governors for the various provinces; but the Governors were in the main tied in with the tribes, and the deep-seated pattern of government continued as before, largely undisturbed. Though the pattern was feudal, not democratic, it was in large measure benign and progressive.

In the eighteenth century disaster struck Persia, a disaster that has been a crippling force even to this day. At that time an alien Turkish tribe, who could not speak the language, seized control of the country and ruled for two centuries. They established the Kajar dynasty, which laid a curse on the land. They ruled and exploited the people; but they did not govern. Seeing the opportunity for profit in Persia's feudal system, they murdered and dispossessed the feudal lords and sold their offices to the highest bidder. The purchasers in turn sold the subordinate positions under them. Sometimes a syndicate would purchase a provincial government and sell at auction to the highest bidder every office way down to the village chief. Thus government became a ferocious, devouring force. It lived on the people. It squeezed every copper possible from them. The feudalism that had been the strength of Persia became the means for bleeding it white.

Justice was for sale. Power was used to exact blackmail. The army and the police were weakened and corrupted. Decay took hold in the moral fiber. The religious ideals that had supplied the generating force behind Persia's great dynasties were discarded.

Not all of the country was despoiled. The Kajar dynasty reached as far into the hinterland as it could, but the fastness of the mountains held treasures it could not reach. These treasures were the main tribes: the Kurds, the Lurs, the Bakhtiaris, and the Ghashghais. They remained independent and largely untouched. Their power in fact grew under the Kajars, for peasants flocked to their dependencies for shelter from the long, oppressive hand of the central government.

For the most part, these four tribes (with unimportant exceptions) flourished in their ancient and accustomed manner until Reza Shah Pahlavi, father of the present Shah—an army officer—seized power in 1925. He undertook to break their feudal system and to settle them in permanent villages. This part of the book touches on that phase of the life and problems of the tribes. But it goes further and attempts to tell what kind of people they are, their worth and position, their role in this momentous period of history.

The books and articles that one finds in our libraries usually describe these tribes in unfriendly terms. The tribesmen are said to be villains —robbers and murderers. Some of the tribes have been used on unholy missions; they have been aroused to fanatic violence; in years past they were instruments through which terror and destruction struck at innocent people. But I walked and lived among these tribes and came to know the lowliest as well as the highest of them. I learned to respect and admire them.

Today they constitute nearly a fourth of Persia's sixteen million people.

They are mostly ruled as they were centuries ago by their tribal chiefs. The Ilkhan is at the top and under him a hierarchy of tribal chiefs—khans who rule a tribe, kalantars who govern perhaps a thousand families or more, kadkhodas who are heads of clans or govern from twenty families on up, and rish-safids, the elders or gray-beards of a clan or village.

These four main tribes are the hard, central core of the nation— proud, passionately independent, courageous, and gallant. They have a deep attachment to their land. They are skilled and resourceful warriors. They could become—if there were the wisdom and political acumen to manage it—an untiring guerrilla force that would relent-lessly harass the invader and over the years make an occupation costly. For they live in wild and rugged mountains where dizzy cliffs and harsh defiles are barriers to all transport but mules. They know every trail, every cave, every spring in that vast and broken land. Patrol of the borders has been their historic mission. In this they have their greatest pride. But time and circumstance—perhaps fate—have con-spired to deprive them of that role in this the greatest crisis in their history, which may also be the greatest crisis in the history of our world.

5. Kurdish Nationalism

THE KURDS are an ancient race located today in five countries—Persia, Turkey, Iraq, Syria, and Soviet Armenia. There are well over a million in Persia alone, largely in the northwest, where they command the Zagros Mountains from Mount Ararat on the north to Kermanshah on the south. The racial origin of the Kurds is not definitely known. Some (including the Kurds) believe they are the original Medes. They are probably from Aryan stock. Those in Persia have a language that has a common root with Persian; but it also has an admixture of Turkish and Arabic.

Ancient Kurdistan is now divided between Iraq, Turkey, and Persia. The Turko-Iraqi frontier cuts through the heart of the ancient country. It has long been the ambition of many Kurds to unite these broken pieces into one nation. At the end of World War I the Treaty of Sèvres provided for a Kurdish state, but events conspired to divide the ancient Kurdistan, not between Turkey and Persia as before the war, but among three nations.

Soviet Russia has played to the nationalist ambitions of the Kurds. Communists go among the tribesmen, posing as their champions. Their propaganda preaches freedom and release; it promises a separate nation for this minority. It was in fact Communist management that engineered a Kurdish state in northwest Persia in 1945.

Divan Darreh is a small village in the southern part of ancient Kurdistan. We stopped there one day for lunch. A spring of clear cool water bubbled out of a pipe into a rock-lined pool in front of a mud-wall house where a detachment of soldiers was stationed. Only a few mud huts lined the dusty village street. A grove of willows by the side of this garrison offered the only shade. As I lighted a gasoline stove and cooked lunch from U. S. Army C rations, we talked of Kurds, of communism, of Divan Darreh.

Divan Darreh means "The Valley of the Devil." How this drab village lying in a defile among low barren hills acquired the name, I do not know. It is a bleak place. In summer there is no touch of greenness to the low-cropped grazing land that extends in all directions as far as the eye can see. Occasional fields of wheat and barley with alternate stretches of fallow land mark a checkerboard in the valleys and on the lower reaches of the hills. This summer the fallow land had not been cultivated, and was covered with a rash of thistles, licorice root, and other weeds which I did not recognize. Men and women were gathering these scrub plants, compressing them into large disk-shaped bundles, and stacking them in the fields. Northwest Persia had had three hard winters, feed for livestock as well as for humans had been short. This next winter the goats, sheep, and donkeys would have to chew on weeds.

A strong wind came up. It was a hot wind with a dry sting. It raced across the fallow land where the farmers were working, swirled dense clouds of dust down the shallow canyons, and whipped through the grove where I cooked lunch. In between its attacks a swarm of yellow jackets descended on our food.

A soldier from the Persian garrison came up to volunteer a story. This village was on the southern border of the country controlled by a Soviet-supported government from 1945 to 1946. The Red Army had established not only the Pishevari government at Tabriz but also one at Mahabad under Qazi Mohammed. During this time many skirmishes took place at Divan Darreh between the Persian Army and the so-called Democrat forces of Mahabad. "Come, I'll show you," said the Iranian soldier.

But I preferred to hear about Qazi Mohammed rather than to review battlegrounds. And so under the dusty willows at Divan Darreh I began to piece together the story of the Kurdish Republic of Mahabad.

Kumela is an abbreviation for Committee of Kurdish Youth. It was a strongly nationalistic secret society formed in Mahabad in the summer of 1943 by a small group of young Kurds. No one could be a member unless he was a Kurd. That meant that both his father and mother had to be Kurds. There was only one exception: the mother could be an Assyrian.

Kumela flourished. It gained wide support among the tribes; it had branches even in Iraq and in Turkey. The Soviets saw in it a chance for sowing seeds of trouble, and before she withdrew her occupation troops in the spring of 1946, she had brought about an important event in the affairs of the Kurds.

Kurds from Russia were attached to the Soviet consulate at Rezaieh as Communist agents, and encouraged Kumela in its nationalist program. The Soviets, who had established in Persia various Iranian-Soviet Cultural Relations Societies, now founded in Mahabad a Kurdistan-Soviet Cultural Relations Society. This society and Kumela worked together. One night in the spring of 1945 they put on a play. The heroine was Mother Native Land; the villains were Iran, Iraq, and Turkey; the heroes were Kurds—the sons of Mother Native Land. In the last agonizing minutes when it seemed that Mother was lost, the sons managed a daring and glorious rescue. The assembled Kurds wept and cheered. It was a moving drama, one that did more than any other single event to unite the Kurds behind the Kumela program.

At this juncture the Soviets took a more direct part, approaching several prominent Kurds with the request that they take charge of the Kumela movement. One of the men they approached was my friend Amar Khan Sharifi, chief of the Shakkak tribe—tall, thin, patrician, now over seventy-five years old. They all refused. Then the Soviets picked Qazi Mohammed of Mahabad, a middle-aged Kurd.

I never met Qazi Mohammed; but from all reports he was a distinguished member of one of the most respected Kurdish families. He was a religious leader among the Kurds and a devout Moslem—indeed, a judge in the Moslem ecclesiastical court. He was well educated and spoke French, Russian, and English. Something of an aesthete, he was a man of deep convictions and great courage; and for a time he was a willing tool of Soviet policy.

The next Soviet step was to supplant Kumela with an organization more amenable to Soviet policy. The Communist party in Persia was the Tudeh party. Qazi Mohammed, after a trip at Russian expense to Baku for a conference with Soviet officials in the fall of 1945, announced the formation of the Democrat party of Kurdistan. He and over a hundred other Kurds signed the announcement, which referred to the victory over fascism; the hope for liberation which all peoples saw in the Atlantic Charter; and the manner in which the Kurds had suffered under Persian rule, particularly under Reza Shah. Its appeal was nationalistic: "We have our own history, language, traditions, customs and habits which are our characteristics. Why should our rights be discarded in this way? Why should we not be allowed to educate our children in their own language? Why will they not permit Kurdistan to be autonomous and to be administered by the Provincial Council which the Constitutional Law allows?"

The Kurds on the whole rallied to the party, many because it appealed to their nationalist pride, others because the Democrats offered an attractive program. The older generation and those in positions of authority with the tribes joined reluctantly and with reservations. They were suspicious of Soviet backing; yet they did not desire to risk liquidation at the hands of the occupying Red Army should they refuse.

The Soviets mustered one rabid band of Kurds behind the Democrats—a renegade group of armed soldiers led by Mulla Mustafa Barzani, a refugee from Iraq. His forces, well-armed and well-trained, reported to Qazi Mohammed for duty and became the central core of his military strength.

On December 15, 1945, the Kurdish Democrat party met at Mahabad, inaugurated a Kurdish People's Government, and raised the Kurdish flag. A parliament assembled; and in January, 1946, Qazi Mohammed was elected President. A cabinet was formed, composed of tribal chiefs, merchants, landlords, and officials. There was no member of the proletariat in the entire government. My friend Amar Khan Sharifi was for a while the Minister of War and for a while Marshal of the Army. Once I asked him why he went into the cabinet. "To save my own neck," he replied wryly.

During 1946 there were skirmishes between the Kurdistan forces and the Iranian Army, some of which took place at Divan Darreh. Mulla Mustafa Barzani supplied most of the army for Qazi Mohammed. Amar Khan Sharifi raised a few troops. But when the Persian Army came in full force in December, 1946, it met with little opposition. Soviet Russia was supposed to have promised Qazi Mohammed military support; but it gave none. Amar Khan's forces offered no resistance. He in fact pledged his loyalty to the Persian government. The anti-Soviet attitude among most of the Kurds was very strong. Only Barzani held out. The Persian Army entered Mahabad on December 15, 1946 without a shot being fired. Their reception was friendly. But the era of apparent good will was short lived. Qazi Mohammed and several of his cabinet were imprisoned; eleven lesser tribal chiefs of the Kurds were shot; and on January 3, 1947 Qazi Mohammed and two of his cabinet were hanged at Mahabad. Barzani, who had retreated to Iraq, swept back into Persia in the spring of 1947, fought his way through the Persian Army, and passed through western Azerbaijan into Russia.

I went to Mahabad on a hot August day. There was not a cloud in the sky and the sun beat down with fierce intensity. There is no sky so clear and blue as Persia's sky. That day it was so bright, so transparent that Mahabad took on a mystic quality—it seemed that one could indeed see into infinity.

Mahabad is south of Lake Urmia—Persia's Great Salt Lake—and east by about seventy-five miles from the main Zagros Mountains. It lies in rolling hill country. The slopes are brown by August. There is some irrigation from a small river; occasional fields are green with corn, melons, tobacco. The only other touches of color are the poplars and willows that line the river bank. When the stream reaches Mahabad it is slow and sluggish. A small dam has been constructed to form a pool in the middle of the town, and the day I arrived dark-skinned, naked boys were playing like porpoises in it. Ladies, dressed in full black skirts and black shawls that hung so low they concealed their blouses, sat under trees tending small children. A few young women dressed in gayer colors pounded clothes on rocks that line the pool.

The streets of Mahabad were practically bare except for grinning boys, ten or twelve years old, who sold sticky, brown-colored candy the size of golf balls, round and bulging with walnuts and covered with flies. A bazaar led off the main street. It was a sort of compound, about a half-block square. Stalls of artisans and merchants were packed close together. There were the smells of coffee, candies, roasting ears, leather, spices, lamb on skewers being broiled over charcoal. There was the noise of hammers striking metal. Deep-throated calls of the stall holders filled the compound.

The traditional dress for Kurdish men is strikingly beautiful: a blue turban, usually made of silk and decorated with tassels; a brightly embroidered vest; coarse wool pants—gray or black—that are loose and baggy; a large sash or *kamarband*—usually bright red

—that is wound around the waist and tied elaborately in front. There is usually a dagger or two sticking out from this waistband and sometimes a pipe.

The men in the bazaars at Mahabad were all Kurds—mostly stocky and broad-shouldered, with white teeth and heavy dark eyebrows, swarthy complexions, high foreheads and prominent noses, dark piercing eyes. Though they were dressed in more somber colors than their traditional costume, most of them wore bright-colored waistbands and some had blue or gray turbans. And practically every one of them had a dagger in his belt. I was to discover that a Kurd is a robust, hearty friend. But that day each of them looked bloodthirsty.

I learned at Mahabad some of the tactics and accomplishments of Qazi Mohammed and his Democrats. During his year of power many things had happened that stirred the Kurds.

The Kurdish costume, which had been banned by Reza Shah, came back into use.

Schools were provided for every child through the sixth grade.

Textbooks for the primary schools were printed in Kurdish.

A newspaper, a periodical, and two literary magazines were published. A printing press had been supplied by the Soviets.

Qazi Mohammed attached to his staff two young poets—Hazhar and Hieman—who wrote not only of Kurdistan and its glories but of Stalin and the Red Army as well.

A constitution was prepared. It proposed a Kurdish state that was republican in character. It pledged the state to defend the interests of Kurdish workers and to create unions for their betterment. It proclaimed that "People should be educated irrespective of race, religion, or sex." It announced that women should have all the "political, economic, and social rights that men enjoy."

The Kurds are Moslems; and under Islamic law women have a very inferior position. But the Kurds in practice have traditionally given women a more exalted role. Kurdish women are not veiled, and have more social freedom than most Moslem women. A Kurdish woman is indeed sometimes found as the head of a tribe. And so the proclamation of equal rights for women was not so revolutionary as it would have been in other parts of the Moslem world.

Qazi Mohammed needed a program of reform if he was to get

mass support from the people. The lot of the average Kurd is misery. Illiterate, and with few or no educational opportunities, he lives at the subsistence level. He knows practically nothing about modern agriculture. Even if he did, he would not benefit from his knowledge, for most Kurds are serfs working for a khan or some other landlord on shares and perpetually in debt. Qazi Mohammed knew the power of the landowners and the political astuteness needed if real measures of reform were to be realized.

Moreover, if his program of reform were to be popular with the people, he had to remove the suspicion that it was the creature of the godless Soviet regime. In general the Kurds are devout Moslems and deeply religious. I have come across them in the remote mountains, on their knees, facing Mecca, and bowing in prayer until their foreheads touched the ground. Many of their affairs are managed by mullahs (priests). The Koran is to them a sacred book. Moreover, the Kurds, unlike most Persians, are orthodox Moslems: they take the Koran literally and completely. And so the Kurd—no matter how wild and ruthless he may appear—has rather strict religious standards.

And so Qazi Mohammed put his scholars to work to find in the Koran and in the teachings of the Prophet principles necessary for his reforms. What he would have done, how he would have proceeded to put through a program of reform no one can tell. We only know that his basic political approach was through the Moslem religion. So far as I could learn he had taken but one specific step under the guidance of the Koran. He had banned usury.

That alone gave him great support among the peasants. In Persia the lawful interest rate on agricultural loans is 12 per cent. But as the story of Karim and Fatima shows, it is not unusual to find loans to farmers at 40 per cent or more. The money lender is usually the landlord. He rents the land on shares that may leave only a fourth or a fifth or even less for the tenant. Once the tenant gets into debt to the landlord he is a perpetual serf. Interest alone eats up the crop and keeps him in eternal poverty. When the landlord is a khan and the tenant a member of the tribe, more considerate terms are apt to be arranged and the tenant not so badly bled. But even legal interest is a heavy cross to impoverished people.

Qazi Mohammed stood, not for separation from Persia, but for autonomy within it, claiming that the Kurds stemmed from the ancient Medes and, like their forebears, had a natural and historic role to perform in partnership with the Persians. He wanted Kurdistan to promote the revival and development of Kurdish culture. There was a good economic reason for his insistence that Kurdistan be tied to Persia rather than to Russia. The Kurds raise much tobacco; and their market for it is to be found in Persia.

There is strong evidence that although Qazi Mohammed used the Soviet power to get his republic established, he planned to develop it along democratic lines. In the latter months of his regime he was in constant touch with the American foreign service in this area, seeking American support and endeavoring to be rid of his dependency on his Soviet sponsors.

But the khans deserted him—not because of his program of reform, but because of his Soviet support. The Kurds have a long memory. They know that Russia is opposed to their religion. They have heard refugees from Russia describe the terror that Russia pours upon anyone who does not conform to the Soviet political creed. They remember Russian troops under the Czar murdering and plundering in Kurdistan and burning whole villages. Their memories of Russians are so poignant that in a Kurdish camp a mother will quiet a crying child by whispering, "Hush or the Russians will hear you."

I forded the river at Mahabad and started out of town to the road that leads down from Maku. In the shade of some poplars by the side of the road a man stood selling grapes. A woman had brought two quarts or so of meal to barter for grapes. The merchant, unmindful of the teachings of the Koran, drove an evil bargain: for two quarts of precious cereal he would give two quarts of second-rate grapes. While this bargain was being consummated, a young Kurd and his wife came down the shaded road. He rode a donkey; she walked proudly by his side. We exchanged greetings.

"Where is your home?" I asked.

"Near Khoy, way up north," he replied.

"What are you doing down here?"

"We are Kurds," he said. "We are making a pilgrimage. We come to pray at the grave of Qazi Mohammed." There was a note of defiance in his voice; and his eyes, as well as the dagger in his belt, conveyed a resolution to meet any challenge to his mission.

The grave of Qazi Mohammed is indeed a shrine; hundreds of Kurds flock there each week to worship. The hanging of this Kurdish hero killed only the man, not the idea of Kurdish independence. His death in fact gave the idea new impetus. In the eyes of the simple peasants who walk hundreds of miles to pay homage to his memory, Qazi Mohammed was a good man who gave his life that their dream might come true.

6. *Once a Kurd Always a Kurd*

MULLA MUSTAFA BARZANI was well received in Russia after the fall of the Kurdish Republic of Mahabad. Having fought both the Iraqi army (defeating it twice in 1945) and the Persian Army, he was a ready instrument of Soviet policy. Moreover, he brought with him a sizable force, numbering about three thousand armed Kurds. Some were tribesmen; others were deserters from the Iraqi army; some were British-trained officers.

From 1947 to 1950 the Russians built Barzani's army up to the strength of ten thousand, gave it intensive training, equipped it with tanks, armored cars, and the Russian repeater gun. It even had an air force. Some eighty Kurds were sent to a Soviet air corps school and given training as pilots.

The Russians curry favor with the Kurds under Barzani, granting them more liberal rations of food than Soviet subjects normally receive. The rations are indeed so liberal that the Kurds have a surplus, which they sell on the black market in Armenia S.S.R.; and Russian officers wink at the offense. The morale of Barzani's army in the summer of 1950 was high for another reason. The Soviets furnished his camps with a liberal supply of girls for the entertainment of the troops.

In the summer of 1950 Barzani's forces were poised along the Russian border in northwest Persia, ready to strike. High-flying planes from Russia dropped leaflets on the Kurds in this area. Printed in Kurdish, Turkish, and Persian, they related how long-suffering the Kurds had been; described the sacrifices and sorrows they had endured; and deplored that their struggle for independence had failed to date. The leaflets went on to say that the Kurds would not have long to wait, that the "democratic forces" of Russia would liberate them, that the Kurds could then have their own republic.

The Soviet timetable for invasion along this southern perimeter seems to have been July 15 to August 15, 1950. There was indeed a great massing of forces at these points. What happened in Korea seemed about to be repeated. I arrived at the Russian border August 18, 1950. A few days earlier Barzani's troops had been withdrawn. The Soviet timetable had been changed. And it was thought at Maku that the change was due to the success (up to that time) of the United Nations forces in Korea.

Maku lies near the tip end of the long finger of land in northwest Persia that is surrounded by Turkey on the left and Russia on the right. It is a town of perhaps five thousand people lying at the mouth of a gorge. On the east a mountain range ends in a towering cliff about a half mile long and twelve hundred feet high; less than a mile to the west is another mountain about as high. In between runs a small shallow stream, the Maku River. Its gorge opens to the north onto a broad rolling plain.

A part of Maku lies along the river bank, where a few homes of the rich fill the spot with trees and lush gardens. But most of Maku lies up the hill under the cliff, which has crumbled and worn at the base to form a huge overhang. The main town is built under that roof. Houses of rocks and mud stand on great slabs that have broken from the mountain. The cliff has numerous caves. Centuries ago a fortress was built here. There is even a spring high on its sides that could in older days keep a beleaguered populace supplied with water.

We passed through the gorge and entered the rolling plain. Straight ahead is Turkey. On the right perhaps ten miles distant is a long stretch of barren hills—a ridge around seven thousand feet high that marks the Russian border. Ahead about twenty miles is Mount Ararat. This mountain, which towers nearly seventeen thousand feet high, seemed dim and remote in the dusk, almost like a mirage of a peak. A streamer of clouds hung below its crest. The volcanic ash, spewed down its slopes from ancient eruptions, had a velvety sheen in the evening's haze. From this angle its sides had somewhat the symmetry of an inverted cone; but the tip was not pointed; like Mount Adams of our Cascade Range Ararat has a false top before the true one is reached. Flecks of snow were scattered on the upper third of the mountain—great snow fields that stay there the year round. To the right was Little Ararat—two-thirds the size of its parent and carved more precisely in the image of an inverted cone. It was dark and somber in the gathering dusk, too low to have any touch of gray on its crown.

We stayed that night about ten miles out of Maku at Baghcheh Jough—a palace built about a century ago by a khan who made it a showcase of his wealth. There are terraces of apple orchards and gardens, and a beautiful pool. The ceilings are high; the rooms spacious; the decorations are gold and cut glass. The walls of the bedrooms have life-sized paintings of beautiful and voluptuous women.

The khan who built Baghcheh Jough not only had great wealth; he had an army as well. He left a son who commanded a principality at the head of this dangerous Persian corridor. Reza Shah, deciding the son should be deposed, sent the Persian Army against him and defeated him in battle; then he stripped the palace clean, taking away all the movable property. I talked to a peasant who worked on the palace grounds at that time.

"It took seven camels to carry the loot away," he told me.

This August night was cool from a wind that swept off Ararat. I watched the stars come out behind the mountain and sat at the edge of a row of apple trees talking with natives about its glories. Ararat is where Noah landed the Ark. Marco Polo called it the Mountain of the Ark of Noah, and to this day many Persians call it the Mountain of Noah. Legend has it that the first vineyards of the world grew on Ararat's slopes. Its grapes made the wine with which survival from the Deluge was celebrated. One peasant at Maku said that it was from Ararat that the wise men saw the star over Bethlehem.

The legend of Ararat and the Ark will not die. The summer before I came to Ararat a group of Bible students had explored it, looking for remnants of the Ark. Some at Maku believe they can be found.

In the morning Ararat was only the ghost of a mountain seen dimly through a mist. The hot air rises early from the plain, strikes the snow fields, and condenses into vapor. That is why in the summer the best views of Ararat are at night. I rode across the plain already drenched in the sunlight of a brilliant day. Persian regiments were practicing their maneuvers on the slopes leading to Ararat.

This is country that the Russians frequently raid, probing and punching in an endeavor to see how strong their southern neighbor is. In the summer of 1949 the raids were numerous. On one foray they captured a half-dozen Persian soldiers in an outpost, and kept them a year. I studied the passes through which the Soviets might someday come and looked down at the gorge at Maku through which they could roar like a flood. The ridge marking the Russian border a few miles to the north looked peaceful and innocent this morning. Behind it lay the famous Araxes River which Russia has closed to all traffic. Between five and six o'clock in the evening people are allowed to come down to it for water at designated places. On its banks are barbed-wire fences that run the length of the border. Behind the barbed wire are land mines—not mines that explode but mines that cause alarms to ring or rockets to rise, exposing the intruders. Great secrecy hangs over this border, and transit across it is forbidden. Even the Kurds have little intercourse with Russia. Years ago the Soviets suspected their Moslem population and throughout this particular region moved them away from the border and resettled them in the back country.

In August, 1950, there was great tension in the region of Maku. Would Russia invade? Would the United States "let" the Kurds have an independent province or state in Persia? Would the United Nations help the Kurds against Russia as it helped the South Koreans?

But a different kind of trouble also brewed. The Maku region has a population as poor as any in the Middle East. A third of the people are Kurds, roaming with meager herds on poor marginal land between Persia and Turkey. Most of the rich bottom lands are owned by a few men who are not Kurds, and who live in Tehran, Paris, London. They represent the worst of absentee landlords. For example, during the severe winter of 1949-1950 the landlords held their grain for higher prices; the peasants starved. How many died in and around Maku I do not know, but the total was in the hundreds. Russia sent relief. Russian relief reached there before the relief sent by the Persian government.

I talked with Mostafa Vakili, Governor of Maku, a young liberal of high caliber and high ideals, a credit to the government of the late Razmara who was pushing for reforms. In reviewing the economic plight of the tribesmen and the peasants in this area, he told me of a challenging program he had under way.

This vast valley has rich land and can produce great quantities of food. Vakili has worked out a plan that will rid the region of some of the evils of absentee ownership. The land is to be pooled so that it can be managed by a co-operative. Modern machinery will be brought in; scientific farming will be introduced; savings on purchases will be effected by central procurement; marketing will be done through the co-operative.

How the land was to be acquired from the landlords or, if not acquired, how their share of the profits were to be worked out had not been determined in the summer of 1950. But Vakili knows that reform in the Middle East begins with the land. He knows that the only political antidote to communism in this region is a program of social justice that is reflected in the lives of the peasants. "We can make Maku an outstanding example of what can be done in a co-operative democratic way," he told me.

As my jeep turned and started its long journey south, Maku and its problems tumbled through my head. There it lies under the shadow of the Russian border, seething with unrest. The unrest stems principally from poverty and starvation. They in turn result from an agricultural serfdom.

Then I thought, why not make Maku the show window of democracy? A land-distribution program, modern houses, schools, churches, roads, hospitals—all these could be had for a tiny fraction of the billions appropriated for foreign aid and lost through the drainpipes of fraud and corruption. We can build factories in Italy to make a few men rich. Why not build on the Soviet border at one of the most troubled spots in the whole world a model, democratic community? Then when people ask, "What does America stand for in her foreign policy?" we could proudly reply, "Maku."

Maku would speak louder than any propaganda; no better barrier to communism could be built. Maku would be a shining example of democratic ideals. It would be a powerful revolutionary force working by its own example to uproot the feudal system that stretches from the Mediterranean to the Pacific. Yet today Vakili makes bricks without straws; and works singlehanded to hold his community against the depredations of the landlords on the one hand and the savage propaganda of the Communists on the other.

All the way to the bleak village of Askar Abad where I cooked lunch this idea pounded in my head. I thought of Washington, D.C., and speeches of democracy and peace and containment of communism. Those words were flat and meaningless in the environment of Maku. Democracy and peace? Containment of communism? Why was not the mighty voice of America raised against governments of landlords? Why was it not pleading the cause of the peasants? No foreign policy would make sense at this farflung outpost unless it was cast in those terms.

Yet in August, 1950, there was still time to keep the masses from going over to Soviet Russia. I learned at Maku that while the border people think the individual Russians are good neighbors, they fear and distrust Soviet Russia. They know that Russia would devour them. In spite of their misery and suffering there are very few Communists among these border people.

Two Kurdish tribes—the Jalali and the Milani, numbering over two thousand families each—live in the neighborhood of Maku. They winter on the Russian border and in the summer move south along the Turkish frontier for grazing. Their khans were imprisoned by Reza Shah, who tried to settle the tribesmen in villages. He had mud houses built for them and underground caves for their cattle. But those restraints were temporary and unsuccessful. Today these Kurds are nomads, hostile to the Persian Army and friendly to their neighbors, the Russians. I learned that Omar Agha Omoei, one of the Milani khans, helped Barzani, for a fee of five hundred gold pieces, find a short cut to Soviet territory when he was fighting the Persian Army. The Jalali and Milani Kurds are said to be in regular contact with Soviet agents who maintain friendly relations with the tribes. During World War II some of these Kurds in fact acted as agents for the Soviet Army. Russia, however, had many allies at that time. She undoubtedly has a hold on some of these Kurds today. But I was convinced that by and large the friendliness of these Kurds to Russia was the friendliness of one neighbor for another, not friendliness born of a common ideology.

I learned three things from my visit among the Kurds. *First*: Kurdish nationalism is in the marrow of these tribesmen—deeper than any creed or dogma. They want a state of their own, one in which they have a degree of self-government. But their basic loyalty is to Persia. There it will remain. They have pride in the tradition that they are the Medes. They have pride in their historic role—border patrol. Neither their misery and poverty nor Communist propaganda have altered those articles of their faith.

Second: The Kurds have a saying, "The world is a rose; smell it and pass it to your friends." That philosophy represents today a yearning for a better life, an opportunity to be freed from a serfdom that often means death, that always means poverty and misery. There are good things in life; and the Kurds propose to have them. The Kurds have never had great political leadership nor known the art of government. But they have staying qualities that others have lacked. They are the ones that harassed and plagued the ten thousand Greek troops under Xenophon who retreated through Persia to the Black Sea in 401 B.C. Today they are true to character. They will plague any power that stands in the way of social justice.

Third: At Maku I talked with people about Barzani. Some feared him. Others distrusted him. A lesser khan of the Kurds, though holding no brief for Barzani, felt that there were extenuating circumstances. As a refugee from both Iraq and Persia, Barzani was welcome only in Russia. This khan argued for Barzani's return to Persia, believing Persia would gain greatly from this move. Russia would be deprived of its greatest Kurdish ally. A Kurdish province could be formed—a province with local autonomy but loyal to the central government at Tehran. Barzani, he maintained, would be a loyal supporter of that regime.

I asked how he could be so sure; why it was not likely that Barzani, if he were brought back, would work for the Soviet interests and turn the Kurdish state into a Soviet puppet.

The Kurd rose and looked at me several minutes before answering. There was pride in his face, and the words came with precision.

"There is one thing people forget," he said. "Once a Kurd always a Kurd. On that I will stake my life."

7. Sons Are an Ornament

THE WELCOME which a Kurdish tribe gives a guest is not only hearty; it is a bloody affair as well. On the outskirts of the village a delegation of men hold a steer ready for the slaughter, and as the guest approaches, one of them stabs the animal in the throat. There is the last agonizing moment when the steer lets loose a bloody, gurgling bellow before it is dragged across the road, leaving a stream of blood in its wake. The guest then steps across the blood. The executioner saws vigorously on the neck of the beast until the head is severed. Then he heaves it to the side of the road and the khan or other ranking host turns to the guest, takes him by the hand, and says in a loud, ringing voice, "May that happen to the heads of all your enemies."

It is a robust, primitive, and genuine welcome. The ceremony is not the Asian equivalent of one of our stereotyped greetings. The sacrifice builds a bond of blood between guest and host. The new arrival is now a member of the tribe. He has special privileges, too. Every last man will give his life to defend him. Every man, woman and child will cater to his needs and show him every courtesy. We of the Western world have no acquaintance with that quality of hospitality. It is a pledge of friendship and fealty.

In origin it was an expression of gratitude that the guest had arrived safely and in good health. The best way of showing thanks was to kill something precious to the host. In ancient days when a Persian king came to a village or a tribe, the head man would go through the motions of killing a son, since an heir would be closest to his heart. And the villagers or tribesmen, playing their part, would rush in and prevent it. The king, understanding the play, would be deeply moved.

I usually managed to avoid the slaughter of the steer by having

an interpreter rush forward with a request that the animal be released. There was no offense in that request. The welcome was still
warm and hearty; and a needless sacrifice was avoided. It was just
as well there was no sacrifice at Zindasht. It would have been a messy
as well as a bloody affair, for we arrived just about dark.

Amar Khan Sharifi stood on the outskirts of the village to greet
us. With him stood his twelve sons—from forty-eight to eight
years old. At a respectful distance behind him stood a group of
villagers.

Amar Khan, over six feet tall, sparsely built, trim, with a head
of close-cropped gray hair, stepped forward to greet me. He took
my hand in both of his and held it for at least five minutes while we
talked through my interpreter.

He opened the conversation by saying, "Welcome to Zindasht."

My reply was, "I bring you greetings from a man who has a real
affection for you and your people—George Allen."

George Allen, present American Ambassador to Yugoslavia, had
met Amar Khan while Ambassador to Persia. That was during the
Kumela days. When Amar Khan joined the cabinet of Qazi Mohammed, he kept in touch with George Allen and threw his weight
against the Soviet influence in that government. After the Mahabad
government fell, and Amar Khan stood in danger of being hanged
along with Qazi Mohammed, George Allen pleaded Amar Khan's
case before the Shah, winning both the case and Amar Khan's devotion.

Undoubtedly the memory of this was in Amar Khan's mind as
he answered: "Anyone who is George Allen's friend is *my* friend."

He motioned to his sons, who came up in the order of their age,
the oldest first. He introduced each one.

"Hossein—Judge Douglas." And so it went—Mohammed, Mustafa, Nasser, and so on—until each had shaken my hand. The sons
now stood in a crescent around Amar Khan and me. Turning to
them Amar Khan spoke as follows: "The Judge is one of us. Our
homes are now his. Anything he wants he can have. Always stay
close to him and protect him. See that no harm comes to him whatever it may cost."

Turning to me he said, "You are now one of us. This is your
home. Come and go as you please. Anything we can do for your
comfort and pleasure we will do."

We walked fifty yards or so, climbing a low height of land where Amar Khan's house stands. It is a large compound built around a garden and housing 103 people.

A dark hallway with a rough stone floor stood at the head of steep stairs also made of rock. To the right was a large room—about thirty by eighteen—lighted by Coleman gasoline lanterns. It was completely bare, except for several Persian rugs on the floor and three straight-backed wooden chairs in a corner. I stood at the far end of the room waiting for some signal. Nothing happened. Everyone remained standing and silent. Kazi, my interpreter, whispered in my ear, "They are waiting for you to sit down."

"Where do I sit?" I whispered.

"The chairs are for you. But Amar Khan always sits on the floor."

Down I sat on the floor, my knees under me. I was on Amar Khan's right. On his left were his sons, seated according to their age, his oldest next to him. Amar Khan seldom wears a hat. But his sons do; and as is the custom in Persia, they kept them on indoors. A short stocky man, dark and swarthy, came in with water and a basin. He too wore a hat; but his shoes were off. He put the basin in front of me, gave me soap, and then poured warm water from the gooThenecked pitcher over my hands. When each of my party had washed, the servant returned with a huge linen table cloth and placed it on the rugs the whole length of the floor. Then he set the table and brought in dishes of food.

While this was going on Amar Khan and I talked. He is a soft-spoken man with a quiet, musical voice. There is not a trace of bluster in him; but he speaks with emphasis and authority. He has a patrician look—high forehead, prominent nose, soft gray eyes, a relaxed, composed face. He is trim and agile, and his seventy-eight years had left little mark on him in the summer of 1950.

He has spent ten years of his life in jail, most of it in Turkey, for he fought the Turks in World War I and went to jail as a consequence. But in spite of his long periods of isolation he has raised a large family. He has had six wives, two of them Turkish. In 1950 he had twelve living sons. How many daughters he had I could not learn. One does not easily discuss the females in the environment of the Islamic faith. Nor do I know how many children were born to him. In urban Persia about 80 percent of the children die before they reach the age of one, usually from dysentery. The mortality among the children of the tribes is probably lower, owing to better water and healthier living conditions in the mountains. Yet even so, Amar Khan's total offspring must have well exceeded seventy-five.

The Kurds of this border area are a taciturn people—reserved and quiet. Their conversation is as cryptic as that of the classic Vermonter. The sons this night did not say a word. And I soon discovered that if there were to be conversation, I would have to supply most of it, as Amar Khan is a man of few words.

I told him where I had been on my trips in Persia. His laconic comment was, "Persia is honored to have you as a guest."

I mentioned that we had used practically every means of travel—air, rail, bus, jeep, horse, and on foot. His comment was brief, "God has given us many modes of travel and we must use them all."

I said that from Zindasht we planned to travel horseback to Rezaieh, a lovely city on the shores of Lake Urmia. He said cryptically, "I cannot discuss that."

I said I would like to get advice from him—how far it was to Rezaieh, the best route, etc.

He answered, "As long as you are my guest I cannot discuss your departure."

I thanked him for the sentiment behind those words but said that we had to do some forward planning.

"Should you later decide you must leave, then we will have time to talk of Rezaieh. But you are now my guest. There will be no more discussion of your departure."

I changed the talk to Communist propaganda, wondering how well-acquainted he and the Kurds were with it. I had been amazed at the number of radios I had already seen south of the Soviet border, where, I had learned, the most popular radio program was the Voice of India. The clandestine Soviet radio in Azerbaijan was second; B.B.C. was third. Now the Voice of America has been reorganized and rates high; but in the summer of 1950 it was somewhere near the bottom. I was anxious to discover if the Kurds also had radios, and if so, what programs they listened to.

I discussed these matters with Amar Khan and inquired if he had a radio. It was as if I had asked a business man in Portland, Oregon, if Portland had a Chamber of Commerce or a Rotary Club.

"Certainly I do," Amar Khan replied in a surprised voice. He said something to one of his young sons who immediately brought a large battery set with a wide short-wave range.

"What stations can you get?"

"Practically any. Which would you like?"

"Let's hear the Moscow radio."

And so for a few minutes we listened to a harsh Russian voice, charged with invective. Amar Khan turned it off and for the first and only time during my visit became talkative. He discussed Korea. At that time it seemed questionable whether the United Nations could gather enough momentum in time to hold their initial beachheads. Amar Khan spoke of this; he expressed the belief that America had temporized too much, that it should never have let North Korea build up its military might. He spoke of the dangers of communism; he discussed its methods of operation and its use of terror as an instrument of government. Here in a border region of Persia I was receiving a seminar on communism—an informed and intelligent discussion of it. There were no newspapers here, no magazines. I did not realize at the time that Amar Khan was practically illiterate and probably could not have read them had they been available. But he has a remarkable facility for analysis and an instinct for the relevant. I complimented him on his understanding of the Communist issue. He bowed and thanked me; and then dismissed it with the words: "We have eyes"—referring to the former Kumela government and the activities of the Soviets in northwest Persia; "We have ears"—referring to the radio.

All this time we sat on the floor. During our discussion the food was brought in. Kazi whispered, "No one will start eating until you do."

It was an elaborate meal: a thick barley soup, several kinds of rice, lamb on long skewers broiled over charcoal, broiled chicken, goat cheese, thin waferlike bread, cucumbers, tomatoes, various jams and jellies, and large dishes of stewed wild plums. I later discovered the wild plum trees as I crossed the ravines behind Zindasht to climb some of the ridges. This evening I followed Amar Khan's example and learned that one of the real delicacies of Persia is stewed wild plums (with plenty of juice) on boiled rice.

After the dishes were removed the servant rolled up the table cloth and returned with a tray of piping hot tea and lumps of coarse sugar. I knew that somewhere in the recesses of this large house were women servants—the ones who cooked the delicious meal, the ones who would wash the dirty dishes. But in my stay at Zindasht no woman of the house ever appeared. Once I looked up at a second-story window and saw the quick withdrawal of a face—a woman had been furtively watching the goings-on. Never once did one participate in any of the festivities, except the dances. I wanted to extend to them through Amar Khan my appreciation for the delicious meal. I said as much and added, "You have wonderful cooks."

He bowed his head and replied, "God has been good to me."

We talked of horses, hunting, Barzani, and the legends of Mount Ararat until fatigue overtook me. I somehow managed to unlock my knees and stand erect. Everyone stood. I excused myself. Amar Khan bowed; so did each of his sons. "God be with you," he said. And the short swarthy servant showed us to our room, which was immediately off the room where we dined. It too was bare, except for rugs. Two small windows about five feet from the floor gave light and air. We laid our sleeping bags on air mattresses, put up our tents of mosquito netting, and went to sleep.

The sun was high when I awoke. A cock was crowing; and there was a chatter of birds I did not recognize from an orchard outside our window. The creek where one washed and the toilet were outside; one had to pass through the dining hall to reach them. I opened the door and found Amar Khan and all his sons seated on the floor, eating their breakfast. They rose at once. I motioned to them to sit; but they remained standing. When I re-entered the room after my toilet, they once more stood up and would not sit down until I joined them.

Breakfast was typically Persian: tea, thin waferlike bread, cheese, marmalade, and cucumbers. This too was a silent meal. In the middle of it I heard in the distance the sound of a horn and a drum. It came closer and closer, until in a few minutes it was right under the window where Amar Khan and I sat.

He turned to me and said, "My people want to put on some dances for you. When you are ready they will start." I was to learn that these dances are robust affairs. This band or orchestra played four hours without missing a beat; and the male dancers danced for ten hours without more than a few minutes rest every hour or so.

The music of the dances is monotonous, loud, and primitive. It is as robust as the Kurds themselves and lacks the plaintive qualities of the music of the south. The horn is a crude instrument. The drum is a conventional type, beaten unmercifully with a sawed-off cane. The themes vary from war to hunting to love. Some of the most popular tunes are *Yarpeyda* (My Beloved Can Be Seen) and *Yar guzal* (Beautiful Beloved).

Three or four men will start off; holding hands, dancing in unison, and moving clockwise around the orchestra. Sometimes they jump high in the air, bend low to the ground, and kick, and stomp with vigor, Russian style. When men and women dance together—the two lines joined—there is no touch of abandon. The steps are then staid and stiff; there is no whirling or stomping; the movement is as simple as our one-step. The women dancers always carry large, bright-colored handkerchiefs tied with a string to one of their fingers. Their costumes are brilliant, their skirts full and flowing.

The Shakkak tribe in olden days migrated with the seasons, coming down to Lake Urmia in the winter and combing the mountains that lie toward Turkey in the summer. But today this tribe, like a majority of the Kurds, is sedentary. Amar Khan lives in Rezaieh during the winter, but his tribe is largely located in villages where they stay the year round. In the old days practically every Kurd in the Shakkak tribe had a horse. Today the need for horses has largely disappeared. Trucks give faster transportation; and the work of the farms is done by water buffalo and a few donkeys.

Amar Khan has only eight horses left—full-blooded Arabian horses, mostly grayish white. They are stallions and mares. I doubt if the Kurds ever had a gelding. Amar Khan's horse is a stallion, a gentle but high-spirited animal. I rode him and thought I never had been astride a finer animal. Then Amar Khan rode him; and I thought I never had seen a better rider.

Horse races were arranged for me. Men mounted on stallions went a mile or more beyond Zindasht and at a signal turned and came back in a mad dash. They leaned forward in the saddles shouting at each other and at their steeds. Their white teeth, dark features, heavy black eyebrows, and scowling faces made them the picture of terror-on-horseback. Maybe, as some chronicles relate, the Kurdish horsemen were never quite a match for the Cossacks. But these riders of the Shakkaks convinced me that whatever the Kurds may have lacked in military skill they made up in daring, gallantry, and grim determination.

Amar Khan is the paramount chief of the Shakkaks. The duties of the office are considerable. He has the peace of the tribe to maintain; he is the father confessor for many of the problems of his people; he sits as a court of last resort in many matters.

Among the Kurds there is a division of judicial and notarial duties between the mullah (the Moslem priest) and the head khan. The mullah supervises all arrangements pertaining to marriages and divorces. Wills must be made before the mullah. They may be oral; but if they are written the mullah is the notary. The mullah also handles minor cases involving civil disputes. Men may quarrel over the location of a boundary line. One may claim a sheep that another has. One or both may take the case to the mullah, who hears each side and renders a decision. The procedure is informal; the decree is binding by force of the word of the priest.

The head khan also sits as a judge. He hears the serious criminal cases, such as assault, manslaughter, robbery, adultery; and he may also take over a civil case involving large interests and potentially disruptive of the peace of the tribe.

Feuding is permissible among the Kurds; it is indeed a point of honor to kill in retaliation. These cases are brought to Amar Khan, who inquires into them to learn if the killer and the deceased were feuding. If he finds there was a feud, he will not entertain the complaint.

If two men row over a water buffalo and one is killed, that is manslaughter. Amar Khan hears the evidence on both sides. Once he is satisfied that the accused is the killer, he turns to the question of damages. He considers not only the wealth of the killer; he inquires into the needs of the family of the deceased. Then he makes an assessment. If the deceased was in the prime of life, $2,500 damages are considered adequate. The defendant normally pays in sheep or goats, not in money.

But the assessment of damages is not the end of Amar Khan's functions. He seeks a reconciliation between the families, for he wants no feuding. The reconciliation is sought in a curious way. He tries to persuade the killer to go to the home of the deceased and stay all night. If he does, the wounds are cured for all time. As I said earlier, Kurdish hospitality is a noble thing. A visit to the home of a Kurd is an honor to the householder and his family. They reciprocate by pledging a bond of fealty.

Manslaughter, robbery, and assault are not punished by imprisonment. And no fine is imposed as we understand the term, only the payment of damages. In robbery, return of the property is first sought. There is a place in Kurdish jurisprudence for murder, but it is a mighty rare occurrence. In such cases corporal punishment by hanging is provided. But there can be no hanging without the mullah's consent. Amar Khan could remember no case of murder. What we would call murders were killings in the course of feuding. Manslaughters were deaths resulting from sudden quarrels.

Adultery is not noticed unless the woman is married, when the offense is most serious. She is at once divorced after a trial before the mullah. The man is tried before Amar Khan. If he is found guilty, he is taken to the village center and stripped. Four men hold him by legs and arms. He then is publicly whipped—one hundred stinging lashes across the back. "Flog each of them with a hundred stripes" is the command of the Koran. Amar Khan says that that is the worst punishment he ever decreed. Adultery is a grave offense among every Persian tribe. I was to learn that it was even more serious among the Lurs. The Lurs from time immemorial stoned the man to death if the woman was married.

Amar Khan's court has no clerk or marshal. It has no records. There are no briefs; and no opinions are written. Amar Khan looked surprised when I inquired if the parties were represented by lawyers. "Of course not," he answered. Each litigant acts as his own lawyer. Each swears on the Koran to tell the truth. Amar Khan stated that after the oath was administered, the question of discovering the right or wrong of the case was easy. "No one can lie after he swears on the Koran," he said.

I suggested that people under oath sometimes commit perjury. Amar Khan was astonished. It was impossible for him to comprehend that a man under oath would lie. I put the case of a major dispute over property—a case brought before him rather than the mullah. The complaining party produces a witness who takes the oath and swears the plaintiff's way. The defense produces a witness who takes the oath and swears the other way. Amar Khan stopped me by raising his hand and shaking his head. Then he spoke with great emphasis: "That is impossible. The truth can be only one way when there is an oath taken."

The more I saw of Amar Khan the more convinced I was that his wrath would bring greater punishment than any of the penalties for perjury given in the Koran. He is the police court and the Supreme Court of the Shakkak tribe. He holds his people with a tight rein. There is no doubt in my mind that if anyone lied in Amar Khan's court and was discovered, he would be publicly whipped.

And so when Amar Khan sits cross-legged on a rug, motions the litigants to sit before him, and administers the oath, I think justice will be done. Yet Amar Khan Sharifi cannot read; and when I asked him for a note with his autograph he said with some embarrassment that all he could write was Amar Khan.

There are apple trees and a rather extensive apricot orchard behind Amar Khan's house. He has also made extensive plantings of poplars similar to the Lombardy. Thus Amar Khan's home sits in shade. But Zindasht, which lies across a narrow valley from Amar Khan, has no touch of greenness. Its houses have mud walls and flat roofs. There is no grass; no vines trail over the houses; not a tree is in sight. Like all other villages and towns in Persia (except Shiraz) the houses have no piped water or plumbing. Zindasht, like the great majority of villages in the Middle East, has the stamp of squalor, as well as poverty, on it.

Most of the people of Zindasht are tenants. Amar Khan or some lesser khan owns the land. Dry farming land is rented to them for one-fifth of the crop; irrigated land for one-third. They grow some melons, corn, and tobacco, but wheat and barley are the largest crops.

The villagers are the poorest of the poor by our standards. They live largely at the subsistence level. Amar Khan loves his people too dearly and has too great a pride in them to let any suffer from starvation; it is indeed part of his responsibility as head of the tribe to see that they do not starve. Nonetheless the villagers of Zindasht have a tenancy that keeps them forever poor. Amar Khan recognized it in one of our conversations. A group of bright-eyed children dressed in rags were playing below the terrace where we sat. I commented that they seemed not only happy but healthy as well.

His reply was slow in coming. At last he said, "Your sympathetic heart makes your mind generous."

Zindasht has no school. There is one in a neighboring village about ten miles distant where instruction for boys is given through the fourth grade.

In earlier years—perhaps as little as a century ago—the rolling hills around this village were covered with oaks. But I scouted great areas of it and found no single shoot. The trees had been cut and consumed by man; the new forests had been eaten by goats before they could get beyond the seedling stage. So today the villagers have no fuel except the dung of their water buffalo, which they make into thick wafflelike disks for use in cooking and heating. This dung makes a hot fire, excellent for cooking. But it should be returned to the earth as a fertilizer. The lands of the Kurds are already greatly depleted. Their depletion increases at a mounting rate.

The salvation of Zindasht is the water that pours from a few springs. It is enough for modest irrigation and for household purposes. One stream also furnishes power for a series of primitive grist mills which are owned by khans. The fee for grinding is one-twentieth of the grain.

The overwhelming economic problems of Zindasht were in my mind the morning I said farewell to Amar Khan. He assembled his sons outside his home and we spent an hour or so taking pictures. He was proud of them and they seemed to adore the old man. He earlier had quoted to me from the Koran, "Wealth and sons are the ornaments of this present life." Now he spoke feelingly of his sons. They would carry on after he had gone; he wanted them always to be my friends; he asked me to bring my son Bill out to his tribe for a whole summer or a year or as long as he could stay.

I extended to him an invitation to visit my home in the States. "Inshallah [if God is willing]," he replied.

I asked him what education his boys had received. He told me that he had sent only one of them to school. That son had finished the sixth grade and gone no further. One boy in the family to read and write and keep account books was enough!

That was for me a sad note on which to leave Amar Khan. Known throughout Persia as "the grand old man" of ancient Kurdistan, he is the embodiment of tribal gallantry and glory. He has character and is the kind of person men will follow to victory or death. Yet those qualities are not enough of an inheritance these days. The overwhelming problems of most of the Kurds are economic, agricultural, and political. Every generation has difficulty enough in working out its salvation through the knotty complex of modern civilization. The chances of finding it under leadership which, though intelligent, is illiterate are practically nil.

8. A New Deal for the Kurds

ABDOLLAH ILKHANIZADEH is the head khan of the Debukri tribe of Kurds. He is a slight man, of middle age and medium height, with a long, narrow face, dark eyes, black hair, and a receding hairline. I met him at Bukan, a town of perhaps eight thousand people, south of Mahabad and Lake Urmia.

He is soft-spoken and quiet. His fingers are long, his hands narrow, his handshake warm. If I had to guess at his occupation, I would say he was a Wall Street broker or banker. The day I met him he was dressed the part. His suit was tailor-made and a conservative gray. His shoes were English; and any American haberdashery might have sold him the shirt and tie.

He and his brother Ghassem together with a group of villagers met me on the edge of Bukan and escorted me to his villa, a ten or twelve room stucco house. An open porch with a roof of peeled, poplar poles runs the length of the house, facing a walled-in garden. At one side is a shallow pool filled with water lilies. Petunias were in bloom; and sunflowers were so high their bobbing heads showed beyond the garden wall.

The house faces west onto a broad wide valley that is rich in soil and produce. Bukan sits at the head of this valley. On the flanks and far in the distance are rolling hills. Bukan is spring-fed. Apricots, grapes, melons, and a wide variety of vegetables are grown there under irrigation. Much grain is grown by dry-farming. There are also many cattle and sheep. But the livestock is coming to be of secondary importance. And Bukan, 100 per cent Kurdish, is fast becoming settled in its ways and a conservative farming community.

Abdollah Ilkhanizadeh has political wisdom as well as business acumen. Most of his people own five to ten acres of land; and those who do not farm have stalls in the bazaar at Bukan and make or sell merchandise.

I sat on the porch of Abdollah's house talking of these things until late at night. He was convinced that ownership of property—land, business, sheep—has a magic curative effect on social disorders. One of the chief troubles in the world is that people do not have a stake, an interest in making their society wholesome and healthy. Ownership—individual ownership—gives that incentive. Bukan, he concluded, shows the stabilizing effect of that program.

Up north the Kurds around Maku and Zindasht are mostly poverty-stricken, as I have said. South of Bukan are the Javanrudis, another Kurdish tribe of very poor people. Their land is owned by a few khans. They herd sheep and goats in snake-infested canyons and eke out a meager existence. I did not visit them. Their rocky canyons, studded with dwarf oak, were closed to visitors when I was in Persia, for they were having trouble with the Persian Army, which wanted to disarm them. They stood on their record of loyalty to Persia and refused. In August, 1950 the Persian Army moved in behind American tanks and artillery. Fierce battles were raging. The Javanrudis were distrustful of the Army, for reasons I will state. Their battles of 1950 were perhaps their last show of independence. The Army was bent on their subjugation, on breaking their tribal authority, a process which the Kajars started and Reza Shah renewed.

The Debukri Kurds at Bukan illustrate how slow that process is, how resistant people are to breaking with their traditions.

As we walked the streets of Bukan in the morning and visited the bazaar every man we met bowed stiffly and formally to Abdollah. I watched their faces, and it was plain that they bowed out of respect and affection, not from protocol or duty.

I spoke of this to Abdollah and he replied with warmth. His tribe is now mostly sedentary, living in Bukan the year round. Many of the old tribal customs have disappeared. Loyalty to the chief remains. Law is administered by Abdollah and by a mullah. Abdollah, like Amar Khan, holds court and applies the ancient law of the Kurds to the disputes arising within the tribe. But as the years go by, more and more of the cases are taken by the civil courts. Whenever possible, however, the tribal court takes hold of a dispute. The Kurds like their own ancient law better than the law of the Governor. They trust their own khans to do justice without discrimination; they are not so sure of the government courts where, they hear, justice is sometimes bought and sold. They also are not quite sure how fair and impartial the judge may be when a Kurd, noted for a troublesome spirit of independence, stands before him.

Abdollah's great pride on this tour of Bukan was *first*, the infirmary and first-aid station, and *second*, the schools. The infirmary had been obtained through the good offices of the Royal Society sponsored by the Shah and his family. The Society establishes hospitals and medical centers. The need in Persia is great, for there are not over seventeen hundred doctors for a nation of sixteen million people; and hospital beds, including those of the Army, are only five thousand. Bukan with its infirmary and first-aid center is unique; few towns of that size have any medical facilities. Bukan has a doctor as well—a German brought in by the Royal Society. Abdollah has made public health next in importance to land reform.

Then come the schools. Bukan had a public school system through the eighth grade, and a high school was soon to be established—one of the few in all rural Persia.

Another night I was at Sanandaj south of Bukan, on the southern edge of ancient Kurdistan. This is the home of the famous Ardalan tribe of Kurds, a tribe that has long been sedentary, a tribe that has given Persia many loyal and capable public servants. We sat in the open at the Officers Club, munching roasted pumpkin seeds and pistachio nuts, drinking cool drinks, and talking of the rumblings of tribal discontent that spread all the way down from the Russian border. I turned to an officer and said, "What do you really think of these Kurds?"

His answer came in a flash, "A Kurd will cut a man's throat as easily as he will drink a glass of water." And he went on to add, "Give a Kurd a horse, a gun, a mountain and about seven women and he'll be perfectly happy."

I had to smile. I thought of Amar Khan Sharifi and the other gracious Kurds I had met. I thought of Bukan and its feudal lord who was revolutionizing his tribal society with a series of basic reforms. That night at Sanandaj as the wind whipped the willows at the Officers' Club, it seemed to me that in Persia, as in our own country, the military mind did not have any real understanding of the ingredients of peace.

9. Independence Is Preferred

THE ELBURZ MOUNTAINS run east and west across the northern part of Persia. They were formed by a mighty upthrust of limestone that pushed Demavend—the highest peak—18,600 feet into the sky. Demavend, flecked with snow, can be seen from Tehran through the heat haze of summer. Lesser peaks of the Elburz—10,000 and 12,000 feet high—are in Tehran's back yard and tower over the city.

The Elburz on the southern slopes are as dry and barren to the eye as any mountains that Arizona and California can show. On their heights one finds numerous springs tucked away in remote recesses of high basins, and an occasional river roaring to the plains. There are at these points touches of green, but they are merely specks on a vast terrain. The total impression is one of immense solitude, desolate cliffs thousands of feet high, lonely parched ridges.

The north side of the Elburz is green and verdant, sprayed by the moisture rising from the Caspian. These slopes produce a wide variety of deciduous trees—oak, plane, elm, ash, beech, alder, cherry, walnut. The lower reaches are jungles, thick with swamps, malaria, tigers, and tropical snakes. The coastal plain, from a mile to forty miles wide and washed by the Caspian Sea, is part of Persia's pride. Lovely rice (the peasant's bread) is grown there; so are tea, citrus fruit, tobacco, hemp. This end of the Caspian produces sturgeon from which premium caviar is obtained.

Here there exists a system of land tenancy which is as oppressive as one will find anywhere in the world. Great acreages are held by absentee landlords who have no sense of responsibility either for their tenants or for the soil. Batman Gelich boasts that his agricultural lands in the Caspian region comprise an area bigger than all of Switzerland. Tenants pay 80 per cent or more of the crop as rent; they are eternally in debt to the landlord; they live in miserable huts with peaked, thatched roofs. They know the pestilence of swamps, as severe as any in southeast Asia.

High above them, along the top of the Elburz and down the parched, barren slopes on the south side, are other people who are just as poor. They comb the dry and rocky canyons in search of grass for their sheep and goats, watching their flocks at night under cold stars and hugging the ground for warmth as a sharp wind comes out of the west and whistles along the ridges. They are dressed in rags; they have precious little to eat; they have no hospitals, no doctors, no schools. Their women lie out in rock cairns overnight, give birth to children, and move on with the tribe the next day. But these tribesmen, unlike the tenants of the coastal plain, have the attitude of free men.

I went into the Elburz to see them.

We entered the Elburz through the villages of Naroon and Afcheh and went out through Plour. General A. M. Djehanbani, a lively, energetic man who speaks Persian, Russian, French, and English, was in charge of our party. We rode Persian Army horses. My son's was named Peacock; mine, Devil. They were almost pure-blooded Arabian horses, fourteen hands high, bay-colored, with small feet and thick shoulders. They were spirited but gentle; and they could run like no horse I had been on.

Afcheh, perched on a high shoulder of the range, is fresh and green. A stream of white water, reminiscent of our Pacific Northwest, fills the place with a roar. There are poplar, plum, and apple trees and ancient walnuts that spread seventy-five feet or more. We stopped at a house with rock walls and a flat roof made of mud laid on top of several feet of thistles, and asked a pleasant-faced peasant for a drink of water. He showed us with much eagerness and gesticulation an ice-cold spring on the edge of a poplar grove. Then he ran to the hut and returned with a Persian rug. Putting it under a tree, he bowed graciously until we sat down. Then he ran once more to the house and returned with a saucer of huge pistachio nuts. He disappeared again and this time brought us grapes—ruby grapes that are very small and sweet and in as tight a cluster as caviar.

We got mules at Afcheh and loaded our pack train. Two brothers came with one mule. The smaller one—age five—had lost his left leg and was on crutches. The older one—age seven—led the mule. He sat by me on a rock wall and started to cry. He cried as if his heart would break. It took time to discover the cause. His father was sick. We would not return through Afcheh. The boy would have to return with the mule all alone. He was scared, for there are wolves in the Elburz.

We released his mule.

Our pack train was an odd assortment. General Djehanbani rode up front; six armed cavalrymen of the Persian Army followed; in the rear were the heavily packed mules—each with a muleteer, shouting, laughing, calling. Bill observed that we were not the only ones well protected; the mules were well guarded also. They had crude charms whittled from wood hanging on their foreheads, to keep away evil spirits and bring good luck.

We were headed for the Lar Valley. The pass we had to cross was between two and three thousand feet above Afcheh. The trail reached there through a precipitous canyon. It was a cruel path, as dangerous as any I wish to travel horseback. It was laid across large smooth rocks which not only were difficult to climb, but often ran in a steep pitch to the side of an abyss. There were cliffs up to one thousand feet high which had to be skirted.

There was no tree or shrub in sight during the three hours of travel. The hillsides had been scoured by goats and sheep, and scrubbed and washed by wind and rain. No grass was left; only thistles and coarse weeds were showing.

The pass is over ten thousand feet high. Below us was a vast treeless valley—the valley of the lower Lar. Across the valley to the north were broken walls of limestone, rising into formidable peaks. To the northeast was Demavend streaked with snow, free of clouds, and forming a perfect inverted cone. On our left in the distance was the great dome of the Throne of Solomon, the third highest mountain of Persia (15,912 feet). Legend has it that Solomon married the Queen of Sheba but could not make her love him. He sent a flock of birds out to find the coldest place on earth. All the birds but one returned the next morning. The last did not come back until dusk of the second day. He apologized to Solomon for his delay and offered the following excuse: he found a summit so cold that, when he alighted, his wings froze to the ground; and he could not free them until the sun was high the next day. Solomon at once moved his camp there. The first night the Queen of Sheba got so cold that she surrendered and moved into Solomon's tent. The next morning Solomon touched the ridge and caused a warm spring to gush forth for the Queen's bath. Natives swear the spring is still there.

We dropped two thousand feet or more over smooth treacherous rock, reaching the Lar at dusk. A huge black oblong tent of a goatherd (typical Bedouin style) lay not far from the trail against the base of the mountain. The sun disappeared, leaving a momentary red glow. Venus appeared. A slice of moon rode above the ridge. Jackals began yapping on the heights above us. A chill wind moved down the Lar. We camped not far from the goatherd and with much flapping of nylon and canvas put up our tents.

For several days we explored numerous valleys of the Elburz—the lower Lar, the upper Lar, and the White Valley.

—We caught medium-sized speckled trout on small black gnat and brown hackle wet flies.

—We went quail shooting.

—One day we kicked out three huge, grayish-white wolves and chased them on our fleet-footed Arabian horses. But wolves are fast and foxy and we never got in range.

—We found huge green and brown snakes (strange species to me) in marshland near the river.

—We looked for scorpions in our boots at dawn but found them only under rocks.

—We caught fast-moving tarantulas in brush.

—We ate delicious Persian food: dolmeh kedoo, which is summer squash hollowed out, stuffed with celery, and cooked in a sweet yellow sauce; boned lamb cooked on skewers over charcoal and served with small, grilled tomatoes; pilau (pronounced pillow), which is rice covered with a juicy stewlike dish of chicken, eggplant, and tomatoes.

One night at the end of a sumptuous meal when the traditional Turkish coffee was passed, an incident happened which illustrates not only Persian humor but the essentially democratic quality of Persian society. General Djehanbani sipped his coffee and then called for the cook. The cook came in and stood awkwardly before the General. The General said, "This coffee is too strong."

The cook's reply was instantaneous, "I know, but it is very good." Everyone including the General and the cook roared with laughter.

It was along the Lar that I first heard of Mullah Nasr-ed-Din, the twelfth-century Persian humorist. Mullah was a practical joker. One day he started a rumor in his village that bread would be distributed free to all villagers at five o'clock the following morning. The village fairly buzzed with the excitement of the news, and people rose extra early to be on hand for the distribution. Five o'clock came and passed and no bread had arrived. One old-timer, wise to Mullah's ways, finally realized what had happened and started up the hill to his hut. He met Mullah hurrying down.

"Where are you going, Mullah?"

"To the village to see if there is any bread."

"But it's all a joke that you yourself started."

"I know," said Mullah, "but I got to thinking about it and decided there might be something in it after all."

The Hedavands are a small tribe of about seventy-five families. They winter on the Varamin Plain, southeast of Tehran, and summer in the high Elburz. When I saw them, they were scattered in various encampments. Each settlement had a few white tents that marked the home of a khan or chief; the rest of the tents (about twenty feet long and eight wide) were made of coarse black wool cloth, and open on one side.

My arrival was unexpected and unannounced. Yet by the time my party had come out of the gorge in the White Valley and ridden the half mile across the high basin where the Hedavands were camped, an interesting ritual had been prepared. A man stood in the trail with a copper tray filled with hot coals. He held the tray high, extending it to me. This was a bit of custom coming down from Zoroaster. Fire on a tray is the warmest welcome the Hedavands know how to give.

We stopped at the home of a minor chief and ate mast (a type of curds) and sipped tea. I went among the Hedavands, talking with them and taking pictures. I even talked with the women, who were unveiled and, though shy and retiring, friendly.

The economy of these people is built around the goat and the

sheep. One afternoon I was with a shepherd boy who had a herd
of a hundred goats or more on the steep slope above White Valley.
I learned that day that the bite of the goat is poisonous. On this
hillside there were only a few spears of grass, one every six or eight
feet. The goats got each one, snipping it off at the ground. Any
remnants of wild flowers that survived June were also taken. Nothing edible above ground was left in their wake; they even ate the
blossoms of thistles.

The sheep—the flat-tailed, Asian species—were almost as devastating. Their eyes never left the ground; they walked tirelessly
with heads down taking every growing thing within reach. These
tired, wasted lands were being prepared for even heavier erosion.

In the afternoon the sheep and goats come off the slopes and
head for camp, where they line up without supervision or direction
for milking. One man and two women service a line. The man holds
a sheep or goat under each arm, while a woman milks. When one
animal is milked the man releases it and another steps up. And so it
goes for a couple of hours until the whole herd is serviced.

The women make mast for the use of the families. Mast is also
dried into hard white balls and stored for winter use. Butter is made
in a goatskin resting on a cradle that hangs from a tripod made of
sticks. Women swing the cradle to and fro; and babies often ride
the cradle during the churning to the tune of plaintive lullabies.

Surplus milk is put into goatskins, which are loaded onto mules
and taken over the mountain to some village where there is a market. The Hedavands were bringing many skins of milk to Afcheh
the day we were there. Merchants met the pack trains, pouring the
milk into fresh goatskins. The milk-filled skins were kept in the
river until nightfall, when they were loaded into caravans and taken
to Tehran. The Hedavands barter most of their milk for cloth,
sugar, tea, grain and the like; some they sell for cash. This milk,
made from the meager growth of wasted mountain slopes, is their
life.

Their one real meal a day consists of tea, bread, cheese, mast, and
perhaps a little meat. They cook over an open fire built in a three-
wall open fireplace and bake bread on a slightly convex copper
plate. Their summer fuel is thistles. Yet these people, as poor as any
in the Middle East, are among the most generous people I have met.

One night in the Lar I was very sick. I had not eaten wisely and

I was spending a miserable night. Word of it somehow went through the darkness to the Hedavand camp. About midnight a ragged, barefooted man of the tribe came to my bed with a bowl of mast. Mast harbors no bacteria hostile to man and has some that kill many unfriendly ones. This mast had a benign influence. After I had eaten most of it, I went to sleep at once; and I woke up well.

I talked with these tribesmen about their economic condition and asked why they did not settle down in villages and enjoy the comforts of life. We ended in a long discussion, the sum of which was this:

A peasant in a village is a slave. He pays four-fifths or seven-eighths or even more of his crop as rent to a landlord. The landlord owns everything—the land and the mud houses where the tenant lives, the village bathhouse where everyone bathes, the animals that work the fields, even the water that is used for irrigation. The peasant cannot leave the village; he has no freedom, no way of escape. He is a serf, bound throughout time to his landlord. His grandfather and father wore those chains before him; his children and grandchildren will wear them after him.

A grimy old goatherd spoke up: "There is one man who owns fifteen hundred villages; and all the people in them. They vote as he tells them. They always owe him money. They are real slaves. When the Tudeh party (Communist party) was growing strong in Iran, rents of farmers were reduced. Now they are up again. A villager is lucky if he has enough after the landlord is paid to keep his family alive during the winter."

"But you are lucky also if you can feed and clothe your family?" I replied.

"Yes," he answered. But his eyes lighted up as he added, "We are free and independent."

These tribesmen, no matter how impoverished, are gallant. They are aristocrats. They love the ridges where the wind blows a gale. The remote peaks take them far above the squalor and filth of villages. There is the thrill of the hunt. The sound of whistling wings of ducks coming down from Russia excites them. They like a crescent moon over a rugged cliff and the roar of a river down a rocky canyon. They like to come and go as they please. They are law-abiding; but it is their own law that they respect. Hence they are often difficult neighbors. They are a force that is in many respects antagonistic to the development of a so-called civilized and ordered society. But even the poorest of them have done much to keep alive in Persia the nation's unconquerable spirit—the spirit of true independence.

10. *I Am a Lur*

THE CHRONICLES divide the Lurs into two main groups—the Lesser Lurs, sometimes called the Feili (Rebel) Lurs; and the Greater Lurs, commonly known as the Bakhtiari. Today in Persia when one refers to the Lurs he means the Feili Lurs; and it is of them I write. Their territory extends from Azna on the south to Harsin (just south of Kermanshah) on the north; from Malayer on the east to the Iraqi frontier on the west. This is a part of ancient Luristan. The capital is Khorramabad, a town of perhaps twenty thousand people, that stands on the edge of a broad plain stretching west twenty miles or so to the ridges of the Zagros.

The Lurs and the Kurds are the closest of any of the present population of Persia to the original Aryan stock. And of these two the Lurs are probably the purest. The Lurs had a place of honor and distinction in ancient Persia. Marco Polo speaks of them as one of the eight kingdoms. They customarily furnished units for the Shah's cavalry. But they remained a principality under independent management. In ancient days they formed part of the council of nobles that ruled with the King of Kings of Persia. With the advent of the Kajars in the eighteenth century their relations with the central government worsened.

Yet not even two hundred years of oppression, corrupt rule, and divisive politics broke the Lurs. They were not finally subdued and reduced until Reza Shah Pahlavi, who was crowned in 1926, threw the force of the Army against them. Even then their final suppression was a major undertaking. And the bitterness that it engendered is today a powerful political force in Persia.

The Lurs are a tribe without much, if any, literature and without a recorded history. Most accounts depict them as a thieving, murderous lot, and there is no doubt that the Lurs stood across caravan routes and looted people, baggage, and freight. Their desire for independence inevitably made them a thorn in the side of every conquering power; plundering was a natural weapon for their defense.

Today there are still lawless elements among the Lurs as there are among every people. I met a group of them near Nour-Abad. They looked like ruffians; their dark swarthy faces and poker expressions were enough for the part. Actually they were smugglers. For a fee they would smuggle anything over the mountains into Persia, anything from a woman to a package of opium. The great bulk of the Lurs, however, are kind, friendly, hospitable. They also have a sense of humor.

The men love to carry arms. These days they have none, except what may be cached away in some secret place, for the Army has completely disarmed these tribes. But the urge to display firearms is still strong. On a visit I made to the Tulabi tribe, northwest of Khorramabad, a young Lur, son of a khan, asked if I would take his picture. I agreed. He put on two bandoleers, borrowed two revolvers and a rifle from our party, and thrust several knives in his belt. First he had me take his picture standing; then he lay flat, rested his gun on a rock, and peered down the barrel. "This is the way we fight," he said proudly.

I stood in front of him, focusing my camera.

"There is one request I will make," I told him.

"What is that?"

"Don't shoot until after I take the picture."

He laughed so hard he dropped the gun. He laughed and laughed and laughed until his face was covered with tears. And all the assembled Lurs roared too.

The Lurs today number about 800,000. About half of them are sedentary, i.e., year-round residents of villages. The other half are migratory. In the summer they are in the high country, grazing mountain slopes and farming the high valleys. In the fall they move south and west to a lower and warmer country.

Though the Lurs today are Shiah Moslems, they have clung fast to some ancient customs dating back to Zoroaster. Thus their wheat and their bread are sacred. A Lur, if he wants to take an oath, is apt to swear, "By the bread we ate together it is true." When the lamp is lighted at night and brought into the room, all members of the family rise out of respect. And their dances at night are near or around a bonfire.

When their tribal system flourished, they had a self-contained system of law. As in the case of the Kurds which I have already described, the mullah handled domestic affairs and minor civil disputes, while the khan handled major civil disputes and criminal cases. Today, however, the tribal structure is almost completely pulverized. The mullah handles marriages and wills, and decrees divorces, but most of the other cases now go to the civil courts of Persia. Only occasionally will a khan hear a case nowadays; when he does it involves a major dispute over property.

The Lurs are as dark as the Kurds but shorter in stature. The men usually wear loose black trousers, an open-neck shirt, and a large colored sash around the waist. For dress occasions they wear a colored jacket that hangs to the knees. Their hats seldom have a brim; these days they are usually gray or black skull caps on the roomy side. Very often they wear instead a dark-colored turban. In older days the men let their hair grow long; today shaved heads are quite common.

The typical woman's costume is a long dress, usually black but sometimes colored, which hangs from the neck to the ankles. She wears a kerchief around her head. Both men and women usually wear cloth sandals.

The dress of the men is sometimes colorful. That of the women seldom is. It may be that in ancient days there was beauty to their dress. Once the Lurs were rich, proud, and powerful. Today they are only proud. The cheapness of their women's dress is a good mirror of their poverty. The best way in Persia to convey the idea that one is poverty-stricken is to say, "I am a Lur."

11. The Six Poorest of Us

THE POVERTY of the Lurs is due partly to erosion. In Kurdistan to the north are mountain ranges practically devoid of trees; for miles and miles there is nothing but high, rolling grassland. From Kermanshah on south into Luristan one finds willow and juniper in the draws and oak on the slopes. The oaks do not form thick forests, but scattered clumps such as one sees in southwestern New Mexico and southeastern Arizona. Few are full-grown. Continuous cutting for centuries has resulted in trees that are mere bushy shoots from roots of monarchs that once commanded the range.

The grass has been so thinned by grazing that now one must take several steps between clumps. Only the thistles seem to have flourished. They stand four and five feet high in the ravines—coarse, spiny stems topped by round, blue blossoms almost as big as an orange. The scene reminded me of some overgrazed areas of our own in Oregon and Colorado.

Quick runoffs of rain and of snow water leave harsh gullies. Floods come in the spring with a mad rush, carrying topsoil with them. The water necessary for irrigation is wasted. The soil in the bottom lands is still rich, but it lacks water. Flood control and irrigation projects are needed. Protection of the ranges against overgrazing, and protection of the forests against cutting are also needed. The latter are as effective for storage of water as man-made dams. But in Luristan none of these conservation measures is in force. The wasting of resources goes on endlessly. Each year the earth is further depleted; each year the pinch of poverty is greater.

Flood control, irrigation projects, and conservation, though critical, are not the whole answer. Landownership and illiteracy are also at the bottom of the economic problems of the Lurs.

The Sagavands are often described in the chronicles of Persia as notorious highwaymen. One would not recognize them as such today. One Porsartib is their khan. Porsartib owns all the land. It lies at the head of a wide valley, fifty miles south and east of Khorramabad. There is scant water for the fields. The mountains that rim the valley on the east and west provide little moisture, except harsh runoffs in the spring. These mountains within the memory of residents of this valley were once green with oak and juniper. Now they are barren.

The tribe is sedentary—permanently settled in thirty-six villages. The menfolk gathered in a village by the road to greet me. They were in rags and tatters; their clothes more threadbare than one saw in our breadlines during the great depression. They stood huddled together, like the sheep they tend, but they held their heads with a pride despite generations of suffering and privation. These men inherited their tenancy. The entire tribe of forty-two thousand people works for Porsartib, paying one-third of the crop to him as rent. They are bound to him by debt as well. It is not extortionate debt; but it is eternal—advances to buy grain during severe winters; loans to meet the recurring emergencies of impoverished people.

Practically all the Sagavands are illiterate. Hence they have no method of escape from the system that holds them tight. Scientific agriculture, cheap means of financing, efficient methods of marketing are unknown to them. They plow with a stick pulled by a cow; they fertilize with night soil; they burn their best fertilizer—cow manure—since that is the only fuel supply they have; they reap grain with a hand sickle; they thrash it by having cows or donkeys pull a drag over it; they separate the grain from the chaff by tossing the straw in the air. This was their fathers' method. And it is likely it will be their sons'. In all the thirty-six villages there are only three schools; and these go only through the fourth grade.

There is no doctor in the entire area. Midwives with primitive methods attend to births; the umbilical cord is cut with a knife from the field. There are no medicines, no first-aid facilities. I talked with a tall, thin man with dark, deep-set eyes about the problem of medical care.

"Suppose you get a pain in your stomach, one that makes you double up. What do you do?"

He answered in a solemn voice. "If God wills it, I live."

More or less the same conditions exist among the other tribes of Lurs in this valley—the Dalvands and the Biranavands.

One August night I sat up late talking with Rustam Bahador, the khan of the Tulabi tribe, located farther to the north. Rustam Bahador owns not only the land; he owns every mud hut, every outhouse, every corral and barn in the area. He talked of the greatness of the Lurs and of their past, of the enduring qualities of his people. He emphasized the richness of their land. But this khan— rich and powerful though he is—is not leading his people out of the wilderness of ignorance and disease. I saw the villages that he owns. They have the mark of squalor on them. They have the fecal odor of the Middle East. There is no sanitation; the wells are not protected; no one is waging a campaign against flies.

Rustam Bahador—talkative, gregarious, friendly—occupies today a strong position of authority and leadership. But, like most leadership in the Middle East, it is irresponsible. He did not seem to be interested in or know anything about the central problems of agricultural production—seed selection, crossbreeding, fertilizers, irrigation, methods of plowing and cultivation, crop rotation, harvesting and thrashing. This Tulabi khan has the virtue of being a resident landlord. But the land and people he commands are merely perquisites of a feudal position.

There are not many landlords in all Persia who have a broad vision and a sense of social responsibility: Abdol Hossein Tavakoli, of Kermanshah, is one; Seyid Zia-Ed-Din of Tehran (former Prime Minister of Persia) is another. But these men are the exceptions.

One day I visited the Direkvan, Baharvand, Mir Baharvand and Papi (pronounced poppy) tribes. As I approached each village or settlement, the tribesmen tried to make a sacrifice in my honor. The Lurs are mostly too poor to kill a steer, even if they owned one; the sacrifice they usually tendered was a sheep. One day I managed to forestall it at five different places. On the sixth stop, when I visited the Papi tribe, several men had a steer tied about the ankles, preparatory to the sacrifice, and were trying to throw it. We stopped them. Beyond them, however, was another group who had four sheep in the middle of the road, ready for the sacrifice. They cut the throat of one before we had time to object. Its bright red blood streaked across the path and Ahmad Khan, their warmhearted, friendly chief, stepped forward to greet me. And when he grasped me by the hand he put in poetic words the ultimate expression of Persian hospitality: "*Ghadam rouyeh tchashm*"—"You may walk on my eyes."

His encampment was high on slopes of the Zagros Mountains, west of Khorramabad, a thousand feet or so below Noozhian, an eight-thousand-foot pass over the range.

We sat on exquisite Persian rugs in his oblong tent of black woolen cloth. An orchestra stood on the open side of the tent. Dances went on as we sipped tea and ate melons, apples, and grapes. After a while four men seated themselves before us and played soft music. One played a long, bowl-like violin; one a flute; two played drums with their hands. And as they played they sang one of the most haunting melodies I have heard. There were seemingly endless verses ending with

> My sweetheart is Kattaneh
> I love Kattaneh
> My sweetheart is Kattaneh
> I love her dearly.

The tenderest of love songs came out of the rags and misery of the Papis. The words came almost in whispers; there was pathos in the voices; each singer poured out his heart; one middle-aged drummer had tears in his eyes. There was more than sadness in their voices; there was supplication too. It was the cry of desperately lonely people for love and affection.

Kattaneh was more than a woman; she was a symbol of justice and mercy. All in this Papi environment that met the eye spelled poverty and suffering. The music rose above the surroundings; it was an avenue of escape from the misery of this life.

The melody has haunted me through all my travels. Goatherds in the high Himalayas of India, the miserable laborers in the date orchards of Iraq, workers in the factories of Isfahan—all these conveyed the same message through their eyes. It was a plea for love—for charity and kindness; a plea which, long neglected, turns into an orgasm of hate and revenge, producing revolution and terror.

After the singing, Ahmad Khan served lunch. There were skewers of liver, kidney, chicken, and lamb done over charcoal. They were perfectly turned by a genial male chef and removed from the fire at the peak of their flavor. We stripped the meat off with our fingers; and as we ate, the crowd of ragged human beings standing before the tent moved closer. They were so marked with poverty—their faces as well as their wretched clothes—that I felt a sharp twinge of conscience.

These morsels of rich food were drawn from the larders of the poor.

This feast was tendered by the poorest of the poor—a meal the like of which they themselves had never eaten.

And as I ate, I thought of the Lurs who had died of starvation the previous winter.

And these were the people who were giving me the feast!

Not far from where I sat nine hundred Lurs out of a village of five thousand had starved to death only eight months before. The central government at last had distributed wheat; but in one village fifteen Lurs were so emaciated they died of starvation after the wheat arrived. And in the spring of this present year the Lurs in some of the villages I had visited had been so weak they could not stand for more than five minutes at a time.

I could eat no more. I motioned to two youngsters who stood in front of me to come near. They had sunken eyes and hollow cheeks. I handed first one, then the other a skewer of meat. They stripped off the delicate morsels and bolted them down. And the whole circle of hungry people moved politely nearer.

I asked my interpreter, Shahbaz, to call up at random six men among these peasants. They stood in front of me, their hands nervously twisting their gray felt skull caps. Turning to the first one I asked, "What is your name?"

"Abbas."

"What land do you own?"

"None."

"What land do you work?"

"None."

"What property do you own?"

"Four calves, ten sheep." (Skinny animals, grazed on barren tribal land.)

"How large a family do you support?"

"Five people."

I asked the other five similar questions.

Abdul. Owned no land, worked no land, owned six cows and 15 sheep, supported a family of 10.

Emani. Owned no land; worked no land; owned four calves and twenty sheep; supported a family of two.

Hossein. Owned no land; rented wheat land from a merchant in Khorramabad and got as his share 20 per cent of the crop which last year was three hundred pounds; owned four cows and thirty sheep; supported a family of five.

Ali. Owned no land; rented wheat land from a merchant in Khorramabad and got as his share 20 per cent of the crop which last year was two hundred pounds of wheat; owned six cows and forty sheep; supported a family of two.

Taghi. Owned no land; worked no land; owned two cows and twenty sheep; supported a family of four.

I will never forget their faces. They were simple men, anxious to speak the truth, caught in a mire of poverty and squalor from which they knew not how to escape. They were eager to pour out their hearts. Their eyes searched mine, as if to obtain a promise of a new future. When I ended the conversation and turned away, the expectation and hope that had filled their faces vanished. They stood before me, ragged victims of despair.

While my questioning was going on, the elders of the tribe seated themselves on the far side of the tent. When I finished, one of them arose and came over to me. What he said was perhaps intended to save face, perhaps designed to relieve my embarrassment. He bowed graciously and then stated, "It was God's will that you should have picked the six poorest of us."

12. Butcher of Luristan

THE GREAT impoverishment of the Lurs is due in part to the pillaging of the tribes by the Persian Army. The tragedy traces back to the policy of Reza Shah, who set about to subjugate them.

Reza Shah was an Army officer who reached the Persian throne as a result of a *coup d'état* in 1925. He did some great and good things for Persia. The famous resort at Ramsar on the Caspian is one. In a few areas he built clean, attractive houses for peasants. The tearing of veils from the faces of Moslem women stands to his credit. Roads, schools, reservoirs, parks—these and other projects have left his stamp on the nation. But his program against the tribes ended in murder and pillage. His plan was to break their feudal ties, rid them of their migratory habits, and settle them permanently in villages—and he used all means to accomplish this end. To what extent Reza Shah was personally responsible for the tragedy that befell the Lurs is a matter of debate. Perhaps he did not know what his army did; perhaps he closed his eyes. But one of the most shameful chapters was written by one of his colonels—known throughout all Persia as the Butcher of Luristan.

In 1936 the government decided to put a paved highway through Luristan. The Lurs opposed the scheme. There were skirmishes between the army and the tribe. Troubles erupted throughout Luristan. An outstanding general of the Persian Army was ambushed and killed by some Lurs at a spot where a short concrete bridge now crosses a ravine a few miles south of Khorramabad. The Lurs at once moved on the city and took it, and occupied the Fort, a huge pillar of fortified rock several blocks square that rises two hundred feet or more from the middle of the town. They were exultant and defiant. They now controlled the heart of Luristan. The plans of

Reza Shah to break up the tribe, destroy its leadership, and resettle the tribesmen on land had received a serious setback.

A young colonel was ordered out of Tehran to Khorramabad. He laid siege to the Fort. Day after day troops poured in and tightened fast their grip on the surrounding countryside. Supplies and reinforcements to the Fort were cut off. The process of strangulation set in. In about a month the Fort capitulated. The leaders of the Lurs—eighty in number—were hanged.

"We kept them on the gallows for three days," an officer told me. "We wanted to make sure that their example was impressed on the Lurs."

The rest of what happened can best be related by an old man—perhaps eighty years of age. I met him on a wind-blown plain of Luristan, in a hut that was open on one side, its walls and roof thatched with boughs of oak. I had come to the hut to inquire if I could take a picture of its interior. On my appearance a woman, who had been sitting weaving, quickly vanished through a rear exit. The man, also seated, looked up with a troubled face and asked, "Is it necessary to take a picture of us in our misery?"

His tired, anxious face had a patrician look. There was dignity in his features, pride in his voice. I was embarrassed and ashamed at my intrusion. I closed my camera and asked if I might come in. He rose, bowed, and with a gracious sweep of his arm invited me to join him on his rug.

We talked of the mountains that lay against the skyline on the west. Wolves, leopards, goats, and ibexes live there. In the lower reaches one finds many partridges and wild pigeons. The old man spoke of his early hunts; he mentioned American Army officers who came up here to hunt during the days of the Persian Gulf Command and told how he helped them plan their trips. He liked the Americans. He spoke of huge fish—perhaps sturgeon—in the Kashgan River which rises in the northwest and flows by Khorramabad to the Gulf.

He rambled on and on. Finally there came a moment of silence when I broke in to ask him about his misery which he had mentioned earlier. He spoke then of the poverty and hunger of the Lurs, of the lack of schools and of doctors, and of those who died of starvation last winter. He himself had barely kept body and soul together. The bitter acorns of the oaks had saved his life.

"And what about Amir Ahmadi?" I asked.

He looked at me quizzically and then shook his head. The story was slow in coming; it took much persuasion and a promise that I would never disclose his identity. Finally it poured from his lips in whispered tones:

"We were camped not far from here. There were twenty huts in all—over one hundred people. We had several thousand sheep and goats, a few hundred cattle, and many dozens of horses. Some of our young men had been with our khans at the Fort. They were all killed. Our khans were hanged. The Army had won. The battle of resistance was over. The road which Reza Shah wanted to build would now be built.

"A few days later I saw a cloud of dust across the plain. Horsemen were coming on a gallop. As they came closer, I saw that they were an Army troop. A colonel was in command. They came right at us, the colonel shouting orders. The men dismounted and started shooting. There were babies in baskets in some of our tents; the soldiers put revolvers to the heads of the little ones and blew their brains out. Women were screaming from all the huts. My wife was cowering in a corner. I stood before her. Two soldiers rushed toward us. I seized a knife. Then there were shots. I was knocked to the earth and lost consciousness.

"When I awoke my wife was lying across me. Her warm blood ran down my chest. She died from bullet wounds in her breast. I had been shot through the neck, and left for dead.

"I did not move, because the colonel and his troops were still there. I could see them through my half-closed eyes. You may not believe me when I tell you what I saw. But by the bread of my house I swear it is true."

There was a long silence before the old man continued. The wind whisked a whirlwind of dust into the hut, stinging our eyes. For several minutes a lizard had been exploring the prospects of joining us. Suddenly he was startled and turned and ran. He ran so fast that his front legs left the ground and it looked as if he might take flight like a miniature jet plane. The old man and I watched the lizard as he disappeared into a patch of licorice root. Then he turned to me and told me the story that still lives in his head like a nightmare.

The Asian ways and means of arranging death and torture are

ancient and numerous. Finely ground whiskers of the leopard mixed with food is said to be good. It causes ulceration of the intestines; and death is a lingering affair.

A good poison is extracted from a beetle. When served in coffee, it causes sure death.

The Mongols had a victim stick his head through a knothole and then twisted it off. Or they pulled the man through an opening only half large enough for him.

Pouring hot lead on top of a shaved head is said to make the eyes pop out.

Starving a victim to death by chaining him in a dungeon half filled with water was painfully revengeful.

One Persian Shah, Agha Mohammed, who had been castrated when a boy, took horrible revenge on society. Once he ordered thirty thousand pairs of human eyes brought to him; and he counted them himself to make certain his order had been obeyed.

The Lurs themselves developed sadistic means of punishment. History records that they sometimes boiled their victims alive.

But the deeds of the colonel, as related to me by the old man, had a unique and hideous twist.

"The colonel had ordered some of our young men to be held as captives. Meanwhile he built a fire of charcoal. I soon discovered what he was doing. He had an iron plate so big [indicating a plate about eight inches long, six inches wide, and a quarter of an inch thick]. He heated this until it was red hot. He had his men bring up one of the Lurs. Two soldiers held the prisoner, one on each side. A third soldier stood with a sword behind the prisoner. The colonel gave the signal. The man with the sword swung. As the sword hit the prisoner's neck, the colonel shouted, 'Run.' The head dropped to the ground. The colonel pressed the red hot plate on the stub of the man's neck. The headless man took a step and fell.

" 'Give me the tall one,' the colonel shouted. 'He can run better than that.'

"The same process was repeated. The tall man, when beheaded, ran a few paces. Lur after Lur was beheaded. Again and again the plate was heated red hot and slapped on the stub of a neck. Once the colonel was slow with the plate; and the blood shot five feet in the air."

The old man stopped to wet his lips.

"The colonel started betting on how far these headless men could run. He and the soldiers would shout and yell, encouraging each victim to do his best."

The old man paused, his anger swelling up as he relived this experience.

"Who won the betting contest?" I asked. He waited several minutes before he would speak.

"The colonel won most of the bets. He won a thousand rials, I think, on the headless Lur who ran fifteen paces after he was beheaded."

The old man seemed exhausted from the telling of the story. He poured tea from an ancient samovar. We sipped it in silence. After we had finished, I asked, "What did the colonel do next?"

"He ran off all our stock—sheep, goats, cattle, and horses. The next day a dozen lorries came. All our rugs, samovars, dishes, jewelry, clothes—every possession was loaded in these wagons and taken away by the Army."

"And what of yourself?"

"I dragged myself to a spring in a ravine and washed my wound. I was too weak to move for two nights. Then I went back to bury the dead. Every man, woman, and child had been killed. Not a living soul was left. The vultures had got there before me."

"What happened to the colonel?" I inquired.

"The colonel? Oh, he became a general and later Minister of War."

"Is he still alive?"

"Very much so. He lives in Tehran. The loot he got from our villages filled dozens of lorries. Tens of thousands of sheep and goats were stolen. How the colonel divided it up among his soldiers I do not know. What higher-ups shared in the plunder I do not know. But the colonel is today a very rich man. He bought several hundred houses in Tehran with the plunder."

There was scorn in his voice, as he spit out the words:

"The Butcher, AMIR AHMADI."

The sun was setting as I rose to go. The old man took me warmly by the hand and held it as he looked deeply into my eyes and asked for reassurance that I would not reveal his identity. After a minute he said, "I am a Persian. I love my country. I would gladly give my life for it. But I hate the Army. God in his time will wreak a vengeance." He dropped his eyes; and when, after a moment he looked up, there was fire in them.

"We fear Russia. We know that the Soviets are an enemy of our people. But we also have one right in our midst."

I met Amir Ahmadi at a garden party in Tehran. He is stocky and erect, and shows the age of a man in his early sixties. He has a fierce black mustache, piercing eyes, and prominent gold teeth. He speaks Persian, Russian, and Turkish. Trained in the Cossack Army in Russia, he still bears some of the marks of its arrogance and daring. It was reflected in a lucid moment of idle conversation.

"What is your relationship to the people of Luristan today?" a lady asked.

"Oh, they think highly of me," he replied. "I am a household word."

"In what way?"

He laughed as he replied, showing his gold teeth, "Why in Luristan if a child cries the mother says, 'Hush or Amir Ahmadi will get you.'"

13. Gun Play at Kuhdasht

THE DAY after I interviewed the six Lurs of the Papi tribe I visited Kuhdasht. Lurs of the Tarhan tribe live there. This day they were in a sullen mood; and a half hour after I left, a pitched battle took place in the village street. The row can be understood only against the background of the Army's relations with the tribes and the manner of conducting elections in Persia.

Kuhdasht lies northwest of Khorramabad about eighty miles. A dirt road follows the long winding valley where the milky Kashgan flows, a river as white as many of our glacial streams. Great limestone escarpments are on the right—sheer cliffs a thousand feet or more high, bizarre-shaped peaks, tall, fluted columns. The road climbs all the way to Kuhdasht; after it leaves the valley it takes a tortuous path, skirting rock debris, and winding cautiously along the edge of dizzy cliffs, coming out at last on a wide plain rimmed by low ridges and eight thousand feet high. Few trees are on the ridges; no peaks are in view. The place looks like a high pocket in the Rocky Mountains of Colorado or Wyoming. Many cattle were in the basin. Wheat and barley were being thrashed. This is dry-farming country, where the moisture of snow must carry through the growing season.

Kuhdasht—a mud village of perhaps two hundred families—lies against the northern edge of the basin. When I arrived, the villagers (men only) were lined up for half a block or so to greet me. It was a grim, silent group. The air was tense; no one was relaxed or smiling. I knew at once that trouble was brewing, but I did not have the faintest notion what was afoot.

The beginning of my understanding came when I started asking these peasants the same questions that I had put to the Papis. I was interested in learning the extent of individual landownership and the standard of living. The answers puzzled me. These men were in rags and tatters, yet each answered that he was a substantial land-owner with large flocks and much grain. As the questioning pro-ceeded I saw a trace of merriment in their eyes; and I realized I was being teased. Then I learned that an officer had preceded me to Kuhdasht and addressed the assembled villagers as follows, "A visitor is coming. He is seeking information. Be careful of your answers. Tell him nothing." A village elder had replied, "We will follow your instructions." The reason for the secrecy unfolded before dusk came and the battle started at Kuhdasht.

Ali Mohammed Ghazanfari represents Kuhdasht in Persia's parlia-ment. I had met Ghazanfari in Khorramabad and he had accom-panied my party to Kuhdasht. He is a slight, dark, middle-aged man, who walks with a limp, a man of wealth and a pleasant, engaging companion. The mayor of Khorramabad is his cousin, Mohammed Hossein Ghazanfari. Apparently an efficient adminis-trator, he practically wiped out malaria in Khorramabad by having every wall, every garden, and every stagnant pond sprayed period-ically with DDT.

The villagers at Kuhdasht had heard that the deputy wanted to make his cousin the Mayor of Kuhdasht. Though both the deputy and the mayor appeared to be enterprising and honest men, the very suggestion of the idea caused emotions to run high. With difficulty I put together from my talks at Kuhdasht with several villagers why this proposal caused a violent explosion.

In the first place, Ghazanfari had large landholdings near Kuh-dasht. Several boundary questions involving his land were being dis-puted. He claimed land that others asserted was theirs. If Ghazan-fari's cousin became Mayor of Kuhdasht, Ghazanfari would win the boundary disputes. That at least was the villagers' thought. But a larger issue smoldered underneath this one.

Elections in Persia are supervised by the Army. Soldiers come with a ballot box and ballots; the men of the village line up and drop their ballots in the box; the box is taken away; and the votes are counted at some central place in the district.

"That is the way Ghazanfari was elected," a young villager said. "Is he not a good deputy?"

"No. He owns a lot of the land. He does nothing for us. Look how dirty our village is. See how miserable our children look. We have no schools, no doctors. If we are sick, we have no medicines."

A middle-aged man interrupted. "Look at those children over there by the wall. They are mine. I love them dearly. But do you know what? They will grow up to be as ignorant as I am." His voice mounted with emphasis and he fairly shouted, "That is not right."

By this time there were a half dozen in the group surrounding me. They all nodded approval of the speaker.

"If your deputy does not pass laws which help your condition, why don't you elect a new one?" I asked.

That statement made the group laugh.

"You do not understand," the last speaker said. "This deputy is a big landowner. He will not pass laws for our benefit. He is not our true representative. Yet he is all we can get."

I turned to the first speaker, the young man, and put my hand on his shoulder, saying, "Here's a good man. I wager he understands your problems. Elect him to the Majlis; then you'll get the laws you want."

My candidate spoke up. "Let me explain. The Army comes with the ballot box and the ballots. The ballots are already printed; there is one name on them—the name of the candidate the Army wants. We line up, receive our ballots, and march by the box and drop them in."

"Write in a different name," I said. "That's what we do in America."

"That is impossible. This is not America. Soldiers are here with bayonets. We must vote for the candidate the Army wants. And the Army always wants the big landlord."

An old man spoke up, "This will change. Our people will not stand it much longer. Did you hear what happened in Lar?"

I shook my head.

"Lar [a town not far from Shiraz] had an election this year. The people would not obey the Army; they had a candidate of their own; they tore up the ballots of the Army and put their own ballots in the box. Then the board came to count the ballots. [The

Ghashghai mansion and gardens, Shiraz

Old home of Ilkhan of Debukri tribe of Kurds, Bukan

Nasser Khan, head of the Ghashghais,
with the author on Namdam plain

Ghashghais on fall migration, 1950

Kurdish women, Debukri tribe, washing dishes in spring, Bukan

Ghashghais on fall migration, 1950

Amar Khan Sharifi, Ilkhan of the Shakkak tribe of the Kurds

Lurs sacrificing steer in honor of arrival of the author

A typical Kurd

Ziad Khan, winner of the Ghashghai
shooting contest

Bakhtiari performing a stick dance

Thrashing floor, Azerbaijan

Bakhtiari women

Morteza Gholi Khan Samsam, Ilkhan of the Bakhtiaris, Shalamzar

Persian goats eat even the blossoms of thistles

Russian border, Azerbaijan, Persia

Persian girl gathering chips for winter fuel

A street in a typical Persian village

Typical tent and family of Bakhtiari goatherd

The author and Ahmad Khan, chief of the Papi tribe of the Lurs

The author interviewing Lurs of the Papi tribe

Maku, Azerbaijan

board, I later learned, is a committee appointed by the Governor of the district.] The word spread that the board was crooked, that the board would count the ballots wrong and declare that the Army's man won. The people of Lar got excited. They formed a mob and stormed the city hall—ten thousand people went after the board. The mob had no guns, only knives and sticks and bare hands. They killed six members of the board. They tore them apart. There was no piece left of one man bigger than his ear." (I learned later that ten villagers were convicted; the convictions of four of these were reversed; and the appeals of the other six were still pending in the fall of 1950.)

There was a tense silence as the old man ended. The young man was defiant as he said, "Our people aren't going to stand this much longer. We are going to have free elections or else."

The tea tendered by the khan of the Tarhans at Kuhdasht was a difficult occasion. The atmosphere was charged. No one said a word. I tried to start a conversation about irrigation projects for the valley, but no one replied except a mullah, and he gave no life to my questions. I had planned to stay in Kuhdasht overnight. But during the tea Shahbaz, my interpreter, whispered to me, "One of the villagers who spoke to you hopes you don't stay tonight. He likes you but fears you may get hurt."

"Why?" I asked.

"The villagers think the deputy is using you to strengthen his position here. They say Ghazanfari is counting on your prestige and your presence to help him in his plan."

I changed my schedule and returned to Khorramabad that night. Thirty minutes after I left a pitched battle took place in the streets of Kuhdasht—Ghazanfari and his crowd on one side, a sizable number of rebellious villagers on the other. Some blood was shed; but no one was killed.

The moon was high over Luristan on our trip down in the jeep. The limestone mountains were big hulks, glistening in the moonlight and making fantastic shapes. The water of the Kashgan had a silver sheen. The whole valley looked like fairyland. Kuhdasht already seemed like a dream. Everything seemed unreal except the Lurs, and they reminded me of embattled Americans.

14. The Bakhtiari Save the Constitution

MORTEZA GHOLI KHAN SAMSAM, head of the Bakhtiari, looks like Monty Woolley and has a range of facial expressions almost as great. He is short and stocky with a round head that sits close to his shoulders. His gray hair and full beard are clipped short. His dark eyes are animated with excitement, laughter, surprise, anger, resentment or any mood which the conversation arouses. He has lived in Europe, and is a man of considerable learning, who would be at home in any American circle. He is robust like West Texas, but there is a gentle and mystic quality as well. He is a devout, God-fearing man.

He is also a considerable political figure. He so managed tribal affairs and tribal conduct that the devastation which hit the Lurs never struck the Bakhtiari. He has been an astute leader. His father, he himself, and now one of his sons has held public office. He keeps the tribe well represented in the Majlis. The beautiful girl whom the Shah recently married is a Bakhtiari. Yet Morteza Gholi Khan is no mere political conniver. He is bold and daring as well. It was he, as I will relate, who in 1909 led the Bakhtiari cavalry against a former Shah, captured Tehran, and saved the Constitution for Persia.

Morteza Gholi Khan dresses in American style with but one difference. He seldom wears a necktie. But a big, gold collar button always shows in his soft, rolled collar.

He had two wives. The first was a Ghashghai. By her he had tall, rangy Jahanshah, present Governor General of Kermanshah. By the other wife, a Bakhtiari, he had three sons—Amir Bahman, Ahmad Gholi, and Fereydoon. I do not know how many daughters he had. The sons are all well-educated. Bahman, like his cousin, Majid, has a pilot's license and flies a Beechcraft.

Morteza Gholi Khan had in addition to his full-fledged wives, four contract wives. Under Persian-Moslem law a man is entitled not only to four regular wives; he may also have as many contract wives as he wants and can arrange for. It is not an idle matter. The mullah must approve the contract, its duration, and the amount of money payable to the woman. Children born under the contract are lawful. At the end of the contract the relation is ended and may not be renewed. The woman goes her way, leaving any children behind and keeping only the consideration which the contract provided. Morteza Gholi Khan tired of his contract wives; but he was deeply devoted to his full-fledged wives.

Shalamzar, the summer home of Morteza Gholi Khan, lies sixty-five hundred feet high in a broad fertile valley of southwest Persia rimmed by high mountains, west and slightly north about two hundred miles from Isfahan. The route from Isfahan lies across a wide plateau strewn with pieces of old mountains. Sometimes a lone ridge will run along for miles; at other times only a relic of a range will be left. One relic is shaped like a loaf of bread, another like a cone or the bristling back of an animal. One sticks up like a spire, another shows a notch like a slingshot. At dusk or in the moonlight they take on a magic quality.

When Morteza Gholi Khan was married about forty years ago he built a castlelike house at Shalamzar, a tall, awkward, stone affair with high ceilings and huge windows. More recently he built another massive house on a ridge to the east. It commands a vast domain. Morteza Gholi Khan at seventy-five rides his spirited Arabian stallion up the steep mountainside that leads to this house. On the slopes below, he is experimenting with apples, quinces, pears, almonds, walnuts.

Water for irrigating the orchards comes from a spring that bubbles out from rocks high on the ridge, but the water for the fields in the valley is obtained through a qanat, an underground type of waterway which one sees from Damascus on east. It is an ancient institution, antedating the Romans. From the air a qanat is a string of mounds of earth that often extends for miles; sometimes there are two streaks of mounds that join together and make a Y.

The qanat supplies water where no spring or stream is in evidence. A narrow well is dug perhaps ten, twenty, or thirty feet deep. If water is found (even though it is only a trickle) another narrow well is dug one hundred feet or perhaps one hundred yards down the slope. Then the two wells are connected by a tunnel. The process is repeated until a chain of dozens of wells all feeding the same tunnel is constructed. A stream that started as a trickle far up the hillside often swells into a roaring underground torrent several miles down the valley. That is the way many villages in Persia build their irrigation systems.

Shalamzar is not only an agricultural settlement; it also has a home industry. The fourteen hundred people who live there have a sizable and respectable bazaar, located in low mud buildings that are shaded by spindly, fast-growing poplars. The Bakhtiari make beautiful Persian rugs in this village.

I visited Shalamzar both in 1949 and in 1950. Morteza Gholi Khan was my host. I did not realize on my first visit that in Persia friendship is sealed by breaking bread together and exchanging stories. Morteza Gholi Khan quickly sealed ours. He swept me off my feet with his stories. They were mostly stories of his adventures with the Bakhtiari cavalry which in olden days he proudly led. Once, he told me, his troops stopped to bury a man who had been killed. They had no shovel or pick; so they dug the grave with their hands. There are quite a few poisonous scorpions in this country, but only one is a deadly species and it is rather tiny. One of these tiny scorpions bit the hand of one of the gravediggers.

"In twenty minutes his arm was swollen so big," said Morteza Gholi Khan, indicating the size of a water melon. "In two hours he was dead; and we buried him in the grave with the other soldier."

I changed the storytelling to a lighter note, and gained a temporary advantage by relating Jack Nelson's mosquito story from the Cascade Mountains of Washington. I told how Jack one night rid himself of the mosquitoes in his tent by putting a candle to them one by one and burning them crisp. All went well until the granddaddy mosquito outfoxed Jack by blowing out the candle.

Morteza Gholi Khan had heard many wonderful things about America—how tall the buildings; how fast the airplanes; how big this; how broad that. But he had never heard of such mosquitoes. He said he thought he had big mosquitoes at Shalamzar; but none of them could perform such a feat. His eyes were wide with amazement as he pondered the spectacle. When at last he realized the nature of the story, he laughed harder than anyone else.

We ended the first evening together by drinking a toast I tendered: a toast to the rearming of the Bakhtiari. The old man stood erect and squared his shoulders, his eyes glistening with excitement. He once more was leading a charge of Bakhtiari cavalry and for a moment relived early days of military glory.

One morning at Shalamzar I persuaded Morteza Gholi Khan to tell me how he saved the constitution for Persia. We sat upstairs in a tremendous drawing room (perhaps thirty by thirty) carpeted with a Persian rug which his Ghashghai wife had made to order. It took two hours for the story to be told. The telling of it was a work of art and revealed an expert's grasp of Persian history. There was the hushed voice when he came to the conspiratorial part, the ringing commands to cavalry, the authoritarian ultimatum to the Shah's general, the charge of the troops when Tehran fell. The story was so beautifully and dramatically told that it almost had sound effects.

At the turn of this century Muzaffar-ed-Din was Shah of Persia. His rule was corrupt; the wealth of Persia was being siphoned off for the extravagances of the Shah and his court, and there was great discontent in the land. When the Shah appointed his son-in-law as Minister of Interior a storm of protest followed; for this man was associated with the corrupt and oppressive practices. The British, who long had been active in Persian affairs, persuaded the Shah to give a Magna Charta to Persia. A constitution was prepared and signed; it was ratified both by the Shah and by his heirs; and the Shah opened the first national assembly in October, 1906. A few days later the Shah died.

The new Shah, Mohammed Ali, was an Oriental despot of the worst type. Though he swore fidelity to the constitution, he plotted to get rid of it. On December 15, 1908 he imprisoned the Prime Minister, had his Persian Cossacks seize the Majlis, and appointed a Military Governor for Tehran. The parliament—designed as the voice of the people of Persia—was destroyed.

Word of the disaster reached Morteza Gholi Khan in France. His father—Najaf Gholi Khan Samsam-Os-Saltaneh—sent for him. Najaf Gholi Khan had moved into action as soon as the Shah had closed the Majlis. He summoned "warriors of a holy war." They came from Resht on the Caspian and Khorram-shahr on the Persian Gulf. They were mostly cavalry, well-armed and committed to the cause of liberty. Morteza Gholi Khan arrived in time to lead them.

The Bakhtiari had had units in the cavalry of the Shah since the time of Cyrus and Darius. The Shah of Persia always asserted the right to levy one horseman and two foot soldiers on every ten families. Actually the recruitments were much less: the cavalry of the Bakhtiari in the Persian Army was limited to a few hundred, and they often served only as hostages for the good behavior of the tribe. There were several hundred in the cavalry of Mohammed Ali Shah. They were sent to persuade Morteza Gholi Khan to turn back and not to attack Tehran.

"This changed my strategy," he told me. "I had one rule: a Bakhtiari must never fight a Bakhtiari."

The Bakhtiari of the Shah's army were on the left flank. Morteza Gholi Khan whirled and attacked the right flank which were mostly Persian Cossacks; and the left flank of the Persian Army did not move into action. Thus he routed the Cossacks at Shahabad and stood before Tehran.

Meanwhile a column had marched down from Resht and joined forces with Morteza Gholi Khan. Speedy action was necessary, since Russia had pledged aid to the Shah and had landed three thousand soldiers at Enzeli on the Caspian. On July 12, 1909 Morteza Gholi Khan struck. He entered Tehran through the Behjit-Abad gate and captured the parliament. A battle inside Tehran raged for three days. Mohammed Ali, who had taken refuge in the Russian Embassy, was deposed; his son was crowned; and two Bakhtiaris went into the new cabinet. In 1911 Najaf Gholi Khan became Prime Minister.

This was a moving story as it was told me at Shalamzar. As Morteza Gholi Khan finished he raised a clenched fist and said, "That was a proud day for Persia. That day we saved liberty and independence for our people. Now our people have a forum where they can complain even against their rulers, where they can pass laws that will improve their conditions."

These words came back to me a few weeks later when I sat in the visitors' gallery of the Majlis.

One deputy purported to speak on behalf of a small village: tribesmen had stolen two hundred of their sheep.

Another deputy was speaking for some of the tribes: the Persian Army was preying on the tribes, practicing blackmail against them, and lining their pockets at the expense of the tribesmen.

Then Mohammed Mossadegh (passionately Persian and anti-Soviet in his leanings, the one who was to be Prime Minister before a year had passed and cause Persia's oil to be nationalized) rose to attack the British oil concession.

The institution, which Morteza Gholi Khan saved from extinction a generation earlier, was still functioning as a public forum.

15. A Goat Does Justice

OREGON, a Bakhtiari village of about three thousand people, lies in a broad, fertile valley about twenty-five miles southwest of Shalamzar. This valley, rimmed by rough, barren hills, has rich bottom land, so that an abundance of springs makes it a fertile place.

Persian clover, wheat, poppies (grown for opium), barley, melons, beans, squash, grapes thrive there. One can see hundreds of acres of wild hollyhocks in bloom, knee-high with heads as big as teacups. There are buff-colored partridge that thrive on the slopes; and if one walks softly he can hear them talking to each other. Walnut, poplar, willow, senjid, and elm trees grow where there is water. One such spot is a small bench a hundred feet above the valley. An ice-cold stream pours from the mountainside and runs through a stand of majestic walnuts with a spread of between one hundred and one hundred fifty feet each. These trees mark a historic spot. Just below them on the edge of the path leading to the bench is a rock where every Ilkhan of the Bakhtiari has sat and held court. Morteza Gholi Khan had not been to Oregon for twenty years. He came in my honor in 1950. Our camp was under the spreading walnuts on the bench. One morning a Bakhtiari came up the path on a run to announce in a breathless voice that the Ilkhan was coming. I went down to meet him and found him seated on the ancient rock with all the village elders at his feet.

Morteza Gholi Khan and I sat on an exquisite Bahktiari rug under the walnuts and talked of Bakhtiari customs and law. These tribes have a hierarchy of chiefs. The Ilkhan is the head chief, the leader of many tribes. Next in order comes the khan, and then the kalantar, kadkhoda and rish-safid. The latter is the elder or white beard of a clan or of a village.

The Kurds and the Lurs divide judicial functions between the khans on the one hand and the mullahs or priests on the other. The Bakhtiari, though very religious and devout Moslems, have no mullahs among them. The khans handle the matters which the mullah customarily administers; and, as among the other tribes, adjudicate all civil and criminal disputes or controversies besides. Their system of rewards and punishments differs in some details from that of the Kurds and Lurs, but in general the concept of justice is similar. There is one important difference. The Bakhtiari, like the northern tribes, assess damages for manslaughter, the family of the killer being required to pay to the family of the deceased from $2,000 to $2,500 depending on the age and condition of the deceased. But the Bakhtiari do not stop there. They require the family of the killer to give a sister or daughter in marriage to a member of the family of the deceased. This custom goes back to immemorial days. Morteza Gholi Khan explained it this way. "The union of blood works in a mystic way. It washes away all desire for retaliation. The two warring families become peacefully united as one."

After awhile the conversation turned to God, the immortality of the soul, the life hereafter. Morteza Gholi Khan believes there is a Heaven and a Hell. He believes the body dies, but not the soul or spirit. He talked of the troubled world, his own advancing years, the threat of Russia and communism. He thought his days of usefulness were about over because his legs were going bad on him and he could not walk with ease. I told him of Franklin Roosevelt, who could not walk a step and yet was elected President four times.

"Yes, but your wonderful man Roosevelt had youth and I have only age," he replied. He went on to say that he felt his death was near. Only the other day he ordered his grave dug. It is right next to his father's grave. He had a headstone prepared; his name and date of birth were engraved on it. "The addition of the date of my death is all I have left the Russians to do," he said.

"You think the Russians will invade Persia?"

"One day the Communists from Russia will come like a flood and sweep all of Persia before them. They will shoot me and all like me, for I am the symbol of all they hate." Then he added with emphasis, "I will not run away. I will stay right here and die with my people."

There was a long silence while the old man sat lost in his thoughts.

He looked up and his eyes were searching me as he asked, "Do you believe in God?"

"Yes, I do."

"Will you believe a story if I tell it to you?" he asked. "I can't tell you unless you promise to believe it."

"I will believe it if you say it is true."

"It is true."

"Then I will believe it." There was a long pause as Morteza Gholi Khan put the pieces of his story together. When it came, the telling had the polish and forcefulness of Walter Hampden.

"It was the fall of the year, perhaps twenty-five years ago, and the tribes had started their migration south. Many groups had gone ahead; I was still at Shalamzar. Word came to me that there was trouble between two tribes. A dispute had arisen over some sheep. Hot words developed into a fight. One man was killed. Since he was killed while a large group of men were milling around, no one could be sure just who the killer was. The khans who were handling the case were troubled and perplexed. They could not decide whether or not the one accused was guilty.

"I sent word ahead to hold twenty men from each tribe including the accused; that I would be there in about a week.

"I reached there by horseback in six days. The khans and the twenty men from each of the two quarreling tribes were waiting for me at a village. Twenty men stood on one side of the road, twenty on the other. They remained standing while the khans and I had a consultation. As we were talking, a herd of goats came down the road. In the lead was a big billy, who led the other goats between the two rows of men.

"When the lead goat got opposite the man who was accused of the killing, he stopped for just a second. Then quick as a flash he put his head down and charged this man. It happened so quickly and unexpectedly that the goat caught the man off guard. He hit him in the stomach with a terrible thump. The man fell to the ground; his eyes rolled; and in just a few minutes he was dead."

Morteza Gholi Khan's voice had been loud as he acted out the drama of the goat and the man and showed with gestures what had happened. Now his voice was hushed.

"When the men saw what had happened they fell on each other's necks and started kissing one another."

"Why did they do that?" I interposed.

"Why did they do that?" Morteza Gholi Khan said in a voice expressing surprise that I need ask. "They did it because all of us who were there knew at once that God had appeared through a goat and done justice."

16. An Audience at Oregon

THE BAKHTIARI are south of the Lurs and north of the Ghashghais. Their lands are 26,250 square miles and extend southward from Luristan to Khuzistan and westward from Isfahan province to Andimeshk. They number today about 600,000 people. About half of them are sedentary; the other half migrate. Merian C. Cooper has told the story of their migration in the book *Grass* and in the movie by the same name.

The Bakhtiari, like most tribes of Persia, have two homes: one is called the garmsir or hot district (which is below thirty-five hundred feet elevation) and the other the sardsir or cold district (which is over six thousand feet). In each of these districts they own land and plant crops. Khuzistan, the garmsir, is very parched and insufferably hot in the summer. But the soil is rich and, when the rains come, will grow grain higher than a horse's belly. Grain is planted in the fall and harvested in March or early April. During that period there is grass for the flocks. The sheep are the flat-tailed Asian species. The feed is so good that by April their tails will weigh twenty pounds or even more. By April the trek starts to the mountain valleys up north. It is a rugged journey. There usually is snow in the passes. There are many streams to cross, streams that are ice-cold and in flood. Women and children and household possessions are floated across on inflated goatskins, tied together to form large rafts and paddled by one or two men who kneel at the bow. It is a cruel, challenging ordeal for everyone, and especially severe on the men when they take the livestock across. Each man has two goatskins tied together like waterwings. He floats on these and paddles, guiding cattle, sheep, and donkeys across the icy waters. (Goats usually ride the rafts.) He does it not only once but dozens of times as he makes trip after trip, holding a wild steer by the horn, keeping a baby donkey above the water by hanging on to its ear, swimming along with sheep to make sure none drowns.

Men, women, and children work their way through marshland above their knees, negotiate steep canyons, and struggle through deep snow as they climb to the passes. The old and the sick ride; women with babies on their backs walk. Calves and lambs must be carried up steep trails and through snowbanks. Babies are born on the migrations; but the mother never stops more than a day to perform the ritual of birth. Camp must be made every night; people and animals must be fed. The pace is slow; there are two hundred miles or more to cover. On the fall migration when the tribe leaves the mountains for the southland they cover this distance in about twenty days. The streams are low, and there is no snow. But on the way north in the spring it takes them better than a month to make the journey.

When the valleys of Shalamzar and Oregon are reached, there is green grass everywhere. Bottom lands are lush; hundreds of acres of multicolored iris and dozens of other wild flowers fill the basins; there is grass on the lower slopes of the mountains; there will be grass higher up as the snow melts, enough to carry the herds into the middle of summer.

In September, just before starting the migration south, the tribes sow winter wheat. When they come back in the spring, the crop is up. This crop is harvested in July. But first, on their return in May, they plant a second crop, grown under irrigation and harvested in late August or early September. Some tribesmen will have stayed the winter at Oregon, Shalamzar, or other villages, taking care of their own property or acting as caretakers for friends or neighbors. There is gaiety and festivity on the reunion. An orchestra of drum and horn, which has played all along the route of the migration to lighten the loads of the tribesmen, now plays for dances in celebration of the return.

Reza Shah succeeded in stopping these migrations for a while. He took all the Bakhtiari chiefs to Tehran and either imprisoned them or put them under protective custody. He sent his army among the Bakhtiari and forced them to settle in villages. But six months after he abdicated in 1941, the migrations were under way once more.

One afternoon at Oregon I was riding with Bahman, son of Morteza Gholi Khan, and several dozen of the Bakhtiari. The Bakhtiari love to line their horses up shoulder to shoulder and then stampede them. I, being the guest, had the place of honor, which was out in front. It's an exciting ride when one is a part of a mass of thundering horseflesh going on a dead run across a plain. Horses, I think, have a mob psychology as well as people. Each runs with fury, intent that no horse shall pass him. Since they run shoulder to shoulder in a mad pace, one misstep would be disaster for both horse and rider.

When we stopped to water the horses on our way home, the discussion turned to the effect on the Bakhtiari of the attempt by Reza Shah to stop the migrations. Some of the tribesmen were settled in unhealthy places and died. Their flocks decreased because they needed both the lowlands and the highlands for grazing. Disease spread and the level of health dropped. And finally, disaster hit the horses of the Bakhtiari. Settlement in one village meant a restriction of pasture. Horses died from the severe cold of the high mountains in winter. Those who were settled permanently in winter quarters had to sell their horses, for forage in the hot low country was sufficient only for a fraction of the year. Stables were badly depleted. Today there are few thoroughbreds left. Bahman and a few of the khans have Arabian stallions. But the bulk of the horses —which are relatively few—are mixed breeds. Now there are many geldings; and dysentery is prevalent.

On the last horseback ride we had together Bahman said to me, "Cyrus the Great loved Persia because of its men and its horses. Now we have only the men left."

There are poor people among the Bakhtiari. There are some so poor they are gleaners in the Biblical sense: they pick up the stems of grain left on the thrashing floor or in the field after the harvest is finished. A picture I can never forget is an old, wizened lady sitting under the shade of a poplar near a Bakhtiari grainfield and picking out the heads of wheat one by one from a handful of straw she had found in the field.

A man of the Bakhtiari is poor if he has only thirty sheep. He is well off if he has two hundred. He is wealthy if he has one thousand, since sheep are worth these days about ten dollars a head. Most Bakhtiari own some land and some sheep or goats. They are not by and large the tenant class. The khans own large acreages; their farms are worked in part by Bakhtiari and in part by Armenians. The khans own oil land and prior to nationalization leased it to British interests. Some of the tribal land includes the slopes and peaks of mountains. These can be grazed by any member of the tribe. Sometimes grazing land of another tribe is used; but that requires a rental of so much a head.

The Bakhtiari are not scientific farmers. They plow with sticks pulled by oxen (and instead of gee and haw they use low, almost inaudible whistles); their methods of reaping and thrashing are primitive; they know little about modern agriculture or fertilizers; the use of sprays is largely foreign to them. Bahman and some of the khans are introducing tractors for the breaking of wheat land in Khuzistan, but the average Bakhtiari, owing to lack of experience, has no feel for machinery and the wheel.

One night at Oregon the kalantars, kadkhodas, and rish-safids asked to see me. About thirty came up to the bench where we were camped under the walnut trees. We sat on Persian rugs facing each other; they on one side, Bill and I on the other. Gasoline lanterns showed faces serious and intent. They sat quietly together, each with a tall, black brimless felt hat on his head.

The Bakhtiari are mostly tall and rangy. They have larger frames than the Lurs but, like them, are dark and swarthy. Yet once in a while the Bakhtiari produce a redhead with blue eyes. There were a few such among the men who came to see me this night at Oregon.

I thanked the group for their hospitality. I compared Oregon, U. S. A., with their Oregon; and I told them of the interest which America long has had in Persia. They had appointed one of their kalantars as their spokesman. He had thought out his speech, and delivered it with sincerity and emphasis:

1. The primary need of the Bakhtiari is medical care. They need doctors. There are only three doctors for every 250,000 people. There is none in Oregon or any nearby village. "If our wives or children get sick," he said, "all we can do is pray. If God wills it, they live."

2. The Bakhtiari have no hospitals, no way to care for sick people.

3. The Bakhtiari have practically no schools. The children grow up, unable to read or write. Thus they are in no position to help themselves.

4. The Bakhtiari have very poor roads. It is difficult for them to get their crops to market (I remember how our jeep almost got washed away in a river on our way to Oregon).

5. The Bakhtiari need to be taught farming. They do not know how to drill wells and irrigate, how to plow, how to use fertilizer and sprays, how to farm with machinery.

6. The Bakhtiari want to be rid of the oppressions of Army rule. Soldiers are quartered among them and live off them, exacting tribute and fines for imaginary misdeeds.

This in a nutshell was the two-hour talk. It was illustrated by examples and episodes; and others occasionally broke in to add their bit. There was complete silence and concentration as the woes of the Bakhtiari poured forth from this eloquent speaker. He spoke of the loyalty of the Bakhtiari to the Shah and the tribal chiefs. He ended by saying, "Ask America if she will help us get doctors and schools; ask America if she will help teach us how to farm."

We drank a toast (in water) to the Shah and then to the President of the United States; and the solemn group of Bakhtiari elders filed down the hill.

My friends, the Bakhtiari, had not heard of the important medical program that is just under way at Shiraz under the auspices of Dr. Sabih Ghorban. Shiraz has a new modern medical school which a student attends for four years. He then must go with a midwife and a public-health man to a village or group of villages for two years. During that period this team teaches public health and first aid to the villagers, treats illnesses, vaccinates the people, and so on. At the end of two years the student returns to medical school for three years. Persia is a large country—a fifth of the size of the United States—and Dr. Ghorban's school will have no more than fifty students. But this start on the public health of Persia is outstanding.

I stopped in hundreds of villages in many lands from the Mediterranean to the Pacific and talked with the peasants. They were invariably as articulate about their problems and their needs as the kalantar who spoke for the Bakhtiari. Concern for the health and education of the family always topped the list.

Communist propaganda undoubtedly has made peasants more rebellious. Even in the remote Bakhtiari country, the tribesmen learn what is going on in the world about as fast as we do. The bounties and riches of civilization are no longer secret to these plowmen and goatherds. And they will not long be denied them.

17. Persian Hospitality

WESTERN CIVILIZATION owes much to Persia. The English-speaking community is especially indebted. Through Persian literature and trade a rich stream of words has entered our language—khaki, divan, hocus-pocus, shawl, julep, sash, awning, turquoise, taffeta, orange, lemon, peach, hazard, and hundreds of others. There are also many words that sound close: two—*do*, six—*shesh*, is—*ist*, daughter—*dakhtar*, no—*na*, brother—*barader*, mother—*mader*, father—*pedar*.

I have mentioned earlier the contribution of Persia to the arts and to medicine. Persia gave the world rug weaving; and it put immortal poetry on the lips of all men. The Persian cat should be added to the list—an animal bred for long hair which is useful in making brushes for artists. And Persia has probably done more to perfect the breeding of the Arabian horse than even the Arabs themselves.

Yet the finest gift, I think, that the Persians have shown the world is hospitality. It can be illustrated by a lunch with the Shah, a dinner with the Prime Minister, a garden party tendered by the Governor of Isfahan, or by the reception of Amar Khan Sharifi or Morteza Gholi Khan Samsam. But as I told the present Shah of Persia, Mohammed Reza Shah Pahlavi, the finest example I experienced was in the Bakhtiari mountains.

We were camped at Oregon and scheduled to climb Mount Kalar the morning of our last day. The aim of the trip was primarily to hunt the ibex and secondarily to do a bit of mountaineering. Kalar, over twelve thousand feet high, rises about five thousand feet above Oregon. Once the approaches are cleared, the mountain itself is a series of cliffs of Jurassic limestone with setbacks reminiscent of New York City skyscrapers. The higher ledges are streaked with snow beyond midsummer. The climbing is mostly rock work, nothing daring or particularly hazardous, only wearing. The cliffs and slopes offer no shade; there's not a shrub or a tree to be seen. The cliffs are warm to the touch from the hot Persian sun; there are practically no springs from top to bottom; one needs to dress lightly and carry a good supply of water with him.

I awoke that morning with a temperature of 101 degrees and a nauseating attack of dysentery. But since it was my last day in Bakhtiari country, I decided to climb Kalar anyway. We had planned to leave at 5 A.M. and finally managed it at 7. We had an hour's horseback ride to the base of Kalar, and took another hour hunting partridge in the thistle-filled ravine where we left the horses. These partridge—buff-colored and a bit larger than our Gambel's quail—have a low, fast, swooping flight. They are difficult to hit. But when they are flushed from thistles there is a split second when they are vulnerable. They must first rise vertically three or four feet before they can take off. It is that instant when the Bakhtiari like to shoot them. We had several from each covey; and a Bakhtiari would carefully slit the throat of each. Otherwise the meat would be unclean by Moslem standards.

By the time we had finished hunting partridge and started the ascent, the sun was burning with authority. It was to be a still, hot day.

I climbed about two thousand feet and then turned back. My canteen was empty, my tongue stuck to my mouth, my temples throbbed. I was sick and weak from fever and dysentery. So far as the hunt was concerned and apart from the item of pride, my turning back made no particular difference. This hunting party would never have bagged an ibex. I was accompanied by a dozen Bakhtiari. The climb for them was a lark; they were like school boys on a vacation. They ran up the rocks with the agility of the ibex, talking, laughing, shouting as they climbed. Any ibex could have heard them a mile away.

When I turned back, they continued the hunt. I cleared the ledges and returned to the base of Kalar where we had left the horses. I was three hours ahead of the time when the horses would return; the sun was relentless; and the fever had me badly shaken. In the distance a black Bedouin-like tent hugged the base of the mountain, and I headed for it.

These tents are made of goat wool. Women spin a thread about as coarse as a heavy string and weave the cloth into black strips about eighteen inches wide and twenty feet long. They then sew the strips together, making the cloth for the back and top of the tent. The other side and the two ends are usually open.

There was not a tree or shrub in sight; no shade but that of the tent. A small spring was a stone's throw away. A man, a young boy, three children, and two girls about fifteen and sixteen years old were by the tent. One girl was spinning wool into yarn; the other was milking the fifty sheep and goats that were patiently standing in line.

The man invited me in. He went to the back of the tent and unrolled a small but beautiful Persian rug and laid it in front of me, motioning for me to sit. He brought out a blanket and placed it under my head for a pillow. He took a large kettle of mast, poured some of it into a smaller pot, and mixed it with water from a goatskin. This mixture is known as dugh, a very healthy drink in this area. He scattered some brownish spice over the dugh and handed it to me. I drank deeply and then lay back to sleep.

Just before I went to sleep, I thought how gracious and genuine a Persian's hospitality can be. When I walked into the tent, it became mine. I was left to myself. The man, the girls, and the children went about their own business. No one stood gaping at me. This was my new home for the moment. I had complete privacy.

How long I slept I do not know. But when I awoke, I was fresh and renewed and I went my way after thanking the man and presenting a jackknife to the boy. The scene came back to me over and again as I passed through the drawing rooms of America, Europe, and Asia. There I met gracious hosts and hostesses—well-educated, charming, and warm-hearted—who showed me every courtesy and consideration. Yet somehow the hospitality of the little goatherd on Mount Kalar surpassed all the rest. He not only turned over his whole house to me, made me a bed, gave me nourishing food, and respected my privacy, but when I first asked if I might rest in his tent, he bowed graciously and said in musical words that still ring in my ears: "My hut is poor and dirty but you may sit in the light of my eyes."

18. A Goatherd Sparks a Revolt

THE GHASHGHAIS (Qashqais) are from a different stock than the Lurs or Bakhtiari. The Ghashghais are Turks. Their home is Fars, the southern province that has Shiraz as its capital and which geographically was ancient Persia. How they happened to come to Fars even the Ghashghais do not know, but they have been in Fars about seven centuries.

The Ghashghais are a strong, wiry, rangy people. They have a Turkish dialect; and they have Turkish features as well, with high cheekbones and prominent noses. Their hair ranges from fair to black. Their eyes are dark—usually brown or hazel. Their name has a Turkish origin: some say it comes from the Turkish verb *ghachmak* meaning to flee; others say it derives from *ghashga*, meaning a horse with a white spot on the breast.

They began to form a strong unity as a tribe under the rule of Nadir Shah (1736-1747), with whom they rode when he invaded India, captured Delhi, and returned with millions of dollars of spoils including the famous Peacock Throne. And they kept their unity through succeeding wars, depredations, and famines. When the central government became weak, near the end of the nineteenth century, the Ghashghais flourished under the leadership of Solat-ud-Dowleh, father of the present khans. They became a nation of themselves, commanding most of southwest Persia, and ruled supreme until World War I. At that time the British organized the South Persia Rifles and in 1918 defeated the Ghashghais; thereafter their power declined.

When Reza Shah came to power, he also moved against them, seizing their Ilkhan and his eldest son, Nasser Khan. The other sons left Persia—Malek Mansour going to England where he studied for six years at Oxford, Mohammed Hossein going to school in Germany, Khosrov staying in Tehran and reporting to the police every morning on his way to school.

Solat-ud-Dowleh, the Ilkhan, was murdered in prison; he was given coffee heavily dosed with poison. Today this is called "Pahlavi coffee" in the Ghashghai country. That was in 1933. For eight long years the heavy hand of the Army lay on the tribes. When the British and Russians in 1941 took over Persia and Reza Shah abdicated, the tribes began to stir. The four sons of Solat-ud-Dowleh returned, and the tribes rallied around them. Nasser Khan, the eldest son, was recognized as Ilkhan. Arms were bought, or stolen, or smuggled into the country, and the Ghashghais became a well-organized, vigilant, disciplined group. By 1946 they had regained their freedom and independence and demonstrated it in a daring and dramatic manner.

The year 1945-1946 was a fateful one for Persia. There was a Russian-sponsored Kurdish Republic at Mahabad, and another Russian-sponsored government at Tabriz, headed by Jafar Pishevari, both of which I have already described. After the Russian Army withdrew from Persia, Europe and America lost interest in the country; its problems seemed solved. But Russia, wise in political strategy, knew that when the interest of the West lagged, it was an opportune time for her to become active. That was an easy formula for Russia to apply to Persia, isolated from the West, lying inland a great distance from the Mediterranean, and pressed close to the southern border of Russia. A nation in a position so remote from friends is susceptible to influence from a more powerful and hostile neighbor. So when Persia ceased to be headline interest in America, she was swept closer to Soviet influence.

In 1946 Qavam-os-Saltaneh was Prime Minister of Persia. On August 2, 1946 he made a move which was a plain indication that he was under the pressure of Soviet power: he made changes in his cabinet to include Tudeh party members and sympathizers.

This cabinet shift had immediate repercussions. On September 23, 1946 the four Ghashghai khans sent a telegram to Qavam, reviewing the complaints of the tribes against the acts of Reza Shah and the growing discontent among the people of Fars. They made several demands: trial of officials who had exploited the tribes; the grant of greater autonomy to the people of Fars; a program of education, health, and road construction; replacement of key Army officials with men of integrity and patriotism; and finally but most important, immediate change and reconstitution of the cabinet and the appointment of men noted for their integrity and patriotism. The telegram set twenty-four hours for action by Qavam and stated that if by then "a definite decision is not taken, we will not be blamed by our conscience and by history for any incident that may occur."

The ultimatum was not met; and the Ghashghais and their tribal allies moved into action. They had several thousand cavalry equipped for thirty days of fighting but armed only with rifles. Their allies, the Hayat Davudi tribe, attacked Bushire on the Persian Gulf, which was defended by tanks. The tribesmen through expert marksmanship peppered the peepholes of the tanks and bombed them with bottles of gasoline. There were heavy casualties among the defenders of Bushire; and it fell in one day. While this was going on, a detachment of Ghashghai cavalry attacked Kazerun (between Bushire and Shiraz). It too fell; and the Ghashghais united their armies and marched on Shiraz.

Meanwhile Jahanshah Samsam of the Bakhtiari (the son of Morteza Gholi Khan and the Ghashghai wife) was supposed to march on Isfahan with two thousand men. Jahanshah, however, had confided his plans to a cousin, Abol Qasim Samsam, who swore to secrecy on the Koran. But Abol Qasim broke his promise and hurried with the news to the Army. (As a result a promise that is not kept is called today in Ghashghai country "an Abol-Qasim promise." The Army arrested Jahanshah, but as matters turned out the failure of his part of the plan was not fatal. As the attack on Shiraz started, the Qavam government negotiated with Nasser Khan through the commander of the Shiraz garrison. The demands of the Ghashghais were in large measure met; Qavam resigned; a new cabinet was created which did not contain the Tudeh members and sympathizers; and Jahanshah Samsam was released. The Ghashghais returned to their flocks.

One gets in Persia various versions of this rebellion.

Some say the Persian Army had no heart to fight and would not do so. They point to General Afshar who resigned from the Army after this episode, allegedly in disgust, and who now drives a taxicab in Tehran.

Others say the Ghashghais were vastly superior in skill and in will to fight.

Some say the rebellion was inspired by the British who feared the spread of Tudeh influence to the oil fields. The Persian government on October 1, 1946 did in fact formally demand the withdrawal of Alan C. Trott, British Consul General at Ahwaz and now British Ambassador to Saudi Arabia, for participation in the rebellion.

Some say the Ghashghais were motivated by the desire for plunder. They point out that, when the ports and custom houses at Bushire and neighboring cities were captured, much property disappeared. They estimate that the property which was seized (mostly sugar) was worth over $20,000,000. This is in addition to more than six thousand rifles, numerous machine guns, and millions of rounds of ammunition.

The Ghashghais may well have profited from the revolution; and other figures may have been working behind the scenes. But I am convinced the project was motivated primarily by the concern of the Ghashghais over the admission of Communists into Qavam's cabinet.

Malek Mansour had studied history and government at Oxford and knew well the Communist techniques. Had not the Communists first infiltrated the governments of eastern Europe by taking over the portfolios of education, labor, propaganda, and industry? Was not the next step to obtain the portfolios of Army and foreign affairs?

With Communists in the government, agents and provocateurs would be sent among the tribes, bribing, breeding dissension, playing one kalantar against another, bleeding the people by blackmail. The Communist influence would be at work night and day among the Ghashghais, Bakhtiari, Lurs, and Kurds. Trouble would be certain to follow. There had been ominous signs already. Tudeh had been calling strikes in the summer of 1946. One strike in the oil fields along the Persian Gulf involved 100,000 employees, resulted in heavy casualties, and caused the loss of 300,000 tons of oil.

These were subjects of discussion in Nasser Khan's tent high in Ghashghai country. The decision to act was reached after full discussion and deliberation, and after appraisal of the chances of winning and the risks of defeat. The decision, though in final analysis that of the Ghashghai brothers, was not imposed on the tribes. They too shared in it. And the way it was reached indicates the basic democracy of this tribal system.

One day when the matter was being discussed in Nasser Khan's tent, many Ghashghais gathered around. They listened as the khans talked. Occasionally a kalantar would speak up. There were arguments pro and con. Finally, Malek Mansour called to a goatherd standing on the outer circle and asked what he thought the Ghashghais should do. The goatherd did not hesitate but said at once, "We must fight."

That settled the matter.

When Malek Mansour told me this tale, I asked him why he sought the advice of the goatherd.

"It's always been that way in our tribe," he answered. "My father and his father, before taking a step important to the tribe, sought the advice of the tribesmen. We have unbounded faith in their loyalty and great respect for their common sense and good judgment. Once our grandfather was suspicious of an invitation extended by the Shah to visit Tehran. He had decided not to go, fearing treachery. A goatherd, who was on the outer circle of the group listening to the deliberations, spoke up and urged him to go. He went and it was best for the tribe that he did. The advice of a Ghashghai goatherd is usually good advice."

19. "By My Mother's Milk"

WHEN REZA SHAH undertook to end the tribal migrations, it might be said he was only accelerating a trend, for the tendency through the years has been for all nomads of the Middle East to settle permanently. But whatever may be said of the merits of his program, it was executed by the Army in a barbaric way.

The Ghashghais were forcibly stopped from migrating. Some settled on the hot, barren, waterless lands in the Gulf area where there is grazing for only a few months of the year. The government provided no irrigation projects. The people wasted away and their flocks perished.

Others who were moved to rice areas along the Gulf fell victims to malaria.

These nomads, who now were forced to become villagers, had no sense of village life. The settlements in which they were placed soon piled high with refuse; springs became polluted; typhoid and dysentery spread; a plague of trachoma hit the tribesmen.

Those settled in the mountain country fared somewhat better, for the climate there is healthier. But these nomads did not know how to build warm houses, nor how to take care of themselves or their stock in freezing weather, nor how to irrigate and farm in settled communities. They suffered greatly from pneumonia, tuberculosis, and other throat and lung infections. Many, many died. The severe winters also killed off their livestock. One year the Darashori subtribe lost almost 90 per cent of their horses when the Army forced them to remain in the mountains all winter.

The property of the khans was confiscated on the theory that the Ghashghais should pay the state the cost of conducting this campaign against them. Further, the central government appointed as khans men who would humiliate the proud tribesmen and who could be counted on to play the government's game.

The tribesmen died at such a rate that many think they would have been wiped out in a few decades had the conditions persisted. To live they had to migrate. And so they began to spend their wealth in bribing Army officers to let them migrate. The Army fastened itself as a leech on these peoples; bribery and blackmail became the fashion and the order of the day.

Qishlaq is a village of about seventy families. It lies northwest of Shiraz in Ghashghai country. The village and all the land around it is owned by a man named Agha Bozorg, who was a sergeant in the Persian Army for about fifteen years. During that time his salary was between seven dollars and twenty dollars a month. A few years ago he bought Qishlaq for $200,000 cash. I stopped at Qishlaq to see him; but he was away. I learned from the villagers that he is married to a woman who beats him and who occasionally takes a shot at him with a revolver. The villagers say that that is justice. They think Agha Bozorg got his $200,000 in a way for which he is now being punished. I do not know how Agha Bozorg got his wealth. But I learned how other sergeants and officers of the Persian Army amassed fortunes under Reza Shah. The following is one example.

A sergeant, with an eye on wealth and fortune, stole a donkey in Ghashghai country. He stole the donkey at night, took it to a distant ravine, and killed it. Then he cut off the front feet, put them in his pockets and returned to his barracks, high in Ghashghai country. He bided his time. As he made the rounds of the tribes, he kept his eyes open for fat flocks, good crops, pure-blooded Arabian horses.

When he selected his victim, he waited until a dark night. Under the cover of darkness he crept into the village, a donkey foot in each hand, and placed hoof prints along all the streets and before every house. Then he withdrew and waited until morning. He returned with troops, searched out the village elder, and said, "There have been donkeys stolen and I am told that some of your people stole them."

The village elder assured him that he was wrong, that there were no donkeys there. The sergeant, looking down, spied the hoof prints of donkeys and said, "You're lying. Here are the tracks. Look, they are everywhere." And with that the sergeant went around the village, followed by his troops, the village elder, and a growing crowd of villagers. And everywhere he went he pointed to the hoof prints. Finally, he stopped and said to the crowd, "Where are the donkeys?"

They assured him they had no donkeys.

"But I have the evidence and the court in Shiraz will convict you."

The denials of guilt became more and more insistent, the accusations were emphatic. Finally the sergeant said, "If no one will confess, I'll have to arrest everyone and take you all to Shiraz." Turning to his troops he said, "Line them up and start them down the road."

Shiraz was one hundred miles away. It would take days to reach there on foot; weeks would be wasted waiting for trial; it would take more days to return. Meanwhile the crops would be lost; there would be no one to care for the sheep and goats. The prospect of losing their year's production and the wealth of their flocks was appalling. Consequently, the village elder sought a way of settling the controversy.

The discussion was long and heated. The sergeant placed a fine on the whole village. There were violent objections. The sergeant answered by once more directing the troops to start the villagers down the road to Shiraz. The village elder slowly and painfully realized that this was blackmail and that he would have to capitulate to save his people. The price then became the subject of negotiation. It was finally reduced to $15,000. Sheep, goats, wheat, money, jewelry were collected and assessed and the sergeant marched off with his loot.

In some villages, he got $20,000, in others $5,000. The donkey hoofs became worth more than their weight in gold. The sergeant grew in arrogance and wealth as he bled the Ghashghais white.

Old habits are hard to break and at the lower echelons there is still a great incentive to prey on the tribes. Salary of soldiers and gendarmes is pitifully poor. A captain of the gendarmes who has ten children and relatives to support practically conceded to me that he had to steal or exact blackmail. His salary is about fifty dollars a month.

The Ghashghais, alert to these practices, are today able to take care of themselves. Almost every man is armed; and their organization is highly perfected. Shortly before my visit the Army endeavored to bring two hundred Arabs into one Ghashghai district for grazing. The villagers protested and refused admission. The Army said it would be back in the morning. When they came, they were met by one thousand Ghashghais, armed and ready to fight. The Army and the Arabs withdrew.

I heard for days on end stories of the depredations of the Army against the tribes and the loot and plunder they had collected. One afternoon I called on a kalantar. We sat in a long open tent, partitioned by carpet hangings. The side part was the *anderun* where the women and children stayed. In our part were beautiful rugs and a backdrop of gaily colored carpets against which were piled rolls of blankets and rugs for sleeping. We had tea; and then the kalantar, an old man with a cracked voice, reviewed the ravages of the Army under Reza Shah. He ended the hour or more of discussion with these words: "We can forgive the Army for some of these things and live with them in peace. But there is one thing which we never can forgive.

"During the reign of Reza Shah there was a captain stationed here who had several thoroughbred puppies. The bitch had died. The captain sent soldiers every morning to one of our villages and demanded two quarts of mother's milk. Our Ghashghai women were forced to submit. Each day dogs drank the milk of our mothers." There was a pause as he gathered emphasis for his final words, "That we can never forgive."

The depth of his feeling can be understood only if two things are remembered: *First.* Dogs are unclean to Moslems. *Second.* The Ghashghai not only have the respect for mothers that is universal; they also have a tradition and custom that this Army captain desecrated. For one of the most sacred oaths a Ghashghai can take is "By my mother's milk."

20. *"Trust in God, but Tie Your Camel"*

WHEN THE Ghashghai brothers returned from imprisonment and exile in 1942, they had many discussions concerning the rehabilitation of the tribes before they finally decided on a course of action. Then their first step was to make an inventory of what every family had and to ask that each put into a pool a designated fraction of his property for distribution to the poor. A family that had one hundred sheep gave one to the pool; if it had five hundred, it gave five, and so on. Donkeys were collected the same way: one donkey out of every twenty was asked for. And so it went for goats, food, and clothes. This was a voluntary, tribal project—no force was used; everyone co-operated.

The khans then distributed the pooled property to the poor families, arranging that each should have a few donkeys (essential for their long migrations) and about one hundred sheep. The tribes were rehabilitated overnight; poverty was wiped out; the Ghashghais gained new unity and cohesion as a tribe; and their loyalty and affection for their khans were cemented anew. This bold political program revitalized the Ghashghais; they had always been proud; now they were confident as well.

Today it is unusual to find a Ghashghai family that has less than one hundred sheep. Most have many more. The lower economic group averages about five hundred sheep. In that part of the world there are two lambings a year. This means at the very least a cash income of $2,000 a year (and there is no income tax to pay).

It is a part of the faith of the Ghashghais that the rifle is the brother of Allah. They live up to it in practice. Thus when the khans returned from exile there was the problem of getting back their property which Reza Shah had confiscated. The Ghashghais demanded it; and when their demands were rejected they armed and went forth to battle. They met the Army and in June, 1943, attacked and captured Semirum, a fort. Thereafter the controversy was settled peaceably.

After the khans got back their property they entered upon a vast program of land distribution. Some land was distributed free; other land was sold with payments extending over a long term of fifteen years or more.

The distribution was extensive. In one summer area over ninety-six square miles of farming and grazing lands were distributed to forty-seven thousand people.

Thus the Ghashghais rebuilt political fences after fifteen years of exile and reaffirmed their worth as leaders of their people.

Not all of the Ghashghais are proprietors. Some work for wages. Most of the servant class, however, are known as gypsies, i.e., outsiders who come from other tribes or from the cities. Though the servants are in most respects the equals of the families for whom they work, and by the standards of that part of the world very well taken care of, the daughter of a cook can never marry the son of a kalantar. Democracy among the Ghashghais does not extend that far. By long custom one marries only in his class. The classes are five: khans, kalantars, kadkhodas, ordinary tribesmen, gypsies or outsiders.

This is a topsy-turvy land when it comes to personal relations. On my many trips by car and jeep with the Ghashghais, the chauffeur was usually a middle-aged man called Najaf. He was short and stocky, and very much a stoic. In all the hours I was in a car with him he never spoke more than a few words. And they were usually a cryptic *"na"* (no) or *"bali, bali"* (yes, yes).

Near the end of my visit I spoke to Mohammed Hossein about the man, complimenting his care and skill as a driver. And I inquired if the khans had difficulty keeping good help of this kind. Mohammed Hossein smiled and said, "This man is not a servant. He's a wealthy man worth hundreds of thousands of dollars."

"Why is he your servant?"

"Because he wants to be." And then he told me that Najaf's father, grandfather, and all the other male ancestors so far as memory went had been attached to the Ilkhan or one of the lesser khans. They were men of property and wealth; but they came to the court of the Ilkhan as volunteer gunbearers, guards, or what not. No pay was given; the position was one of honor. The relation was almost a filial one.

"Najaf would be insulted if I offered him pay," Mohammed Hossein said, "and yet he'd do anything for us."

He went on to relate an episode in connection with the 1946 revolution. He had had to go to Isfahan on a secret mission, preparatory to the assault on Bushire. Najaf drove him; another man went along as guard. Najaf, one of the best shots in all the Middle East, sat in the dark outside the Isfahan house which Mohammed Hossein entered. He had a rifle across his knees. His orders were to let one hour pass. If Mohammed Hossein did not appear by that time, Najaf was to break into the house and rescue him.

"But if there were a plot to hold you, your rescue by one man would be a hazardous venture."

"Yes, but Najaf is equal to any ten men."

Malek Mansour, the older brother, who had been listening to our conversation, interrupted to say, "The personal relations within our tribe are intimate and strong. An American or Britisher might not believe what I will tell you but it is true: if we commit ourselves to a project, we carry through though it means death. There is nothing a brother won't do for a brother, nothing this chauffeur won't do for us or we for him. We'd gladly die for one another."

There was no boasting in this statement. It was a quiet assertion of an article of faith—an article of faith that is deeply moving in a world where deceit plays a major role in world affairs.

21. The Ghashghais on Horseback

THE GHASHGHAIS have the finest Arabian horses I have seen. They are probably unequaled in the world. For centuries the Ghashghais have bred them for the hunt. At present they are a bit over fourteen hands, larger than the normal Arabian. There are not many geldings in the tribes. Stallions, spirited but gentle, are preferred for the hunt, since they have more stamina for the long, hard runs. But mares are also used in the less strenuous hunts.

Ghashghai saddles are a bit reminiscent of McClellan saddles; they have a low cantle and no horn, but a front that is slightly raised and padded. The usual stirrup is the English type; sometimes triangular side plates are used, one corner of which serves as a spur.

The Ghashghai men, normally tall and rangy, have an odd-looking tribal dress. It is a long robe which looks much like a dressing gown with a sash around the waist. Over this they wear a leather vest. The hat is usually brown felt with turned-up flaps, front and back.

The tribe of the Ghashghais most famous for its horses is the Darashori. Its head is Ziad Khan, a short, slight, middle-aged man, who loves horses as a man loves his sons. He also loves to ride them; and Ziad Khan is one of the best riders and hunters and one of the best shots on horseback of any of the Ghashghais. To be rated with the Ghashghais let alone to be placed at their head is high praise.

Ziad Khan constantly brings new Arab blood to his stables from Khuzistan. The Arab blood most desired is the Khersan. Stallions in his string will sell anywhere from $2,500 up. And Ziad Khan in 1950 could produce on twenty-four hours' notice twenty thousand cavalrymen, mounted and armed, with provisions and ammunition for thirty days.

The tails of the horses are cut when they are six months old and again when they are a year and a half. This makes them fluffy and full. The effect is striking when the tail is arched. Petals of a species of mallow, rubbed on the tails, give them luster and are said to promote their growth.

The horses are first ridden when they are a year old. This requires no breaking of the horse, as we use the term, for they never buck or rear. They are as gentle as household pets when they are colts; indeed, they are pets from the time they first walk. I was in a long, open Ghashghai tent having tea, when a young colt came in and nuzzled me looking for sugar. He kept coming back as a dog might, friendly and intimate, a regular member of the family.

The first riding of the horse is at a walk, no trotting or running. This is done only occasionally, just enough to get the animal used to the feel of a saddle, bridle, and rider. When the horse is two and a half years old he is given a wider experience. This is when he is broken to fire, music, and gunpowder.

He is led around bonfires at night until he no longer jumps or shies at the noise, the flame, or the heat. He is then exposed to Ghashghai orchestras of drum and horn (oboe) that play for the dances. Finally he is exposed to fire and to music, because the Ghashghais' wedding dances are at night around bonfires.

He is led near a firing range. When he no longer is startled at the noise, he is brought closer. In a few days his trainer is shooting a gun next to him; then there is shooting across the saddle and finally from the saddle. Any horse goes wild when a gun is shot off right over his ears, as many a hunter has learned. Ghashghai horses are broken to fire with studious regard for their sensitivity.

In a week a stallion is broken to fire, music, and gunfire. Then he is ready for a full measure of tribal life. When a stallion is used for riding and for the hunt, he is not put at stud. His days at stud come after his hunting days are over when he is eight or nine years old. Ghashghais have the theory that a stallion at stud loses the keen edge necessary for the hunt.

These horses are wiry and tough. There are no barns or stables to shelter them. Most of the time they stand tethered by a halter and by the rear feet. They receive generous portions of barley; and they are exercised every day.

When I hunted with the Ghashghais, I learned what magnificent animals the Arabian stallions are. They have an instinct for the hunt that is keen and sharp. All that needs be done is to point them to the game and they hold to the prey as a greyhound does to a rabbit.

They and the Ghashghais make the most skillful hunting combination I have ever known.

One day Malek Mansour and I headed across the Namdan Plain. I was riding Mohammed Hossein's white stallion; Malek Mansour, his own bay. About eighty mounted Ghashghais were on our flanks and in our rear. Each had a rifle and a shotgun, one of which was carried by a bearer. We were headed for an ibex hunt.

Namdan Plain is almost as flat as a floor and extends two hundred miles northwest and southeast. It is around fifteen miles wide. The plain lies about six thousand feet high, which makes the ridges that cover its flanks eight thousand feet or better; and the mountains that lie behind the ridge on the west rise to fifteen thousand feet. The hills have no trees in the vivid sense of the word, but there are wild peach trees—shrubs from two to eight feet tall—and other coarse shrubs of camel thorns and thistles. But by late summer these mountains look naked to the eye.

The plain itself is covered by grass that is stirrup high in the spring. There will be miles and miles of wild iris and hollyhock in bloom. In the spring a meandering stream flows through the plain; by fall this stream is a winding, dark streak of marshland. Dogear rushes, twelve feet tall, grow in it. It is a favorite haunt of the wild boar.

The ibexes are in the hills above Namdan Plain and they were our hunt that day. As we rode, Malek Mansour spotted a hawk traversing our course about a half mile ahead. He took a shotgun from the bearer, pointed his stallion toward the hawk, and leaned forward in the saddle. The stallion ran like the wind. Though the hawk changed its course, the stallion kept in pursuit and came under the hawk. The stallion was still on a hard, fast run when Malek Mansour dropped the reins, stood slightly in the stirrups, and brought the hawk down with one shot. That afternoon other Ghashghais performed similar feats, chasing hawks, vultures, and low-flying ducks on horseback and shooting from the saddle on the dead run. They must on the law of averages sometimes fail to get their bird; but this afternoon they seldom missed; and the most shots anyone took were two.

We did not get our ibex that day. They are found above the plain in ravines, rocky gorges, and open slopes of the high mountains. Careful planning is required to drive these fleet animals so that they come in range. Several converging parties worked one huge valley and mountain; but the ibex raced up a cliff rather than around it and got away.

I had ridden the white stallion on a hunt in the valley. Never had I been on a faster steed. When he ran it was as if he had his belly to the ground. His feet sounded like machine-gun fire. He went with the wind and as freely. There was joy and abandon in the run—an all-out, enthusiastic burst of energy. The run had a beautiful rhythm; horse and rider became one; it was a wild, exultant co-operative project. The pounding of the hoofs, the feel of the wind, the tenseness of the pace, the thrill of the chase make going at thirty-five miles an hour aboard a stallion an exquisite experience. But to the uninitiated the run of a Ghashghai horse through broken country is on the startling side. Those horses take brush, rocks, gullies as if they did not exist. There is no break in the stride, no change of pace. Uphill and down they go as if propelled by Satan. Then it is that one knows why stallions are preferred for the hunt. Mares cannot endure the grueling speed. Once in a while these hard-running stallions have an accident, but injuries are rare. These fleet animals with tiny feet and strong shoulders can go almost anywhere on a dead run. Only marshland breaks the beautiful rhythm of their pounding pace.

I took movies of one gazelle hunt. Advance parties sent out by the Ghashghais turned a mass of gazelles from the mountains onto Namdan Plain. There were several thousand of them in one herd, racing over thirty miles an hour. Through the glasses they looked like waves of a vast sea that filled the basin in a mirage. Their backs rose and fell in perfect symmetry as the great mass raced across the valley.

Some were finally cut from the herd and my group went into action. Few of our western horses would ever get within range of a gazelle. This member of the antelope family, with short, straight, pointed horns and tiny legs, weighs about forty pounds, is hardly higher than a big shepherd dog, and can do fifty miles an hour. I have clocked them at that speed on the Namdan Plain. No horse ever born can run that fast. Some therefore resort to the criminal practice of hunting gazelles in a jeep. Ghashghais strenuously object to that practice and make life miserable for any jeep hunter who enters their domain. They get their gazelles by cutting out a few from a herd, coming in on them from an angle, and shooting from the saddle on the dead run. This afternoon the fifteen in my party got forty gazelles; and every one was the result of magnificent riding and shooting. They were all saddle shots, where the hunter has to know the rhythm of the horse, the arc his gun is traveling, and the split second when he's on the target. That's hard enough with a moving target when the hunter is stationary. It's an exacting skill beyond most hunters when both target and hunter are on the run.

When I was in the Bakhtiari country I had seen a nice exhibition of shooting on a gallop. I had in fact put up prizes for a contest. Bahman Khan was judge. He laid out a course about two hundred yards long and ran horsemen by a stationary target about fifty yards distant. It was good shooting; but Ghashghai shooting was even better. The Bakhtiari have been disarmed so long they are out of practice. Once they were equals of the Ghashghais, and Bahman of the Bakhtiari today can ride and shoot with any of the Ghashghais. But the average Ghashghai is now far ahead of any tribesman not only in Persia but in the whole Middle East.

I gave prizes for a Ghashghai shooting contest. Malek Mansour arranged it. A bush on a side hill was the target. The contestants rode by it at a distance of fifty yards, shooting from five different positions on their three-hundred-yard course—once as they started, once at the quarter, once when directly opposite, once at the three-quarter position, and once at the end. These were hard fast runs, the riders never once touching the reins. The last two shots were made going away from the target, the rider shooting over the tail of the horse.

Over twenty entered the contest. Not one shot from the entire group went astray. There were misses; but every shot either hit or rimmed the target. Ziad Khan, famous horse breeder, won the contest against two sharp, clean-cut youngsters in their teens. Ziad put five bullets in the center of the bush on the run down; then he turned the horse, came back on a dead run, shifted his rifle to his left shoulder and put five more bullets in the bush. Others followed suit and many had records almost as good.

I had never seen such shooting, even by circus experts. The skill of these Ghashghais made the rewards seem woefully inadequate: all I could contribute as prizes were a carton of American cigarettes, a pair of sun glasses, a jackknife, a whetstone, and a key ring. To my surprise Malek Mansour made the key ring the first prize and gave the rest in reverse of the order I had listed them.

I thought that exhibition was the most superb shooting I had ever seen, but I was to see more. Returning to camp one afternoon with Malek Mansour and a host of Ghashghai hunters, I galloped ahead to get a picture of the group coming across Namdan Plain. They, however, stopped a quarter mile away and sent a rider after me, who came with a clatter shouting "*Gros, gros.*" Before I could translate his message Malek Mansour and the rest of us were off on a hard fast run across the plain in pursuit of a wild boar who had broken out of the marshland and headed across the basin. The boar had a two-mile start and was loping at full speed. We had to cross the marsh and so for a few moments were slowed to a walk. When we finally negotiated it, Malek Mansour had a long lead and was going like the wind. In five minutes or so he got within two hundred yards of the boar, stood in his saddle, and fired. The bullet hit the boar in the right shoulder. The animal's front legs collapsed momentarily; but he was up in a jiffy and on his way.

Now Malek Mansour had a dangerous venture on his hands. A wounded boar has no equal in ferocity. To chase a wounded boar on horseback is suicidal, for a boar in full flight can turn faster than a horse can turn; when he does, he comes up under the horse, ripping him with the tusks and killing him and probably the rider too. So Malek Mansour pulled out about fifty yards and ran parallel with the boar. In a few minutes he was abreast of the animal.

This was the tense and telling moment of the hunt. The boar now turned and charged the horse. A wounded boar on a short charge goes much faster than even an Arabian horse can run. If this stallion bolted and ran, the boar would be under him in a matter of seconds, ripping open his belly. This was the crucial test for the rider as well, for he had only one shot before the boar would be under the horse. The Arabian stallion never wavered though death would reach him in seconds. He went pounding across the plain, holding his course as though he were a guided missile. Malek Mansour had dropped his reins and was now low in the saddle, leaning sideways. He waited until the boar was seventy-five feet away and then dropped him with one bullet between the eyes.

I never have been able to decide who was more of a champion—Malek Mansour or the bay stallion with the arched tail.

22. The Ghashghais on the Move

THE GHASHGHAIS probably number around 500,000 people, a half of whom migrate. In the summer they are in territory south of, and contiguous to, the Bakhtiari. Their summer quarters head up in the Kuh-i-Dina range of the Zagros Mountains, dominated by a peak fifteen thousand feet high. Here they have grazing land and farmland. There is much dry farming and some irrigation. Ghashghai rent is on shares; and it usually is five parts for the farmer and one part for the landlord. Wheat and barley are grown in great quantities. There are many vegetables produced; and some of the tribes raise poppies for opium. The agricultural industry also includes exploitations of the thorny tragacanth bush from which the famous gum is obtained. Tapping the roots of this bush is a large part of the summer industry of the tribes. The Ghashghais market tons of this gum every year. Ghashghai women are expert weavers. They produce rugs, carpets, blankets, feed bags, and rope that find their way into bazaars and constitute a source of substantial income for the tribes.

By and large the Ghashghais still use primitive methods in farming. Some tractors have been introduced; but they are new. The khans are enterprising, inquisitive, and progressive. They have brought from America many species of oranges, lemons, grapefruit, and other citrus and developed large orchards. There are wild peaches in the mountains, as I have said, and farther south one sees wild almond and wild pistachio trees. Like the wild peach they are coarse shrubs five to eight feet high. They make excellent browse. The khans have been experimenting with them, planting strips of them both as a soil erosion measure and as browse belts. The Ghashghais do not know why these plants are good for stock; but they know that stock which feeds on them is always healthy.

(The Persian government has also started an afforestation program. It planted two million trees in March, 1951.)

The khans are interested in scientific agriculture. Nasser Khan's son at present is in California's agricultural school. Time seems to stand still with some of the tribes, as I have indicated. And so far as schools, doctors, hospitals, and general modernity are concerned the average Ghashghai is where his ancestors were a hundred years ago. Not so with the khans. Their khans are trying to keep abreast of the times; soil erosion, crop rotation, pest control, new types of plants are engaging their interest. Yet in spite of their emphasis on science in developing the economy of the tribes, tribal life keeps pretty much the pace it had centuries ago.

The tribes move north in the spring and south in the fall. Their migrations are the longest of any Persian tribe, extending in some cases 350 miles. The people start down from the high mountains in September and take a month or six weeks to reach winter quarters. They pour down many valleys, following ancient migration routes. These routes converge at Guyum, about twenty miles northwest of Shiraz and thus, as Reza Shah knew, become very vulnerable to any power that would want to interfere with the migration. From Guyum the tribes fan out—some west to Behbehan, some south to Dashtistan, some southeast to the loop of the Mand River on the border of Laristan. Here they stay until April when they start their northward trek.

I was with the Ghashghais on one fall migration. It is as colorful a sight as one can hope to see. The first and superficial impression is that of a pack outfit moving through our western mountains. But it is not as carefree as such an expedition. These migrations involve moving the entire family and all its worldly possessions. Everything that is needed is transported on foot twice a year three hundred miles or more. The old folks and the babies ride. Tents, cooking utensils, looms, poles, fuel, blankets—all the belongings are loaded on donkeys and camels. Chickens are tied on top of donkeys. Gay colored blankets and saddlebags make the camels look as if they were on dress parade.

The families move early on the march. They stretch out as far as the eye can see; great clouds of dust hang over the procession and mark its course.

Dozens of dogs keep up front or scour the flanks for rabbits or fox. They are mangy, nondescript animals—ugly to look at but heroic. They guard the flocks, fight in packs against wolves, and often give their lives in gallant battle.

One sees mostly women and children on these marches. They walk in front of the camels or follow behind the donkeys, beating them with sticks and shouting hoarse commands. The men are largely missing. The reason is that the main procession follows the valleys, while the flocks must seek higher ground. The Ghashghais have at least seven million sheep, which must eat as they move the three hundred miles or more. Feed for that quantity of grazing cannot be found in the thoroughfares; thus the flocks spread out along the ridges on both flanks of the main procession. There are appointed camping places; and here the families usually reunite at evening. Then the flocks must be milked, cheese and butter made, and mast prepared.

This is a gigantic project, run pretty much on clockwork, and efficiently managed.

But the migration is not only of people and their possessions. The migration is well-nigh universal. Almost all the animals migrate with the Ghashghais.

There are ibexes and mountain sheep in the hills. They too move south with the tribes. So do the gazelles. So do the foxes.

The predators follow suit—wolves, leopards, and jackals. They slink through canyons by day and walk the ridges at night, following their prey.

Thousands of birds move south, even the hawks and vultures. For me the most thrilling sight of all is the migration of the partridge. These buff-colored birds move by the thousands under some mysterious command. They walk in mass formation—several thousand in one group—headed south. They hold their heads high, and as they march along they talk with each other just as the Ghashghais do.

Men and animals alike seem to receive from nature the same signal. They start south together. They move as a group to the land where the days are warm, the nights are cool, the grass is high, and other food is plentiful.

Only the wild boar stays behind.

23. It's an Old Ghashghai Custom

MULLAH NASR-ED-DIN, the legendary Persian humorist, had served the Shah long and faithfully. When at long last he got an audience, he asked His Majesty for a favor. He wanted a royal commission, authorizing him to go about the realm interviewing the people and collecting one hen's egg from each man who feared his wife. The Shah, to humor Mullah, wrote out the commission and Mullah went his way.

Mullah traveled the length and breadth of Persia (which in those days was several times its present size). Everywhere he went the eggs rolled in. He traded eggs for flocks of sheep and goats; he traded eggs for Arabian stallions and mares; he filled the markets with eggs and with the money built a summer castle for himself high in the Zagros Range and a winter palace in Shiraz; he sold eggs and purchased plants and shrubs from all over the world and built himself beautiful gardens. Mullah was rich; he had dozens of servants, wonderful baths, luxurious food, and a good-looking harem.

Finally he finished his tour of Persia and sought an audience with the Shah to give him an accounting. He reported at length of his journeys and his achievements. When he finished the Shah said, "Mullah, I am ashamed of you. You have got rich from the royal commission I gave you and you have not even brought me a present."

Mullah, raising his voice, replied, "Your Majesty, I am most grateful to you for your great favor. As I went about the country I kept thinking of you."

"Yes, I know," said the Shah, "but you didn't bring me a present."

"Yes, I did, Your Majesty," replied Mullah. And then in a voice that could be heard throughout the castle, Mullah added, "I brought you a beautiful, young Turkish girl."

"Sh-h-h-h," whispered the Shah, putting his finger to his lips.

"This Turkish girl is the loveliest you have ever seen," Mullah roared.

"Sh-h-h-h," the Shah once more admonished.

"She has beautiful eyes, silken hair, a shapely figure," Mullah bellowed.

"Not so loud, not so loud," whispered the Shah. "My wife is in the next room."

Mullah rose, bowed graciously, held out his hand and said, "Your Majesty, now you too owe me an egg."

Nowhere is this story more greatly appreciated than in Ghashghai country. And nowhere in the Moslem world do women have a stronger, more authoritative position in family and tribal life than among the Ghashghais.

Like other tribal women in Persia, they go unveiled. Like them they do most of the manual work of the camp and of the migrations; they also work in the fields, harvesting wheat or barley with hand sickles. But these women, many of whom are strikingly beautiful, look one in the eye, confident and self-possessed. And as they do so they scan the intruder with a searching look as if to say, "You can't possibly be as brave, and strong, and versatile as our men." They are, in other words, proud and independent.

In one respect, however, Ghashghai women are inferior to other tribal women. The other tribes usually have laws of inheritance that leave one part of the father's property to a daughter and two parts to a son. Under Ghashghai law the sons take all, the daughters nothing. Daughters, however, are under the protection of their brothers until they marry, and on marriage receive a dowry.

There is a very superior and dominant woman behind the management of the Ghashghais. She is Khadejeh Bibi, mother of the four khans. She has wisdom and power and wields it wisely. But the reasons for the unique position of Ghashghai women in the Moslem world strike deeper. The Moslem religion permits divorce; but the Ghashghais do not. If a man undertakes to divorce his wife, her family takes matters in their hands. They may kill the husband with impunity, for his act is an insult to their house.

Ghashghais for all practical purposes are monogamous. Marriage to more than one woman is rare. It can happen and sometimes does. If a couple, though married for five or six years, have no children, a second marriage may be arranged. But it is managed by the kalan-

tars or khans and is done only with the consent of the wife. If a
second wife is taken, she takes an inferior position in the home. The
first wife remains in full control of the home, including the discipline of the children.

Ghashghai children incidentally are not whipped or beaten. They
are punished by being denied what they want most—participation
in a wedding dance, horseback riding, or a hunting party.

The boys are raised in the women's quarters until they are seven.
Then they are circumcised in a public ceremony by a tribal barber
who uses a razor and slit bamboo. A unique hemostatic dressing is
used—the ashes of a cremated rabbit. When the boy is a son or
relative of a khan or kalantar, the circumcision is the occasion for
feasting by the whole tribe.

Ghashghai courts are close to the people. The Ghashghais, like
the Bakhtiari, though Shiah Mohammedans, have no mullahs in
the tribes. The khans adjudicate all the disputes. Ghashghai law is
well developed. Years ago the khans had it reduced to writing,
and it is now contained in several volumes, covering all phases of
tribal and personal relations. It has some interesting variations from
other tribal law. For example, if it is publicly known that a young
couple is guilty of fornication, which is forbidden, both may be
killed by a relative. If only the families know, a marriage will be
forced.

In case of rape the whole tribe takes up the chase. The man is an
outlaw and when captured is killed at once.

Feuding is a point of honor. If a man is killed in a quarrel, it is
the duty of his family to hunt out the killer and kill him. Once
revenge is had, the khan steps in. He goes to the home of the last
man killed and asks the family to forgive their enemy. A khan by
tradition commands rather than requests; so when he asks a favor,
his desire is always respected.

The khans serve as priests and father confessors to their people.
They have a paternal relation to the lowliest of them. A goatherd
may have a grievance against someone who took his goat; if he
feels he was not accorded justice by the kalantar, he complains to the
khan. The khan sends a trusted employee to investigate. If the employee does not make a fair report, he is punished. The goatherd,
dissatisfied with the report, appeals to the khan. The khan sends
word that he will come in person. It may be a 50 or 100-mile

ride; but he goes. He holds court and hears both sides. If he rules for the goatherd, he will order the return of the goat and fine the offender. He then gives the goatherd a letter saying that he has won and that no one should ever touch his goats. A goatherd armed with such a letter has great prestige. No kalantar will dare touch him. He carries in his pocket the key to immunity from all raiding.

The goatherd cannot sit before a khan; he must stand. A kalantar on the other hand may sit. But goatherd and kalantar have equal status before the law.

Even in so personal an affair as marriage the khans play an important role in the lives of their people. When a Ghashghai couple decides to get married, they ask the khan's blessing, and take him a kid or an ibex as a gift. It is a symbol of good luck for them to accept something in return from the khan. The khan's wife or sister will make an article of clothing for the bride; the khan will give the groom a horse, gun or sheep depending on the groom's interests or needs. The khan becomes the "spiritual godfather of all the children of the marriage." He may give his blessing to the marriage even though the families of the young people oppose it. In that case the khan takes it on himself to work out a reconciliation. It may require years; but his ingenuity and diplomacy are tireless in devising ways and means of bringing ultimate approval from the parents.

The wedding festivities last three days or more, and are enlivened by a variety of night dances. (Dances of the Ghashghais are commonly held at night, against a backdrop of a huge fire built in a rock cairn. In this custom, one recognizes the trace of Zoroaster's philosophy and teachings. It is revealed again in a Ghashghai oath: "By bread and salt" or "By the fireplace"—the equivalent of our "Cross my heart and hope to die.")

In one of the wedding dances, women and girls dressed in brilliant colors dance clockwise around a fire. Then the men put on the stick dance. I first saw this dance in Bakhtiari country. The men at Oregon performed it, and ended by making Lowell Thomas, Jr. and me participants. One man holds before him a heavy wooden staff five to six feet long, resting one end on the ground. He keeps it stationary and tries to use it as a shield against the attacks of the other participant. The latter has a willow stick. His aim is to whack the defender across the ankles or calves. There is much weaving and jumping, while feints and false passes are made. The attacker has only one blow. Then the dancers change positions, walking and strutting around the ring until the holder of the staff places it in front of him and gets ready for the attack. This is all done to music; and often the crowd keeps time by clapping. There is great competition for the places at the end of each dance. There are many casualties; a smart blow on the calves has sometimes put a good man to bed.

Dancing during wedding festivals continues from dusk until 11 P.M. or so. Then the father of the groom tenders a dinner to all the assembled guests. On the last day the bride arrives, mounted on a white horse which she has ridden three times around her camp before departing. She has a young boy seated behind her—an omen that her first child will be a son.

Among the Ghashghais, to come across an unexpected wedding when one is traveling is an omen of good luck. One's trip will be pleasant; his hunt successful. Another sign of good luck is having water unexpectedly or accidentally spilled on one. (That happened to me late one afternoon just before I went to wedding festivities at the camp of a kalantar; and at the dinner which followed I ate some mountain goat which made me ill for six days.)

On the other hand, a sneeze is a warning. If a group is planning a trip (say for hunting) and one of them sneezes before they start, they give each other knowing looks and wait. They will wait perhaps a half hour; or if anyone has any particular feeling about it, they may wait a whole day.

When I went to visit the Ghashghais, I passed through the village of Kaftar where Ghashghai families live the year around. A group of men were on the edge of the village with a sheep which they sacrificed before I could stop them. Behind them were a group of thirty or forty women. When I dismounted and walked up to the village elders, the women gave their greeting. It was a shrill cry—a sharp, piercing trill made with the tongue alone, not by moving the hand against the lips. The trilling resounded again and again. It is the way Ghashghai women extend a formal welcome.

I had experienced this type of welcome in the Bakhtiari country. On my first afternoon at Oregon I had gone for a horseback ride. Coming back we skirted the village. Group after group of women had assembled and gave this piercing cry. One woman would say, "Happiness be with you," and the others would respond by trilling.

This trilling usually is not a short cry like a whistle, but more like a melodious chant. It rises and falls and fades away; then it returns with a great crescendo. It is startlingly beautiful.

It is used by the Ghashghai women when their men go into battle. In case of war the women go with the men as caretakers of the camps. When the Ghashghais charge, the last they hear is the shrill trilling of their womenfolk. I asked about the custom and the reason for it.

Malek Mansour replied, "When we hear that cry, we know we must win. If we fail, the enemy will have our women. That's why the Ghashghais seldom fail."

PART III

Rumblings in the Arab World

The Arab world embraces Lebanon, Syria, Iraq, Trans-Jordan, Saudi Arabia, and Egypt. All of it is ancient and historic land, though some of the nations are new.

Until recently Lebanon and Syria were out. Beginning in A.D. 1516 they were under the rule of Turkey for almost four hundred years. By the turn of this century Arab nationalism was growing in intensity, and during World War I plans were laid for an independent Arab state of Syria. Those plans were subverted; international politics called the play; and Syria and Lebanon ended up in 1920 under a French mandate. They remained under the French mandate until 1941. On September 26, 1941, the Free French granted Syria independent status and on November 26, 1941, they did the same for Lebanon. It was not until November 22, 1943, that full independence was achieved, after small uprisings in Damascus and Beirut following the attempt of the French to impose conditions.

Iraq was formed after World War I when pieces of the Ottoman Empire were being reshuffled. Mosul, Baghdad, and Basra, three Ottoman provinces, were united to form Iraq.

Trans-Jordan was also an Ottoman province until World War I. The British at that time conquered it; in 1920 England separated it from the Palestine mandate and in 1921 put it under the rule of a king. It remained a British mandate until March 22, 1946, when England finally recognized its independence.

This is also the land of the invader. The part I traveled had been subdued in whole or in part by the Egyptians, Assyrians, Hittites, Persians, and Greeks. Then came the Romans. In the seventh century the Moslems took over. In the eleventh century came the Crusaders who conquered the coastline and for a century or more maintained a series of feudal states—Edessa, Antioch, Tripoli, and Jerusalem. Saladin defeated the Crusaders at the end of the twelfth century. The Mongols invaded in the thirteenth. The Mamelukes of Egypt drove out the Mongols and ruled until 1516, when the Ottoman Turks conquered it. The heavy and corrupt hand of the Turk lay on the land until World War I.

These are the four Arab countries I traveled in my journeys, partly by foot, mostly by car. Some stretches of desert and the upper reaches of the Tigris and Euphrates I explored by air.

Lebanon lies on the eastern shoreline of the Mediterranean, just north of Israel. This is the famous Phoenician coast, a long, narrow domain. At points the mountains meet the sea. At other places there are wide valleys and gentle slopes running to the ocean. Monasteries and convents look down on the littoral from high ridges. Domes of mosques and spires of churches dot the coast.

The air along these shores is warm and humid in the growing months. Sugar cane and bananas flourish. Olive orchards and vineyards creep up the low spurs of the Lebanons.

Here the Phoenicians made merchant ships and established commerce with the world. It was down this coast that the First Crusade came overland from Europe. It conquered some of the walled towns that stood in its way, swept around others, and poured on to Jerusalem. It was the last Crusade to get through by land. Later ones tried but failed. The only other Crusades that reached these shores poured in by sea.

At the time of the Crusades the Arab civilization was in many respects further advanced than that of the West. In the tenth century the Arabs had a rural health clinic operating out of Baghdad. They introduced the hospital and traveling clinics. Rhazes, a Persian by birth and leader in the Arab medical world, was like Osler in our own. The Arabs led in astronomy, philosophy, mathematics, chemistry. These influenced Europe mightily. So did the compass which the Crusaders brought back from the Middle East. From the Arabs the Crusaders learned of carrier pigeons, gunpowder, chivalry. From them they also got damask, satin, and muslin, as well as various new plants, fruits, spices and perhaps most important of all, sugar, the Arabic sukhar.

Castles of the Crusaders dominate strategic military and commercial points of the coastline. High-arched Roman bridges of stone—which still look sturdy—mark the course of ancient passages over gulches or streams. At Dog River are plaques and carvings going back to Nebuchadnezzar and showing the records of victories of every conqueror who came this way.

Along the ocean are remnants of square, stone blockhouses of ancient age. These were fire houses, placed a few miles apart from Palestine to Constantinople. Queen Helena, who was excavating in Jerusalem, had them erected. If she found the true Cross, fires were to be built on these towers. The keeper of the first tower got the good news and lit his fire. The next one down the coast saw the fire and lit his; then the third, and so on. Thus the message was relayed, fire tower by fire tower, from Palestine to Constantinople in but a few hours.

Friezes, cornices, pillars, relics of statuary, huge stone blocks are scattered here and there, pieces of cities and sanctuaries long buried. Reminders of the death of mighty civilizations are on all sides. Here glory and power died; new forces consumed the old and were in turn destroyed. One walks among ruins that mark the savagery of man to man; ruins that are visible evidence of the unlimited lengths to which man has gone throughout history for power and wealth.

Yet from this coast there also came the creed of Him who taught brotherhood and love.

This coast has other contrasts. While age and antiquity have heavily marked it, so have modernity. A refinery, fed by a pipeline that taps the oil of the interior, stands at Tripoli. A railway that connects Constantinople with Cairo runs along the coast. Huge shallow concrete basins dot the shore. They are settling pans. Salt water is pumped to them; salt is deposited by evaporation. And automobiles (mostly American) roar down the hard-surfaced highway, dodging burros and caravans of camels loaded with produce.

Lebanon is divided into two parts. The Lebanon Mountains rise from the ocean and at their highest point reach around ten thousand feet. East of this range is a great fertile valley called the Boqaa, which at points is twenty-five miles or more wide. It is a long valley, heading in Syria to the north and emptying into Palestine.

The Boqaa is an intermountain valley, for it is bounded on the east

by the Anti-Lebanon Mountains—the range that ends on the south
in Mount Hermon of Biblical fame, the one called "Lebanon toward
the sunrising" in the Bible (Joshua 13:5).

The east side of the Anti-Lebanon Mountains flattens out into a
vast desertic steppe. Damascus (capital of Syria) lies at the bottom
of this range and on the edge of the desert. Damascus is an oasis.
Beyond it to the east is a vast, empty land that runs five hundred
miles or more to Baghdad and Babylon. Baghdad, robbed of its ancient splendor and as drab as the poverty of its people, sits at the
bottom of the V formed by the confluence of the Tigris and Euphrates. These rivers, filled with silt and filth, flow sluggishly to
the Persian Gulf. To the north of Baghdad is the mountainous country of ancient Kurdistan. It has alpine climate; but Baghdad is hot;
and Basra, south of it on the Gulf, is one of the hottest places on the
earth. The 120 degrees which I found oppressive in Baghdad is the
temperature the date growers at Basra pray for in August so that the
dates may ripen.

This part of the world has virtually no rain during the summer
months. Its rains are distilled over the Atlantic Ocean and come in
the winter with the strong west wind, providing around ten inches
of rainfall a year. In the summer those winds are parched and they
whip up tremendous sand storms. One day, when we were coming
to Baghdad from Tehran by plane, we were swallowed by a dust
storm several hundred miles wide, five hundred miles long, and eight
thousand feet deep. The dust was as thick as fog and blotted from
view the tips of the wings of the plane. The airport at Baghdad was
closed, so we made an emergency landing in the desert at Habbaniya,
east of Baghdad. This is a base built by the British—an oasis that is
a vivid reminder of how glorious a garden Mesopotamia once was,
and an impressive example of how rich and green the valleys of
Iraq could be. When at last we landed at Baghdad, the ceiling was
only one hundred feet. The dust storm was so great that Baghdad
was practically in darkness by midafternoon. We found the airport
by skimming the ground and following a highway. The curses of
camel drivers were on us for doing it. The low-flying plane caused
panic among camel caravans. Under the roar of our motors camels
broke ranks and ropes and dashed madly across the desert.

There is rich color in this land. But it is color which, since the
seventh century, could not be painted. Mohammed had a prohibition

against the making of graven images. Decorative art flourished in the Islam world but not painting of people and scenery. Under the Turkish rule it was a misdemeanor to paint. Only since Lebanon obtained her independence has art flourished. Only since that date have Saliba Doueihy and other Arab artists been allowed to show their talents.

The limestone of the Lebanon and Anti-Lebanon Mountains has as many different hues as the moods of a summer day. There are patches left of the majestic cedars of Lebanon, clinging to high, steep pockets of limestone, adding dark green to a background of mauve. There are wind-blown peaks and deep gorges. On the eastern side of the mountains there are sunsets that rival Arizona's. The stars at night have a glory that we of the West do not know. They hang low and shine with a candle power of great brilliance. A cool wind usually sweeps the desert at night, whining through harsh gullies and making the coarse camel thorn hum. The days which are free of dust storms have a brilliance that is almost blinding. The infinity, which we see in the azure blue of the sky the world around, seems less remote in this parched land. There is austerity in every view—rocks, gullies, dry plains, bristling thistles. From the desert side the Lebanons and Anti-Lebanons seem almost a mirage. The universe presses in on every living soul; it is a weary land where man finds no escape from a relentless, burning sun. It is hard to find escape from poverty too. Perhaps there is psychological significance in these physical phenomena. It was in this region that some of the great religions of the world were born.

24. It's a Small World

WHEN I FIRST saw the Middle East it seemed strange and mysterious.

My son Bill and I had come to Lebanon by way of Athens. When we flew to Athens from Rome, I felt strangely alone in a faraway foreign place. Then in the brilliant light of early morning I had seen the Acropolis, the marble pillars atop it fairly glistening. Its most imposing edifice, the Parthenon, stirred nostalgic feelings in me. That building had served as the model for our own Supreme Court building. The sight of it gave me an intimate and friendly tie with a strange land.

Later, as I gave the Acropolis a farewell look on our flight out of Athens to Beirut, I had an empty feeling. Most connections with the past would now be broken. The land for which we were headed, its people, their culture and customs would all be strange and new. And I was to discover that in large part it was indeed as strange and foreign to Americans as it had been to the Crusaders who in 1095 answered the call to march against the infidel.

We landed briefly at Rhodes, where dozens of windmills with white cotton wings were feverishly pumping water in a green valley. Then came Cyprus of legendary fame. In less than an hour out of Nicosia (its capital) the shoreline of Asia had loomed up—a thin dark line that gradually grew into a high mountain range that seemed to drop to the ocean.

Soon Beirut came into focus—as gaily colored as Paris. And in a few moments we were over the beach, rich red in the dazzling sunlight.

"This is where St. George killed the dragon," someone said. "The beach was stained by the blood."

We circled the airport twice and finally came in on a short runway, barely skimming the roofs. I saw a bearded Arab in a courtyard a few hundred feet below us. As we roared by his tarboosh flew off, his beard stood out, the hair of his head seemed to stand up; panic was on his face.

"I sympathized with him," the pilot later told me. "We practically had to scrape the housetops to make the landing."

We spent three days in Beirut. Beirut has the touch of Europe on it. It is a great port for the vast interior. It faces the West and is affected by Western habits and thoughts. American University, founded in 1866 and now headed by Dr. S. B. L. Penrose, is one of the reasons. The Lebanese merchants—probably leading all in shrewdness—are another. Here are modern hotels and telephones approaching European efficiency. Western goods flood the market. Light cars made in Detroit scatter donkeys, camels, and people as they race down highways using their horns more than their brakes.

We spent the three days with Dr. and Mrs. Penrose. This June was hot and sticky in Beirut—uncomfortably humid like Washington, D.C. We swam in the Mediterranean with Arab boys who grinned at us when we spoke to them in English. Beautiful gardens run down from the Penrose home to the sea several hundred feet below. Here we explored new species of plants, came to know the sturdy, flat-topped stone pine, the acacia, and the Aleppo pine, and experimented with color film.

Yet there was still the atmosphere of the Arabian Nights about the place.

Porters carrying bales, desks, pianos, huge packing boxes on their backs with the aid of a head strap.

The call of the Moslem priests to prayer.

A kneeling man on a rug in a courtyard bowing toward Mecca.

Veiled women peering timidly from windows.

The babble of strange tongues in the market places.

Stately caravans of camels swinging down highways.

Burros loaded with bundles many times their size.

Families on the move—the husband out front on a burro; the wife on foot, with children and baggage, bringing up the rear.

Veiled women carrying jugs, pots, baskets, and trays on their heads.

A fakir on the street corner putting on his act of torture for the crowd.

Dark, immobile, inscrutable faces; strange food; music with an exotic lilt.

All these and more gave an air of magic and mystery to the place. But by a curious turn of events I suddenly came to feel at home in Beirut.

I attended the commencement exercises at the University. I saw men and women in the familiar cap and gown step forward and get their degrees in the humanities, in medicine, in philosophy, in engineering. The scene took me back to all the commencements I had attended in this country. This was the familiar, the known.

Then came the speakers. The first was Dr. Costi K. Zurayk, noted Arabian scholar. He spoke warmly and fervently in Arabic. He spoke of the Arab culture and civilization. He told how it had its roots not only in the revelations of the Prophet Mohammed but also in the works of Plato and Aristotle. And he spoke of the "unity of humanity" across the various boundaries which divide peoples and religions. He spoke of the Arab philosopher who wrote, "I follow the religion of Love, whichever way his camels take. Love is my religion and my faith."

I was the second speaker. My first words were in appreciation of the hospitality of Dr. Penrose and American University. Dr. Penrose had gone to my college—Whitman. And when I was a student there his father—also S. B. L. Penrose—had been its president. It was my purpose to mention these matters. So I opened my talk with the statement, "I, too, went to Whitman College, Walla Walla."

The whole audience—three thousand Arabs—burst into laughter.

I was embarrassed. I searched for a clue to the humor. My mind was a blank. I turned to Dr. Penrose for some indication of what I had done. He had joined in the laughter and was of no use to me. I swallowed a couple of times, adjusted my mortarboard cap, and launched into my address, which was devoted to a discussion of the Four Enemies of Man the world around—Illiteracy, Poverty, Disease, and Misgovernment.

After the exercises were over I got Dr. Penrose aside and said, "What the devil did I say or do that was so funny?"

He laughed again and said, "In Arabic Walla Walla means By God, By God."

A walking trip that I took in the Lebanon Mountains made me seem very much at home in this strange land and taught me that the

Arab peasant, who can be roused to fury, is a simple, uncomplicated, trusting soul. I also learned that this peasant, who plows an inhospitable soil and is bowed by poverty, carries the weight of the world with grace and dignity.

It was the last week in June, 1949. There were five in the party—Dr. Penrose and Professor William West of American University, Dave West, son of Professor West, my son Bill, and I. Professor West was our interpreter. We started at Biskinta, a village which lies forty-eight hundred feet high in the Lebanons north of Beirut and we ended five days later at Hadeth, above Tripoli. Mules carried our baggage; and three peasants from Biskinta were our muleteers—Raji Tannus Tannouri, in his forties, tall and lean with a patrician look; Faris Usuf Hajj, short, stocky with a round and joyous face, also in his forties; Khalil Yusuf, handsome son of Faris, in his teens.

These men wore the typical peasant costume. The trouser legs fit snug and tight and the crotch is full and baggy, hanging almost to the knees. Their shoes were of leather and low, sandal-like. Their shirts were nondescript; their headdresses colorful. They wore the kafiyeh which covers the head and hangs below the shoulders. It is held on the head by a band, called the aghal. The color of the kafiyeh and aghal varies with tribes, professions, and the like. I thought at first that the kafiyeh was folderol, a silly vestige of ancient custom. I learned differently. The headdress protects the neck and face from the burning sun, and keeps dust from the mouth. It is an article of amazing comfort on hot and treeless slopes and plains.

I learned other things from these muleteers. I sat with them at night in our camps along the skyline of the Lebanons, watching the stars come out. Jupiter would hang like a brilliant flame in the sky, travel a low arc, and soon drop below a ridge. There would be the tinkle of bells on the mules, staked out close by. I could hear the soft trill of their lips as they talked back and forth. Some nights there would be the roar of a stream—the milky Neba Leben (which means Fountain of Milk) or the clear River of Adonis. When we were camped high at Laqlouq all distant sounds floated in like faint echoes from the valleys below us and the ridges above. There was the yapping of a jackal and the response of a dog and the braying of a mule. The muleteers and I sat cross-legged on the ground, mostly in silence; but our session always ended in a seminar. They could not speak English nor I Arabic. But we taught each other. I taught them light, match, cigarette, water, mountain, star, thank you very much, hello, how are you?, yes, no. They repeated the words after me and laughed in an embarrassed manner at their clumsy pronunciation.

They taught me *m'kary* (muleteer); *baghl* (mule); *jelal* (pack saddle); *neba* (big spring or fountain); *ain* (small spring); *anzih* (goat); *nar* (fire); *moy* (water); *shems* (sun). Their faces were serious—a wonderful study in complete concentration. An error on my part would cause a flicker of disappointment to cross Raji Tannus' face. It was the disappointment of a teacher whose star pupil fails. He would shake his head, pronounce the word in the deep guttural that distinguishes the Arabic tongue, and hang eagerly on my next attempt. I remember he had great difficulty getting me to associate *moy* and water. When at last I did so, he jumped to his feet with the joy of a teacher whose pupil has just won a Pulitzer Prize. "*Moy, moy, moy,*" he shouted approvingly and gave me a yard of Arabic of which I understood no part.

Near the end of our journey I ended a class by proposing a toast: "A toast to teachers the world around." The four of us drank from an old tin cup, they knowing only that it was some act of American friendship.

I wished many times I could have had a recording of our last half hour together. It was at Hadeth, a small village of a few hundred people. This was the end of our journey. Cars were there to pick us up; the muleteers would return to Biskinta. After the mules were unloaded, we gathered in the village square to say good-by and to settle accounts.

Bill West stepped forward with a handful of Lebanese bills to pay the muleteers. Raji Tannus was their spokesman. He and Bill West were long in conversation. We had advanced Raji Tannus money along the way to buy eggs and cheese. That amount had to be computed and agreed upon. Then there was the question of the amount of compensation of the muleteers. The rate was clear—5 £ ($1.50) a day per mule. That meant $6 a day for the muleteers. But when did the days start? A full day at Biskinta though we arrived at noon? When would the days end? Now or when the muleteers got back to their home at Biskinta? If the latter, how long would it take to return? We came in five days. Would three days be adequate for the return?

These questions were finally answered to the satisfaction of Raji Tannus, who from time to time consulted his associates. Bill West agreed. The sum of money owed was computed, and Bill started counting out the bills to Raji Tannus.

By this time two dozen men had gathered around. Their dark faces were serious and intent. One of the men was a coal-black Sudanese. Another was an Arab wearing a helmet on which a white cross had been drawn, the sign that he was deaf and dumb. All kept their eyes on the counting of the money. Raji Tannus counted out loud. At first he spoke softly. Then a few of the crowd joined him in the counting. Soon all of them but the mute were counting. Their voices picked up in volume. Soon it was a loud male chorus—fifty, fifty-five—sixty, seventy, seventy-five, eighty-five. There was a swing and cadence to it.

Counting the money had become a community project. The villagers were there in part to help Raji Tannus—to see to it that he was not mulcted. But there was more significance than that in the event. No such money had ever been seen in this village. No wages of the kind we paid our muleteers had ever been paid there. This was a new order, a new economy come to Hadeth. These men scoured the bare hills and worked terraces on dizzy slopes to eke out a living. Some left their scrawny farms and worked for the government on the roads, breaking rocks with hammers for ninety cents a day. But the wages we paid were much better. These villagers were celebrating the occasion. Each was an excited participant in the adventure of Raji Tannus.

The trail which we had traveled on our walking trip was always close to civilization, though it followed the skyline of the mountains. Every available foot of ground in the Lebanon is cultivated. Men and women often climb high to reach a narrow terrace of grapes, apples, or cherries or walk far to plow a nub of a ridge for beans or potatoes. And so it was that we saw many farmers even though we kept well above the villages.

One day we came to the high plateau at Laqlouq where a stone house with a flat roof stood desolate in an open field. It was the summer home of Sheikh Saleem el Hashem.

Hollywood had taught me that a sheikh (pronounced shake and meaning the elder) was a man in flowing silken robes with a large harem. But there was not a touch of glamour or romance to this sheikh, who wore the ordinary trousers of the area, not a flowing robe. He was like any of ten thousand farmers the world around. My fantasy of a Hollywood sheikh was gone forever.

There were occasional goatherds on the ridges above us. I could hear them singing from distant points of rock or lookouts. Strange, unfamiliar melodies—pieces of folk songs which were old when Christ was born—came floating down the wind as if from another world—melancholy, lonely, sad. One day I heard an exultant one—a song with a lilt, the music of laughter, gaiety, abandon. I could see the singer standing on a ledge high above me. He was singing his heart out. His music, like Pan's, was full of trills.

The singer stopped and, after eying us for a spell, came dashing down the ridge, yelling as he ran. He stopped directly above us and shouted something. Bill West replied. The goatherd's face fell. We had declined a luncheon invitation.

"What would we have had to eat?" I inquired.

"Bread, cheese, and olives," Bill replied. "This man made a particular point of his cheese. Said it was good."

I occasionally looked back as we moved along the trail. For a mile or more I saw the goatherd standing on the ledge where we had left him—a lonesome soul, watching us until we were out of sight.

At one point the trail crossed a rough gully or ravine and then climbed steeply, clinging precariously to a steep mountainside. One of the mules went down. His front feet were over a ledge running crosswise of the trail and his belly was stuck on it. As a result of his struggles he went over on his side. The muleteers had to remove the pack.

While our fallen mule was being repacked, we waited at a farmhouse beside the trail a few rods forward. A small spring had been enclosed by rock so that it poured over the lip of a ledge in a tiny cascade. A Cretan beam tree which resembles our mountain ash stood below the spring. A woman—Christian—came down to the spring to get water. She carried a jug of the type commonly seen in this region—wide base, narrow throat, holding a quart or two of water. Its distinguishing characteristic was a small short beak about the size of a pencil extending from the side of the narrow throat. One does not put his mouth to this nozzle; he throws his head back, taking the stance of a sword swallower, and pours the water into his mouth. When I first tried to drink from one, the water missed my mouth completely, hitting my chin and running down my neck. And when at last I managed it, I almost choked to death.

In a few minutes the man of the house appeared on the knoll above us. He shouted to Raji Tannus and came down to join us. Almost his first words were: "Are you Americans or British?"

When told that we were Americans, he asked, "Have you come to take over the country?"

We shook our heads and roared with laughter.

His face fell. After a few minutes he said, "It's too bad you are not going to take the country over."

"Why is it too bad?"

"Because someone should take it over and run it."

Then followed a long complaint:

Everywhere, he said, was corruption. Hashish was grown here. Hashish is against the law. But someone high up controls the hashish.

In one village, he said, was a forest, owned by the villagers. It was communal property where everyone could cut wood for his needs. Wood was very important here because the winters were cold; it was the only fuel for warming houses. It seems that there was a project for bringing electricity to this village. The lines got within a mile of the place when construction stopped, and the village was told that it could not get electric power without payment of a bonus of 20,000 £. The village did not have that amount of money. To get it the forest was cut down and the wood sold. The money went to a contractor and some officials, this man said.

The government, he complained, did nothing about the irrigation system. Water went to waste; the ditches were not good.

His complaints came in a torrent. They proved, he maintained, that America would do well to take over Lebanon and run it.

The inquiry of this simple peasant is worth a whole volume on the psychology of the Middle East. From time out of mind some foreign power has been running these countries or meddling in their affairs. When there were persecutions or massacres or any other major trouble, Turkey, France, England or Russia stepped in either to give asylum to a minority or to take the reins of government in its own hands. Today when trouble brews in the Middle East, the peasants begin to wonder what foreign power will rescue them. The democratic tradition of self-help is just starting to take hold among these people. They must not be judged by political standards which we espouse and which took Englishmen at least seven hundred years to mature.

At Biskinta, the start of the walking trip, I met Mikhail Naimy. A man by the name of Sol Fard stepped out of the crowd and in perfect English invited me to Naimy's house. As we walked through a peach orchard to Naimy's home, a square stone building with a tiled roof, I learned that Sol Fard was a native Lebanese, now living in Portland, Oregon, and home on a vacation. Naimy also spoke perfect English. He too had started at Portland, attended the University at Seattle, and lived in New York City.

As we sipped Turkish coffee, he told how he had graduated from the University of Washington School of Law and had been admitted to practice law in Washington. After serving with the U. S. Army in World War I, he was granted citizenship by Congress. He was a member of a literary colony in New York City. There he lived and worked with the late Kahlil Gibran, who wrote *The Prophet*. Naimy spoke of his recent book *Mirdad* and its theme—that freedom comes through love and understanding.

Naimy is a philosopher, a poet. He has the face of an aesthete. His fingers are long and delicate. His deep dark eyes were somber and reflective as he talked. When he finished I asked why he had turned his back on law and literature in the United States and retired to Biskinta.

"Will you come to my farm near Mount Sannine? It's on your way. There I will answer your question."

The farmhouse was a low, stone house that lay below the trail on the right. The farm was perhaps twelve acres and all in cherries, plums, peaches, pears, and apples. We sat on a terrace built around a giant oak that was about 150 years old and one of the loveliest trees I have seen. To the north a mile or so as the crow flies was Mount Sannine, 8,600 feet high with patches of snow all the way to its top. Below us to the south were the peaked, red-tiled roofs of Biskinta and the outline of the rocky gorge called the Wadi Jmej or Valley of the Skull.

We ate the sandwiches we had packed for lunch; and then Naimy's brother—who worked the orchards—brought us a platter of cherries for dessert. As we ate, Naimy talked of Biskinta and Lebanon; how the war in Palestine had lost for the Lebanese their best market for fruit; how the French in their long occupation had saddled an enervating bureaucracy on Lebanon; how America, if she was to make progress against Russia in the Middle East, had to promote and back programs of social and economic emancipation for the masses of the people there.

There was quiet for a few moments after he finished. Then I repeated the question I had put him in the village.

"I needed the quiet of the hills," he answered. "That is why I returned to Lebanon."

The song of the meadow lark floated up from a pasture below the orchard. Then came a softer, sweeter song.

"Do you recognize it?" he asked. I shook my head.

"Goldfinches." All conversation ceased while the place was filled with the melody of their singing.

Naimy touched my arm and pointed to Mount Sannine towering over us. Clouds were drifting in from the Mediterranean and casting shadows over the great limestone wall, flecked with snow. The cliffs turned gray to pink to purple.

"America is a beautiful country and I love your people," he went on to say. "But I could not endure your great cities. I felt the whole weight of New York City on my shoulders."

"We have lovely mountains, too."

"For me there's no mountain like Sannine. It belongs to my people. It has seen their sorrows and disasters. It is a symbol of their strength—and of their hopes and aspirations, too!"

There was tenderness in his voice as he ended, "The call of Sannine was too strong to resist. I can find peace and harmony only when I live in its shadow."

Three days later we were camped at Monk's Spring at Laqlouq over sixty-five hundred feet high in the Lebanons. It was late afternoon and I had gone to the spring for a drink.

As I rose I saw a man coming up the slope toward the spring. He was almost running. He appeared to be an Arab but his headdress was different. Instead of the flowing kafiyeh he had on a knit cap without a visor. He was dark and swarthy—stocky and about five feet eight. His black hair was slightly gray. He stopped before me out of breath.

Then he said in broken English, "Are you Joostis Dooglaw?"

I told him I was.

"I am Yacoub Bishara."

I took him to camp.

"Where in the world did you learn to speak English?" I asked.

"Portland, Oregon."

I had to smile. Another Oregonian had popped up from nowhere in the high mountains of Lebanon.

Yacoub Bishara told me that he had gone to Portland when he was a young man and had worked in a cement factory. Then he worked on a farm. In fact, he had undertaken to buy the farm. It was a wonderful farm—soil three or four feet deep, "not like thees rocks of Laqlouq."

I asked him why he left the United States. He told a long rambling story—how his mother in Lebanon got sick, why he had to support her, how he got stranded and could not return. It seems he had married and had eight children.

"How wonderful!" I exclaimed. "What a lucky man!"

"No, no, no, not lucky," he sadly replied.

And with great feeling he went on to say that he must have sinned terribly to have been forced to return to Lebanon. I asked why. He said that the thirteen years in America were heaven—the great happiness of his life. Return to Lebanon was punishment— punishment for some sin. In Lebanon he had to slave to grow food among rocks. In America the plow sank deep; anything would grow. There were schools and plumbing in America. There were doctors for everyone, and hospitals. Yes, America was the most wonderful country in the world. In America he was happy. In Lebanon he was overworked and harassed.

Then Yacoub spoke of his sons. He wanted them to go to America. He wanted them to have the opportunities he had missed. Perhaps, Yacoub suggested, I could help. Perhaps his sons could escape the punishment of having to earn a livelihood on rocky, wasted land.

I spoke up. "Yacoub, I think you might not feel so depressed if you had a shave. You haven't shaved for a week."

He rubbed his chin and nodded his head.

"How would you like to be shaved by an electric razor?"

"'Lectric razor?" he asked. "There's no 'lectricity in Laqlouq." And with that he shrugged his shoulders and looked around.

"Oh, yes, there is. We bring it with us."

My son got out our battery and electric razor. As the buzzing of the razor started Yacoub's dark brown eyes got wider. He was too polite to refuse me. But he feared nothing worse than what awaited him. There was near panic in his face as I raised the razor to it. He looked as I imagine a man looks who takes his seat in the electric chair.

Yacoub jumped when the razor touched his face. Then he relaxed and enjoyed the shave. I finished one side of his face and started on the other. The razor ran like a lawn mower through deep grass, leaving a single narrow path down his cheek. At that point he made me stop. He wanted his face left like that so that he could prove that he had been shaved by my razor, not by his own.

During the shave other Arabs had appeared from nowhere—eight or ten of them. They stood silently in a crescent around Yacoub. When I had finished, they pounded Yacoub on the back. They shook him by the shoulder. They shouted and gesticulated, all talking at once. When quiet had been restored, I got the gist of the conversation:

"Yacoub Bishara, an honor and distinction has come to you that no one in the long and glorious history of Lebanon has ever had. What has happened to you never happened even to any king or prince of Lebanon. You are the first man in the whole kingdom ever shaved by an electric razor. You must go home at once and tell your children and make sure they tell their children, so that people will know throughout all time that the first man in the history of Lebanon to be shaved by an electric razor was Yacoub Bishara."

My son Bill was meanwhile busily engaged making something.

"What are you up to?" I inquired.

"Making a barber shop sign. Maybe we can earn some of our expenses."

We then took pictures of Yacoub. He asked if I would send him some. I promised. He said I would probably forget.

"Forget? Forget Yacoub Bishara? Never."

He wanted the pictures by Christmas. Would I promise—really promise?

"Yes, I'll promise. I'll send you three of each by Christmas."

And with that Yacoub bade us good-by. He put out a gnarled and rough hand and took mine, thanks and gratitude on his face. Then he went down the mountain to his village of Akoura.

In a few moments another Arab came walking rapidly toward us, his kafiyeh flying in the breeze. He too was coming on the run. All of us stood watching him for several minutes. Finally Dave West spoke up.

"First it was Sol Fard from Portland, Oregon. Then Mikhail Naimy from Portland, Oregon. Then Yacoub Bishara from Portland, Oregon. If this newcomer is from Portland, Oregon, I'm going to shoot him."

When I returned to the States I remembered my promise to Yacoub Bishara to send him prints of the photographs before Christmas. But an intervening event—being crushed by a horse while riding the high Cascades—laid me up for months. Finally one day in the Yakima hospital I thought of Yacoub. I was distressed because my promise to him would be broken. So I had my secretary in Washington, D. C. write Yacoub and tell him of my accident, and say that the pictures would be sent as soon as I could find them and arrange it. Several months passed. Near the end of my convalescence the following letter arrived:

Akoura Labenen
feb. 5-1950

Dear
Justice W. O. Douges
I racifd you wallcan letter and I was verey surey wen I know you fol of the Herse and he ralled ouer you bet I wos gllad wen I knau you get well I wesh you the best the helet Know I an stel weten far the pickres you pramised tau send tau me I lack tau hau you send me sam nams from u.s.a. I gad nat ansur you leter san.

Mey bey have thrabll bet he cam out o.k. I tank the god We have 3 yard snaw an the leallmo I sen Dog. Benrowy,* in Beyrauth and he is o.k.

I wash I gatt Mad trek to U.S. for set Manes   I well writ to you Maur the Nixt time   I wesh you will return tou Wash. D.C. and har from you I send Mey best greetigs and best wishes. to you famelly

    Very truly yours
    Yacoup Bashara
    of Akoura Lebanon
et kous Mey writen and spolem

* The Arabic alphabet has no letter **P**.

25. The Poisonous Bite of the Goat

ONE HAS to walk the Middle East to know the full impact of over-grazing of land and unlimited cutting of trees. Here one sees the end product of erosion. A trail that follows the contours of the ridges passes only a few trees a day. In summer one is under a blistering sun the whole day through. Great areas show nothing but ugly gullies. The topsoil of the upland basins has rushed to the sea. Only bare rocks are left or fields which show little soil until tons of rocks are removed from them. The slopes have been washed by millions of rains and robbed of their fertility, so that today nothing remains but miles of rocky expanse. Some of the rocks have fantastic shapes —towers, mushrooms, pyramids, needlelike pillars, cliffs with great overhangs produced by a weathering of the base. A changing light turns this land into an artist's paradise, as colors turn from blue, green, gray, and brown. But it is land that is no better than marginal and often sterile.

The tragedy grows as the pressure of people on land continues. The pressure is great; every possible bit of ground is used. Across the Neba Leben River there is a gracefully arched, natural bridge eighty feet or more above the water. The natural bridge supports a good-sized potato patch, fifty by one hundred feet. Scabby hillsides are turned into meager terraces. Marginal land, scab land, submarginal land are all used as the demand for food increases. This is not a new problem. Two thousand years ago Romans were building terraces along these same hillsides; and many of the stone fences they laid are there today.

While the chief villain in the story is the goat, even he has a few redeeming features. He showed me, for example, a wondrous sight the night we stayed at the headwaters of Neba Leben. We were camped right under Mount Sannine, out of whose rock wall Neba

Leben pours with a roar. Its northern cliffs rose over three thousand feet above us and flared out at the base forming a rough amphitheater. We had indeed front-row seats for a beautiful spectacle.

A herd of goats dropped off the mountain. I first saw them when they were fifteen hundred feet or more above us. These goats are different from ours. They are smaller than our goat—wiry and robust, shiny black with ears that are long, narrow, and thin.

This was a herd of several hundred goats. Behind them was the herder dressed in flowing robes and a dark kafiyeh. He had two dogs with him. The goats came off Sannine mostly in double file. They were spread out several hundred yards, forming shiny black streamers down the limestone slopes of Sannine.

Bill West turned to me and said, "Do you remember what Solomon said about his lady's hair?"

I confessed I did not recall.

"'Thy hair is as a flock of goats.' That is from the Song of Solomon."

Memories of Sunday-school days came back to me. I remembered how puzzled I had been over that expression. Hair like a flock of goats? It must be some allegory. It could not possibly be flattering. Goats smell; goats are dirty; goats are coarse and ugly.

But now I knew that Solomon complimented his lady. The prophet had doubtless seen sights such as this, evening after evening, as shepherds brought their goats off limestone and basalt mountains for bedding down in the valleys. The sight was indeed a beautiful one. Black, lustrous, rippling streamers of hair down a mountainside! A more graphic description of beautiful hair would be difficult to achieve.

Most of the activities of the goat, however, are on the debit side. Once the Lebanon and Anti-Lebanon Mountains were covered with thick forests of cedars, pine, juniper, and oak. Some were cut for timber, some for fuel, and some to run slag furnaces. These mountains had small iron deposits that were worked centuries ago. No new forests grew up when the old ones were cut. The goat was the reason. He ate the seedlings. We know that is the reason, because the ridges that are kept free of goats grow new forests today.

A goat will eat practically anything and does. One ate a part of my plant press when my back was turned and while I was taking pictures. The people cannot live without the goat, since he supplies their meat, milk, butter, cheese, leather, and wool. They cannot live with him because he makes them poorer every day. The problem of the goat is basic and fundamental. His bite is poisonous; he is a scourge to the earth unless tethered. To rebuild the economy of the Middle East so as to leave the goat as the poor man's cow and develop other means of livelihood is a major problem not only in agricultural planning but in politics as well. An economy that is as old as man is hard to change.

I talked with many goatherds about the problem of the goat, but they had no understanding of it. The goat was their livelihood; what was good for the goat was good for them. One day in the high Lebanons above the village of Akoura I sat with an Arab boy about twelve years old who showed two missing teeth when he smiled. He had a flock of goats grazing on a washed and sterile hillside where only yarrow and thistles grew in the summer. As I sat with him memories of an experience in my boyhood flooded my mind.

I was traveling the Conrad Creek Trail of the Cascade Mountains in the State of Washington on my way to the Goat Rocks. I was several miles above the lush Conrad Meadows where grass grows stirrup high when I saw a campfire on the edge of a small wet meadow that abounded in beaver. A ranger of our Forest Service was cooking a meal. He invited me to join him. During this meal I received my first lecture on conservation.

My ranger friend told me of the telltale signs of erosion which he had discovered in a meadow below us. Sheep had caused it. He explained why it was; sheep had been on these slopes in too great numbers and for too long a time.

"Nature has constructed reservoirs in every meadow and on every slope of these mountains. On the slope below us are millions upon millions of fine roots of grasses. There are also coarser roots of shrubs and greater roots of trees. They hold rain water back; they impound it and release it slowly. Moreover roots of grasses, shrubs, and trees build soil. They create it through chemical processes and through their own transformation into humus. Heavy grazing of the grass and the pounding of the turf by the hoofs of too many animals uncover the soil. Then the ground is ready for destruction. When the soil is bare, water runs off fast, taking the topsoil with it. If it is held by grasses and roots, it seeps out slowly and is as crystal clear as Conrad Creek down there in the meadow. The grass makes cover for the soil too, protecting it from erosion by rain and wind."

I went with my ranger friend as he inspected some misused meadows, and he told me about the seed time of grass too. He said that stock should be kept off until the grass is about ankle deep; that some grass seed should ripen each year. "Get next year's grass seed in the ground," he said, "and you're beginning to lick the problem of overgrazing."

He explained how it was that next year's grass crop is injured if all of this year's crop is eaten. A good part of the green leafage should be left. The green leaves manufacture the food which makes the grass grow. In the winter it is stored in the roots. The next spring new growth comes from the stored food. If all the green leaves are eaten, the grass starves.

"That nourishment is carbohydrates," he added, "like potatoes and bread and ice cream that people eat. Grass must have the nourishment made by the leaves if it is to remain strong. Sheep have been eating too much here. Use of this area should be much lighter."

That was why fewer plants were growing in this high basin. There were bare spots between the clumps of grass. The humus cover of dead vegetation was being washed away. Very little was left to decay and to enrich and make new soil. There would be a greater runoff next spring.

"Muddy water'll pour into the South Fork," he said. "We can see that kind of damage. But there's other damage that is not so easy to see."

He went on to explain that when there is good cover for the soil, water seeps through leaves, humus, and roots into the topsoil underneath. Topsoil is granulated and porous. It absorbs the water and sends much of it into underground reservoirs. These underground reservoirs are hooked up into great uncharted and unseen river courses that are tapped for wells, that come bubbling out of the ground in springs, and that feed lakes and streams. Once the plant cover of the topsoil is gone, swift runoffs take the topsoil with them to the ocean. The ground under the topsoil becomes hard. It is packed, not porous. It will not absorb water. There are no leaves and plant tops to decay and form new rich, porous soil.

"When the rains come," he explained, "the water will not soak through. The underground reservoirs will not be filled. Some wells a hundred miles from here will go dry."

This ranger also told me about forests and lumber.

"Asparagus is fast-growing," he said. "You can cut stalk after stalk in the same bed without danger. Pine, fir, and cedar are the same, except that it takes fifty to one hundred years for them to do what asparagus can do in a few days. One crop of lumber after another—that's what the nation must have. Cutting must be planned. Only mature trees must be cut."

He stopped and pointed out the red and white fir around us that were too young to cut and other trees that were ripe, if not overripe.

Then he continued, "There must always be a crop of lumber in the ground. There must always be a crop maturing. The demand for lumber will increase. The forests must be cut. But the forests must always have as much or more timber in them as they had when we started. We can grow richer rather than poorer in timber, if we will use our heads."

What my ranger friend described to me was the lumbering method known as the sustained yield. Since he spoke some thirty years ago it has gradually attained a wider adoption in the United States.

I thought of this lesson in conservation as I sat with the Arab boy on the slope above Akoura.

No ranger had ridden the hills of Lebanon to watch for telltale signs of erosion, to say what basins should be grazed, to mark the trees that could be cut. For centuries there had been no guardians of the public interest in topsoil. Men and goats—both greedy— took what they wanted from the earth.

The early Phoenicians cut the forests, especially the cedars, for the construction of their merchant ships that plied the ocean. Solomon built his Temple at Jerusalem with cedars furnished by Hiram, King of Tyre:

And Hiram sent to Solomon, saying, I have considered the things which thou sentest to me for: and I will do all thy desire concerning timber of cedar, and concerning timber of fir. My servants shall bring them down from Lebanon unto the sea: and I will convey them by sea in floats unto the place that thou shalt appoint me, and will cause them to be discharged there, and thou shalt receive them: and thou shalt accomplish my desire, in giving food for my household. (I Kings 5:8, 9.)

Solomon also built his own house

of the forest of Lebanon; the length thereof was an hundred cubits, and the breadth thereof fifty cubits, and the height thereof thirty cubits, upon four rows of cedar pillars, with cedar beams upon the pillars. And it was covered with cedar above upon the beams, that lay on forty five pillars, fifteen in a row. (I Kings 7:2, 3.)

It was a mighty host that gathered the materials from Lebanon for Solomon's project:

And Solomon had threescore and ten thousand that bare burdens, and fourscore thousand hewers in the mountains . . . (I Kings 5:15.)

At that time the mountains of Lebanon must indeed have been lush with cedars and other trees. Eighty thousand woodcutters! "Today—June 1949," I thought, "eight woodcutters could make short shrift of all that is left of the famous cedars."

As I rose to go I thought that any sheepman, cattleman, or lumberman in America who complained of the regulation of grazing or cutting of trees should be given a free trip to the Middle East so that he could see with his own eyes what erosion can do.

26. Cedars of Lebanon

"As THE shadow of a great rock in a weary land." One has to travel in a barren, naked land under a blistering sun fully to appreciate that Biblical expression. On mountain trips in the Middle East light and heat are everywhere. There's no escape from them—no retreat, no solace, no relief. One watches the angle of the sun in the sky, praying for its early disappearance. The earth is a hot griddle—fair-skinned man is the victim. His energy is sucked out of him through all his pores. Shade is haven to a man pursued by light, as land is to the drowning.

We had walked four days under a sweltering sun. There was no cover of any kind—for man, birds, or beasts. The Mediterranean sky was cruel. When at last I reached the cedars at Hadeth, I had an interesting psychological experience. I lay on my back under the first cedar and thanked God for trees. I felt as if I had reached home, as if protective arms were around me. I had escaped an enemy that pursued me with a hot breath. I, a refugee from the sun who was burned to a frazzle, was at last safe.

The cedar of Lebanon is the true cedar. It has dark-green needles similar to our red fir. At Hadeth the cedars are wind-blown, about thirty feet high, with three- or four-foot trunks. Most of them have been topped, and as a result of cutting they have split trunks. The effect is a chewed-off, mutilated forest. But the cedars of Bsharreh, which we visited after we left Hadeth, are perfect specimens. They are east of Hadeth at the head of Qadisha Canyon, a harsh, rough defile about fifteen hundred feet deep and famous in the Middle East for its danger and beauty. The local name of these cedars is Arz-ar-Rubb—Cedars of the Lord.

These cedars rise a hundred feet or more. While the trunks are usually four or five feet thick, like our tamarack, some are over thirty feet in diameter. These are the monarchs of the forest, perhaps a thousand years old. The branches are long and swooping and cover the ground for fifty feet or more around. A forest of them is so closely woven with branches that it is difficult to get a picture of a single tree. At Bsharreh there are only about four hundred cedars left, packed together in a small ten-acre tract, the remnants of a mighty race. And they barely survived, even after the church that owned them threatened excommunication to any who cut the trees. Still the grove steadily diminished in size for generations. Now it is a government preserve.

When I saw the true and perfect specimens of the cedars, the praise which the Bible bestows on them had new meaning for me.

Moses knew the hot breath of Palestine and Arabia in summer. He had felt the oven heat of basalt rocks in the hills; he had known the searing of desert sands. He too had walked treeless plains looking for shade. He had stood on naked ridges and looked into valleys barren of green meadows, lakes, or streams. He had crossed saddles where in a whole expanse of dreary land there was not a bit of shade, no clump or line of trees to break the monotony. The land of Moab is parched and dry. The treeless plains of Bashan are often scorched; its lava rock remains hot the night through.

So Moses looked north to Lebanon where patches of snow capped the highest ridges; where the slopes were dark green with the thick stands of cedars; where Neba Leben and other cold streams gushed from limestone cliffs. And he said, "I pray thee, let me go over, and see the good land that is beyond Jordan, that goodly mountain, and Lebanon." (Deuteronomy 3:25.)

When Solomon said, "His countenance is as Lebanon, excellent as the cedars" (Song of Solomon 5:15) he meant that their majesty suggested repose, tranquillity, and nobility.

The mountains of Lebanon were the hills to which the Psalmist raised his eyes and from which came his strength. Here were snow peaks, roaring brooks, green forests, abundant springs, luxuriant meadows, brilliant flowers. Here was the source of life and livelihood. Above all else here was solitude sublime, the place of meditation and communion. "The righteous shall flourish like the palm tree: he shall grow like a cedar in Lebanon." (Psalms 92:12.)

And so the destruction of the cedars became the symbolism of dire calamity and disaster. It was the ultimate in expression of the wrath of God.

"Lebanon is ashamed and hewn down." (Isaiah 33:9.)

"And I will prepare destroyers against thee, every one with his weapons: and they shall cut down thy choice cedars, and cast them into the fire." (Jeremiah 22:7.)

"Open thy doors, O Lebanon, that the fire may devour thy cedars." (Zechariah 11:1.)

The Prophets knew what the scourge of deforestation could do to a land—that it was the ultimate in destruction. The cedars are mostly gone. Topsoil that their roots once held back has rushed to the Mediterranean. The gullies become harsher and deeper, the land more impoverished every year. The goats keep new forests from rising. Yacoub Bishara has to rise at 3 A.M. to eke out a living from the thin and rocky soil that is left. Poverty has permeated the land.

27. The Agrarian Problem

WE IN America think of the Arabs as a nomadic people. The Bedouins are. But at least 90 per cent of the Arab world is even more firmly settled than our Iowa farmers. The economy of the Arab world is predominantly agricultural. The most acute and pressing problems in this area are therefore rural ones.

Poverty is foremost in the Arab world. Poverty in that region, as elsewhere, breeds malnutrition, unsanitary conditions of living, miserable housing, high infant mortality, and a long list of preventable diseases. But poverty in the Arab world is not the temporary kind that a depression produces in our country; it is permanent and abiding, the product of age-old and deep-seated ailments.

The reasons for this poverty are several. First is the system of land ownership. In Egypt about four million people are actively engaged in agriculture. Of these, three million own no land or own less than a feddan—slightly more than an acre. In Syria about 55 per cent of the land is owned by landlords and cultivated by share tenants. These holdings are large, 25 per cent of the land being in units of five hundred hectares or more—one hectare being roughly two and a half acres. In southern Iraq practically all the land is owned by landlords who lease it, through an intermediary called the sirkal, on shares to the cultivators. In Lebanon there is more land owned by the farmers who till the soil than in any of the other Arab countries. But in Lebanon there are great landholdings along the coast and in the interior valley of the Boqaa.

The system of share-tenancy gives the tenant little feeling of security. He is subject to eviction at the will of the landlord; he has no fixed tenure. The rent he pays varies; usually it is a percentage of the crop. One way of dividing the crop is by fifths: one for the land, one for seed, one for water, one for beasts of burden, one for labor. It is not unusual for the tenant to retain only 20 per cent under that system, since the landlord will often furnish not only the land but the seed, water, and work animals as well. But the tenant's share of the crop is customarily higher. He may pay only one-fifth, one-third, or one-half of the crop as rent. His actual share, however, is usually much less than the share to which he is entitled under the lease. The reason is that there is little bank credit available for agriculture. In Syria some agricultural bank loans up to a thousand dollars are available at 9 per cent interest. But the farmer who owns land as well as the landless tenant must usually resort to moneylenders, who have extortionate rates of interest—15 and 20 per cent are customary; 100 per cent is sometimes charged. A tenant soon gets in debt to a moneylender or to his landlord. In most cases he is unable to repay the principal and meet the heavy installments of interest. He becomes in substance a serf, irrevocably tied to a master by debt. Though his share of the crop may on its face seem generous, what he is able to retain is only enough to keep him and his family at a subsistence level.

This system of tenancy not only makes the great bulk of the farming class perpetually poor; it also has a devastating effect on the land, for the tenants feel no responsibility for the use of fertilizers or for the adoption of long-range programs of land improvement. The system leaves no room for incentive—for the prospect that increased activity will bring new rewards.

The methods of farming are in the main still primitive. Egypt is an exception. The areas where farmers own their own land, as in parts of Lebanon, and where large holdings are devoted to the raising of cereals, as in north Syria, are another exception. But the habits of farming are for the most part what they were in the days of Christ. Plowing is done with a stick, harvesting with hand sickles, thrashing by rolling a spiked drum over grain piled on the ground, separating by tossing the wheat or barley in the air with a fork, the chaff being blown to one side. Olive trees will produce a crop every year. But in this region the farmers get a crop every two years. The reason is that they harvest the crop by knocking the fruit off the trees with long sticks, which destroys a large percentage of the buds from which next year's crop derives.

A few of the Arab countries have oil, but the natural resources of most of them are skimpy. There is no iron and very little coal.

The region is arid: the coastal ranges get around twenty-one inches of rain a year; the interior from six to ten inches. In the interior only one crop in two years or two crops in three years may be grown except where there is irrigation as in the valleys of the Tigris, Euphrates, and the Nile. Most of the major streams have not yet been harnessed for flood control, irrigation, and electric power. Soil erosion and the uneconomic use of water have gone on for centuries. They continue to deplete the land.

The pressure on the land increases yearly. The area has a potential capacity to care for many more millions of people, but to do so it must have numerous TVA's and other handiworks of science. Today the continuous increase in population merely serves to intensify the conditions of poverty.

In many sections of Egypt and in the dry-farming areas of Syria, Transjordan, and Iraq the agricultural worker—the fellah—is on a seasonal basis. He sows the cereals in the spring and harvests them in the fall, working a half or perhaps only a third of the year. He and his kind are not migratory workers; they barely exist on the few hundred dollars which their partial employment produces each year.

In the rural areas illiteracy is high—perhaps 95 per cent. There are few rural schools. The peasants have no avenues of escape from their conditions—no keys to knowledge that will show them improved methods of plowing and irrigating, the use of fertilizers, the way to balance the economy of a farm with livestock, the control of disease among fruit and vegetables, the prevention of disease among humans.

The governments in these areas are alive to these conditions, but the measures taken to date have not touched the fundamental conditions on which the destitution of the masses grows. Remedies employed either have been minor in nature or, where more ambitious, have chiefly aided the landlords. The United States Agricultural Mission made a comprehensive study of agricultural conditions in Syria and submitted an excellent report in 1946. The report is highly praised on all sides. But by 1950 nothing had been done to implement it.

The measure closest to actual land reform in the Arab world is the provision of the new Syrian constitution that, "A maximum limit for landownership shall be prescribed by law." But that touches only future acquisitions, not present holdings, since it has no retroactive effect.

The Arab peasant has long been a fatalist and still is. But he is beginning to understand his problems—the causes of his misery and the remedies for it.

Part of his understanding has come from the dissemination of ideas about America and its way of life; part has been due to Soviet propaganda. Soviet propaganda reached the peak of its influence in the Arab world in 1944. A picture of Stalin then hung in almost every Arab home. The expression Abou Shanab—"the man with the mustache"—came into common usage. Abou Shanab became a sort of Robin Hood. A peasant who was angry at his landlord, an employee who had been discharged by his employer, a person who was indignant over the acts of a crooked politician—each of these would threaten vengeance. He would say that Abou Shanab would see that evil was punished, that the cause of justice was served.

When on November 29, 1947 the Soviet Union voted in favor of partition of Palestine, the wooing of the Arabs by the Soviets received a serious setback. The Arab governments at once outlawed the Communist party; and their publications were banned. Six Communists were burned to death in Damascus. The Communist party in the Arab world went underground. The party was purged; the intellectuals were weeded out. Control of the party in the Middle East was given to professionals whose endurance to suffering and whose loyalty to the Kremlin had been thoroughly tested.

Communist propaganda has to date failed to make Communists of the masses. It has, however, made them politically conscious. It has created an acute awareness of their troubles and dissatisfaction with the *status quo*.

Illiteracy, disease, poverty, and misgovernment—these are real, personal enemies of the Arab peasant. The Moscow radio tells about them. It speaks of the corruption in high places; the struggle of the Arab at the bottom to escape his cruel fate; the eagerness of the Soviet people to help the oppressed; the savagery with which the ruling class, aided and abetted by the "Anglo-American imperialists," thwart every move by the masses to free themselves from the feudal system. The Moscow radio speaks in Arabic:

"Tonight you Arabs sit in your mud huts eating unleavened

bread, cheese, and olives. Tonight your masters who are supported by the Anglo-American imperialists feast on the fat of the land. You live in filth and misery; they dress in silk and live in comfort. They and the Anglo-American imperialists will not let you be freed from your misery and your suffering."

What Sir Oliver Franks, British Ambassador to the United States, recently said of the peasants of southeast Asia can be appropriately applied to the Arab peasants as well: "We can no longer assume, as they no longer assume, that generation after generation will come and go in unchanging ways, lost to all comforts but the meagre one of traditional fatalism."

28. Zayim

THE FAMOUS gardens of the Middle East are those in the palace of Azm in Damascus, built two hundred years ago by a noted governor. Today its fountains still produce the music of cascades. A mass of jasmine, hauntingly fragrant, blooms against a brick wall; sour orange trees, loquat trees, the thin dark cypress sway in the wind that sweeps off the desert; goldenrod and morning glories give a dash of color to drab clay walls.

Azm represents the peak of splendor. Yet every Arab, no matter how poor, has his garden or courtyard. In the typical village the home of a poor Arab opens on a courtyard of hard-packed dirt surrounded by a mud wall about eight feet tall. It has no tree or touch of greenness. An open ditch carrying waste water from the house runs through it, the assembly point of a host of flies. The courtyard carries the smell of goats and donkeys. Yet the garden is home, the place where privacy begins.

One July night in 1949 we sat in a more pretentious garden in Damascus. A rich lawn filled the space, and willow and apple trees bent before a wind that swept from the west off the Anti-Lebanon Mountains. It had been blistering hot that afternoon. Now it was cool—so cool that it was uncomfortable to sit long without a wrap.

A group of us had discussed at length the economic plight of the peasant in the Middle East, the remedies for his ills, Soviet propaganda, the prospect of effective political action to combat it. One of the group—a large landowner—deprecated the suggestion that modern agricultural methods should be introduced. He described in detail the primitive methods of harvesting grain, how women worked all day on their knees to cut with a hand sickle a small plot of wheat, how boys and men stacked the sheaves on camels and took them several miles to a thrashing floor, how that thrashing method caused a loss of a fifth or more of the grain. But then he added, "If farm machinery were introduced, the peasants would have more leisure time. Think of the trouble they would get into then."

Another spoke up and said that ownership of land had nothing to do with productivity, that in Syria the larger the estate the more efficient the management of it, that the answer to the land problem was the introduction of scientific methods by those owners who had the necessary skill and imagination.

Still another added in general agreement with the others that before land was distributed to the peasants each peasant should demonstrate that he was worthy to be a landowner.

Most of this group were business and professional men representing a conservative point of view. They doubtless shared the sentiments of the dominant political groups in the region.

Beginning in March of 1949, however, one loud and powerful voice had proclaimed a different attitude. It was the voice of Husni Zayim, dictator of Syria, who had seized control of the government in a bloodless coup. Whether he was in earnest about his political program, I do not know. Damascus seemed to be divided in opinion. But if he were serious, he was a grave threat to the *status quo*. He promised

—redistribution of the land to the peasants

—slum clearance

—low-cost housing

—emancipation of women

—resettlement of 100,000 Arab refugees from Palestine on Syrian land

—a tax program to carry forward these projects.

He also seemed to be working for peace with Israel. That at least was what he professed to be doing. And he had taken one step in that direction by signing an armistice.

I tried to see Zayim to make up my mind about his sincerity, but he was moving around too fast for me to catch up with him. I did, however, see his Prime Minister, Muhsin Barazi. Barazi seemed smooth and suave and full of intrigue. I did not get from him a feeling of sincerity. He pressed me to help Syria get from the United States equipment for a modern army.

"We promise not to use it against Israel," he said. "We must be strong against the threat of Russia to the north."

But there did not seem to be in Barazi's mind the idea that the real show of strength against Russia would come in a social revolution that effectuated a program of rural reconstruction such as Zayim talked about.

Within the month Zayim and Barazi were dead. They were seized and executed by the Army on the morning of August 14, 1949. A new government took over. Up to then the Damascus radio had been broadcasting everlasting praise and tribute to Marshal Zayim. Suddenly it switched its theme; now Zayim was everything wicked in the book, from traitor on down.

The Moscow radio blared at length in Arabic about the episode and offered as usual a conspiratorial theory involving the democracies: "We now know why and by whose hand these acts were accomplished. In order to grasp this case we have carefully observed whom this Syrian event displeased and whom it pleased. To decide this subject we do not need to look into the simple faces of the Syrian people, but perhaps the countenance of some diplomat in London, Washington and Paris must be scrutinized. Everything is read in those countenances. In some of the British faces a smile of satisfaction; in some French faces, regret and nervousness; and in American faces, disappointment and displeasure. The Britishers consider themselves masters of the Arab countries. French capital lost its influence in Syria, but is hopeful by serving the Americans who are attempting to oust the Britishers from these countries and replace them, to remain in its position."

Many believe that Soviet propaganda even to this day. The British are readily suspected in the Middle East. Some say Zayim and Barazi were shot because the Zayim government was too friendly with Israel. That also is too easy an answer. Zayim had given asylum to a political refugee from Lebanon and then in a moment which many thought to be treacherous, returned the man to Lebanon to be shot. Zayim had become, like most dictators, a braggart—bold and boastful in his attitudes. The common Syrian explanation is that he was therefore shot because he was dangerous to the nation. That was the excuse.

The truth is that Zayim's announced program struck at the heart of the feudal system that holds Syria in its grip. The Moslem clergy, the landowners, the industrialists, and the die-hard Anti-Zionists were aligned against his reforms. Zayim's political strategy and astuteness were not equal to that revolutionary occasion.

But, the ideas which Zayim espoused live on in the Arab world.

29. Jebel el Druze

WE LEFT Damascus by car one hot bright morning, heading south by west for Soueida, Amman, and Jerusalem. In a few minutes the greenery of Damascus was behind us. The black-surfaced road lay like a snake across the blistering plain of Bashan. There was not a tree as far as the eye could see.

The plain was basalt. Dark lava rocks, from the size of eggs to the size of barrels, were scattered across the fields. Some had been piled to form fences. Others lay on the surface. The ancient wooden plows still used to work the land plowed around them. They stood like islands in a sea of skimpy crops that stretched to the horizon.

The crops were mostly sorghum, wheat, melons, and sunflowers. This is an area of dry-farming. There had been no rain for two months. We stopped briefly at the small village of Sheikh Meskine. There was no shade except inside the flat-roofed, ill-smelling mud huts. The village had not even a shrub or a tuft of grass. A searing sun had scorched the earth and left it brown. The stone walls on the roadside had a furnace heat in them. Beyond the walls camels were being unloaded of the sheaves which they had brought to the thrashing floors. Their masters stopped work and stared—their faces dark and inscrutable but marked with the almost unendurable effort of producing food and raising families on arid land carrying the marks of centuries of abuse.

The plain of Bashan gets rockier and rockier as it approaches Jebel el Druze—the Mountain of the Druzes. This is a low-lying barren ridge, perhaps two thousand feet high. It lay ahead of us to the south and seemed from a distance to be no more than a drab foothill. It is historic ground, where the Argob and Geshur are located. This is where Absalom fled after the murder of his brother (II Samuel 13:38). It has been a refuge for countless others who fled before the law. A great many Druzes settled here in the nineteenth century, coming from Lebanon where they writhed under the rule of the Turk.

The Druzes have always been a religious minority in the Arab world. Today they constitute about 4 per cent of Syria's three and a half million people. Their resistance to authority has made them a thorn in the side of almost every government of Syria. Their record as warriors is renowned. They sided with Islam and fought the Crusaders. They have massacred Christians and warred on divers groups. In much of this—especially in the killing of Christians— they were inspired and directed by the Turks who ruled Syria for four hundred years. In other instances—as in case of their resistance to the French in the 1920's—they were inspired by intense nationalism. And when it came to war with the Bedouins, they fought in self-defense.

The Bedouin and his flocks have walked this region together for centuries. Bashan used to be covered with oaks. They are mostly gone. A Bedouin never leaves a tree standing. He cuts it down by setting it on fire; then he waits for the wind to blow it over. He uses that extravagant method even though he wants only a few boughs for his cooking. If there were only one tree left in a basin, he would destroy it. The Bedouin figures that if he doesn't appropriate it, someone else will.

It was the lack of conservation that bled Bashan—and more. There has been great insecurity in its civilizations. There was continuous raiding and pillaging. Men took what they saw. There was no incentive to build and construct for the morrow. Men lived from day to day. The earth and soil were resources to plunder. If one did not take today, the raiding Bedouins or the corrupt Turks would take tomorrow. It paid to cut trees, for the Turks placed a tax on them. Thus irresponsible management of water, topsoil, grass, and trees became the norm.

The Druzes who bordered the Bedouins on the west were constantly armed. They even took guns to the fields.

We were the guests of the Druzes at Soueida, a clean, pleasant town of about ten thousand. We had been invited by Said Taky Deen, who spoke for Sultan Pasha Atrash, the head of the Syrian tribe. The Governor of Jebel el Druze, at whose office we reported, took us on a tour of the city, and afterward gave us lunch in the Governor's mansion. The menu consisted of the following:

Djaje mihshi (Roast chicken stuffed with a dressing made of rice, ground lamb meat, spices).

Koosa and *leban* (*Koosa* is squash, stuffed with rice, ground lamb meat, and chopped parsley. *Leban* is milk which when processed thickens as it sets).

Kibbeh (*Kibbeh* is made from finely crushed wheat, ground lamb meat, and spices. This is pounded together until the mixture has an even texture, and then fried).

Rice and *yakni* (*Yakni* is prepared by boiling okra until softened. The okra is then drained. Onions browned in olive oil and tomatoes are then added).

Hummos bithiini (Chick peas with sesame. Chick peas mashed and mixed with *hummos* which is diluted and mixed with olive oil, lemons, and parsley).

Salad (Mixed vegetables with a dressing made of olive oil and lemons and highly seasoned).

Mixed assorted fresh vegetables (Olives, fried eggplant, tomatoes).

Dessert (Fresh fruit and *baklawa*. *Baklawa* is a pastry made of thin layers of crust with a filling of crushed nuts and honey).

After lunch we retired to the drawing room where Turkish coffee was served. Then we received the dignitaries of the tribe. To understand what transpired at the reception a bit of Druze history must be given.

The Druzes constitute a secret, religious sect. Syria and Lebanon have been their home ever since they first appeared late in the tenth century near Mount Hermon. Always an agricultural people, not interested in industry or commerce, they are organized today as they were in the beginning—in a feudal society. Villages are under the control of local sheikhs—a word which, as I have said, connotes old age, seniority, respect. The sheikhs are in turn under one or more amirs or princes. Land is for the most part owned by the members of the hierarchy.

The Druzes consider that Christianity, Judaism, Islam, and all other religions were forerunners of Druzism. Adam, Noah, Abraham, Moses, Jesus, and Mohammed were all prophets. But to the Druzes Mohammed was Lucifer. For them Al-Hakim (A.D. 996-1020) is the Messiah. The name Druze comes from Darazi, the first missionary of the faith.

The Druzes have predestination as a philosophy of life. There is little place for the free will of man. They also believe in the transmigration of souls. When a Druze dies, he is supposed to be reborn in China. Little actually is known, however, of the Druze religion. It is part of their religion that nothing of it should be divulged or promulgated. The door of their religion was indeed closed in A.D. 1031. This step was taken in order to save the Druzes from being delivered into the hands of their persecutors by converts with subversive tendencies. Since that date no one has been admitted to the Druze nation; nor has anyone been allowed to leave it.

The Druze religion thus became wholly hereditary. No outsider, and few insiders, know the secrets of this religion. Some of the theology is transmitted secretly by word of mouth to succeeding priests or wise men. Moreover, the words in the religious texts of the Druzes have double meanings that only a select few know.

The art of dissimulation is a legitimate technique. The Druze religion was fashioned with an eye to survival in a hostile world. Hence a Druze may profess any other religion as a means of protecting himself. He may in appearance and profession be a devout Moslem or Catholic. But at heart he is always a Druze, forever a member of a homogeneous group, bound by religious and fraternal ties, tied to a feudal system of government, united to an indissoluble family.

The feudal system of the Druzes of Jebel el Druze was imposed by the Hamdans—Kurdish families who are part of the tribe. But since the Atrashes ousted the Hamdans last century, the social and political structure in Jebel el Druze has been democratic. The Jebel is divided into Makarin (districts) and each district is governed by the largest family. Party politics are family politics. Whenever an emergency arises the unity of the various districts and families is achieved by the religious leaders. In ordinary administrative matters the priests or wise men never interfere except where a religious question arises. Discussions on public matters are usually conducted at the Madafaat—equivalent to our town meetings, and complete social equality is maintained there.

In nine centuries there has on the whole been little change

in the Druze way of life—religious, political, social, and economic. But the Druzes do not live in a vacuum. They are part of the dynamics of the Middle East. Their hopes and aspirations are tied to those of all Arab peoples. And so it is that Russian propaganda, the advances in Israel, and the contagion of liberal ideas sweeping the world have penetrated the feudal walls of Jebel el Druze.

After the luncheon at Soueida we received the dignitaries of the Druze tribe in the drawing room of the Governor's palace. The first to enter were five Druze priests or wise men. Taky Deen introduced my son and we shook hands with each one. The priests then sat opposite us on a sofa. I expressed our gratitude for the hospitality of the tribe, and for our luncheon at Soueida.

The spokesman for the priests replied simply and formally. He spoke feelingly of the happiness of the Druzes in having us as their guests, expressing the hope we might stay longer. As he spoke I studied the five faces. It is written in the religious code of the Druzes, "The Mind is the Pen which writes upon stone, and the stone which it writes upon is the Soul." The souls of these Druze priests shone through their countenances.

Seldom have I seen such aesthetic, spiritual faces as two of them had. Mr. Justice Cardozo had such a face. So did the Rev. William Robinson of the Congregational Church at Yakima. So did Father. The faces were faces of dedicated men. I had seen preachers with the harassed look of a bedeviled sergeant of a police force. These men were serene inside. They had deep and everlasting devotion to some idea or ideal which to them was more precious than life.

The next delegation numbered about a dozen. They represented the ruling families of the Druzes. They were mostly men in their thirties and forties. Their faces carried the mark of the sun and wind. Their hands were firm and gnarled.

After expressing our gratitude for their hospitality, I went on to say that ever since I had reached Damascus I had felt strangely at home. First, there was the similarity between the setting of Damascus and that of Yakima—each an oasis in the desert. The great plain of Bashan was much like the sagebrush area of the Inland Empire in eastern Washington. The basalt formations were similar. The treeless expanse of eastern Washington—the area to be irrigated by Grand Coulee Dam—might well be Bashan.

"That is why I have felt a bit homesick in your country," I concluded.

The spokesman for the group expressed his pleasure that this land had such a strong appeal to me. Then he asked, "Have you seen the Arab refugee camp at Soueida?"

The refugee camp at Soueida had at the time about a thousand refugees. It was located in warehouses on the outskirts of the town. Families partitioned off space—about eight by twelve—by building low walls of stone or of boxes or packing cases. There was no plumbing; and water had to be carried from the village.

My son and I had visited the camp earlier in the day. A group of a hundred or more gathered around us.

"Are you Americans?"

"Yes."

"Well, help us get back home. . . . We have nothing to do here. . . . What has happened to my vineyard in Palestine? . . . Can't we be given new homes in Syria? . . . There are no schools for our children here."

These were the kind of questions and problems put to us by the refugees. They flooded my mind as the spokesman for the Druzes asked me if we had visited the camp.

I told him we had visited it.

"Then you will understand the feelings of the refugees. This land of ours makes you homesick. Think how homesick these poor refugees are."

With that he proceeded with an exposition of the refugee problem—a denunciation of the Jews, a criticism of the United States, a plea that these "innocent victims" be given justice, a warning that unless they were given justice they would grow as "festering sores" in the Arab world.

The statement he made was a forceful, polished plea by a good advocate of the Arab side of the controversy. When he had finished, he expressed the wish that Bill and I would stay with his people for a while and not rush away as we were scheduled to do that evening.

When we returned from the courtyard where we had been photographed with these men, another group awaited us. They too numbered about a dozen. They were young men in their thirties. Their spokesman was a handsome chap—tall and lean, well-proportioned, with sharply chiseled features. There was an earnest, sincere expression on his face.

I was to learn from him the meaning of an old Arabic expression, "The beauty of man lies in the eloquence of his tongue."

After we had exchanged formalities he made a speech. It lasted perhaps fifteen minutes. At first he spoke quietly and slowly. As he progressed, his delivery quickened, the volume of his voice increased. There was now great emotion in his speech; it welled up from deep within him.

Arabic is a guttural language, like German. It comes from the throat, not the lips. Often it sounds harsh. But the speech we were hearing had the fullness of the organ in it. The rhythm of it rose and fell. It would build to a great crescendo and then fall like something soft and liquid. Then it would start building again. It would have the roar of the wind through forests of pine and fir. It would drop to a whisper as soft as an echo from a distant cliff. There was tragedy, pathos, suffering in the voice. It was a rhythmic outpouring of a soul. It was a symphony from the vocal chords.

I didn't have the least idea what the man said. But it was the most moving, eloquent speech I ever heard. It carried an important message—one that would shake the frame even of a strong man. There were tears in many eyes when he finished.

I had experienced what is known in the Arab world as "lawful magic." No language seems capable of exerting such irresistible influence over listeners as Arabic. In this melodious tongue it is easy for a master to stir an Arab audience to the depths.

When Taky Deen turned to me after the speaker had finished, I noticed that he too was filled with emotion. He wiped his eyes and said,

"Mr. Justice, that is the most beautiful Arabic I ever heard. I must apologize to you, for I cannot possibly translate it as he spoke it."

I asked him to summarize it as best he could.

Taky Deen sat in silence for a moment and then said:

"This man traced for you the history of the Arab people. Conqueror after conqueror overran the land. They exploited the resources—cutting trees, permitting overgrazing, wasting the water resources. They also brought graft and corruption into high places.

Government in this country has long been a heavy, oppressive yoke on the people.

"The people, moreover, are held under a vicious feudal system. They do not own the land. They pay excessive rent. They have few doctors, few hospitals, and not many schools. They are too ignorant to help themselves."

Taky Deen stopped for a moment and turning to me said, "He made one statement that he hopes you will remember above all the others. He said the French when they ruled Syria took many acts of vengeance toward us Druzes. They jailed and shot us. They violated our women. They raided our villages and carried off our stock. They sat up all night trying to figure out ways and means of breaking our resistance, of subduing us. But the French were not smart. There was one way—and only one way—they could have subdued us. They could have closed our schools. That would have been the greatest punishment of all."

Taky Deen went on to say that this man's plea was for education. He wanted teachers for his people, teachers who would show them how to plow, irrigate, and farm; teachers who would show them how to prevent disease, how to cure illness; teachers who would show them how to read and write and become intelligent citizens of a democracy.

"Teachers are what we need—education, not money. Only education will raise my people from the poverty and ignorance in which you see them."

The speech of this Druze had not only moved me emotionally; it had expressed a philosophy with which I had been associated in the States. I felt a kinship with the man. I felt it so keenly that I walked across to him and grasped him warmly by the hand. As we filed out to have our pictures taken with this group, Taky Deen added: "This is the Populist element of the Druzes. They are working hard within their tribe to bring about the reforms of which this man speaks."

A further word about the Populists is necessary.

The largest family in Jebel el Druze has for years been the Atrashes. This family is headed by Sultan Pasha el Atrash, who led the revolt of 1925 against the French. When that revolt failed, the Sultan left Jebel el Druze for Saudi Arabia. Among those who accompanied him were outstanding leaders of Jebel el Druze, the most famous being Hamzi el Darwishe. Those who remained among

the leaders in Jebel el Druze were the relatives of Sultan Pasha.
They allied themselves with the French mandate, and monopolized
most of the administrative, judicial, and military jobs of the Jebel.

The Populist movement gained its impetus when the Atrash
family allowed only members of that family to become candidates
for parliament. The other families among the Druzes, members of
the Socialist and Syrian Popular parties, mobilized their arms and
fought the Atrashes. The Populist movement won, and then in turn
denied the Atrashes the right to any political office. In the election
to the Syrian National Parliament the Populist candidates won the
four seats allotted to them.

Jamil Abou Assali—from Soueida—was the prime mover of the
Populist revolt. We met him at Soueida—the only Druze there
who was dressed in European clothes. His thin, eager face watched
us closely. He furnished the dynamics to the Populist cause.
Since we saw him in 1949, he was killed in an automobile accident.

Leaders of the Popular movement are either men who fought
with the Sultan against the French or young intellectual Druzes.
Of the leaders, Hamzi el Darwishe was the best known. He grew
to be the strongest fighter among the Druzes. His stories are like
legend; but the Druzes say they are true. In the battles in which he
engaged he used to take his sword and with one stroke cut a horse
and a man in two, four pieces falling to the ground. And before
battle he used to break a sword by swinging it, a device he used
to make the men enthusiastic. But Darwishe also died in the winter
of 1949. He too was killed in an auto accident.

After the reception at Soueida was over we drove about ten miles
to the small, desolate, treeless village of Krai to call on the famous
Sultan Pasha. This man—now in his early fifties—was, as I have
said, a great hero of the resistance movement against the French, and
had helped Lawrence take Damascus in 1918. His deeds, like those
of Hamzi el Darwishe, have a heroic quality that makes them almost
unbelievable. It was Sultan Pasha who charged on horseback a
French tank. He charged it alone; and he captured it. The tank crew
was apparently too bewildered to act. The Sultan drew up to the
tank, jumped off his horse, opened the door, and tossed in a hand
grenade. The French Foreign Legion to their sorrow came to know
the cunning and daring of this man.

The Sultan greeted us at the door of his simple cottage on the edge of Krai and ushered us into a spacious and rather barren drawing room that looked out on a treeless, rocky expanse of land.

He has the face of a stoic—immobile without a trace of expression. He is a man of few words, and conversation was difficult. After we had finished our Turkish coffee he asked if he might show me his horses.

We went outside and he ordered two Arabian horses to be led out from the stables in the rear. They were beautiful stallions—gentle, well-proportioned, with small legs and feet and husky shoulders. He walked around them, caressing them gently and speaking to them as a father would to a child.

Our visit was coming to a close. It was late afternoon and Bill and I had to drive to Amman, capital of Trans-Jordan, that night. It was only seventy-five miles, but we would have to pass through the Syrian and Trans-Jordan army lines, which were apt to be time-consuming.

I turned to the Sultan and told him how much we had enjoyed our day with the Druzes. I added, "The Druzes, you know, are well-known in America. Your people are particularly remembered for their courage and bravery, for their ability as warriors."

The Sultan replied instantly, "I know that is true. But I wish we were remembered differently."

"In what way?"

"I wish we could go down in history not as warriors but as teachers."

He took me by the arm and led me to the edge of a field. It was a rocky stretch of ground out of whose thin soil the Druzes had to make their living.

"See what poor land my people have," he said. "To farm it they should know modern methods. They do not know about fertilizers, about plowing—do you call it contour plowing?

"They do not know about co-operatives—about financing and marketing their products. They may have a good crop and be robbed by merchants in Damascus. My people are smart but they do not know these things. They need to be taught."

He touched on most of the subjects which the U. S. Agricultural Mission covered in its report on Syria in 1946—matters which to date had received no attention in Soueida.

Turning to me he said, "Can't America teach my people? We don't want America's money. We want merely to learn how to live. If my people knew that, then they could take care of themselves."

As I turned to go he said, "Show my people how to do all these things. Then they will be able to teach others. Teachers are more important than warriors."

30. Kemal Djumblatt

EL MOUKHTARA is a small Druze village in southern Lebanon about halfway between Beirut and Sidon. It sits high in the Lebanon Mountains, facing west to the Mediterranean. Its perch is a precarious one, for the slopes run away fast, some at forty degrees. Mulberry, apple, and a variety of soft fruit trees grow on tier after tier of terraces that follow the contour of the range. Grapes and vegetables are planted in like fashion. Water brought many miles down the valley in a canal is fed ingeniously into these terraces on its way down to the village, where enough is left on arrival to run a power plant and to turn a grist mill.

El Moukhtara has been the home of the Djumblatt family for three hundred years. The Djumblatt houses are its most prominent features. One is a lonely castle high on the ridge; two are halfway down, all commanding a broad sweep of the valley for miles and miles. Each is made of rock and looks from the distance like a fort that clings precariously to the mountainside. The rooms are spacious, with stone floors and high ceilings, and doubtless very draughty in winter.

The head of the Djumblatt family today is the thirty-year-old Kemal, who is married to the beautiful May Arslan. She, an Arslan, and he, a Djumblatt, unite the two leading families of the Lebanese Druzes. Thus Kemal occupies a strategic position in their destiny.

We came by car from Beirut to El Moukhtara. Kemal Djumblatt and the other leading Druzes of Lebanon were there to greet us. From the point where the road ends, wide stone stairs wind their way for perhaps one hundred feet up to the main floor and gardens of Kemal Djumblatt's house. Both sides of the staircase were lined with men and boys—all Druzes. As we approached they started clapping and they never stopped until we reached the top. Their clapping, echoing and re-echoing off the stone walls of the castle-like house, was so loud that I could not hear Kemal Djumblatt. The clapping continued in the garden until Mr. Djumblatt raised his hand. After he had introduced me it started again and was stopped only at his intercession.

The priests or wise men were there to greet us. I sat with them in an alcove while some of the men danced outside. A flute provided the music. These dancers, like Persian tribesmen, formed a line, each holding on to the other's waist or shoulders. They kicked, and bowed, and went through many gyrations, moving clockwise as they danced. There were no womenfolk of the Druzes present except Kemal's wife. Druze women, like most Moslem women, are not seen on such occasions. They dance, but only in private. No male eyes are allowed to observe them. At Jebel el Druze there had been no women present at any of the functions. May Djumblatt, educated in France and speaking English and French, was throwing off the old customs. She was the hostess at El Moukhtara. She bowed to convention only in one respect; she wore a veil over her hair and shoulders, though not over her face.

Lunch was served buffet style. A whole calf had been roasted. Servants tore off slices with their hands and loaded our plates. We were surfeited with other delicious Arab food and ended with huge white grapes, crisp apples, Golden and Red Delicious, grown locally, and Turkish coffee.

After lunch the several hundred guests assembled in front of an alcove off the garden and listened to speeches. Addresses of welcome were given; and I replied. Then Kemal Djumblatt introduced Ramiz Abi-Suab, a young man in his twenties who spoke of the principles and achievements of the Progressive Socialist party.

Kemal Djumblatt is its founder. A member of the Lebanon Parliament since 1943 and for a while Minister of National Economy, he is well-educated both in government and in religion. He rises at five o'clock every morning, goes to the tower of his home high on the ridge above El Moukhtara, and sits in prayer and meditation for two hours. He is a devout man and somewhat of a mystic, greatly influenced by Hindu philosophy. The destiny of the Arabs in a fast-changing, revolutionary world is uppermost in his thoughts. He has in fact dedicated his life to their welfare.

He studied Marxism in Paris but was not convinced. Yet he

believes that the "capitalistic phase" of society is passing and that a new form of economic, social, and political democracy must be designed. He gave this project many months of thought.

In the winter of 1949 he organized the Progressive Socialist party in Lebanon. One of its sponsors describes its aims as follows:

An economic democracy: bread and work, Justice and Freedom.

A social democracy: neither right nor privilege without a corresponding duty—a society without classes.

A political democracy: neither dictatorship nor anarchy, but an organized people's democracy.

Every citizen is an owner.

A worker is the partner of the owner of the enterprise.

The fatherland is a happy country: social security assured to all citizens, education accessible to everybody.

The party sponsors socialization of a select group of industries, equality of men and women with respect to civil and political rights, compulsory voting, social security, universal education, hospitals and clinics, a degree of socialized medicine, protection of water supplies, elimination of malaria, income taxes, industrialization programs, freedom of the press, formation of trade unions, an independent judiciary, and dozens of other reforms, most of which have had a familiar ring in this country from the time of the elder La Follette to date. And not the least plank in the new party's platform is:

Partition of large landed properties into small lots and acquisition of these lots by tenants, farmers and workers in agriculture, the sales price being paid on long term installments. Abolition of the system of sharecroppers which is tied to medieval feudalism; encouragement of agricultural co-operatives; establishment of a suitable system of agricultural credit.

It is this program that Kemal Djumblatt calls the Third Force—a group of measures which reject the fanaticism of Soviet communism and the unrestrained activities of private enterprise.

His party has established rural health clinics in a few dozen villages where its members live. It has arranged medical service on an insurance basis for its members in the cities. In villages where the party is organized it is establishing libraries, tennis courts, swimming pools, and football, basketball, and volleyball fields. Consumer co-operatives have been started in some villages. Marketing and credit co-operatives are planned. It is launching genuine collective farms at the villages of Btekhnay and El Moukhtara in Lebanon. And perhaps most important of all, Kemal Djumblatt's party cuts across all religious lines. Among the fervent men who talked, one was a Russian Orthodox; another was a Maronite.

Kemal Djumblatt is a tall, thin, soft-spoken man. His high fore-head, unruly black hair, deep-brown eyes, his long, delicate hands mark him as an intellectual. He speaks slowly. His responses to questions are thoughtfully methodical, not quick. He is the thinker, the teacher, the philosopher. How he will succeed as a political manager no one knows. But in the first few months of his political activities he fired some fifteen thousand young men and women with zeal and enthusiasm. Theirs is not a passion born of narrow nationalism or class hatred. It has a distinct moral flavor. To paraphrase Kemal Djumblatt, their movement borrows from the philosophy of Jesus, Mohammed, Confucius and Buddha—all products of Asia. It is genuinely Asian. It is spiritually akin to every true democratic movement in the world.

Kemal Djumblatt, with his wife May, is providing leadership of a revolution from within the feudal system itself. Their management is high-principled and sincere. They—Arabs of the highest aristocracy in the Arab world—are devoting their lives to the improvement of the lot of the lowliest Arab. The Arabs who joined in this seminar held for my benefit at El Moukhtara had not only admiration for this courageous couple, but love and affection as well. It was evident in every gesture, in every word.

During this long discussion my mind went back to an earlier visit I had paid to Beit-ed-Dine, a pretentious castle a few miles up the valley from El Moukhtara. The President of the Republic of Lebanon tendered my son and me a luncheon there in 1949. We ate in the garden, with the full sweep of the valley at our feet. Beautiful terraced gardens fall away from the castle on the west. Here grow many botanical wonders of the Middle East including one I especially liked—the tiger's mustache, a coarse, broad-leaved grass that grows a few inches high and then droops. It looks a little like the squaw grass (bear grass) of our Pacific Northwest.

After luncheon we sauntered through the historic castle. Of all the wonders we saw, one caught my eye.

Emir Bachir Shahab, the ruler of Lebanon who built the castle near the beginning of the nineteenth century, had an Arab poet attached to his entourage. This poet would not only read the Koran to his master; he also wrote inspiring poems for him. The choice lines—the ones which the Governor thought the best—were carved in stone on the walls or written over the doorways of Beit-ed-Dine. As we moved through a spacious salon I asked that the inscription over one of the doors be translated. What it said came back to me as I watched the sensitive face of Kemal Djumblatt at El Moukhtara while he explained his political philosophy. The engraved words were these: "One hour of justice is worth three thousand hours of prayer."

31. Siblene—the Magic of Ownership

ELON GILBERT and I stayed the night with the Djumblatts at El Moukhtara. Kemal Djumblatt's mother Nazira (since deceased) held court. Sheikhs and other dignitaries from Druze villages far and wide came to pay their respects. Nazira was of the older generation. She still wore the veil, for though she let it drop occasionally, she could not bring herself to reject it entirely, as does May. A princess by birth and by bearing, she spoke English and French fluently and was as witty and lively a conversationalist as I have known. It was always hers to command; and she ruled over El Moukhtara like a queen.

But Kemal worried her. She wondered if he was not going too far and too fast with his political projects. Kemal also worries his wife's branch of the Druzes, the Arslans. They are wealthy, feudal lords. Kemal is decidedly out of favor with them because of his "radical" views. What upset both them and his mother the most was the thing Kemal did at Siblene.

Siblene is a village of about two hundred people which overlooks the Mediterranean eight miles or so north of Sidon. Siblene is not on the coastal plain, which is rich with the topsoil carried from the mountains as a result of centuries of erosion; it sits in the foothills. At that point the hills look as if they have been scrubbed and scoured of earth. As one approaches the village there seems to be nothing but bare limestone in sight.

Siblene has been a Djumblatt village for at least two hundred years—a Moslem not a Druze village. That is to say, a Djumblatt has been its owner, renting the land to Moslem tenants on a share-cropping basis. Some of the families of these tenants have been there as long as the village. Most of the present tenants were indeed born there, as were their fathers and grandfathers.

Siblene from time out of mind has been a feudal estate, the tenants no better than serfs, eking out a bare existence on this rocky ridge. Siblene's olive and fig orchards have the mark of antiquity on them. Somehow or other wheat and barley were raised in small amounts on rocky slopes that appear to be not even good pasture land. Since there is no well or creek, all water must be carried from a spring ten minutes distant.

Kemal Djumblatt distributed the land at Siblene to the tenants. He first asked the peasants to appoint a committee to value the land and to allocate the acreage among each of the families. When he received their report, he took one-third of the valuation they had placed on the land and sold it to them at that price on a ten-year installment basis. Each family ended by owning about four acres of land; and in each case it was the ancestral plot that his family had worked for generations.

This distribution of land to the peasants was the bombshell that rocked the Arab aristocracy. And the fact that it was done by an aristocrat made it all the more ominous. I had heard reports of the effect that it had had among the peasants and wanted to see for myself. That was why I went to Siblene.

At Siblene I saw young new apricot and peach orchards which the peasants planted just as soon as they became the owners. These orchards will treble the production of the land in a few years.

Siblene had been a village of mud huts marked with squalor. The Djumblatts, as landlords and owners of the huts, had never done anything to modernize them. I saw a village transformed. In a few months after the peasants had acquired ownership of their homes a miracle had happened. The mud houses were now spic and span; yards were tidy; shrubs and flowers had been planted; new stone fences had been erected; there was fresh paint on the gates and doors. Curtains gave dashes of color to the windows. Siblene was now neater and brighter than any Arab village I had seen.

Siblene had never had a schoolhouse. Within a few months after the peasants became the owners of the land they built a school-house—a one-room affair reminiscent of our country schools.

It had never occurred to the villagers to have a village recrea-tional center. Under the feudal system which they had known the landlord had the initiative; their duty was to work for him; they had either no consciousness of demands which they could rightfully make or insufficient courage to press them. Once they became owners of the village they had a new viewpoint. This was now their true home; it was theirs to do with as they pleased. And so they made big plans for it. Their recreational center was no more than a large room in a building on the highest point of the ridge, but it provided a place for games, for reading, for small assemblies, as well as a gathering place for the elders when village affairs needed settlement.

I walked among these people, talking with them, studying their faces. It was plain that something dramatic and deeply important had happened to them. I had first learned in Puerto Rico that a person moving from a house made of packing cases and sheets of tin into a house that was clean and modern underwent a transformation. Even his face was changed. I saw in Siblene something even more fundamental. I saw what magic widespread private ownership could produce. By reason of it a village had been remade almost overnight.

People who own land have a stake in their community; they have a new sense of citizenship; they acquire a feeling of responsibility. And with it all comes an attitude of confidence, of dignity, of well-being. This showed on all sides at Siblene. A quiet social revolution had taken place. It seemed to me a dramatic illustration of how quickly the character of the Middle East could be remade if the peasants were permitted to inherit the earth—on the installment plan.

I talked at length with Kemal Djumblatt about Siblene and its meaning in the Arab world. "The starting point for social reconstruction in the Middle East," he said, "is land reform. All else flows from that."

He went on to point out that only when the peasants are given a stake in their country can a truly democratic society be developed. Only then can any sense of citizenship and feeling of responsibility for community and national affairs be developed. Otherwise the peasant is bossed by some overlord, whose responsibility it is to determine what shall be planted, how the land shall be worked, and so on. In those matters the tenant has no voice. He never learns the lesson of initiative and enterprise. There are none of the rewards that increased effort can produce. The lack of incentive conditions all his activities.

Such is the peasant's fate. The facts of daily life teach it. Soviet propaganda hammers away at it.

There are those in the Middle East who jeer at Kemal Djumblatt and say that he is merely a politician who seeks popular support by what he did at Siblene. He is a politician; but he is of a different breed than the Middle East has ever known. He has spiritual qualities quite foreign to the political arena. He believes deeply and sincerely that the future of the Arab people depends on the quality of Arab leadership. That leadership has not been progressive; and prominent elements in it are to this day corrupt. That leadership, whether or not honest, has never yet fashioned for the peasants of that area a full-fledged democratic program such as Nehru is sponsoring in India. Government in the Middle East has been of the landlords, by the landlords, for the landlords.

"If we want to bring peace and security to our people we must adopt democratic methods," says Kemal Djumblatt. "Before we do that Arab leadership must cleanse itself."

"Is that why you decided to distribute the land at Siblene to the peasants?"

"Yes, that was one of the reasons," he replied. "If I am to lead the Arab peoples to a life of social justice, I myself must be worthy. I myself must live that life."

There was a long silence while he sat in meditation, his head bowed.

"What was the other reason?" I asked.

He lifted his face and turned to look at me. His eyes now had the fire of the Prophets.

"The other reason that I distributed the land to the peasants was that it is right that he who works the land should own it."

PART IV

Cross, Star, and Crescent

Mohammed is a name borne by more boys and men in the world than any other, including John and Bill. The most famous person who bore it was born in A.D. 571 at Mecca. To him was revealed the word of Allah; and he reduced that word to the Koran. He died in A.D. 632, leaving behind a militant religion and a group of fanatic followers who used the Book and the Sword to conquer the earth.

Mohammed taught a new brotherhood—the Brotherhood of Islam. "Know ye that every Moslem is a brother to every other Moslem, and that ye are now one brotherhood. It is not legitimate for any of you, therefore, to appropriate unto himself anything that belongs to his brother unless it is willingly given him by that brother." Through this creed he fashioned a Pax Islamica that united the faithful and inspired them to mighty conquests.

In the decade or so after his death the little nation of Arabia conquered most of the then civilized world. Damascus fell after a six months' siege. The Byzantines were routed at Yarmuk, a tributary of the Jordan. Arabian armies pushed north to Turkey and into Armenia and Georgia. They moved east and conquered Iraq and Persia. By A.D. 643 the Arabs were on the borders of India. They swept south and west, taking Alexandria and then most of Egypt and sweeping along the coast of North Africa to Tripoli. By A.D. 711 they were in Spain. On the first centennial of Mohammed's death Islam had reached the zenith of its temporal power.

While that political empire lasted, a great civilization prospered under Islamic influence. Science, art and literature flowered. The political empire, however, lost its cohesiveness and unity after five centuries. The dynasties it established crumbled from within. Mon-

217

gol hordes attacked the empire on the east; Crusaders attacked it
on the west. The world of Islam shrank. Yet even so it left millions
of converts behind. Today one-eighth of the peoples of the earth
believe that the Koran is the embodiment of wisdom and truth.

Five times a day there is the call to worship:

> la ilaha illa—'llah:
> Mohammed rasulu—'llah
> No god but Allah: Mohammed
> is the messenger of Allah

Men from the Mediterranean to the Pacific, from Africa to Russia
then get on their knees, face Mecca, and offer prayers to Allah.

The brotherhood of Islam still persists. It is a brotherhood that
draws no line at color, race, or nationality. In that sense it is universal. Islam draws only one line—the line between the faithful and
the rest of mankind.

The Middle East is predominantly Moslem. In Persia and Iraq
about 95 per cent of the population is of the Islamic faith; in Syria
about 80 percent. Only in Lebanon are the Christians in a majority.
There they have a slim lead, perhaps 51 per cent.

The Arab village is governed by a council. Representation is along
religious lines. The religious vote is on the religious "party line." Thus
Lebanon is divided into religious districts, which means that when
delegates to the Parliament are chosen a Druze must be elected from
one area, a Moslem from one, a Maronite from another, and so on.

Religious differences cut deep from the Mediterranean to the
Pacific. The region is filled with records of religious wars, persecutions,
and massacres. Less than a century ago, eight thousand Christians
were massacred in Lebanon, eight thousand in Damascus. That
history injects a subtle influence in all community and political affairs;
it lurks in every dispute; it may whip up into a bloody affair between
a Bedouin goatherd and a Christian villager; it is an influence in international politics. It was only the other day that Moslem and
Hindu alike forgot Gandhi's teachings and fell on each other in
bloody slaughter. The religious factor was responsible for breaking
India in two and creating Pakistan.

32. *Hattin*

ONE OF the most effective speeches ever made in all history was delivered by Pope Urban II at Clermont in the fall of 1095. It was the summons of the faithful to a war against the infidels; it was a plea to save the Christians of Asia Minor, Syria, and Palestine from persecution. The plea of Urban II to the faithful was—"Enter you the road to the Holy Sepulcher, convert it from the wicked race, and subject it." It was a holy cause. "God wills it" was both the summons and the battle cry. The cross was the badge all wore. Jerusalem was the road of salvation.

And so in 1096 about 300,000 soldiers marched east, headed over-land for Jerusalem. Finally the Crusaders stood before it, praying, "O, Sepulcher, help us." They marched around the city, blowing their trumpets, as Joshua had done at Jericho. But the walls did not fall. Then started a month's siege. On July 15, 1099 under the blows of the broad sword and battering rams, Jerusalem fell. "God wills it." The Sepulcher was in the hands of the faithful. The Cross on which Christ was crucified was the standard carried into battle, as the remaining citadels of the Moslems along the Phoenician coast were subdued.

From 1099 to 1187 Jerusalem was held by a series of Crusader kings, who built and maintained great commercial and financial empires in the region and fastened a heavy yoke of political and social feudalism on the country. The Crusaders in their daily lives set no noble Christian example for the Arabs. Moreover, the military hold they had on the region was tenuous; actually what they held were citadels and provinces scattered like islands through a vast region. An Arab leadership watched them closely—and waited. This was a leadership driven by a religious fanaticism. With them the jihad (holy war) was a duty.

In preparation for my first trip to the Middle East I had reread the history of the Crusades and learned how much the Crusaders took from the culture of the East—and how little they contributed. My reading had made the Crusaders more real to me and less romantic than they had seemed to be in my youth. Their reality became even more vivid as I saw their castles and crosses in Lebanon and Israel and their handiwork at the Church of the Holy Sepulcher in Jerusalem. But it was a strange coincidence that made me feel on intimate terms with them.

In July, 1949, my son Bill and I were traveling down the Jordan Valley by car with Colonel Yochana Ratner of the Israeli Army, an able, middle-aged architect turned soldier in the cause of Zionism. We were approaching the Sea of Galilee (Gennesaret). In the days of Christ the region about the Sea of Galilee was heavily wooded —oaks on the ridges; olives, sycamores, grapes, figs, walnuts on the slopes; palm trees at the lakeside which is about seven hundred feet below sea level. Today the hills around the Sea of Galilee are mostly bare. Only oaks, carob trees, plane trees, and oleanders in the ravines are clues to the thick forests that once covered these slopes. But about the only vegetation I saw this July day were thistles—dry stalks about waist high.

We first saw the Sea of Galilee from a distance. Hermon's snowy head looked down on us from the north. Below us to the south was the deep blue water, shimmering in the haze that overhung the hot land of Galilee that afternoon. The lake is about thirteen miles long and eight miles wide, a broad and deep expanse of the Jordan that flows in on the north and out on the south to its sepulcher in the Dead Sea. When we reached the lake, we stopped to sit in the shade of a clump of willows that grew near the water. An east wind was blowing; white caps showed on the water; a modest surf pounded at my feet. The gravelly shores were covered with smooth pebbles. Many were colored—some flat, some round. They were the pebbles that were here when Christ walked these shores. I pocketed a few for a Sunday-school class back home.

We had not passed very far on the west side of the lake when the source of the haze which overhung the valley became evident. A raging fire was racing up a valley that pours into the lake.

"Thistles," said Colonel Ratner. And after a pause he asked, "The thistle fire is at Hattin. Do you recall Hattin?"

I shook my head. He stopped the car, pulled out a map of Palestine, rested it on the hood and fender of the car, and traced some lines for me.

"At Hattin Saladin defeated the Crusaders. Now do you remember?"

I still shook my head. So he went on to describe the battle. It took place July 3 and 4, 1187.

Saladin, a Kurd, led the Arabs. He was probably the greatest of all Arab military leaders. He was also more than a general; he was a statesman of character and stature—one of the great men of all time.

At the beginning of the battle of Hattin Saladin seemed to be in a disadvantageous position. His back was to the Sea of Galilee. The Crusaders, under the command of Guy, King of Jerusalem, Raymond of Galilee, and Reginald of Kerak, for a reason not explicable left their camp near Tiberias, where they had good supplies of sweet water, and moved out to the heights of Hattin where they had neither water nor shade. The Christian soldiers were blistering hot under their armor; and the heat became unendurable when they ran out of water. Saladin capitalized on their predicament, giving them no surcease from attack during the long, grueling night of the first day of the battle. Then with an east wind blowing at his back Saladin set fire to the thistles. The fire roared up the heights, roasting and suffocating the Crusaders. The Cross was soon lowered by the Moslem horde. The Crusaders—parched, bleary-eyed, scorched, singed, and burned—were decisively beaten. The Moslem battle cry, "God is most great," "There is no other god but God" came in exultant shouts from the heights of Hattin.

Seven hundred sixty-two years later—almost to the day—my son Bill and I saw a raging inferno, fed by thistles, once more sweep up Hattin. As I stood there watching the billowing smoke from a fire that raced faster than a man could run, the Crusaders became real men to me. I was with them and Saladin and relived for a moment the drama of Hattin.

Jerusalem was the real prize won at Hattin. Saladin went on to take the Holy City. It fell on October 2, 1197 and Saladin tore down the Cross that stood on the Dome of the Rock. Where the Crusaders had shown cruelty, Saladin showed mercy. In 1099 the Crusaders had marched into Jerusalem killing every infidel they could lay their hands on. When Saladin took Jerusalem, he asked a large ransom for the lives of the Christian inhabitants, but he released free of charge all old people; and he also left unharmed people too poor to pay. For his philosophy, as spoken to his son, ran as follows: "Do the will of God, for that is the way of peace. Beware of bloodshed; trust not in that, for blood never sleeps."

Then came Richard the Lion Hearted to reclaim Jerusalem. He landed 250,000 on the shores of Palestine. No warrior was ever braver. Richard's prowess on the field of battle filled the Arabs with terror. Near the end of the battle of Jaffa Richard rode out in front of the whole Moslem army, his lance uplifted. He trotted up and down, taunting the Moslem hosts, challenging any one of them, any ten of them, any hundred of them to come out and fight him. But so great was his reputation that none dared move against him.

Yet in spite of Richard's victories along the shores, his troops never even saw the walls of Jerusalem. Richard was opposed by Saladin, who was too great a commander and leader to be undone by bravery alone.

One day in 1192 when Richard was storming the plains below Jerusalem he sent word to Saladin, demanding the surrender of Jerusalem. Saladin's historic reply soon came:

"Jerusalem is as much to us as it is to you, and has more value in our eyes—for it was the place of the Prophet's night journey to Heaven and will provide the place of assembly for our people at the Judgment Day. Do not think that we will give it up to you. The land was ours in the first place, and it is you who have come to attack it."

The conflict that Richard the Lion Hearted and Saladin did not resolve in 1192 lives on. It is as sharp today as it was then. It is generated by forces deep in the emotions of men. Those forces cannot be crushed. They survive the victories of armies and the raging fires of thistles.

33. *Josef and Fouda*

DAMASCUS IS an oasis. It is surrounded by bleak and dreary foot-hills on the north and west and on the east by a barren wasteland that stretches five hundred miles to Baghdad. In between lies a lush, circular garden thirty miles wide. The oasis yields annually thousands of tons of apricots, wheat, barley, vegetables, and grapes and thousands of pounds of walnuts, hemp, apples, and other fruit. The surrounding country, though dry and barren and showing only camel thorn and licorice root in the summer, is a rash of colorful wild flowers and green grasses in the spring. Anemones, poppies, iris, and the purple-headed onopordons give streaks of color even to the desertic steppe on the east. But by July all the land surrounding the oasis is brown. A dry, stinging heat has seared and baked the ground, sapping the strength from every bit of stubble that the Bedouins leave behind.

For centuries the Bedouins have roamed the desertic steppe to the east of Damascus with camels or sheep. Both the sheep men and the camel men are called Bedouins; but a Bedouin in the strict sense is a camel-breeding nomad and a member of one of a dozen tribes.

Nomadism is a necessity in this barren land. Wells or springs are few and far between. The grazing is so sparse that one must keep on the move. The winters are cold, the summers hot. One moves north to the hills in summer and south to valleys in the winter.

A Bedouin seldom runs caravans for the transportation of goods. He is a breeder of animals—principally camels, but sheep, goats, and horses as well—which he sells in the markets. To the Bedouin, manual labor—on farms or in town—has been an ignominy. To call him a worker or fellah was to insult him. In recent years, however, the pinch of circumstances has changed that attitude. It has driven many of the poorest Bedouins into work for hire.

The Bedouins in modern days are poor folks. The wealthiest sheikh these days probably has an income of no more than one hundred dollars a month; the poorest Bedouin has perhaps three dollars a month. He lives almost entirely on flour, rice, and dates. When grazing is good he will have milk and cheese from his goats and sheep. He will have a sack of wool and some butter to exchange on the market for coffee, olive oil, sugar, and perhaps tea.

Yet this man—poor and on the edge of starvation—has the attitude and philosophy of an aristocrat. By his standards there are two occupations fit for free men—hunting and warfare.

There is considerable game in the desertic steppe east of Damascus —gazelles (fleet animals weighing around forty pounds with legs as small as dogs'), hares, black partridge, sand grouse, and a small species of the famous bustard. The Bedouin hunts chiefly with hawks and greyhounds. But his main preoccupation has always been war and raiding. He was a mercenary who would hire out to any ruler. He might forsake one ruler for another who paid a higher fee, but if he did so he had no traitorous intent; it was like a man in this country shopping around for a better job.

The Bedouin liked it best when central authority was weak. Then he could make the raiding of adjoining tribes his profession. It was a sport in which there was honor and excitement. The Bedouin entered it with fanaticism. There was always the prospect of untold wealth in flocks of camels, goats, and sheep. There were long night marches across the desert and the attacks at dawn. There was the strategy of smaller raids—waiting until a herd was far from camp and then driving it off before an alarm could reach the owner; or stealthily entering a camp in dead of night and running off a few horses or camels.

If the venture was successful, the raiders became wealthy overnight. If they were apprehended and failed, the consequences were not apt to be serious. If they survived the fighting and were captured, the chances were that the intended victims would then tender them a dinner, give them quarters where they could rest, and supply them with food for their return journey across the hot desert. Such is the chivalry of raiding. Raiding persists to a degree to this day, though it is on the decline.

Formerly the Bedouins were the sole masters of the desert. They alone had riding camels that could melt into the desert and travel days without water. The Bedouins alone knew every acre of the desert: the water holes, the wadis, the places where men and herds could hide. A man on horseback could not follow them many miles into this waterless wasteland. Hence the Bedouins were in command of the vast desert area, and collected tribute from travelers and from those who lived along the edge of the steppe, promising safety of passage and immunity from raiding.

That monopoly of the Bedouins has been practically broken. Motorcars manned by high-powered rifles have put even raiding parties moving on fast camels within reach. The patrol cars have been particularly successful when manned by Bedouins, and Bedouins have been increasingly available for those jobs. The economics of the desert has made work for the army and the police very attractive.

But the bulk of the Bedouins are today as they were centuries ago. They are on the move—free men owing allegiance only to their own tribe. They move as silently as the dawn; when the sun rises their night encampment is empty with no trace of their departure.

At night one will see lights on the desert hundreds of miles from nowhere. The lights are from small fires built of camel chips, marking a Bedouin encampment. Here these camel men sit far into the night sipping their slightly bitter coffee from small cups. Around these fires plans for new raids are laid and the history of old ones retold. Much of the telling is in the recitation of poetry, for the Bedouins, though largely illiterate, have their poets and venerate them.

I have been among the Bedouins and learned something of their hospitality. Generosity may well be at its best among the desperately poor. In India I saw people on the edge of subsistence make such generous division of their meager food with a guest that they would go without for days. The same is true of the Bedouins. One of these nomads may own but one goat or sheep and be wholly dependent on it for milk and cheese. Yet for a guest—a casual guest who comes as a stranger—he will kill it and prepare a feast. This is a hearty hospitality—a hospitality with abandon. The Bedouin also has other extremes of character. He is a cruel and ruthless person when it comes to killing. If he has his enemy in his grasp, he can sit on the man's chest and cut his throat out as easily as a New Englander can shuck an oyster—and with the same unconcern.

One evening in late August I returned to Damascus from a visit to some Bedouin encampments in the desert. The smell of the camels was on these people, for there is little water for bathing in the desert. It was still in my nostrils as I found the black asphalt highway that runs to the edge of this wasteland. It was dusk when I reached the outskirts of town. Here are large fields of grapes, each patch being marked by platforms on stilts—platforms that hold tiny thatched houses. These are lookouts where watchers stay night and day when harvest is near to protect the crop against the Bedouins. As I passed, many farmers were climbing crude ladders to these platforms to start the night's vigil.

I drove through the city and north along the highway that leads over the Lebanon Mountains to Beirut. I was headed for a tea house on the Barada.

The rivers Barada (formerly called the Abana) and Pharpar are the life of Damascus. Damascus—founded by the grandson of Shem and by many thought to be the Garden of Eden—has had staying qualities that other cities lacked. Damascus was old when Rome was young. David captured Damascus; so did Alexander and Pompey. Wave after wave of the invaders swept over it and around it. They sacked and burned it and yet left it strangely untouched. Palmyra— two days' ride east of Damascus—was the home of Queen Zenobia. It was indeed a capital of splendor. Today it is a ghost. Baalbek— across the Anti-Lebanon Mountains—was built when Damascus was teeming with life. Damascus lives on, while Baalbek is lost in the mists of history.

The staying qualities of Damascus have come from its two rivers.

Long, long ago in the days of Elisha, Naaman was the King of Syria. Like the present-day rulers Naaman lived in Damascus. He was a leper who came to Elisha for a cure. Elisha said, "Go and wash in Jordan seven times, and thy flesh shall come again to thee, and thou shalt be clean." (II Kings 5:10.)

Naaman eventually followed that advice and was cured. But his initial reaction was one of anger. He said, "Are not Abana and Pharpar, rivers of Damascus, better than all the waters of Israel? may I not wash in them, and be clean?" (II Kings 5:12.)

The Barada boils out of the limestone of the Anti-Lebanon Mountains about fifty miles north and west of Damascus. Its water is clear and cold and carried by gravity flow through a system of canals into every house and garden of Damascus. In its lower reaches it is lined with cafes which hang on its edges under groves of willow and poplar. At one of these I stopped.

A cool wind swept down the valley. My table was at the water's edge. The babel of tongues from adjoining tables where a few men smoked water pipes was drowned in the roar of the river. I was roused from my thoughts by a tall, dark young man standing by my side. He spoke English, and asked if I would permit him to join me.

He was an Arab and his name was Josef. He was in his twenties—thin, athletic-looking. His black hair was curly and combed straight back. His brown eyes had a troubled look and the thin line that marked his lips seemed grim and determined. I asked him why he seemed so downcast. He hesitated before replying and then said, "I have no one I can tell my problem to. You are a Christian. May I talk it out with you?"

Then came Josef's story. He, like about 12 per cent of Syria's three and a half million people, was a Christian. Josef—a Russian Orthodox—was in love with Fouda, a Bedouin girl about nineteen years old.

Bedouins are Moslems, but they have modified the standards set for Moslem women. The custom of the veil is not closely followed. In a Bedouin camp the women share in the entertainment of visitors, and enjoy a social freedom denied most other Moslem women.

But as Josef learned, there are other Moslem practices which limit their freedom. As Josef described Fouda to me my memories of Bedouin girls came flooding back—beautiful, untamed creatures, with no mark of convention on them; wild in the sense that a doe is wild. Barefooted, wearing ragged skirts full and flowing and a red and white kerchief on the head. Eyes filled half with fear and half with eagerness for friendship. Fouda was such a girl. Josef had first seen her when her father brought sheep out of the desert to graze above Damascus, crossing the highway not far from this cafe. When Josef stopped to stare, she ran like a gazelle and joined her father.

Her face haunted Josef. He returned day after day, searching the slopes of the foothills for her. One evening he was rewarded. Fouda was carrying water from the river. They met in a grove of poplars. Thereafter they had several hurried, secret meetings that were fleeting seconds for Josef, who knew now that he was desperately in love. Finally one night, while a southern moon rode high over Mount Hermon, Josef took Fouda in his arms. It was early morning when Fouda crept back to her family's encampment. It was a week or more later when they met again in the grove. Now she had bad news—heartbreaking news for Josef. She could not marry him. She had discussed the matter with her mother, who had talked with a mullah in Damascus. The decision was clear. Marriage with Josef was out of the question. Fouda was a Moslem; Josef a Christian. If Fouda married Josef, it would be the duty of her father or brother to kill her. That was the law of Islam. "Nor marry [your girls] to unbelievers until they believe." On marriage a woman took the religion of her husband. Fouda would in Moslem eyes become a Christian if she married Josef. There was only one way to avoid the calamity. Would Josef become a Moslem? If so, all would be well.

Josef's uncle had been a priest in the Russian Orthodox church. Josef's father and mother were devout, religious people. They had been raised in Damascus, where they were always a religious minority, in an environment that bred doubt and suspicion concerning the designs of the Moslems. The Moslems were men whose swords were part of their religion. All who were not of their faith were infidels against whom the sword might be used in a holy cause.

Here in Damascus eight thousand Christians had been massacred less than a century ago. Josef's father and mother had never forgotten that massacre. That was a holy war or jihad. There had been no jihad since 1914, and that a failure, but Josef's father feared the jihad might be used again any day or night.

Josef himself shared these fears. They had indeed been inculcated in him since childhood. The idea of becoming a Moslem would never have occurred to him even in a fantasy. The religion was an alien one; its philosophy seemed to him raw and vulgar. Its creed violated his Christian sensibilities. It was crass and crude, a handmaiden of force and violence. At least that was his belief. He had spent the torture of sleepless nights thinking about it ever since

Fouda had given him the conditions of their marriage. His opinion remained the same; he could not embrace the alien religion with true fervor; his heart would never be in it. Yet love of Fouda was the most important thing in his life. He would join the Moslem faith as a matter of form; he would sacrifice his scruples for love.

These things he first talked over with Fouda; then he steeled himself and broached the subject to his father. Josef had difficulty in describing the scene to me. It was as if he had dealt his father a mortal blow. The news shocked the old man so deeply that he suffered a stroke. Josef, heavy of heart, brought the word to Fouda. They sat in the poplar grove discussing their fate while another southern moon rode a high arc above the Anti-Lebanons. Fouda broke a long silence with the words, "Josef, you must not hurt your father more. I will become a Christian."

"But you will be killed?"

"We will flee."

"Where can we go? Before we could get a passport the terror of the Bedouins would be on us."

While Josef talked, I munched the large, sweet pistachio nuts that flourish in the Middle East. Now the waiter brought green English walnuts cracked and ready to eat except for the thin skin that covers the meat. It had been ninety degrees in the sun that day; now the temperature was under sixty degrees. A chill wind swept down the Barada, whipping the willow trees that line its banks and swinging the overhead cord of electric lights to make weird shadows dance across the garden where we sat.

Josef, too wrought up to eat, toyed with the nuts. His face revealed the torture of the decision that plagued his mind. There was a silence of perhaps five minutes. At last he lifted his eyes. They had an imploring look that asked for release from agonizing indecision.

"You are a stranger," he said. "But you are a Christian. You have understanding, I think. Tell me, what should I do?"

34. "Thy Faith Hath Made Thee Whole"

ONE DAY in and near Damascus I had some experiences that caused the memory of a host of Sunday-school lessons to tumble through my mind in colorful and dramatic fashion. I had gone down to visit the bazaars, which like most markets of the Middle East are under covered streets and composed of numerous stalls packed close together. There are sections for goldsmiths, silversmiths, coppersmiths, candymakers, shoemakers, textile workers, woodworkers, and the like.

These bazaars have a strange fascination for me. There are the mixed smells of spices, candy, nuts, fruit, tobacco, and leather, the cries of the stall holders, the sound of hammers striking metal, the hum of a thousand tongues, and people of many races dressed in colorful costumes who pour silently and endlessly through the dimly lighted ways. At frequent intervals along this covered street are doors which open on courts where the caravans or trucks are unloaded. The doors are heavy wooden affairs faced with metal and about fifteen feet high. In each door is a smaller door about three feet high. These small doors are designed for the passage of men and made small enough so that a camel cannot enter. They are the "eye of the needle." "It is easier for a camel to go through the eye of a needle, than for a rich man to enter into the kingdom of God." (Mark 10:25.)

The main thoroughfare of the bazaar which I visited in Damascus is a street famous in the Bible. It is "the street which is called Straight." (Acts 9:11.) Mark Twain said that that expression was the one facetious comment in the Bible. The street, about twenty feet in width, is far from straight. It wobbles in its course like any trail that a calf will make in a meadow.

This was the street that Paul had often walked. The story is told in Acts of how he came to Damascus with hatred in his heart, bent on ridding the city of the Christians he despised. But before he reached the city he was stricken; there was a great light and a voice which even the soldiers who were with Paul heard. Paul fell to the ground blinded, and when he arose his mission was different. He went on to Damascus—now, however, to convert more people to the doctrine of brotherly love.

But because of his past record, the Christians did not trust Paul, and plotted to kill him. He escaped at night, lowered in a basket over the wall of Damascus, and then hid among the rocks of the dreary plain that extends on the south until his pursuers gave up the chase.

The walls of the old Damascus still stand. We went out through the east gate and around the outside to the south gate, where Paul made his escape. I went inside the gate and examined the walls. They are massive things—about thirty feet thick and eighty feet high. They would be formidable even to modern artillery.

Then I stood across from the gate under shade of some poplar trees bordering a field of sorghum. This was a morning of such dazzling sunlight that the yellowish walls of old Damascus gave off heat waves. I stood for a moment lost in my thoughts of Paul.

His example I thought had meaning for democrats today—if we too will only keep the faith. We are filled with apprehension because the totalitarian world grows larger and larger while the democratic shrinks. The democratic countries where real freedom of thought and expression is known become indeed more and more like islands in a world of tyranny. Dictatorship, Russian style, promises to hold the great bulk of the people of the world in its grip. Because of this we are apt to take a counsel of despair.

There is no hope, we hear, to check this gargantuan growth of tyranny—no hope except through war. But Paul had been faced with a prospect even more dismal. There was then no spot on the globe offering any haven or refuge, comparable to what the democracies offer today. Paul had no friendly base of operations. In the days of Paul Judaism was a militant, missionary faith. It was sacrilegious to put the word of Christ against the law of Moses. Before his conversion Paul had been active in persecuting Christians. Now Paul was the persecuted. But he always maintained the initiative.

Under regimes that were hostile and suspicious he spread the faith throughout Asia Minor, Macedonia, and the islands of the Mediterranean. He was mobbed and flogged, driven from cities under threat of death, persecuted and jailed. Finally he was beheaded in Rome in the first of the Christian persecutions under Nero, shortly after he had written "I have fought a good fight, I have finished my course, I have kept the faith." (II Timothy 4:7.)

Elon Gilbert and I talked of these things. And as we turned to go these were the questions in our minds: Have we of the West lost our faith in everything but dollars and military might? Have we forgotten that the most powerful weapons are ideas? Why do we not preach the gospel of freedom and justice in the villages of Asia?

We went by car south and west of Damascus. The villages we saw often rested on the edge of beautiful olive or walnut orchards, but they themselves were usually miserable.

Squalor in the Middle East is like squalor in India. A fecal odor hangs over the village. Filth is fried daily under a burning sun. It cooks up into a permanent stench.

The reasons for this are not many. The outhouses are shallow affairs and often are forsaken for the yard or field. The drainage of waste water from the houses is in open canals. The canals get clogged and stopped up and the water stands for days in the open, an uncovered cesspool. Control of flies and other simple sanitary measures are not known or understood.

One summer will see fifteen generations of flies, carrying dysentery and typhoid. They cling like lice to people. We stopped at one village where I saw little children whose faces were matted with flies feeding on open sores. Older children had ringworms on their faces as big as saucers. There was no doctor near, no first-aid station where simple medicines could be obtained.

In village after village I saw the same sight; and as I went among these huts I got a new understanding of Christ at work in this area. I realized for the first time what Christ the Healer meant. To rise from any sickbed is a miracle. To rise from a sick bed surrounded by the squalor and stench of the Middle East without the aid of drugs or science is superhuman. I appreciated for the first time what hold Christ must have had on the ordinary people of this area. These disease-ridden folks had no doctors, no medicines, no hospitals; but He knew how to cure them. They saw Him make the afflicted whole with a word; and so they worshiped Him and flocked in multitudes after Him. His deeds were the talk of the nation. One day the host that followed Him was so great they had to let a sick man down through the roof because the doors were blocked. At Galilee the audience was so large He had to preach from a boat pushed out from the shore. It was Jesus the Healer whom they adored. No wonder there was a great commotion in a city when the word was passed, "They say that Jesus of Nazareth is come!" No wonder the ecclesiastical powers of that day trembled at the thought of Christ's great popularity. By their standards a man who had such a hold on people was a dangerous man, a subversive influence.

Though squalor is characteristic of most of the villages in this region, there are notable exceptions. Down in the Jordan Valley near Jericho is a model village newly built under the supervision of Musa Bey Alami.

The Jordan at this point is about thirteen hundred feet below sea level. In the summer the valley has the heat of our Death Valley in it. The limestone and basalt walls of Judea on the west and Moab on the east make an oven out of the gorge. Here the Jordan is a slow, muddy stream half as wide as a city street. The soil on either side looks as lifeless as sand. Jericho—on the west side of the river—is an unattractive village of clay and adobe huts, parched and dry in the intense heat. Below Jericho a few miles is the Dead Sea on whose shores stood Sodom and Gomorrah. The July day I was there it was a blue shimmering spot in a thick haze. It is tepid and so salty that when I washed in it, the water clung to my skin like scum. The Dead Sea—in fact the whole valley where Jericho is located— seemed to me a symbol of death and sterility.

Others have felt the same way about the spot: it was long maintained that this stretch of the Jordan was sterile. But Musa Bey Alami, looking for a way to take care of two thousand Arab refugees, proved the contrary. He dug four wells each one hundred feet deep and got pure, cold water. After washing the land several times he planted cypress, pine, bananas, and palms. They flourished. He found that eggplant and all the other vegetables would grow there. Hence he started his housing projects.

His fifty housing units have mud-brick walls and thatched roofs for coolness. The ceilings are high and the rooms have cross ventilation. The floors are concrete. Each house has a concrete sink, concrete drain boards, an indoor toilet, and a shower. The village has a school and a first-aid center. Musa Bey Alami conceived the project; the Arab refugees did all the work. A garden now blooms on the edge of the most desolate spot in creation—a garden that is clean, fresh, and healthy.

Kaber Essit and Babbila are ancient villages near Damascus that have gone through similar transformations through the efforts of the Near East Foundation, which has a highly successful agricultural experiment station in Damascus. Among its other projects it helped institute a marketing co-operative in these villages, and helped form the Arab equivalent of the Future Farmers of America. But I was particularly interested in the measures it has taken for public health and education.

Control of disease starts with control of sewage. These villages are equipped with modern pit latrines, nine feet or so deep, lined with rock, and covered with a concrete slab. The watchmen who are hired to guard the villages at night put disinfectants in the pits. The waste water from the houses that formerly gathered in open canals is now run off in ditches that are lined with concrete slabs and covered over.

The walls of every structure that men or beasts occupy are sprayed twice a year with DDT or BHC to keep down the flies.

The water supply comes from wells. Regular tests are made to ascertain if the water is pure. Shortly before my visit one well was found to be polluted and was closed.

In Babbila there is a school for women and girls. Though it gives the equivalent of five years in our grade schools, only three years are required to finish it, school being in session eleven months out of the year.

At Babbila there is also a midwife clinic and a first-aid clinic, as well as a delivery room and a laboratory. The day before I visited Babbila in September, 1950, fifty-two patients—mostly women— had gone through the clinic.

The moving spirit in this health project is Sanyieh Zafari—a middle-aged Arab woman. When war between Israel and the Arab countries began, she was a midwife practicing in Haifa. Then she came to Damascus, and was induced by the Near East Foundation to head up the work at Babbila.

She is a plump lady with a kind face and a ready smile, and showed her projects to us with pride. We went through the laboratories and the school, and into her model kitchen, where she served us Turkish coffee. The cupboard in her kitchen was screened, the shelves had paper or oil cloth. The furniture was simple and plain, everything was in order, and all was spic and span. She described the unsanitary kitchens in the typical Arab village. The Arab peasant wife seldom knows the rudiments of housework and of cleanliness, but now they come by the hundreds from miles around to see this model kitchen, and are fast duplicating it in their own homes.

In this region close to 50 per cent of the children die before they reach the age of one. Miss Zafari spoke feelingly of the fact that for over a year no infant had died in the villages she served. She praised the midwives who had come for training, and the mothers who were under her care.

As I walked through the village and talked with people, I learned that everyone loved and respected Miss Zafari. Her word was taken as the gospel. She is an outgoing person who gives her affection to the humblest. Day or night she will travel to remote places by bicycle to help a pregnant woman or a sick child. She is mother to thousands of people who respond like children to sympathy and affection.

On my way back to Damascus I talked about this unusual lady, the good work she is doing, the affection she commands. I mentioned to an Arab friend how rare it is to find such a servant of good will with both skill and understanding and a willingness to devote her life to a selfless end. He said that only an Arab can provide that leadership to the Arab people. Ideas can come from outside but their execution must be in Arab hands. Miss Zafari is not only an Arab; she is an Arab of technical competence and high idealism. But beyond that—and even more important to her effectiveness—she has made two pilgrimages to Mecca and Medina. In the Arab world she is known as a hadjie. Her word therefore carries great weight and her example becomes a powerful influence, even when it comes to persuading housewives to put screens on their cupboards.

35. Moslem Women

AFKA is the headwaters of the Valley of the Ibrahim of the Lebanon, the fabled River of Adonis that empties into the Mediterranean near the ancient city of Biblos, now known at Jbeil. Afka lies in an amphitheater ringed with limestone cliffs that rise one thousand feet or more on two sides. The river comes with a deep-throated roar from the base of one of the cliffs. Its waters are said to be the tears of Venus, shed over the death of Adonis, who met his fate while chasing a wild boar on this ridge.

The river runs red each year and discolors the Mediterranean at its mouth. Milton wrote that "smooth Adonis from his native rock ran purple to the sea." The discoloration is due to iron deposits, but legend says it is the blood of Adonis.

The place is rich in female symbolism. Long before the Romans, it was the seat of a sect worshiping Astarte, the Phoenician goddess. One cult that worshiped at this place made the prostitution of both sexes a sacred practice. The Romans erected a temple to Venus, which later became a Christian holy place, dedicated to the worship of the Virgin. Its ruins are still there.

It is a place of worship even to this day. Fig trees (sacred, to the Phoenicians) grow near the foundations of the old temple, where a cold spring boils from the ground, and hang wide over the river. The day I was there women had come to this shrine to pray; and as they left, they tied pieces of cloth to the branches of the fig trees—a votive offering for a sick child or for some other sorrow. There were dozens of bits of cloth on the trees, each representing a heartache, a hope, a supplication. Every flutter of the cloth renewed the prayer. This temple in ruins does not belong merely to ancient days. It is a living church.

We camped on the bench above the river under a walnut tree.

Next to us was a Moslem camp where two young couples, a half-dozen children and an elderly lady stayed. They were operating a small store for the benefit of the shepherds and goatherds who grazed the ridges, selling cheese, eggs, and wine.

Our arrival caused considerable curiosity; and Arabs gathered around to watch us make camp. The two young wives of the Moslems in the next camp stood together watching us. Their husbands squatted behind them over a charcoal fire, their backs to us. The ladies wore veils of coarse black cloth, and plain black dresses. Their feet were bare. Long black strands of hair loosely braided hung over their shoulders. They were engaged in animated conversation, but there was no flirtation in their demeanor. This was lively, feminine conversation over an exciting event.

We were the event; our fancy gasoline stove, mattresses filled with air, cameras, field glasses, sleeping bags, etc., were packed with curiosity. They pointed to one article and then another. Their eyes danced with merriment.

When they started to talk, only their eyes were visible, but as time passed their veils slowly dropped until in a few minutes their faces were bare.

Most of the women of this region have a queenly posture. It comes from carrying baskets, jugs, and boxes on their heads. These two young ladies under the walnut tree were stately. They were tall—perhaps five nine—their features finely chiseled, their teeth a beautiful white, their dark eyes warm and vivacious. The two looked so much alike they may have been twins.

They were, I am sure, quite unconscious of being unveiled. They were conscious of us only as moviegoers are conscious of the play unfolded on the screen.

Suddenly one of the husbands turned around. Seeing the women unveiled he shouted something in an angry voice, and both wives quickly covered their faces. They stood quietly for a few moments. Then in their interest they became once more forgetful; and as they talked the veils gradually dropped until in five minutes or so they again stood barefaced before us.

Then a forked tongue struck. The same husband who had given the previous warning turned and saw the women unveiled again. He was on his feet at once in a terrible fit of rage with an oath on his lips.

The curse in the Arab world has a touch of art to it. We in America get at an opponent through his womenfolk. So do the Arabs. Their curses run as follows:

A curse on your house.

A curse on your religion.

A curse on your sister's religion.

A curse on your sister's sister's religion.

The oaths grow increasingly insulting in that order.

Which one the husband used I do not know. It was probably the first; and being directed at his wife, it meant that he hoped her family was cursed. His face was livid; he lunged at his wife with closed fist, hit her on the side of the face, and knocked her to the ground. Then he stood over her, pouring out his denunciations in an angry torrent of words. He pointed with his finger to the hills and in a thundering voice gave a command.

The wife, who had been groveling at his feet, stood up, brushed off her clothes, took one small child in her arms and another by the hand, and went up the hill through a thin stand of oak and juniper, followed by the other woman and several small children. The one who had been struck looked furtively over her shoulder from time to time. Once she stopped and said something that was not audible. There was scorn on her face and the words she spoke were spit out. The husbands brought up the rear but were not in pursuit. No one was left under the sprawling walnut tree but the old lady. She was unveiled; and she smiled at me showing toothless gums, and went about the spot tidying up.

The couple of dozen Arabs who had gathered on the opposite side of our camp watched us until our supper was over. Then they melted away. By dusk there was no one in sight except the old woman and our own muleteers.

About dark the Arab who had knocked his wife to the ground reappeared. He had a few whispered words with the old lady and then approached me.

He smiled, placed his right hand over his heart, bowed before me, and delivered a short address. His actions were a mystery to me. Bill West, to whom I turned for enlightenment, chuckled and gave me the following explanation:

In this part of the world, among the Moslem peasants, a wife is property—pretty much like a donkey. She can be used and abused in the same way. There is no accounting to anyone, except public opinion, whatever damage may be suffered. A good Moslem wife is never unveiled before a man unless he is her father, husband, brother, or son. These women committed a grievous sin when they became unveiled before us, and their act reflected on their husbands. Husbands are supposed to train their wives better.

"What will you think of *him* when his wife is so loose with her moral conduct?" asked Bill. "You will doubtless rate him as a second-rate husband."

"Doesn't he realize that I think he's a louse for knocking the good woman down?"

"Certainly not."

What the husband was doing was apologizing for his wife's conduct. He was also stating that he hoped I would not think too badly of him for what she had done. He hoped I would forget her transgressions and accept him as a friend. This was my rude introduction to the problem of the women of the Moslem world.

Most Moslem women live in an environment of insecurity. That insecurity stems from the philosophy of the Koran that "Men shall have the pre-eminence above women, because of those advantages wherein God hath caused the one of them to excel the other and for that which they expend of their substance in maintaining their wives." In the Moslem view that pre-eminence of men rests on their superior understanding; their greater strength; their preferment for the offices of church and state; and their role as warriors for propagation of the Moslem faith.

The Koran commands obedience of the wife to the husband. It allows husbands to beat their wives. "But those, whose perverseness ye shall be apprehensive of, rebuke; and remove them into separate apartments, and chastise them."

The Koran allows a man to have four lawful wives. Some sects, as I have said, permit any number of contract wives in addition to the four legal ones. A contract marriage is subject to the approval of the priest, the term of contract being specified, as is the amount of money or property which the woman gets. If children are born during the term of the contract they are lawful heirs. At the end of the contract, the wife goes her way. The contract may not be renewed. The children stay in the home of the father.

The husband can have as many concubines as he wants or can

afford. There are markets in Mecca where this can be arranged—where merchants try to please their customers by providing girls that meet the most fastidious taste.

Under Moslem law a wife cannot get a divorce for any reason. On the other hand a husband can get a divorce any time he wants one and for any reason he may advance. The Koran speaks of maintenance for a divorced wife "on a reasonable scale," but the law in the Arab world provides alimony for only four months, to make sure the wife is not pregnant. After that, the duty to support ends. The length of time children must be supported is also greatly curtailed by law. Thus in Iraq it extends until boys are seven and girls are nine.

The divorced wife gets the children only as a matter of grace; the husband has the right to keep them if he desires. The short of it is that on a divorce the woman goes empty-handed, retaining only the money or property that the marriage contract provided. In every marriage arrangement there is a provision for dower—the transfer of property from the husband to the wife—as the Koran admonishes the man to seek a woman in marriage "with gifts from your property."

The Koran also commands that women "restrain their eyes, and preserve their modesty, and discover not their ornaments except what necessarily appeareth thereof." Women are to live in a retiring manner; no jewels, no make-up, no attractive clothes are to be worn. The Koran indeed says, "Let them throw their veils over their bosoms," taking care to cover their heads, necks, and breasts. They are directed not to show their ornaments except to their menfolk or other women.

Women do not vote. They are not qualified for office. Under Moslem law women inherit property as men do, but the share of the man is double the share of the woman.

There are of course happy marriages in the Moslem world—perhaps as many as elsewhere. Polygamy has greatly declined. Women are expensive, and the economics of the Middle East has driven more and more men to monogamy. Even Abdullah, the late King of Trans-Jordan, had only three wives.

But the inferior position of women in the Moslem world makes a profound impression on one who, accustomed to the sex equality which we know, walks the streets of the Middle East, frequents its restaurants and hotels, and is entertained in its drawing rooms. In every public place the women are shy and furtive, drawing their veils tightly over their faces and usually showing only one eye. One becomes accustomed to that. But it was much more difficult to get used to the total absence of women at the social functions.

Every lunch, every tea, every reception, every dinner is a stag affair. There is no woman to greet you; the wife of the host is not to be seen. Once in a while the eye will catch a slight movement of a shutter or screen where a woman has been watching. Women will of course be in the kitchen, cooking the meal; in the dining room, setting the table; in the sleeping quarters, making the beds. But they are discreetly absent—unseen and unheard—during all of the social activities. I recall a stay at the home of a prominent official. I was unaccustomed to the house and mistook the dining-room door for the door to the suite which had been assigned to me. As I entered, pandemonium broke loose. Women of the household, their faces uncovered, were setting the table for dinner. When they saw me, they were seized with fright and ran from the room like does in a panic.

The stag party usually lacks the grace and charm that feminine company contributes. There is not the same thoughtfulness, the same attention to the guest's comfort as when the lady of the house is the hostess. The talk is apt to be neither so profound nor so frivolous and gay. Women, with their keener perception of the atmosphere of a room, their greater awareness of the mood of a group, their more discriminating taste, give a balance to a social occasion which a stag party customarily lacks. The atmosphere of hospitality they create is more intimate and personal.

When one is a guest in a home it goes without notice if the lady of the house does not turn up for breakfast. But when for days on end one never sees, let alone meets, the womenfolk, the home acquires an emptiness.

Some of the well-to-do people and the professional classes are breaking with custom. Their womenfolk appear at social functions even outside the home, unveiled and bejeweled. I remember a garden party in Isfahan, Persia, on a clear August night when a full moon rode high in the west over the Bakhtiari country. Among the eighty people present were many beautiful women, both Moslem and Christian. But the Moslem ladies all sat together in one corner of the garden. No one was introduced to them. None of them danced. I inquired if it would be proper for me to invite the hostess—wife of a Moslem—to dance. There was a whispered conference on protocol and word came back, "No, it's not done."

My dinner partner was a Moslem lady, a beautiful creature in her twenties with long, black silken hair, lovely skin, deep brown eyes, and long black eyelashes. The dinner took an hour, but not once did she look up from her plate. I kept up a running conversation, plying her with questions, and she answered each one politely with a yes or a no where possible. But not once did she take a thread of the conversation and weave it into a thought of her own. Not once did she look at me. And when the meal was over she quickly left without a word and returned to the protective corner where the other ladies of the Moslem faith sat.

This attitude of Moslem women has at times rather serious practical aspects. One of the pressing problems of the Middle East is health. Hospitals and first-aid clinics are as essential as doctors. But hospitals require nurses; and women who must keep their necks and faces covered and who must not look upon a man outside their family obviously cannot do the work of a nurse.

The problem of nurses is not as serious in Persia as in other parts of the Moslem world. I visited a nurses' training school at Shiraz where traditions are fast being broken; many young women are available for the course. But the Persians, who were converted to the Moslem faith at the point of the sword of Islam, have not taken the Word in all its rigors. In Iraq the conditions are quite different. I visited a hospital at Basra (which is near the Persian Gulf) and learned from the chief medical officer—an Arab of distinction—some of the difficulties of getting women for nurses. There are a few; but the majority of the nurses are males. Thus the Arab world, which was the first in history to have hospitals, which centuries ago brought traveling health clinics to rural areas, which introduced scientific medicine to Europe, now lags far behind. The religion which gave it the unifying, driving power to conquer the world now hampers it in solving its major problem of public health.

I mentioned earlier that when I was a house guest of Kemal Djumblatt in Lebanon, his mother, Nazira, appeared for a tea. Except that the Druzes do not sanction polygamy, Druze women have as inferior a social position as Moslem women. Hence Nazira's presence at the party was a break from tradition. She acted bravely. Villagers from miles around were there for the reception, and villagers have strict notions about women; they adhere steadfastly to precedent. The tea went off nicely, however, in spite of my hostess's defiance of custom. But she showed restraint. She never let her veil drop clear of her face.

As the party broke up Nazira walked to the front porch to bid some of the people good-by. I asked her to stand facing the sun so I could take her picture. She said, "The picture of me that you can have is the picture you will carry in your heart."

"I will always carry your picture in my heart," I replied. "But I also want one to carry in my pocket."

She laughed, shook her head, and went into the house. Later she took me aside and whispered, "If I had let you take my picture, every villager here would have used it against me. Overnight I would have the reputation of being a loose woman."

She must have noticed the amazed look on my face for she added, "It's the men. They have old-fashioned ideas about us. They want us neither seen nor heard."

It is difficult for an outlander to talk to a Moslem woman; it is especially difficult to get her to talk about the Moslem customs that keep her in serfdom. But I finally persuaded a few to talk; and the outpourings were so moving that I believe I found the truth.

Moslem women do not wear the veil of their own accord. It is not, as some suppose, anything like the American woman's custom of wearing hats. The veil is the product of pressure by the husband and of discipline by the clergy. Her position of inferiority is impressed on the girl from the time she is in the cradle. The example of all the womenfolk, the quick scoldings of the mother, the admonitions of the holy man, all combine to condition the girl when she is still a child. By the time she has grown to womanhood, she has fixed patterns of conduct. To deviate from them is not only grievous error; it is outright sin.

I visited a rug factory in Isfahan, Persia, where beautiful Persian rugs were being made by little girls, some six years old, sitting on scaffolds and tying knots in the warp and woof of the rug hanging in front of them. Their tiny fingers worked like machine-driven shuttles. Each wore a veil; but since they were alone, they had let the veils drop free of their faces. When they saw me, fright came to their eyes; they instantly covered their faces and held the veils in their teeth as they bent with renewed vigor to their work.

I told this story to May Djumblatt, the charming Druze lady who is breaking with tradition. She nodded with understanding and then said, "These Moslem and Druze women of ours are frightened, timid souls. A terrible sense of sin hangs over all of us whenever we try to be free."

She discussed what Reza Shah had done in Persia, defying the clergy and ordering the police to tear the veils from the women on the street.

"That's the only way it can be done," she declared. "We are too frightened, too timid to do it on our own. Force must be used."

She went on to emphasize how deep-seated this timidity was; it would take several generations for Moslem women to overcome their fear, she thought, even if heroic measures were used. She illustrated her point with the Persian example. Reza Shah had torn the veils from the women—but when Reza Shah passed from the scene, the Moslem women under the pressure of custom and the church resumed their ancient ways.

We talked about the place of women in the world of affairs; the desirability of granting them the right to vote and so on. But she was not optimistic. "The poor, miserable, frightened dears must first learn to face the world unafraid. That will be the first step."

She spoke of the plank in her husband's Progressive Socialist party platform which gives equal rights to women. (Under the new Syrian Constitution women are given the right to vote and some of them are exercising the franchise.) "But it is very difficult to get women into political work. Their menfolk frown at any such doings. Women are to remain behind the scenes to rear babies, cook, and keep house."

I expressed surprise that both Moslem and Druze women were not thrilled at the proposal of equal rights. There was a wry smile on her face as she answered. "They want to be. But they're too frightened to be openly thrilled." She went on to describe the difficulties of getting Arab women active in any community or political affairs. "Listen," she said, "I have worked days on end, talking with our women. I say, 'Look, I'm free! I discarded the veil.' That's what I tell *them* to do. But there are very few who have the courage to take the step."

There was a mounting emotion in her voice as she spoke and there was fire in her eyes as she turned, "Why do men do this awful thing to us? Why do they keep us subjugated, filled with the terrible sense of inferiority?"

The Russians are too astute and wily to direct their propaganda against this treatment of women in the Moslem world. One can comb through all the Russian broadcasts and literature prepared for this area without finding a word that challenges or defies either the custom or the teachings of the Koran. The Soviets do not want a clash with the clergy (the mullahs). Their technique is much more subtle and their methods of attacking the problem are more indirect.

The Moslem woman, though socially and legally inferior in the Moslem scheme of things, exerts a powerful influence behind the scenes. When the French moved into Syria, she thought the new-comer would be her emancipator. And so she whispered to the menfolk, discouraging them from resisting. Perhaps the greatest political mistake the French made in Syria was to endorse the Moslem code and to support the system that held women in an inferior position. As a result, it was not long before the women were stirring the men to new resistance. But for British protection, the French forces might have been entirely wiped out in the last violent months of their occupation.

The Russians seem to appreciate the moral of that story.

There are thirty million Moslems in Russia, largely in Turkistan. Accurate reports of their conditions are hard to get. We do know that Russia has used terror to hold them in line. Genocide is part of the Soviet technique among its minorities. Dispersal of groups is another. In the case of Moslems the Soviets have practically barred pilgrimages to Mecca, allowing their Moslems no opportunity to effect a tie with the Brotherhood of Islam in the countries south of the border. But from sources that I deem reliable I have learned some of the things (apart from terror and other police practices) that the Soviets are doing inside Russia to wed their Moslem population to Soviet communism.

First. They have had a hand in selecting mullahs or priests sympathetic to the Soviet cause—priests who will preach conformance not rebellion.

Second. All but two million of the thirty million Moslems in

Russia have been settled on the land. Extensive desert areas have been brought under cultivation; and the economic lot of the Moslem population—what they wear and eat and the physical conditions under which they live—has been improved.

Third. More important perhaps than all the other measures has been the emancipation of the Moslem women. The Soviets have had a whole generation to work on the problem. The old folks cling to ancient habits. The new generation of women have a new freedom; they have been given recognition that Moslem women have never known. Veils are not worn. Women occupy posts of importance; all avenues of activity are open to them; there is no discrimination against them in education; their talents are given opportunities even in government. Their achievements are praised; even their pictures are carried in the Communist press and given much prominence. The Soviets publicize the number of women employed by the Communist party in its organizational and administrative work, the number who hold positions with trade unions, those who have become engineers, technicians, nurses and doctors, those who hold posts as deputies in government.

The Communist party in the Middle East, mostly underground, has branches for women. Women secretly spread the doctrine of equal rights and work clandestinely for the cause of feminism. The Tudeh party in Persia has many young women among its leaders. They are in fact the main pillars of its strength.

The recognition of women is a powerful factor in breaking the resistance of the thirty million Moslems inside Russia. The women like their new freedom. No amount of religious or other propaganda can induce them to surrender it and resume the lowly position which their faith reserved for them. As a result the Brotherhood of Islam no longer presents a completely united front to Soviet Communism.

36. *Sukhneh's Arab Refugees*

"PRAISE BE to God, the Lord of all creatures; the most merciful, the king of the day of judgment. Thee do we worship and of thee do we beg assistance. Direct us in the right way, in the way of those to whom thou hast been gracious; not of those against whom thou art incensed, nor of those who go astray."

This was the singsong chant in Arabic Bill and I heard coming from a group of peaked tents that dotted the barren plain at Sukhneh in Trans-Jordan. The tents were neatly arranged, forming a village about twelve blocks long and six wide. Flying high above this tent city was the flag of the International Red Cross. It marked the administrative headquarters (also in tents): admission office, hospital and first-aid clinics, living quarters for the doctors and nurses, kitchens, and, perhaps most important of all, a milk-distribution center.

This was an Arab refugee camp housing sixteen thousand people, of whom two thousand were children under the age of twelve. The cluster of tents nearest us formed the public school system.

The plateau on which the camp was located was rolling land without a tree or bush to relieve its monotony. There was scant vegetation, only a few straggling spears of dry grass. To the south a herd of camels under the management of a Bedouin searched the scorched earth for nibbles of nourishment. To the north a mile or so was a touch of green deep in a ravine—perhaps some willow trees. They marked an ancient spring of pure cold water that the Red Cross pumped up to the village. There was no other sign of greenness as far as the eye could see.

This plateau is a part of Moab, sometimes known as the Mount or Mountains of Abarim.

It was from Moab that Moses first saw the Promised Land. This is a land of scorpions and vipers—the region of the fiery serpents of Biblical fame (Numbers 21:6). Moab has little rainfall—from six to ten inches a year. The land is dry and parched in the summer. Here the Israelites had to dig for water as they sang, "Spring up, O well; sing ye unto it." (Numbers 21:17.) Here in the land of Moab at some unknown spot Moses lies buried (Deuteronomy 34:6).

The plateau around Sukhneh is typical of western Trans-Jordan. But, though barren to the eye, it is more productive than most of Trans-Jordan's land. For as the low hills roll east they become more and more desolate, joining the desertic steppe of Iraq far to the east and rolling into the sands of Saudi Arabia on the southeast.

A wind swept down from the northwest, whipping the tents and sending little whirlpools of dust dancing across the ground. It was a hot wind with the warmth of a furnace in its breath. Some of the flaps of the tents broke loose and made such a noise as almost to drown out the chant of the Arab prayer. Dust whirled into the tents and out again. But the chanting went on without interruption.

Karl Reiser, head of the Red Cross in Amman and our host, told us about the educational adventure which we saw in operation on the hot plateau of Sukhneh. It was inspired by the Arabs themselves. Among them were many educated people—doctors, lawyers, teachers, clergy and the like. They proposed that schools be established to absorb some of the energies of the restless group under twelve years old and to give direction to their lives. The Red Cross cooperated by furnishing the tents. Arabs volunteered to serve as teachers.

As is customary in the Moslem world, girls were taught separately from boys, but each was given in the main the same course of instruction. It started with the Koran. The prayer that we heard was from the first book. It came in soft female tones from the tent next to us; then we could hear it in a more robust male chorus across the way. Older girls were chanting it in a measured beat. Young lads five years of age were singing it in piping tones.

I stood at the door of one tent and listened to a class of boys recite. There were twenty of them, sitting at the feet of a young male instructor who held the attention of the class in spite of our intrusion.

"I have five apricots and I eat one. How many do I have left?"

Four fingers went up from each student except one, a tiny tot perhaps six years old, who showed five fingers.

We moved to another tent. Girls were having a spelling lesson.

"Mary, how do you spell Allah?"

"Elizabeth, how do you spell *anzih* [goat]?"

In another tent boys around the age of six were having a reading lesson. From a distance the pamphlet from which they were reading had a familiar look. I walked up to a lad seated on the floor and looked over his shoulder and had to smile at what I saw. He was reading the story of the "Three Little Pigs." He turned a few pages and there was an illustrated story of the "Three Bears."

In another tent we listened to boys reading a lesson from the Koran. One ten-year-old stood reciting. He read in a faltering unsure way but with dignity and seriousness: "Praise be unto God, who hath created the heavens and the earth, and hath ordained the darkness and the light."

In another tent, young girls seven and eight years old were being given sewing lessons. In still another older girls were writing—copying from the Koran. Across the way was a boys' class in history—a young instructor (without a history book) reciting some early chapters in Arab history.

As he spoke the dust swirled under his feet and blew into the faces of the youngsters seated before him on the ground. When we were outside, Karl Reiser spoke of the problem of the dust in this desolate place. He said it was particularly hard on the students when they were in their classroom-tents. The students and volunteer instructors had decided on a course of action: they would build brick walls three feet high around each tent to protect the classes from the dust. But such a project required money. Clay and straw would have to be brought in; forms would have to be made; some tools would be needed; and the help of brickmakers obtained.

There were brick-makers in the camp who contributed their services. The students raised the American equivalent of twenty-five dollars and, with the help of the Red Cross, the needed supplies were obtained. The day we were there bricks were being made. One tent had already been walled. An enthusiasm which was contagious had swept the school. This school in the wasteland—housed in tents with dirt floors, and located in an oven filled with dust from the wings of a torrid wind—had an *esprit de corps* which is often lacking in more luxurious surroundings. Building mud walls together had created a community attitude.

We inspected the kitchen where milk (made from a powder) was dispensed once a day. A pint for each child each day was the ration. The kitchen, tightly screened and open at the sides, was neat and clean. The line formed where a Red Cross worker ladled out the milk from a waist-high window.

The scourge of the Arab world, so far as small children and others who have not built up an immunity are concerned, is dysentery. Dysentery and undernourishment go hand in hand. In the Moslem world if there is not enough food to satisfy the hunger of the whole family, the boys and men are fed first, the girls and women last. It's a man's world; and every advantage from birth on through life is granted the male.

We saw at Sukhneh an example of this. In one of the hospital tents British nurses were giving intravenous injections to some babies less than a year old.

"What is the trouble?" I asked a slim, blue-eyed, blonde nurse.

"These are girls who were about to die from undernourishment and dysentery," she replied.

"Many cases like this in camp?"

"I've been here a month; and I would say we have saved the lives of at least two hundred little girls this way."

The cry of one little tot receiving the injection was so feeble that it seemed to come from the other world. The dark face of her tall, thin mother showed a complete absorption in the work of the nurse—so complete that her veil had dropped, disclosing her whole countenance. At first she was not aware of our presence. When she saw us, she quickly covered her face. But in that moment I had seen a face full of grief and suffering. It showed more than the deep concern any mother would have when the life of her child hung in balance; it mirrored the suffering of a woman in a world where the odds were against her at birth, where she bloomed and flourished early in life, and where under the burden of work and drudgery she faded early and was apt to be old by her middle thirties.

The ration for the Arabs in this camp was fifteen hundred calories daily. Most of it was consumed by the recipients. Some of it found its way into a black market that had sprung up in the camp.

I inquired through a native if I could get chocolate, powdered milk, coffee in that market.

"Come with me," he said, motioning with his head.

I did not accept his offer. Instead we toured the dusty streets and saw the life of the Arab camp. Women were carrying water from the central hydrant for cooking and washing. Men were lolling in the shade of the tents—some asleep, some in groups talking, others sitting in solitary meditation. I asked Karl Reiser what they did all day, how their morale was.

He said that inactivity in a camp rotted people—ate away at their inner core and made them bitter, or else robbed them of initiative and made them indolent and irresponsible.

"It hurts the fiber of a person—whether a prisoner in a war camp in England, a concentration camp in Germany, or a refugee camp in Trans-Jordan," he added. "One who has been behind a stockade for a year usually needs rehabilitation."

Many of these refugees wanted to be rid of Moab and Judea and find homes elsewhere—in Baghdad, Damascus, Beirut, or along the Tigris or Euphrates rivers. But the pull of Palestine was still strong. I had visited the Shaieba Refugee Camp located in another bit of wasteland out of Basra in southern Iraq where three thousand Arabs from Palestine were housed. The heat at Shaieba had a sticky, humid quality. From the camp I kept seeing vast expanses of blue water that beckoned from the south. They were mirages. So had been the expectations of the refugees for settling in Iraq. But when at last the Iraqi government offered them land, they refused. The call of Moab and Judea was still too strong to resist.

I sat in a tent at Sukhneh discussing these matters with the administrative staff. After the doctors and nurses joined the group, the talk turned to the psychosis that developed in people who are hemmed in by stockades.

It appeared that the problem in Trans-Jordan was not quite so acute as in other Arab countries. Abdullah had been liberal in granting the refugees in his country freedom to leave the camps and find employment—if they could. Some had been able to find outside work. But opportunities for employment in a society based predominantly on a Bedouin economy were quite limited. A young Arab doctor, graduate of American University at Beirut, who was on the medical staff at Sukhneh, spoke up:

"There is in each refugee camp a cross section of people in Palestine. There are peasants of the lowest economic class and professional and scientific people of the highest. There are doctors in a camp in Lebanon who are not allowed to minister to the sick in Beirut. There are engineers, pharmacists, architects, lawyers rotting away in this camp."

One of the Belgian nurses added that these people would all be sick people—sick emotionally and maladjusted—unless resettlement was effected quickly.

The young Arab doctor nodded assent and with a wry smile added, "Yes, and the only ones to gain are the Communists. They spread the poison of discontent, building in the minds of these people anger against every person or group or party in power. The Communists whisper that the enemies of the refugees—those responsible for their plight—are the Jews and America, Abdullah and England, Zayim and France, Wall Street and the Vatican."

After a pause he added, "This camp is like an infection. We run it as best we can. But no camp is healthy. Each breeds a virus that medicine cannot control or cure."

Back in Amman we saw Abdullah. The King was not well, a condition made worse by the fact that this was the month of Ramadan, the fast month when the Moslems neither eat, drink, nor smoke from dawn until dark. It was midday and blistering hot. Yet on short notice Abdullah received us, dressed in a white gown and turban.

He was a short man and slight, vivacious and lighthearted; and his eyes danced with merriment.

Turning to my son, Bill, he said through an interpreter, "I have a job for you."

Bill, greatly surprised, said, "A job? What is it?"

"It's a job here in the palace."

"What will I have to do?"

"Teach me English."

"What is the pay?"

"I'll pay you by teaching you Arabic."

"It's a deal," Bill replied. "But I want Saturdays and Sundays off."

Abdullah threw back his head and laughed. Then turning to me he said, "I like your son. Is he going to be a lawyer too?"

"I don't know," I replied. "I wish he would become a teacher."

"Of English?" he asked. And we both laughed.

Then the conversation got more serious.

Was there a chance for an early peace with Israel?

An armistice had just been signed, Abdullah said; and he hoped that a peace settlement could be worked out satisfactory to both sides.

And what about the Fertile Crescent—the project for uniting all the Arab countries from Egypt to Turkey in a grand federation? Abdullah a short while previously had made a bid to head such a league. Zayim, dictator of Syria, had replied scornfully.

Abdullah spoke lightly of Zayim—as if Zayim were a mere whippersnapper or smart aleck who had no possible claim to the loyalty of the Arab world.

The conversation wandered off into pleasantries; and we left shortly.

It had been cool and dark in the room where we had been received by the King. Outside it was dazzling bright and the sun touched the skin with a sting. As our car turned from the driveway into the highway I said to our interpreter, "The amazing thing about that interview with Abdullah is that there was not a word of bitterness against the Jews. Maybe there is a real chance of peace. Or was he merely putting on an act?"

We returned to the Philadelphia Hotel at Amman, where we were staying, and found Musa Bey Nasser waiting. He is a Palestinian Arab—bright, able, soft-spoken—who had recently been made Minister of Communications in Abdullah's cabinet. He spoke more feelingly than Abdullah about the Arab-Jewish issue. But reconciliation was his theme.

"We need the Jew and the Jew needs us. There is no reason why we should not have peace. But it must be peace based not on force but on a fair political settlement."

Wells Stabler, U.S. Chargé d'Affaires at Amman, invited us to his house for lunch. Amman, the original Philadelphia of the world, is a town of perhaps ten thousand located on both sides of a deep gulch. So far as I could see its mark of distinction was the ruins of a Roman amphitheater opposite the Philadelphia Hotel where we stayed. But Amman has also a warm spot in our hearts which came from Stabler's home. He lives on a height overlooking the city. Bare, rolling hills are on all sides with hardly a tree to break the bleakness and monotony of the countryside. It was blistering hot in the sun but cool in the shade of Stabler's porch.

A congenial group gathered there for lunch. Those I best remember, apart from Wells Stabler, were Karl Reiser of the Red Cross and Father William, Franciscan monk.

Francis of Assisi had gone with John of Brienne, King of Jerusalem, on the Crusade of 1218-1221. This was the first attempt to take Cairo, and it failed. But St. Francis, barefooted and hatless, appeared in the camp of the Sultan as an apostle of poverty and gentleness, as a missionary of peace. He walked unafraid through the unfriendly camp of the Arabs, and the Sultan ordered that he pass unharmed. The Franciscans have been in the Middle East most of the time since then.

Father William, short and roly-poly with dark thinning hair, is a lively conversationalist and wit. He set the tone of the luncheon. There was some serious talk—the vicissitudes of the Franciscans in Palestine; their educational work among all races of the region; the great numbers of martyrs (some fifteen hundred of them had been killed in seven centuries of service in the Middle East); the new school under construction at Amman, an institution of which Father William had charge. We could in fact see the new school on a hill above Stabler's home—a large white building still covered with scaffolds.

Then the conversation livened and hit a lighter level. Someone asked if we had met the favorite of Abdullah's three wives—a Sudanese.

Another whispered, "She runs the black market in Trans-Jordan."

"Don't whisper," Father William said, his round face beaming, "or the Douglases will think Stabler got this delicious wine through her."

After a pause, Father William, turning to Stabler, said, "You know, I think our friend Reiser here is becoming a very apt pupil."

"Of what?"

"Of the Arab world and its ways."

"And what in particular?"

"In particular, of the Bedouins," Father William replied with a twinkle in his eye. He went on to tell how in the first days of the Red Cross no one knew for sure who was an Arab refugee and who was not. Great numbers of people were drifting over the border.

Most were legitimate refugees; others were merely looking for a bread line. The problem of the Red Cross was to separate the one from the other.

"One day," Father William added, "a number of Bedouins came to Karl and asked that he go with them to the outskirts of Amman to enroll a group of Bedouin refugees on the Red Cross roll. Karl went. The first day he enrolled two hundred. The next day he enrolled three hundred. The next day he enrolled over five hundred. He came to me to ask if it were possible there were so many Bedouin refugees in this region. I suggested that there might be one hundred.

"So the next day Karl hired an Arab to mingle with the Bedouins and do some espionage work for him."

"With what results?" Stabler asked.

Father William was chuckling from his waist up as he said, "Karl found that the Bedouins who enrolled went off on their camels behind a hill about a mile distant, reorganized their group, and reappeared as new Bedouin refugees."

We roared with laughter. Then Father William added as he wiped his eyeglasses, "Some of those bunnies had registered twenty times under different names, while they looked Karl straight in the eye."

"Is this the truth?" I asked. "Or is it a bit of skullduggery magnified many times by good wine?"

"It's the whole truth," said Karl. "All a Bedouin with a mustache had to do the second time was to cover it with his kafiyeh. They'd appear with different women and children each turn around. A man with a donkey would ride a camel the next time, and so on."

"People are pretty much the same the world around," said Father William in a more serious vein. Turning to me he asked, "Are those reports of padded unemployment rolls emanating from Seattle any less bizarre than this account from Amman? Or was it Jersey City?"

37. *The Eternal City*

BILL AND I stood by the wall of Jerusalem at St. Stephen's gate and saw the sun rise above the Mount of Olives, where Christ was accustomed to go for the night when He taught during the day in the Temple at Jerusalem. At the bottom of the Mount of Olives is Gethsemane, the garden where He was wont to pray and where He was betrayed by Judas. Now as then it is an olive grove; and today the olive trees are relics of an ancient age. Their trunks are gnarled, twisted, and hollowed, and many times thicker than any I had seen. A Franciscan church is located in the garden; and one of its Fathers (whose name I never knew) spoke feelingly of the olives. This man, like the olive trees, was aged. I asked him how old he thought the trees were. Though he had doubtless been asked the same question a thousand times, he stood in reflection awhile and then reverently replied, "I have come to believe they were young trees when Christ first came here to pray."

We crossed the Valley of Judgment below us on the west. It seemed that each available plot of ground was already occupied by a grave. Tombstones are packed tight through the whole reach of the valley and on both slopes. It is an odd-looking cemetery. There is no expanse of trees, no green lawns to break the desolation of the spot. As we crossed the valley a funeral procession was coming down from the north, the participants on foot, strung out a block or more.

We entered the Old City of Jerusalem through St. Stephen's gate. In the days of the Old Testament it was known as the Sheep Gate, since it was through this gate that sheep were brought for the sacrifices in the Temple of Solomon. But it has been called St. Stephen's Gate since early Christian times, for near here St. Stephen met his death. He was tried before the Sanhedrin (famed Rabbinical court) for blasphemy—for maintaining that the Word of Christ replaced the Law of Moses. He was found guilty, and hurled from a height so that his back might be broken. But he survived that ordeal, and was stoned to death, his last words being, "Lord, lay not this sin to their charge." (Acts 7:60.)

We followed a narrow winding street called the Way of Sorrow to the Church of the Holy Sepulcher. This street is too narrow for automobiles to pass, and is used mostly by pedestrians and by camels and donkeys. This morning it was packed—members of the Arab Legion swinging jauntily along; veiled women with jugs, platters, baskets on their heads; donkeys loaded with lumber, stone, wheat, straw, bales of undisclosed produce trotting in orderly fashion and directed from behind by men or boys with sticks; Moslem clergy going to a mosque; a few camels walking gingerly, their heads high and sneering, their backs loaded with bales; beggars in rags, deformed, blind, emaciated, crying for alms—"Backshish, backshish."

There are some shops along the Way of Sorrow; but most of the buildings are adjoining residences or offices with no courtyards in between. Near the start we passed the house of Pontius Pilate. Then we came to the so-called "stations"—the places where, it is said, Christ fell or stopped to rest as he carried the Cross to Calvary. The "stations" have been given the semblance of authenticity by plates set in the walls.

We had as a guide a tall, rangy Arab who wore his tarboosh at a jaunty angle and spoke English with a British accent. There is a dent in a stone wall where, according to him, Christ stumbled and fell, hitting the stone with his elbow. We passed the home of the Wandering Jew who would not let Christ rest on his stoop, and also the former home of St. Veronica. The so-called twelfth "station" is the church, a massive building, mainly distinguished in appearance by a rotunda with an open dome. First built by Emperor Constantine in A.D. 335, it has since been destroyed and rebuilt several times, but has stood substantially unchanged for the last century and a half. It is the property of five Christian sects—Catholic, Armenian, Coptic, Greek Orthodox, and Jacobite—which for years have not been able to agree on its management. Consequently Moslem soldiers have guarded it and today Moslem priests have the keys.

The church has been built over the holy places and is filled with shrines and altars of the various faiths. Priests stood in attendance, asking alms and handing us candles to light our way. We went down into caverns that had a damp chill about them. We climbed stairs and groped our way through cellars and passageways that were Stygian black. The whole interior seemed damp and gloomy.

There is marked the place where Christ appeared to his Mother after the Resurrection; the place where the crosses were found by St. Helena; the pillar to which Christ was bound when he was scourged; a chapel hewn out of rock where Christ was confined prior to his Crucifixion, the place where the dust was collected from which Adam was made; the tomb of Adam; an altar marking the spot where the soldiers divided the raiment of Christ; another dedicated to the centurion who cried out when the veil of the temple was rent in twain, "Truly this man was the Son of God" (Mark 15:39); the grotto where the walls and roof drip water, still weeping over the tragedy of the Crucifixion; the piece of marble on which Christ sat when he was mockingly made king and crowned with a crown of thorns; the rift in the rock made at the time of the Crucifixion by the earthquake; chapels on end, plain ones hewed out of rock, ornate ones with lights and gilded screens.

My first reaction to all this was that man by his inventions had somehow cheapened these historic spots.

But all that feeling passed as I stood at the scene of the Crucifixion. One sees the spot where the true cross stood. And then looking up he sees the picture of Christ engraved in gold and studded with gems. The two thieves flank him on lustrous crosses. The Virgin and Mary Magdalen are there. It does something to one of my faith to stand in that place. I experienced an overwhelming feeling of humility and reverence. This place may not be the true site of the Crucifixion, as some maintain. But hundreds of thousands gave their lives for it. The history of it is written in blood and tears shed out of the adoration which for centuries men of many languages have had for the Prince of Peace.

We climbed the wall of the Old City near the Damascus gate and walked it for a distance under the guidance of a fat, good-natured Arab policeman of Jerusalem. The top is about as wide as the average sidewalk; its sides are lined with little parapets. The day we were there the Arab Legion was at strategic points along the wall; and sandbags marked machine-gun emplacements. For war with Israel was still on; an armistice had merely marked the end of the shooting.

It was a clear day, cool in a breeze that swept the heights of Judea. All the historic spots lay at our feet—places crowded with events which only volumes could relate. Our Arab guide pointed them out one by one, rattling on in the monotony of one who has learned his piece by heart and is bent on reciting it to the end. As he talked, the memories of my visit to the Mount of Olives, Gethsemane, the Valley of Judgment, the Golden Gate, St. Stephen's Gate, the Way of Sorrow, the Church of the Holy Sepulcher swept over me. They were so poignant that they crowded out all other thoughts.

A young, well-educated Arab who was on the staff of our consular service accompanied us on this tour of the Old City. All morning he had been most attentive to our needs. Turning to him I said, "All of Jerusalem seems to me to be a Christian shrine. How can the Arabs lay claim to it?"

Our friend spoke to the guide in Arabic and then replied to me, "Come, we will show you."

We descended the wall, passed through a labyrinth of streets filled with tiny shops, made a short detour to see the famous Wailing Wall of the Jews, and then came out on an immense open paved court. In the middle of the court stood a mosque.

"The Dome of the Rock," our Arab friend said. "Holier to us Moslems than any place except Mecca."

The guide took over and explained that under the huge rotunda of the mosque is a rock. This is the rock where Abraham was going to sacrifice Isaac (Genesis 22:14); it is the rock where the angel stood who threatened to destroy Jerusalem and was deterred by David (II Samuel 24:16). It is the rock from which Mohammed made his night journey to Heaven. The Dome of the Rock, located on the site of Solomon's Temple, was built for the Arabs in A.D. 688 by Byzantine architects.

The young Arab interrupted to say, "I noticed that you were moved when you stood at the scene of the Crucifixion. We devout Arabs have as great an attachment to this spot."

We rented sandals from a priest at the door and put them on over our shoes before we entered the mosque. Inside it was dark and cool. The rounded dome was covered with exquisite mosaic work and beautiful colored windows, each of a different design. The floors were carpeted. In the center of the room under the dome was the Rock of Ascension, enclosed in a high wooden fence. There was nobility and grandeur in the scene.

The guide pointed out the mark of a foot on it—Mohammed's foot. I wrote in my notebook at the time "size 15 or 16." Later I read that Mark Twain (*Innocents Abroad*) had called it size eighteen. Anyway, it was a big foot. The guide's story was that the rock tried to follow Mohammed; but Gabriel seized it. The guide showed us the prints of Gabriel's fingers on the Rock—huge indents. But as Mark Twain said, "Very few people have a grip like Gabriel."

Our Arab friend must have noticed a look of disbelief on my face, for he politely said, "Those of a different faith often make jokes about the gossip of guides who show this place to tourists. But like Mecca it is a holy place to millions of us Arabs."

Opposite the Dome of the Rock is the Temple from which Christ expelled the money-changers. We passed it and came to another mosque. There was a fountain in front, playing into a large pool. Here men were washing their hands and feet preparatory to entering for prayer. This mosque is younger and lesser and not as exquisitely done inside as the Dome of the Rock. Nor was all the mosaic of the walls finished in 1949. I paused for a moment at the door. A dozen or more men were on their knees, facing Mecca, bowing up and down, saying their prayers. Others were lying on their backs, reciting the Koran in a singsong way.

The guide paid no attention to these worshipers. He went on, like a phonograph with a loud-speaker, announcing the points of interest. He even shouted something in Arabic at one chap who was in our path that evidently meant "Get out of the way." For the man broke off his praying and scampered. I felt uncomfortable and unhappy.

"If this is a House of God to these people," I whispered to our young Arab friend, "we also should treat it as such." He nodded and he, Bill, and I turned and went to the door, leaving our guide talking to himself in an alcove.

We went out of the Old City through St. Stephen's Gate and stood at a vantage point overlooking the Valley of Judgment. The guide pointed to a slab of rock projecting a few feet high on the eastern wall of the Old City. He explained that it is the belief of many Arabs that on the Day of Judgment Mohammed will stand on that slab and Christ will stand about a mile across the valley on the Mount of Olives. Each will hold the end of a horsehair. The dead will rise and walk the hair. The wicked will fall into the valley. Only the righteous will reach the heights.

I turned to our Arab friend for confirmation of the legend. He nodded and then said, "I have a mullah for a friend. He believes this legend. He thinks that on the Day of Judgment he will walk the horsehair. That's why he grows long curls for sideburns."

"What have the sideburn curls got to do with it?" I asked.

"You see, when my friend starts to walk the horsehair, angels will come down—one on each side—take hold of the curls, and help him keep his balance."

This time I looked to the guide for confirmation; and at once I was sorry I did. For he nodded his head in violent approval.

"This guide of ours," I whispered to Bill, "would believe anything."

"Ask him about the moon and green cheese," Bill said.

We started back to the American Colony, a hotel in the Old City where we were staying.

We had not gone far when churchbells began to ring. They were announcing sundown.

This was Ramadan, the month the Koran was sent down from Heaven. During this month (which comes at a different time each year) a Moslem cannot eat or drink from dawn to sunset. From this fast none is excused, except travelers and sick persons. The latter, however, must fast an equal number of days when the impediment is over. The bells I heard announced that the period of fast was done for the day. Other bells would ring at 1:30 A.M. to warn the people to start preparing breakfast before sun-up. My Arab friend excused himself, saying as he left, "Ramadan is severe on many of our people. Since they do not eat, drink, or smoke from dawn to sunset they get nervous and high-strung. There are apt to be street fights. It is well for Christians during Ramadan to be discreet and moderate when they are in crowds or near holy places.

In the morning we passed from the Old City to the New through Mandlebaum Square. On one side of the square were the Arab lines; on the other, the Israeli. The positions were marked by sand-bags, barbed wire, and concrete posts set in the pavement to form tank traps. The houses bordering the square bore the marks of fighting—windowpanes were out, stucco had been broken by shells, sandbags covered the edges of roofs, all walls bordering the square were pock-marked from bullets.

Passage through the lines had been arranged. We presented our papers to Arab Legionnaires, and in a few minutes they were back in our hands. Then we moved one hundred feet across the square and Israeli guards went through the same process.

The attitude in the New City was strikingly different from that in the Old. The Old was held by the Arabs who had lost the war. The New was held by the Jews who were the victors. The Arabs had been quiet and reflective. The Jews were bursting with energy, ideas, plans. I was to learn that there was more to this psychology of theirs than victory on the battlefield, but victory had given a lift to their spirits. Yesterday had been Israeli Army Day. The parade near Tel Aviv had been the best of its nature that our military observers had seen. The Jews held their heads high; there was spring in their steps.

The talk too was exuberant. A story (told to us by a member of the Israeli government) is typical of the attitude:

A Jew who returned from Tel Aviv to New York City was asked how the Jews accomplished so much in Palestine. First, they created Israel; second, they won a war; third, they took in all the Jewish immigrants who applied for admission.

"How could the Jews achieve so much?" the puzzled friend inquired.

"There are two reasons," the returning Jew replied. "One is natural and the other is supernatural."

"What was the natural one?"

"The Jews had God and justice on their side."

"And what was the supernatural one?"

"The Jews knew how to shoot."

We toured the battlegrounds on the south and west of the Old City with the famed Colonel Moshe Dayan of the Israeli Army and his wife, Ruth, both of whom speak excellent English. The colonel, known to millions by the patch worn over one eye socket, is a young man in his thirties. He has two main enthusiasms—his family and his farm not far from Nazareth. Fighting was for him merely an interlude. He is a quiet, soft-spoken man, short, slender, and wiry.

He explained the tactics of infiltration of small forces—the key to the military success of the Israeli Army. This was a tactic well known to Arab armies, one in which they had long been skilled. Yet it was this tactic which defeated them, while they were trying to master the modern technique of mass maneuvering which Patton used so brilliantly in France.

There was one hill, never taken by an attacking army in nineteen centuries, which Dayan and seventy soldiers took. They went at night in waves of not more than five. It was brave and daring fighting. Twenty of the seventy were lost. But the Israeli flag flew over the hill at dawn. That hill commanded a strategic spot on a line of attack against the walls of the Old City.

We saw position after position which had been taken, lost, and retaken in the fighting. Perhaps the bitterest fighting of all was at the Hill of Rachel. A Jewish kibbutz (communal settlement) had been located here. During the fighting it had changed hands six times. It had been fought over building by building, room by room, foot by foot by the Egyptians and the Jews. The structures—all stone or concrete—were a shambles. The place had been utterly destroyed.

"All except the orchards below us on the east," said Colonel Dayan. "Come and I will show you."

We started to the orchards when a young Israeli noncommissioned soldier came running out of a lookout post and talked excitedly with Colonel Dayan in Hebrew. The colonel turned to me and said, "He says we can't go any farther."

"Since when has a sergeant overruled a colonel?" I inquired.

Colonel Dayan smiled as he replied, "This alert young man just told me that the orchard is still mined. Now wouldn't that be a bit inhospitable—for me to get you blown to bits?"

We returned to a shell-marked rampart overlooking the walls of the Old City and stood in silence for a long while watching the distant sky line of spires, domes, and towers. Far in the background was the Mount of Olives, a dark-green spot on the low-lying Mountains of Judea. There was not a movement of life anywhere to be seen or heard. The city looked vacant, a city of papier-mâché built on a model for some Hollywood production. But behind those old walls an ancient Arab civilization thrived. Life droned on and on with the rhythm of the centuries. Religious fanaticism grew in the breasts of many. The fervor and zeal of Arab nationalism mounted. The Arabs behind those walls stood committed to defend with their lives the shrines holy to them.

I was thinking of these things when Colonel Dayan, pointing, said, "There is the Church of the Holy Sepulcher. Along the ridge to the north are our medical school and university. Below them and out of view is Gethsemane. These historic spots must not be harmed or destroyed. They are ours and we must occupy them."

We visited Ein Karem, a village of three thousand people about twenty miles from Jerusalem. It is a quiet, country village, built on a ridge at the head of a draw. The village is flanked by churches—a Franciscan church and school at one end; a Franciscan and a Greek Orthodox church at the other. Olive orchards fill terraces that line the sides of the ravine. Tall, stately cypresses with their dark-green spires and pine of a lighter hue line the ridge. Father Carrol of the Terra Santa College (Franciscan) of Jerusalem, a bright-eyed, brilliant priest in his thirties, was our guide.

Ein Karem, an Arab village for hundreds of years, was the birthplace of John the Baptist. In the recent war it was never attacked by the Israeli Army. It was indeed not on the path to Jerusalem. It had no apparent military value. Yet it was evacuated by the Arabs. Every man, woman, and child left—all except eight old women. The refugees put a few personal belongings and what food they had in their cupboards on the backs of donkeys. They walked out of their ancestral homes in Ein Karem, shut the doors, and turned to the east. They did this, though no shot was fired, though their village was neither encircled nor threatened. Some went through Jerusalem to Jericho down the corkscrew road on the east that drops off Judea. Most went around the Eternal City, seeking a path down the precipitous Judea Mountains, fording the Jordan, and climbing the hot and blistering ridge of Moab. We had met some of them in the refugee camp at Sukhneh.

I inquired why the exodus, and was taken to two of the old women in a mud hut on the edge of town. They were wrinkled, wizened, and shy, and hesitated to talk. But finally they gave the following explanation:

First, there was the massacre by an irresponsible, lawless element of the Stern Gang at Deir Yassin in 1948, when men, women and children—all but one in the village—were killed one night. The massacre struck terror in the hearts of villagers throughout the region.

"Some thought all of us in Ein Karem might also be killed some night," one old lady said as she twirled the ends of a black shawl.

Second, the villagers were told by the Arab leaders to leave. It apparently was a strategy of mass evacuation whether or not necessary as a military or public safety measure.

"They all left during one week," said the other lady. "Every morning there were more who had gone. Finally only a few of us were left behind. We were too old and feeble to go." There were tears in her eyes and her face had a weary look.

I expected to see a ghost town. But as we started down the main street of Ein Karem I heard singing.

"New arrivals from Europe," Father Carrol said.

In a few minutes we stood at the door of a large building transformed into a synagogue. A cantor was singing. A rabbi was bent over a lectern. Men and women were bowed in worship.

We walked down the street. Another service was being held in another makeshift synagogue. We came upon yet another. The whole village had gone to church. An overflow of young people was in a class being conducted on the edge of an olive orchard near the center of town.

As we returned from a visit to the chapel of Elizabeth, mother of John the Baptist, on the far side of the village, one of the synagogues was emptying. People were going back to their new homes; children were doing a hop, skip, and jump along the road; a rabbi, bent in meditation, walked slowly through the village. The men and women pouring out of the synagogues had faces that were happy and relaxed.

"Not many months ago these people were housed in awful camps in Europe," Father Carrol said. "Many barely escaped death at the hands of Hitler's henchmen."

For them this was, indeed, the Promised Land. Here refugees from terror and agonizing death had found security, freedom, a peaceful valley, and opportunity to work and live and worship as they chose. Their new freedom was reflected in their eyes, in the spring in their walk, in the laughter of their children.

To them this village was a haven, a refuge. It did not then matter that Arabs at Sukhneh, some forty miles away, sat in tents dwelling with anger on the evacuation of Ein Karem and on the occupation of their ancient village by newcomers from Europe. For Ein Karem had been won in war. The victorious Israeli Army that swept the village within its lines would defend it to the death.

To the newcomers at Ein Karem the Holy Land was a sacred place where scatterings of this ancient people would regather and reunite for the preservation of the race. Here they would bring a new civilization. Here they would return to the soil and rebuild a devastated land into a rich and flourishing garden. Here they would destroy the feudalism that had held the peoples of the region in slavery from time out of mind. This region would become a new home of democracy.

Those who reclaimed the land in this way would establish their right to it, their worthiness to survive.

This was a Cause, a Crusade. It swept all before it, including innocent Ein Karem. It moved on to Jerusalem. Like the earlier Crusades it traveled on the wings of tremendous enthusiasm. Its call summoned men from all parts of the world. There was fervor in those who faced toward Jerusalem, a fervor that would neither brook delay nor allow defeat.

In 1949 the contest for Jerusalem as capital of Israel and as seat of the Arab government of Palestine was raging. As I have said, the Arabs held the Old City; the Jews the New. The Jews had not only pushed their front lines into Jerusalem, they had also brought a part of their government there. The Supreme Court of Israel, created in 1948, sat in Jerusalem. And on July 22, 1949, the first anniversary of its creation, I sat with it at a special session.

It was Call Day—when lawyers are admitted to practice. Herman Cohn, State Attorney and formally dressed, presented each candidate. In our high court admissions are moved in short cryptic motions. In Israel the ceremony was more intimate and personal. Mr. Cohn would say, for example, "Martin Diga. Mr. Diga is, comparatively speaking, a new immigrant. He came here from Bulgaria in 1944 and he has already acquired a knowledge of our language and has passed all his examinations. He was a lawyer for a number of years in Sofia, Bulgaria."

Each candidate was presented in that personal manner. Each rose when his name was called; and then the Chief Justice, Moshe Smoira, granted their admissions and delivered an address of welcome. In his message he referred to my presence, said a word in eulogy of Mr. Justice Murphy, who had just died, and spoke of Mr. Justice Cardozo, quoting from his writings. He closed by saying that he hoped that Isaiah's prophecy would be fulfilled in Israel: "And I will restore thy judges as at the first, and thy counsellors as at the beginning; afterward thou shalt be called, The city of righteousness, the faithful city."

It was a friendly, intimate session—dignified but not austere— and it had a warmth that was uncommon. For here was an ingathering of exiles from many lands. They had come to reclaim Jerusalem and the Holy Land, to dedicate it to the freedom of man, to make this city a righteous one and thus to fulfill the prophecy. Like the Jews who manned the outposts of the Israeli Army or tilled the fields, these lawyers and judges were also inspired. They had a zeal, a drive, a purpose, a cause. They were dedicating themselves to a crusade in this, the Eternal City. They were laying in Jerusalem the foundations for the capital of the new state of Israel.

The first meeting of the Knesset (the Israeli parliament) had also been held in Jerusalem. But after Jerusalem came under siege, the seat of government was moved to Hakirya near Tel Aviv where it still was in the summer of 1949. Later in 1949 when the United Nations decided that Jerusalem should be internationalized, David Ben-Gurion, Premier of Israel, made an important announcement about the seat of the Israeli government. Ben-Gurion, short and stocky with a shock of white hair, is dynamic, idealistic, and courageous. He has some of the zeal of the Prophets. His announcement carried back to an age-old conflict between Moslems and Christians over Jerusalem.

Ben-Gurion first promised free access to all the holy places and the religious buildings of Jerusalem. He denounced the "enforced separation of Jerusalem," which he said violated without need or reason "the historic and natural right of the people who dwell in Zion." He said that under the stress of war the seat of government had been moved from Jerusalem to Hakirya. But he added, "For the

State of Israel there is, has been, and always will be one capital only, Jerusalem, the Eternal. So it was three thousand years ago, and so it will be, we believe, until the end of time."

We had seen at Jerusalem, Sukhneh, Ein Karem, and Hattin, part of the story of that conflict.

PART V

Israel

38. Into Israel from the East

My son and I came to Israel from the back country. We left by car from Amman in Trans-Jordan and corkscrewed off the barren, hot ledges of the Moab Mountains to Jericho and the Dead Sea where it was over 120 degrees. The dry hills of Moab on the east of the Jordan and those of Judea on the west were as hot as furnace walls. I could feel through the soles of my shoes the heat of the gravel on the shores of the Dead Sea.

We had been in a blistering heat for most of our journey: Syria, Iraq and Persia had seared us; and some mornings on our pack trips in the mountains of Persia I had wakened with my face swollen and eyes closed from sunburn. We were refugees from the sun who had traveled treeless ridges and basins for days on end.

We had seen in the country to the east of Israel the most ancient of agricultural methods. There were exceptions. But almost every farmer was using a wooden stick and oxen to plow, hand sickles to reap, and primitive thrashing floors for separating the grain from the chaff.

I had seen the heavy mark of government of the landlords, for the landlords, and by the landlords on the land. People lived in squalor with no opportunity of escape. Some men owned two hundred, six hundred, fifteen hundred villages apiece. They owned every piece of property in these villages: the mud houses, the community bathhouses, the fields, the animals and the water that serviced them, the farming utensils. They even owned the people who, for all practical purposes, were their serfs. The peasants voted as their landlord dictated. Some landlords controlled 500,000 votes and cast them in a way that would perpetuate their control.

This is the sordid side. There are wonderful things about the Middle East—the people and their civilizations. But the features I have mentioned—heat, treeless land, primitive agriculture, and the squalor of a vicious tenancy—were prominent in my mind the day I traveled the tortuous road that climbs thirty-eight hundred feet from Jericho to Jerusalem.

One who reaches Jerusalem in that mood undergoes a transformation. Jerusalem, standing on top of the Mountains of Judea, is a refuge from the torrid heat of the interior. There are cool breezes here and the shade of pepper trees, cypress, and pine. Historians say that the location of Jerusalem makes no sense by any standard of commerce, trade, or economy. But when one reaches it from the desert side it has special spiritual values.

When I dropped off the Mountains of Judea down the road to Rehovoth and Tel Aviv, I began to get the feel of a different environment. It came in simple ways. The western slopes of Judea are as heavily eroded as the eastern side. It has in many places been scrubbed clean of soil and one sees for miles only the exposed shoulders of limestone. This is typical Middle East scenery. But now I saw a change. There were occasionally new stands of pine twelve feet high! I saw freshly planted forests on barren limestone ledges!

Next I saw a hay baler in operation in a field—the first sign of modern agriculture that I had seen in weeks. It was being run by a young Jewish farmer. Soon I saw tractors; they too were being run by Jews. But shortly I came to a farm operated by an Arab whose kafiyeh was flying in the wind as he too plowed with a tractor.

There were neat modern houses next to old mud huts where poverty-ridden villages had stood for centuries.

I saw chicken farms, compact, highly modernized.

I saw bare slopes being planted with young orchards.

When I reached Rehovoth I saw the Weizmann Institute, a highly modern laboratory for research. I talked with its founder and the President of the Republic. He is a chemist turned politician. He said with feeling that politics was the more important part of his life, much more important than his earlier career as a chemist.

When I saw the Institute I wondered if he were correct. His genius as a scientist has loosed on the manifold problems of the Middle East a whole arsenal of talent. I saw the staff at work on various projects in physics and chemistry—for example, a plan for making nylon out of the castor bean and developing a species of the tree that will make large-scale production possible. Others were working on a low-cost method of taking salt from water, not only for drinking purposes but for irrigation. (Present methods cost about $1.40 per cubic meter of water.) This project strikes at one of Israel's basic problems, for the lack of surface water in the plains is as acute as the loss of soil on the hillsides. Israel's agricultural problems are indeed reducible to those two simple facts. Perhaps the laboratories at Rehovoth will produce a formula that will in time make Israel self-sufficient.

Some of the gains I saw had been started by the British under the mandate. The British had instituted the tethering of goats. They also created forest reserves and made many plantings of pine, oak and carobs. They planted cypress as windbreaks and they covered sand dunes with acacias and tamarisk. What the British did in this respect the early Jewish colonists did to an even greater degree. Out of 50,000 dönüms (4 dönüms equal 1 acre) afforested during the period of the mandate 37,900 dönüms were afforested by the colonists. And the people of the new State of Israel took it up with tremendous zeal and energy. The whole nation is tree conscious. Everyone plants trees, as did Abraham, who "planted a grove in Beersheba, and called there on the name of the Lord . . ." (Genesis 21:33.) In the three years following independence ten million trees have been planted.

The road is long and the undertaking is tremendous. In December, 1950, there were 1,336,000 people in Israel of whom 1,161,000 were Jews. In the time of Jesus the larger area of Palestine had 5,000,000 people. In A.D. 1000 it was double the number today. What were pine forests even one hundred years ago are sand dunes now. Several feet of topsoil have rushed to the ocean. It will take time and the best of science and land management to restore the ancient fertility of the land and to create industrial wealth.

Today everyone in Israel seems conservation minded. There is a passionate endeavor in each community to reverse the cycle of erosion, to rebuild the land, to grow food for an expanding society.

Some 20 per cent of the total Jewish population of Israel is engaged in farming. Those people make conservation their first business. So does everyone else, whatever his calling. Every man, woman, and child is united in the cause, as though putting out a fire that would consume them.

It is this atmosphere of great events in the making, of unity of purpose and activity that I felt as I reached the coastal plain of Israel. Grim causes had united the Jews in this endeavor. If the people in the countries to the east of Israel were given the incentive to reclaim their lands, if the same release of energies and direction of power could be achieved there, the whole of the Middle East would experience a renaissance. In every country I had visited there were people eager to undertake it.

39. Israel Experiments

ISRAEL'S ATTITUDE is experimental, not dogmatic. One can be as passionate for private capitalism as he chooses, or he can espouse and practice a socialist philosophy more extreme in some respects than even Soviet Russia's. Israel's tolerance is indeed one of its most impressive qualities. The Soviets thrust their dogma down the throats of all men. Israel leaves the choice to the individual; no creed is forced on anyone. And in Israel, unlike Soviet Russia and most Middle East countries, one finds the finest traditions of civil liberties as we know them in the Anglo-American world. One may write and speak as freely as he wants, within the bounds of decency. The legislative and executive branches of government do not have free rein. The Supreme Court of Israel sits in review of their actions. One of the first acts of the newly created Supreme Court was to enjoin a cabinet officer who exceeded the authority set by law.

An Arab, Abu Luban, had been arrested and held incommunicado for some weeks. The Court held the arrest illegal and said, "The government is subject to the law in the same manner as any citizen of the state."

Israel has a wide variety of economic organizations.

1. Many *individual farmers* and *businessmen* own and run their farms or factories and embrace private capitalism as devoutly as anyone in America. They have a Farmers Federation which functions somewhat as a Grange in this country, and which also offers services in the marketing of produce, the purchasing of supplies, and the rental of machinery. Forty per cent of the agricultural population is in this category.

2. Many farmers (27 per cent of the agricultural population) are organized into formal *co-operatives*. The individual owns the land; the co-operative does the procurement or marketing or both. The

273

aim is increased efficiency and lower costs. A co-operative among poultry farmers will market the eggs and the meat, and buy the grain and chicken coops. A co-operative among dairy farmers will own the creamery, process the milk, and make the butter and cheese.

3. The *kibbutz* is a communal settlement (30 per cent of the agricultural population live in these); and it is probably more strictly socialistic than the collective farms in Russia. In Russia, while all farmers are on collective farms, most of them have a small plot of land. There they may grow what they like and sell it on the market. They also have separate homes and kitchens.

In a kibbutz, however, everything is communal. Families have no separate houses, kitchens, gardens, or bathhouses. The kibbutz has a common kitchen and a common dining room where everyone eats. It has a nursery where all children are placed shortly after birth, and nurses who care for them. Parents are with their children only at day's end and on week ends. The kibbutz has schools and playgrounds; furnishes doctors and medical services; owns all the land and all the produce. It is managed by a council or board (usually five members) elected annually by a vote of all the members. They determine the allotment of work for the members—in the kitchen, the machine shed, the orchards, and so on. They also determine what crops shall be raised and how the funds shall be invested.

No member of a kibbutz receives any dividend at the end of a year or any other period. He has no need for cash while he is in the kibbutz. The communal store supplies his wants—clothing, cigarettes, shaving cream, shoes, writing paper, needles, and the normal range of consumer goods. Members of some of the older kibbutzim are not on rations; they may draw as heavily on the store as their needs dictate. In the new kibbutzim, however, the resources are so limited that rationing is required.

Each member of a kibbutz receives an annual vacation—usually two weeks; and he is allowed so much cash for that purpose. Each member is cared for until he dies, whether he stays well or becomes a cripple or is bedridden. He receives the same food, the same store privileges, and all the other perquisites of the kibbutz that every other member receives. The kibbutz, in other words, offers security through sickness and old age.

There are many types of kibbutzim—some formed from religious groups, some small and restricted, others large. Though each kibbutz is always an agricultural organization, it often has an industrial aspect too. One kibbutz may have a creamery, another a fruit-processing plant, another a printing plant, and so on. These industrial projects are also collectivized; the governing committee assigns members to work in them; and their profits are owned by the community, not by the individuals.

4. There is an agricultural organization known as the *moshav-shitufi* which has elements both of the kibbutz and the co-operative. This too is a communal settlement engaged in farming; and like the kibbutz, it frequently has an industrial or commercial project also. Each family, however, is maintained as a unit; there is no nursery for the children; each couple has a house with a private kitchen and dining room; each family has a small plot of ground where vegetables and flowers can be grown, though none may be sold on the market. All production is for the account of the community; and in other respects too the pattern of the kibbutz is followed. It has drawn to date 3 per cent of the agricultural population.

5. The *Jewish National Fund*, another unique institution, was founded by the Zionists in 1901 and was incorporated in England for the purchase of land in Palestine and for its cultivation and maintenance. The land acquired is to be chiefly agricultural. It is never to be sold or mortgaged but remains the property of Jewish people for all time. It is rented on forty-nine-year leases at low rates with renewal provisions—2 per cent of the value in case of rural land. The scheme has manifold purposes: to return the Jews to Palestine and settle them on the land; to keep the land under Jewish management; to avoid the large landholdings which result in many workers' becoming hired hands; to avoid mortgage foreclosures and the loss of land; to avoid death duties and the liquidation of estates; to dedicate increased increments of value to the community rather than to the individual landowner.

The purchases of land by the National Fund have been extensive. Today it owns close to 25 per cent of the arable land in Israel and about two-thirds of the acreage actually cultivated in 1949-1950. It started early to plant trees and has since its beginning promoted afforestation projects. It has drained swamps and reclaimed land, constructed roads, installed water systems, and engaged in extensive building.

Most of the land is rented to Jews, although the National Fund leases to some Arab tenants. For example, in July, 1949, the first Arab kibbutz was formed on land of the National Fund. Whoever the tenant may be, the National Fund watches over the management of the land. The leases provide that the National Fund may reduce the acreage. Twenty-five acres may prove to be too much for one farmer to operate; a new water supply may make the need for the large unit unnecessary; a different use of the land may produce more food or food whose shortage is critical, etc. During recent years when immigration to Israel has been high, the National Fund has reshuffled many leaseholds, working for the best utilization of the land. I visited a chicken farm at Ramataim (not far from Tel Aviv) where the National Fund had reduced holdings down to one acre per family. Modern American equipment had been introduced and a highly concentrated operation was under way. New immigrants were assigned to the excess land.

6. *Histadrut* is a trade union of unique character and great proportions. It has so many projects, so many different lines of activity, so diversified a membership that some in Israel call it a state within a state.

The Histadrut goes back to 1920 when several unions with a membership of forty-four hundred merged to form it, the purpose being to establish a Jewish laboring community in Palestine. Taking in all workers, it served the conventional ends of trade unionism—better working conditions, higher wages, and the like—but its purpose did not end there. Formed when the British controlled the land under the mandate, it undertook to prepare the land for the return of the Jews to Palestine and to help bring them there. Its program was to aid the mobilization of the country around the Zionist cause. And so it launched into manifold activities. Today Histadrut has departments or branches that cover a wide range of activities and directly affects the lives of all the people in Israel.

For instance, it has formed well over one hundred co-operatives in the fields of transportation, waterworks, metalworking, electrical products, building materials, printing, woodworking, tailoring, restaurants, weaving, and the like.

Histadrut furnishes medical care not only to its trade union members but to anyone in Israel who pays the monthly fee. This service covers all the ills of the family, dental and medical, and takes care of operations, obstetrical cases, physical therapy, X-rays, and everything in the medical and surgical line. Histadrut has sanitariums, pharmacies, and hospitals. When new settlements are formed, Histadrut contracts for the furnishing of medical care to them, employing the doctors and nurses and assigning them to one or more settlements, depending on the population and needs. The settlements pay Histadrut an annual fee. All in all, in 1950 Histadrut was furnishing medical care to 50 per cent of the people of Israel.

Histadrut's educational branch has established many schools which provide instruction from kindergarten through high school. It also has numerous trade schools, and conducts extensive physical education projects. Its youth movement trains young men and women for life in Israel, finds placement for them, provides summer camps, excursions, forums and the like. Histadrut has a women's branch, training women for the farms and for absorption in other phases of life in Israel. It also has established child welfare centers.

One of its most interesting projects is at Onim—a youth center near Tel Aviv where children whose parents are missing are assembled. In this school there are eight beds to a room, modern kitchens, excellent sanitation, beautiful lawns and gardens, playgrounds, a swimming pool, and skilled psychiatrists. Three hundred children were living there the day we visited the place. Some had come from behind the Iron Curtain, many had been picked up in Germany, Morocco, and Yugoslavia. They are kept here for about six months; then the healthy ones whose parents are not located are turned over to settlements. Those poorly adjusted are given special treatment.

Jacob Aronson, twelve years old, came from Yugoslavia. His mother found him here six years after her search began. One boy had lost his speech; one boy had been tied to a tree since he was young and now walked like an ape; many had nervous disorders from the terror and suffering they had known.

Histadrut has an organization that contracts with settlements for the purchase of their supplies—foodstuffs, feed for livestock, farm machinery and the like—its fee varying from 3 per cent upward, depending on the article. This wholesale purchasing provides great savings. It also has marketing agencies that sell the produce of the fields both at home and abroad, the fee for this service running around 6 or 6½ per cent. These agencies market well over 70 per cent of the agricultural produce of Israel.

The policy of the National Fund is to lease to one person no more land than he and his family can work. If a lessee has so much land that he needs a hired man to help out, the amount of leased land is reduced. It is a cardinal principle in Israel that when possible every man shall be an owner, that the employee class shall be kept at a minimum. This is designed to increase the dignity and worth of all work and to prevent the exploitation of the employee class. Nevertheless, some agricultural crops, notably citrus, require considerable labor, both regular and seasonal. Histadrut undertook to organize and protect that labor supply. It formed a branch which contracts with farmers to pick, pack, and ship fruit for a price. This branch organized settlements for these unattached workers and in addition to contracting for their labor, founded new industries for them (fruit canning and manufacture of tiles and pipes).

Histadrut has a department engaged in finding water and distributing it to settlements. It has numerous wells and vast distribution systems throughout Israel.

It also owns some industries and is a partner with private capital in others. It is owner or part owner of companies making oils, soap, shoes, sugar, rubber goods, bricks, cement, sanitary earthenware, glass, pharmaceutical supplies, electrical machinery; owner or a partner of wool processing and weaving plants, a sugar-beet factory, a large modern foundry, a tool and machine factory, a ship-repairs plant. It has daily newspapers and periodicals, a publishing house, and a theater.

These days one department of Histadrut, the owner, negotiates with another department of Histadrut, the trade union, over working conditions and wages. There is real collective bargaining and vigorous trade union representation. But in Israel when labor is a partner in industry there seems to be a large degree of industrial peace.

Histadrut likewise has departments that do almost every kind of construction work—road building and paving, quarrying, draining swamps, laying rails, building factories, houses, and apartments. The housing unit operates on a nonprofit basis. It plans development work and housing projects.

The Workers Bank formed by Histadrut has supplied credit for

vast agricultural projects, industrial enterprises, producers and con-
sumers co-operatives, housing, etc. Histadrut has credit and savings
co-operatives that make loans to workers. It also has an institution
(Nir) to extend agrarian credit, to finance workers' housing units,
and to establish new agricultural settlements and help finance their
manifold activities. And finally Histadrut is in the insurance business
through Hassneh—life, fire, accident, burglary, workmen's compensation, and maritime insurance.

The supreme body of Histadrut is the General Convention, to
which all affiliated groups send delegates on a proportional basis. The
Convention, which meets every three years, elects the General
Council. The managerial group is the Central Executive Committee
appointed annually by the General Council.

Histadrut may in time have many of its functions taken over by
the government of Israel. To date it has rendered invaluable services
to the cause of Zionism, translating into concrete measures the
idealism of the Zionists. More than any other group, it is responsible
for the actual reclamation and settlement of Israel. It has developed
the co-operative form of organization to a degree not equaled anywhere else in the world.

Israel is experimenting in numerous ways with the ancient
problem of landownership and management. Its experiments are not
ideological ventures; they were born of the necessities of the Zionist
cause. The needs that gave rise to the various forms of co-operative
projects are manifold. What served Israel may well be of slight use
elsewhere. But Israel is a vivid demonstration center showing that
there is no one road to economic salvation and social justice.

We in America are apt to think that the world is choosing sides
between private enterprise and communism. Vast portions of the
world—notably the Middle East and southeast Asia—feel no such
compulsion. They seek solutions best suited to the genius of their
people. Their way will not necessarily be our way when it comes to
economic organization. This does not mean it will be any the less
devoted to democratic standards or any the less respectful of human
rights and the dignity of man. What Israel has done proves that.

40. *"From Dan even to Beersheba"*

ISRAEL IS a small country geographically. Its length as the crow flies is about 260 miles; its width varies from 5 to 70 miles. It is indeed a thin and irregular stretch of coastal plain pressed against the Mediterranean. Jerusalem—partly held by the Arabs and partly by the Jews—is less than 40 miles from the sea and lies at the end of a long finger of land protruding into Arab-held territory. Israel runs east to the Jordan from Dan on the north to a point below Kefar Rupin on the south. But the rest of the Jordan Valley is in Arab hands. Israel extends halfway up the west side of the Dead Sea, the upper portion being held by the Arabs. And Israel includes the whole of the Negev (the wilderness of Zin) that runs through sand and wasteland to the Gulf of Aqaba.

It is only 175 miles or so from Dan to Beersheba; and it is in that long narrow corridor of land that most of the people live and that Israel's agricultural and industrial projects flourish. Yet the Negev is important to Israel too; and there are significant developments even in this desert south of Beersheba.

Dan is at the head of the upper valley of the Jordan, the furthest north of any village in Galilee. Mount Hermon towers over it on the northeast. Here the Jordan rises and starts its journey to the Dead Sea. In these headwaters it is a small purling stream pouring through deep channels lined with grass and shrubs. The valley that it enters is hemmed on the west by the Mountains of Judea and on the east by the Mountains of Moab. It is a place that is pleasant to the eye. The hills, though mostly bare, are soft and rolling, and below them in the valley is some of the rich topsoil that has washed down. There is the mark of fertility on the basin. It has long stretches of marshland that presented acute malaria-control problems; some of it has been reclaimed, and some has been developed into fish ponds where carp are raised for food. Most of the land, however, from Dan to the Sea of Galilee and from the Sea of Galilee on south along the Jordan is cultivated.

It was just below Dan at Kefar Giladi that I saw my first kibbutz. This kibbutz was one of the earliest, having been founded in 1914, and for years had only several hundred members. By 1949 it had grown to 750 as a result of the absorption of new immigrants. This collective owns a few thousand acres, most of which is reclaimed wasteland—one thousand acres or more in grain, one hundred in fodder, one hundred in fruit, one hundred in vegetables and one hundred in fish ponds. It has four hundred sheep, two hundred cattle, four thousand laying hens, but few horses or mules, the entire farming operation being mechanized. Kefar Giladi is a modern farm, well-managed, and beautifully maintained—a thriving, hustling, prosperous place.

Kefar Giladi is governed by a board of five, elected annually. Under the board of five is a committee composed of representatives of each division of labor—cooks, mechanics, orchard men, etc. These groups handle all administrative matters—assignment of work, contracts with the Histadrut, investment of funds, and the like.

One of the elders of this kibbutz is Elizer Kroll who looks like Moses. He is a quiet, dignified, pleasant man. When I was there, he was over seventy years old; his responsibilities for work had ended and the kibbutz would care for him the rest of his life. He had seen dozens of babies born at Kefar Giladi—babies who were delivered on birth to the communal nursery and raised by nurses rather than by their parents. I had heard friends say in Tel Aviv that they would not want their children raised that way. At Kefar Giladi I talked with boys in the late teens who had been raised in its communal nurseries and were now members of the kibbutz. The kibbutz to them was the ideal life. They flourished in it and wanted their children raised by the same formula.

I talked with Yetta Caller, who came out of Brooklyn some years back to join Kefar Giladi, and is now one of its guiding influences. She said that a few had tired of the kibbutz and left. (A withdrawing member receives no liquidating dividend.) Yet the vast majority had stayed on for thirty-five years, growing old and spending their declining years in idleness and relaxation.

I asked Yetta Caller what happened when a member of the kibbutz turned out to be a gifted pianist or engineer or showed other talents that the agricultural enterprise of the kibbutz would not satisfy. That is a problem with which the kibbutz is wrestling. A more prosperous kibbutz sends its gifted members to the university at the expense of the kibbutz; others try to provide some sort of training within the limits of their means and the availability of teachers. Yetta Caller was not sure what the adjustment would be at Kefar Giladi.

Below Kefar Giladi are other kibbutzim—orchards of pears and apricots, wide fields of cucumbers, large fishponds. Men and women, working in the fields, almost invariably wear shorts of blue, the color that marks the agricultural worker in Israel. We stopped and talked with them and made a long visit at Ashdot Yacov, a kibbutz south of Tiberias on the Sea of Galilee. It was started in 1935 and now has a membership of twelve hundred people, six hundred of whom are below nineteen years of age. This kibbutz comprises about a thousand acres, in grapes, fodder, bananas, vegetables, citrus, and mixed produce. It has hundreds of sheep, goats, and cows, thousands of chickens, and several fishponds. It also has a fruit-processing plant where fruit juices, jams, and jellies are made, and where fruit and vegetables are canned. Fruit and vegetables from a wide area are processed here.

I sat in the shade eating watermelons and talking with Jacob Schur about this collective farm and its problems. He was proud of this thriving project; there were plans afoot for bringing new lands under cultivation; new water pipes were being laid and bulldozers were doing grading. He spoke of these things and he also mentioned with pride the development of a library for the kibbutz. People come in from the fields at 5 P.M.; there is the problem of their entertainment and recreation. The kibbutz is on a circuit of music, operas, and movies; there is a program of dancing and games; there are some sports for the younger set.

I talked with Jacob Schur about the problem of pleasing every individual in a kibbutz, of having enough variety to satisfy the great diversity of tastes.

"Could I get at the store of the kibbutz my favorite brand of cigarette?"

"No, we have only one kind."

"Same for toothpaste, lotions, underwear?"

"Yes. A member can have as much as he wants in quantity; but we have to standardize our purchases and restrict the variety."

"Suppose I don't smoke but enjoy a cocktail. Can I get it or the ingredients at the kibbutz?"

"No. We sometimes have wine; but no hard liquor is distributed."

"Some would not like that."

"That's true; but the collective farm in Israel, unlike Russia, is voluntary," Jacob Schur replied. "One need not join unless he wants to."

We had come to the Sea of Galilee by way of Haifa and Safad. Safad is an ancient town that sits like a fort on the dome of a high hill. It looks impregnable; yet the Israeli Army took it one night with a small group who knew the tactics of infiltration. Safad has interesting features: an ancient synagogue and old colorful houses set along narrow passageways that climb at dizzy pitches up the hillside. It is also distinguished for a beautiful rest center which the Histadrut maintains there. In summer it is always cool in the shade of cypress and pine that flourish on this high hilltop.

We returned to Haifa from the Sea of Galilee by way of Nazareth. Someone said that Nazareth clings "like a whitewashed wasp nest to the hillside"; and so it does. And to one of the Christian faith it is a hallowed place where the cries of hawkers and the clanging of artisans seem discordant.

Below Nazareth is Nahalal which lies at the head of the valley of Esraeldon. This is a pleasant, fertile spot where the famous Colonel Moshe Dayan and his attractive and brilliant wife Ruth live. Nahalal has eighty families, each having twenty-five acres leased from the National Fund. Dayan has chickens, turkeys, cows. These farmers pool their resources and own farm machinery in common; they also purchase co-operatively and market co-operatively through the Histadrut. At Nahalal one hears only praise for this form of organization. "We are more independent than members of a kibbutz," Ruth Dayan told me.

I visited numerous co-operative villages in the central part of Israel: Ramot Hashavim, where seventy families have forty thousand chickens; Beit Yitzhak, settled by professional and business men from Europe, who raise chickens, eggs, and dairy products; Kefar Warburg, where one hundred families do diversified farming and raise mostly hay and grain; Richon Le Zion where citrus fruit.

almonds, and grapes are raised and where the community owns a co-operative winery; Nira, where two hundred families have a knitting mill and raise fruit, vegetables, and chickens on small holdings. Most of these use Histadrut to make their purchases and to market their produce.

I heard in each of these co-operatives what Ruth Dayan had said: that the co-operative method of farming is the best of all because the members have more independence. Mrs. Sonia Rosenblum summed it up. She lives with her husband and three children at Kefar Warburg, but before that they had been in a kibbutz for seven years. She and her family like the co-op best. "We're not tied down by the rigid life of a collective," she said.

I learned at Beit Yitzhak that the professional men make the best farmers; that they are far superior even to those who were farmers in Europe. And to my surprise I learned that of the professional men probably the lawyer has turned out to be the best farmer of them all.

At Ramot Hashavim I found that one of the major tasks of the co-op was to provide movies, lectures, and concerts for the villagers. William Stern, one of the leading villagers, who moved to Palestine from Germany when Hitler first came to power, talked with me about the cultural and educational life in these villages. He summed it up in these words, "A German Jew must always be learning something."

At Nathanya, I learned something of the pull of Palestine. I talked with M. D. Lipsitz, a United States citizen whose home had been in Detroit for years, a prosperous businessman, who had pulled up all his roots in Michigan and is now operating a four-acre chicken farm in Israel. I told him I could understand why Jews from Poland, Germany, Austria, and Russia flocked to Palestine. "But why did you?" I asked. "You had happiness and security in America, nothing from which to flee."

He thought awhile and then said, "I guess it was the call of the blood."

Mrs. Leah Landu and her husband had lived in a kibbutz for thirteen years, then left it and joined the Nira co-op. Their son, however, hastened back to a kibbutz when he turned eighteen. She talked about the pros and cons of the kibbutz. She and her husband had hated to sacrifice the contributions they had made to the kib-

butz during those years; they had made the change and incurred
the sacrifice only after much deliberation.

"What finally induced you to leave?"

"The lack of privacy. My husband got terribly tired of sitting
down at the same table with the same people three times a day year
after year."

I asked her why her son returned to a kibbutz. Her reply, which
was verified the length and breadth of Israel, was revealing.

"The people who like the kibbutz best are those under thirty and
over fifty."

Those under thirty are caught up with a new idea and a crusade.
Those over fifty have the longing for security: no worry about
rent, heat, food, clothes, medical care, or insurance. Those between
thirty and fifty want to be on their own.

I asked Mrs. Landu if she and her husband regretted their resig-
nation from the kibbutz. Her answer was slow in coming because
she was perplexed.

"We are near fifty now; and the work does not let up a bit. We
go from dawn till dark. Last winter my husband was very sick. I
do not know how long we can continue at this rate." She added
rather wistfully, "It would be nice to be back in the kibbutz with
everything provided for—if my husband could only stand eating
in the community dining room."

This matter of privacy for the family has transcending importance to many. The privilege of withdrawing from the community
at day's end and reuniting the family group for exchange of confidences, bestowal of sympathy, and renewal of affection is necessary for some. It was the force behind the moshav-shitufi movement—the combination of the kibbutz and the co-operative in
which each family has its own house, garden, dining room, and
kitchen.

I visited this new and different kind of settlement. One of the
leading ones is Kefar Monash located not far from Tel Aviv. Started
in 1946 by young soldiers, it now has around fifty families who cul-
tivate three hundred acres. Rye and vegetables are grown; the collective has quite a few milk cows, a growing dairy industry, and a
printing plant with modern, up-to-date machinery. There is no
community nursery. Each family has its own house—a man and
wife with one child has a one-room house with kitchenette; if there

are two or more children, the family gets another room. A young man named Ahron Goren with whom I talked told me that this kind of collective is growing in popularity; it offers the security people crave and the privacy that many must have. He summed it up this way: "Now we can have our eggs burned if we want them that way."

But at Kvutsat Saad and Revivim in the Negev I saw the kibbutz in new perspective. Kvutsat Saad is west of Beersheba, a few miles from Gaza. It is a kibbutz of a religious group; thirty families operate about five hundred acres and grow mostly hay and grain. There is an altar in the communal dining room and on it a lighted candle in memory of one of their members killed in battle. Kvutsat Saad was behind the Egyptian lines for a year. The members lived underground in dugouts after their village was destroyed in battle. Thirty-five men and women held out until the Israeli Army retook the place. I visited their underground homes and found the prize unit of them all—an underground bakery run by a Diesel engine. This kibbutz was supplied by convoys of armored cars that ran the Egyptian lines at night.

A group of young men and women—eager and devoted—gathered round as I left. I asked why they stuck it out during the war, why they risked the running of the lines. A young chap answered me, "You see we are more than a settlement. Our kibbutz had military value. So long as we could keep an active unit behind the enemy's lines we were a thorn in his side."

Beersheba, a bustling town of ten thousand, lies at the head of the desert that stretches to the Gulf of Aqaba. Here is where Abraham pitched his tents at the end of his long, hot journey from Babylon. A paved highway runs south to Egypt through one of the most desolate stretches in the Middle East—a desertic steppe from one thousand to two thousand feet high, cut with gullies and washes and dotted with *haloxylon articulatum*, a low shrub that looks like the bitterbush, and a saltbush (atriplex). No matter the time of year this is a dreary, unattractive region. Yet a group of youngsters from the Histadrut are trying to make some of it into a garden. One such place is Revivim.

About twenty-five miles south of Beersheba is a small deserted village by the name of Bir Asluj. One turns right here and goes two and a half miles on a dirt road to the dusty kibbutz of Revivim.

This is rich loamy land with dirt as fine as flour that rises around one when he walks and swirls in clouds with even a light wind. Wind here is a considerable problem. The kibbutz has planted many rows of trees for windbreaks: tamarisk and acacia which are native to the region and the long-needle, dark-green *casuarina* imported from Australia.

The only water at Revivim comes from a well that is slightly salty. The hundred members of the kibbutz drink the water and now prefer it to the sweet water they could have if they operated the distiller that they possess. The salt water is sufficiently sweet for irrigating olives, date palms, and pomegranates. Young orchards of these fruit trees seem to be thriving. The only other water supply is the flash floods which usually come off the Judea Mountains in March. The members of the kibbutz have built concrete diversion sluices, which carry the water into a reservoir lined with asphalt. This supply is usually sufficient for their vegetables and Sudanese hay, which grows knee high and is very nutritious.

Revivim, like Kvutsat Saad, was underground in dugouts during the war. It was behind Egyptian lines for several months, and was supplied with food by air and by convoys that ran the lines. During this period the men of Revivim would raid the Egyptian headquarters at Bir Asluj at night, getting guns and ammunition. Despite eight casualties, about thirty men and women stuck it out, manning the dugouts and fighting pitched battles by day and raiding at night.

When we were there, they were in the midst of a building program. They had moved out of the dugouts into tents and temporary buildings of stone and wood. A makeshift shower room (with plenty of salt water for bathing) had been constructed. A large square stone tower that served as a lookout and citadel during the war had been converted into a library and a small factory for making clothes.

We stayed all night and had tea, bread, jam, sausage, and potatoes for dinner. These were young people in their twenties, most of them married. They were zealots—hardy, intelligent, determined. Most of them had never been to America; and they were filled with curiosity about it—curiosity and bewilderment too.

Why was America getting ready to fight Russia? Did America think that war was the only way of solving an unemployment problem? Why is America against everything that is socialistic? Why isn't a kibbutz a wholesome project? Is there anything evil in collective security? Why do some Americans think Israel has gone communistic because it has promoted co-operative schemes and collective farms? Isn't America willing to receive new ideas? Must we all be private enterprisers and worship capitalism?

These were the questions fired at me after dinner, as we sat for a couple of hours holding a seminar on world events. These were youngsters who had lived underground in a parched desert and fought for their new freedom. They were militant cross-examiners. They would not take platitudes about democracy without question. They were interested in solving the problems of the Middle East to avoid the ugliness and oppression of communism. Yet they wondered why America thought it could remake the world in its image.

After the discussion I stepped out into the darkness and walked the desert. The stars hung low this night and shone with the brilliance of Persian stars; a thin slice of the moon showed over Egypt; a cool wind swept in from the ocean. On my return I mounted a small hillock and stood listening to the night sounds of the desert. Suddenly a tremendous chorus sounded from the dining hall. These young folks were singing. The voices were exultant and triumphant; they had the ring of determined men and women marching to victory. This was a chorus of crusaders who would not be turned back.

Israel is the product of a crusade. It has many problems, including that of making a just peace with the Arabs so that taxes can go to the land rather than to armaments. Not all of Israel's political problems are easy of solution, for its eleven political parties have made a coalition government necessary. There is the problem of water and topsoil and the development of productivity so that the economy need not be subsidized. Israel needs food, and industries that can manufacture for export. But Israel has conquered the main problems that plague the Middle East—land tenure, illiteracy, disease, and corrupt government.

It seeks to provide schools for every child and medical care for every family. Malaria has been wiped out and other public health programs flourish. Workers have strong unions; and the agricultural economy is so organized as to give every farm laborer a stake in his country. The standards of the public service are high.

If Israel survives, as it will, these achievements are certain to give impetus and direction to revolutions that are well under way in other parts of Asia. Israel does not exist in a vacuum. It is an integral part of the Middle East. Its contagious ideas are certain to spread.

PART VI

India

41. A Girl and a Basket

I HAD LEFT New Delhi for the Himalayas. I was going as far as
Bareilly by train and then by car to Ranikhet—an old British Army
hill station located on a 6,000-foot ridge opposite a 120-mile stretch
of snow-capped Himalayas. The train was slow; and it stopped
at all the way stations. At every stop I swung open the door of
my compartment, which, European style, was on the side of the
train, and walked the platform.

The platforms were packed with people—Sikhs, Moslems,
Hindus; soldiers, merchants, priests, porters, beggars, hawkers.
Almost everyone was barefoot and dressed in loose white garments.
I would ask not more than three people before I found one who
spoke English. We would talk world affairs and Indian affairs—
Korea, communism, Nehru, America, Pakistan, food, and every
major topic the news of the day produced. In this way I was trying
to get a feel of the pulse of the nation, checking opinion against
official attitudes and reports.

The route lay through one of the richest of India's agricultural
areas. This was the plain of the upper Ganges River, a thousand
feet above sea level but tropical. The Ganges was brown with silt,
swollen with flood waters, its overflow inundating thousands of
acres of rice. To the north were jungles—great expanses of grass
higher than a man's head and unbroken except for an occasional
clump of trees—the home of tigers, elephants, pythons, and cobras.
Everywhere else there was flat land running to the horizon as in

Indiana, but dotted here and there by the sacred banyan tree or by rows of pakars—trees shaped like elms and having thick, twisted trunks. Hot, humid air was moving in from the southwest. Monkeys —some of them mothers with babies clinging to them and riding underneath—swung off trees at the stations looking for food. The villages we passed had walls made of mud mixed with water and cow dung. Their peaked roofs were thatched—bundles of grass tied to bamboo poles stretched across the rafters. That day the pumpkin vines that grew over them were in bloom, trailing streaks of yellow over drab walls.

At one station my routine of talking with the natives was interrupted. As soon as I alighted, a group of young children gathered around me. They were selling baskets—hand-woven, reed baskets with simple designs and patterns. They held the baskets high, shouting words I did not know but conveying unmistakably their desire.

These were refugee children. When partition between India and Pakistan was decreed, hundreds of thousands of people pulled up their roots and changed their residences. Nine million people left Pakistan and came to India, driven by the fear of religious fanaticism. They were poor people to start with; they were poorer as they began their long trek, for all they could carry was a bit of food and a few belongings. Soon they were out of food. A few days after they started they began to fall by the wayside from the weakness of hunger, and died where they fell. The highways were so thickly lined with bodies that the vultures could not eat them. And so the corpses bloated and rotted in the sun, the smell of putrid flesh filling the valleys.

The children selling baskets were sons and daughters of these refugees. They or their parents or relatives had gathered in the cities, setting up stalls, manufacturing simple articles, trying to make a living in markets already overcrowded. They lived in cloth and grass lean-tos that lined the streets. The peasants among these refugees had been accustomed to little all their lives, for the annual income of an agricultural family does not on the average exceed one hundred dollars a year. The average unskilled laborer makes thirty cents a day or less than two dollars a week. There is one meal a day—an onion, a piece of bread, a bowl of pulse (lentils) with milk, perhaps a bit of goat cheese. No tea, no coffee, no fats, no sweets, no meat. One hundred dollars a year is not two dollars a week, yet even that small amount is hard to earn by selling baskets to people too poor to buy them. That no doubt is the reason these little children descended on me like locusts. I, an American, was doubtless the most promising market they had seen.

I bought one tiny basket for a few annas, another fruit basket for a bit more, a beautiful wastepaper basket for a rupee, a lovely sewing basket for a rupee, a few fans for an anna or two apiece. My arms were filled and I had spent not fifty cents. The children pressed in, shouting their wares. I was a prisoner, completely surrounded, unable to move. The most diligent, aggressive vendor was a beautiful girl of nine right in front of me. She had a lovely basket with a handle; and she wanted a rupee and a half for it or about thirty cents. She was an earnest pleader. There were tears in her eyes. She pleaded and begged in tones that would wring any heart.

My arms were full. I had no room, let alone any need, for another basket. Balancing my baskets and fans on my left arm. I reached into my right coat pocket and got a handful of change—perhaps fifteen cents in all—which I deposited in the basket that the young girl held imploringly before me. I tried to explain that I could not buy the basket but extended the gratuity as a substitute. I realized at once what offense I had given. This child of nine, dressed in rags and on the edge of starvation, raised her chin, reached into the basket, and with all the pride and graciousness of a lady handed the money back to me. There was only one thing I could do. I bought the basket. She wiped her eyes, smiled, and dashed down the platform, headed for some grass hut that would have at least thirty cents for food that night.

I told this story to Prime Minister Pandit Jawaharlal Nehru. I told him it was one reason I had fallen in love with India.

The people I saw in India—those in the villages as well as those in high office—have both pride and a lively sense of decency and citizenship. They also have a passion for independence. This beautiful child—born in squalor and poverty, uneducated in both grammar and manners—had given me a glimpse of the warm soul of India.

42. India and Asia

THIS SPIRIT of true independence is the dominant note in India's life today. It expresses itself in many different ways.

The villagers, for example, have a passionate desire to own their own land; collectivism—the religion of Communists—has not the slightest hold in agricultural India.

Moreover, Indians do not want their country to be the tail to any kite. British imperialism bled them. They still maintain that British capitalism first mutilated and destroyed Indian industry in order to give the imperial factories a monopoly. They saw the profits made in India under the British (sometimes three hundred per cent a year) exported abroad rather than used internally to improve living conditions, to build schools, and the like. They want to be independent of that kind of capitalism.

Their passion for independence expresses itself in foreign as well as in domestic policies. An Indian official summarized it for me in an after-dinner discussion at Nehru's home:

The world is choosing sides—America or Russia. Both America and Russia are wooing the nations of the world. The search for allies goes on; there is the pressure of loans and trade agreements, diplomacy, the threat of the big Red Army, a Communist-controlled strike, and so on. India feels these pressures. Russia is a neighbor on the north. Communists inveigh against Nehru and bomb the railways that the Indian government recently nationalized. Americans often criticize Nehru for playing Russia's game, for not aligning India with America against the forces of evil that walk the world today.

But India's position, he went on to say, like that of the ancient kingdom of Judah, is not one of neutrality in the insipid sense in which we use the word today. India by instinct, by tradition, by religion is opposed to totalitarianism; but India does not want to become either a staging ground for American military defense against Russia or a Russian base. The teaching of Gandhi on nonviolence is a powerful force in India. That doctrine does not mean a passive submission to terror and aggression, but is based on the principle that the human spirit is more powerful than tanks and aircraft. It proposes nonviolence as an affirmative force. As Nehru put it, the doctrine of nonviolence is "an active and positive instrument for the peaceful solution of international differences."

This is a matter of deep conviction among leaders of Indian thought. And it has intensely practical aspects. India has too many internal problems to solve—problems that will take all her resources and all her energies—to become committed to a military doctrine of force and armed might. She cannot afford to launch into a military program.

People often ask how India's neutrality in the mounting conflict between East and West can be reconciled with her great friendliness toward and sympathy for Communist China.

Nehru's answer to me gave insight which those who have never visited Asia usually lack.

"China is at last tackling her basic economic problems. The Communist government is honest. It is on the side of the common people. It is taking measures against the ownership of land by the few. It is for mass education, public health, rural reconstruction. The Chinese peasant at last has a champion."

Such political projects in Asia are inspiring to Asians, whoever undertakes them. Asia has been under despots for untold centuries. Asians have been exploited beyond the imagination of most Americans. The day of liberation is a notable day in Asian annals whatever the political creed of the liberator. That was the spirit behind Nehru's leadership of the Asian Conference in 1949 that came to the aid of Indonesia.

My discussion with Nehru turned to Russian aggression, its plan to subject the world to communism, and the place of China in the Russian orbit of influence. The answer was both honest and genuinely Asian. In Asia, China is more Asian than Russia is. There is an Asian consciousness that ties India, China, and all the other colored races of that continent close together. Russia, as well as England and the United States, is excluded.

This color consciousness is a major influence in domestic and foreign affairs. The treatment of colored peoples by other nations is an important consideration in the warmth of India's relations to the outside world. It is on the tongues of those who meet a new arrival. Thus the first question at my first press conference in New Delhi was, "Why does America tolerate the lynching of Negroes?" The attitude of the United States toward its colored minorities is a powerful factor in our relations with India. That is why a speech made in New Delhi on August 16, 1949 by Mrs. Edith Sampson, able Negro lawyer from Chicago, created such a profound impression. She made it clear that while she would fight for the rights of her people at home, she would stand for no criticism of America abroad by reason of the color issue. She proudly proclaimed that in the last eighty years the Negro has advanced further in the United States "than any similar group in the entire world." That speech created more good will and understanding in India than any other single act by any American.

One runs into this color consciousness in the villages as well as in the cities. The peasants of India have no conception of the global strategy of Russia, of the appetite of communism that would consume the earth. And so they saw the events in Korea in the summer of 1950 from a limited perspective. And what they saw troubled them. They like America; they also feel a kinship to the Koreans. Their conflict of emotions was best expressed by a man on the station platform at Bareilly, "Won't America please stop killing Koreans?"

This Asian consciousness has many manifestations. Officials in Uttar Pradesh could not imagine that China would ever be the tail to any Russian kite. One of them at a luncheon in Bareilly said, "China is communistic; but her communism will be indigenous to China. It will reflect the character of her people." After a pause he added, "The Chinese people are the most democratic people in the social sense the world over. What they make of communism will be very different from what the Russians make of it."

Later Nehru told me, "Communist China has produced a greater crop of capitalists than any previous Chinese government."

"And what do you mean by that?" I asked.

"The Communists have distributed the land to the peasants. They are making landowners out of every Chinese farmer. And there is no more staunch capitalist than a landowner."

Throughout India there is this attitude of warmth and friendliness to China. Both nations have long known the morass of poverty and squalor that ignorance and a swelling population created and that an oppressive government either countenanced or promoted.

There may turn out to be bitterness in India's cup by reason of her encouragement and support of Communist China. But there is a close affinity between the two peoples that only stern and bloody events can destroy.

India's philosophy and approach to problems are mostly democratic, not totalitarian. India's constitution, adopted November 26, 1949, provides a parliamentary system of government, with a President who appoints the Prime Minister, and with an independent judiciary. It guarantees freedom of conscience and religion, the right of peaceable assembly, immunity from discrimination on the grounds of religion, race, caste, sex, or place of birth, separation of church and state.

India in her original Constitution also guaranteed freedom of speech and expression. But in 1951 she took an antilibertarian step. The Constitution was amended so as drastically to limit the right of free speech, the legislature being granted broad powers to restrict freedom of speech in the interest of the security of the nation, public order, friendly relations with foreign powers, decency or morality.

India in its philosophy and law is tolerant of minorities. But India in its domestic policy has little tolerance for Communists. There are not many Communists in India—in the northern agricultural areas probably not six out of a million people are Communists. There are more in the south and in urban centers but still not sizable numbers in proportion to the population. Thus the All India Trade Union Congress—Communist-dominated since 1942 and the only Communist union in India—in 1949 claimed about 600,000 out of 3,000,000 organized workers in the nation. But all the 600,000 certainly were not Communists; and that membership was heavily drained by other unions during 1950. The Communists, however, are noisy and troublesome and are bent on destroying the liberal program of Nehru and his government. They sabotage the railroads, causing wrecks and derailments, and they have killed hundreds in terroristic activities. High government officials know the long-range program of the Communists.

The government decided it could not risk the stresses and strains incident to violent Communist agitation, so the Parliament early in 1950 enacted the Preventive Detention Act, permitting among other things detention of a person up to one year in order to keep him from acting in any manner prejudicial to the defense of India, to the relations of India with foreign powers, to the security of India, or to the maintenance of public order. Many Communists have been jailed under this law; and the Supreme Court in the famous Gopalan case recently held that system of detention constitutional.

India, in its treatment of Communists, is following the teaching of Gandhi engraved on the walls of the government radio station at New Delhi: "I want the cultures of all lands to be blown about my house as freely as possible. But I refuse to be blown off my feet by any of them."

43. Nehru's Welfare State

NEHRU IS not India any more than Roosevelt was America. But each has represented in a warmhearted way the humanity of his country and made vocal its aspirations.

Nehru is the spiritual heir of Gandhi. Gandhi is a saint, a holy man. His picture occupies the place of honor in every hall, school, home; his writings fill the schoolbooks; his thinking dominates the politics. Rajghat—the place of the cremation—is a sacred place.

I visited it at sunset. At that hour each day Gandhi held a public prayer meeting no matter where he was, reading passages from the Gita, Koran, and Bible and ending in community singing, sometimes with his favorite Christian hymn, "When I Survey the Wondrous Cross." He conducted an evening prayer meeting at Rajghat not far from New Delhi. There in a broad expanse of lawn is a low concrete pyre surrounded by an iron rail—Gandhi's samadh. Here people come by the thousands at dawn and sunset to pray. I took off my shoes and walked up a few steps to lay a wreath. On the samadh were printed Gandhi's last words—"Hai Ram [God be praised]." They were printed in dark blue flowers, freshly picked by some worshiper.

Gandhi has probably even more influence in India today than when he lived. He gave India a unity of purpose. He taught tolerance for all minorities; to him India was a mother who had a full measure of affection for each member of her diverse family. But Gandhi taught more than that. He thought of India in terms of the common man—the poor, the oppressed; those who lived amid squalor in mud huts, as well as those who lived in palaces. His mission was to raise these downtrodden masses, to lead them to a new life. His devotion to that ideal was so great that he even adopted their way of life and their manner of dress so that none in the whole land might feel lowly or inferior.

Nehru's inheritance of the Gandhi tradition is genuine. His aim is to make India's 400,000,000 people equal partners in all the dividends of freedom, to give to India a broad democratic base by raising the standards of the masses.

Nehru is an inspiring leader. When he travels people flock by the thousands to see his train; and they crowd around him in public places trying to touch his garments. This is genuine affection to which Nehru is sensitive. He makes incessant tours of the country, talking, talking, talking. He knows and loves his people; and they know and love him. Nehru—educated at Oxford and western in many attitudes—gives his people the feeling that he belongs to them and that his government is theirs. There is sincerity in this attitude. Nehru is no demagogue; he speaks from the heart. What he seeks to represent is the finest in Indian traditions. He tries to make his people think noble thoughts even amid their squalor and poverty. He sets high aims for them—ideals that challenge the best that is in them. His words of sympathy to the victims of the recent awesome floods in Kashmir are typical: "It is no good allowing ourselves to be overwhelmed by any catastrophe however big. Perhaps all this provides a testing ground for a people and ultimately strengthens them."

A more silent partner in these endeavors is Dr. Rajendra Prasad, first President of the Republic. His quiet dignity carries tremendous prestige in India. Prasad, like Nehru, spent many years in jail during the resistance to the British. Thirty years ago he gave up a lucrative law practice to join Gandhi. He is a solid pillar of strength —honest, humanitarian, liberal, and steadfast—a symbol of the long-suffering, enduring qualities of the Indian peasant. The people seem to realize it; for Prasad commands their respect and loyalty.

In recent years the third main character on the Indian political stage was the late Sardar Vallabhbhai Patel, Minister of State and Home Affairs. Nehru devoted himself primarily to foreign affairs, Patel to domestic matters. He, like Nehru, was an able campaigner, but he did not have the broad base of popular support that Nehru enjoys. Nehru is philosophically a Socialist. The leaning of the intellectual group who today determines India's policy is in that direction. But Patel leaned toward the philosophy of private enterprise; he was the main, political counterweight to socialism in India.

Political leadership in India poses different questions than in America. In Travancore 75 per cent of the people are literate. That is the exception. In the rest of India only 5 per cent can read and write. There is no tradition of the party system; in the two hundred years of British rule there was no universal exercise of the franchise. Thus Indians have had no political experience in the democratic way of life. Democratic standards, however, are written in the new constitution. Every person, male or female, 21 years of age or over, can vote. Nehru and the entire Indian administrative service—educated in British ways of thought—are committed to these standards. But Nehru, to make the democratic system work, has made compromises. He did not think that India was ready for the two-party system. All parties were brought together under the Congress party. This alliance of parties was welded in the fight against the British for independence. It has largely survived in the four years since independence was achieved. The Communists—a negligible group—are not included.

In 1948 the Socialists seceded. They have a small but vigorous party—perhaps the most effective, single one in India. It is under the leadership of Jaiprakash Narayan, once a Communist but now a Gandhian who has democratic principles. He has a strong hold on labor and he is insistent about the abolition of landlordism. He broke with the Congress party to provide democratic opposition to the weight of its conservative elements.

The Congress party under Nehru's leadership has forged a political program for India that is more challenging than any I saw from Beirut to Bangkok. Both New Delhi—the nation's capital —and the capitals of the provinces (the states of the federation) are humming with it. There is great ferment in the country. Every problem is being attacked; new ideas are pouring out; short-range, long-range programs are being devised; the capitals are bristling with energy. There is nothing orthodox or dogmatic about the approach. It is as unorthodox and as dynamic as Roosevelt's first term. This is a crusade and everyone is in it.

The burden of it is being carried by the Indian Administrative Service—the real legacy which England left behind. This service was the "steel structure" of the government even when the British were there. It was the main support for the operation of the British government. When independence was declared on August 15, 1947, and India became a sovereign state, tremendous responsibilities fell upon this Service. It was drawn upon to staff the Indian delegation to the United Nations and every Indian embassy and legation around the globe. That was a heavy drain. Enough experts had to be left to run the internal affairs of the country. These men and women rose to the occasion. The Service doubtless has deteriorated to a degree, but that is a concern of government and is being given attention. Certainly at the top Nehru's government compares favorably with what I have known either here or abroad.

First among the many acute problems of India is *food.*

The pressure of India's population on the land is increasing. There are about 400,000,000 people who are increasing by 3,500,000 a year. It is not uncommon to find 1,000 people living on one square mile of land. Every square foot is cultivated. The search for additional acreage has led to the destruction of most of India's forests as new land was opened to the plow. With the loss of the trees, the climate often changed. Hot winds now blow in from the southwest and burn crops. With the destruction of the trees there have been even more tragic losses. Now there is no fuel. The price of kerosene is too high for the peasants. So they burn cow dung which should be used as a fertilizer. Thus for years the land has become poorer and poorer.

There are 257,000,000 cattle in India. Among these are dairy herds that compare favorably with the best; but most of them are thin and scrawny, their ribs plainly visible. Since the land can support only 60 per cent of the 257,000,000 cattle, there is not enough food to go around; consequently the cows give on the average only a quart of milk a day. Cows are sacred in Hindu religion. They may not be killed; the meat may not be eaten. And so hungry cattle get a bare subsistence on fodder that should go to humans. When I was in Uttar Pradesh a riot broke out in a village because of a rumor that someone had killed a cow. About the same time the government's project to reduce the herds was brought to a halt. A leading politician made a denunciatory speech. "They say that economic ruin will come to India unless our herds of cattle are reduced. I say, let's have economic ruin rather than a sacrifice of our religious principles."

To increase food production, modern methods of agriculture

are needed. But many of the holdings of peasants are pulverized and scattered, e.g., the two acres a man owns may be divided into several tiny units and widely separated. The introduction of modern farm machinery is impossible under those circumstances.

The greatest ravager of soil and food is the flood. Most areas of India have plenty of rain—one, over four hundred inches a year. But the rain is seasonal, coming mostly in the monsoon period and running off quickly. The run-offs carry soil and crops with them; then a people who already are near a subsistence level drop to starvation rations. As President Prasad told me, the most important single measure for increasing the food supply is "to train the rivers." Flood control and irrigation projects rank high in priority—next to care for the nine million refugees from Pakistan.

Here are a few of the important steps which Nehru's government has taken on the food problem:

1. Food is rationed from surplus areas to deficit areas. About 130 districts (over 112,000,000 people) are on the ration list, receiving regular quotas of basic foods. This includes all the urban population.

2. Many surplus cows are being sequestered in state forests, kept segregated from bulls, and allowed to live their natural span. (Cows, by the way, like the leaves of India's oak trees.)

3. Fuel forests are being planted near villages in sufficient size and numbers to supply wood for cooking and heating. The fast-growing acacia—which will produce fuel in ten years—is widely used. As these forests become available, cow dung will be saved for fertilizing India's old and tired land.

4. India is tackling the tree problem. Each August there is a week devoted to a tree-planting festival—Van Mahotsva. During this week schools, villages, and other organizations are encouraged to plant trees, which can be bought for a few annas from government nurseries. In August, 1950, twenty million trees were planted by individuals. For the first time in centuries Indians are becoming "tree conscious."

5. There has been an encouragement of co-operatives and a great development in their use. The problem of small, scattered farm holdings is being solved in some places by a pooling of all village land, which is then managed by co-operative methods. Each farmer's share of the crop is measured by his proportion of land cultivated.

Some farm machinery is being introduced, but this must proceed slowly, since spare parts and trained mechanics are needed for its repair. I saw 500 tractors in Uttar Pradesh, 175 of which had been immobilized for weeks for lack of parts and mechanics.

6. Ancient jungle lands are being opened up with tractors and bulldozers. Thousands of farmers—mostly refugees from Pakistan—are being settled on them. Many more new lands can become available when irrigation projects are completed.

7. Great flood-control and irrigation dams, with substantial hydro-electric power, are being built. Many had been built by the British, including one hundred dams over one hundred feet high. Larger ones—inspired by TVA and following its pattern—are under way. Four were to be in operation within a year—Bhakra, Damodar, Hirakud, and Tungabhadra. Nine others of smaller proportions are under way. Tremendous ones are in blueprint. There is, for example, the Kosi in northeast India which will overshadow our own Grand Coulee.

The *health problem* in India is staggering. Life expectancy at birth is about twenty-seven years (as compared to over sixty years in the United States). There are no accurate statistics of infant mortality; but it is estimated that close to 75 per cent die before they reach the age of one year. The mortality of women during pregnancy and birth is twenty-three times that in this country. There is one doctor to every 6,300 persons; one nurse to every 43,000; one midwife to every 60,000. The doctors are mostly in the cities. The great population of India—perhaps 90 per cent—is in the 500,000 villages; and these are substantially without medical care except for midwives. The doctors are mostly local herb doctors—not trained in western diagnosis. The midwives are largely untrained; sanitary conditions are lacking.

The health program of India—based on the Bhore report of 1946—is under way. It is under the auspices of a learned, dynamic woman (a Christian), another disciple of Gandhi—Rajkumari Amrit Kaur. It has manifold phases—malaria control, vaccination, increasing the supply of doctors and nurses, midwife clinics, first-aid clinics, education in preventive medicine, protection of water supplies, and so on. It is a long-range program, but it is being managed with a missionary zeal—though like most of India's projects, it is being slowed by lack of money.

Public health programs are certain to cause the population curve to shoot skyward—just as it did in Puerto Rico, where the rate of natural increase jumped from 15.2 in 1910 to 24.9 in 1945.

How can a land already hard-pressed for food support more people?

Nehru is convinced that India is in truth underpopulated.

The answer to the population problem is in part the development of new land and the better utilization of the old. The irrigation and flood-control projects will greatly help. But that will be only a partial answer. *Industrialization* is necessary for the standard of living under which India's new freedom will flourish.

India has vast natural resources. There is a tremendous hydroelectric power potential in the country of which only 1½ per cent has been harnessed. India's developed hydroelectric generating capacity is 615,000 kilowatts as compared with our 17,700,000 kilowatts. India's undeveloped hydroelectric generating capacity exceeds 111 million kilowatts, of which 40 million seems economically feasible. One has only to see the Himalayas to realize that the power they hold surpasses anything we know in America. The dams which to date have been constructed harness only a fraction of it. There is some oil in India, and its iron ore is richer perhaps than any of our deposits. There is a seemingly unlimited coal supply. And there are manganese, titanium, and numerous other metals. There is a steel plant in operation with a 900,000-ton capacity. But it is quite insufficient.

One of Nehru's points of emphasis is scientific research. Scientific inquiry and the use of technology to unlock the secrets of the universe and put them to work for the people are indeed almost a religion with him. He sees science as a revolutionary force, as the instrument of change, as the handmaiden of political freedom and independence. While the struggle for independence went on, the political leaders treated science as Western, as alien, as an agency of imperialism. That was Gandhi's view. But during this same twenty-five year period Indian scientists were running a parallel course—they wanted freedom and opportunity to develop science in India; they were striving to put modern technology to work on India's problems.

In Nehru those two forces have merged—the man of science and the political leader. Nehru's right-hand man and executive in this venture is Dr. S. S. Bhatnagar, a distinguished chemical scientist. He is now promoter and manager of vast research centers. There will be eleven national scientific laboratories established in India by 1952. Those research centers perform the functions of our Regional Research Laboratories, Bureau of Standards and the Mellon Institute. They include all fields of science—physics, chemistry, fuel, glass and ceramics, and the like. The emphasis of Hindu philosophy has been on the search for truth. The mystics and the scientists now have a new partnership. There are opponents of this new trend; but they are in the minority. The tide of science rolls over India.

Capital for new enterprises has been hard to get. Historically capital in India reaped a rich harvest; a 25 per cent or 30 per cent return on investment was not unusual. But with the advent of India's independence capital has been scarce. American business has scouted several projects and turned each down. Much of the local Indian capital is in hiding. Fortunes were made in the black market during the last days of the British. That money, being a refugee from taxes, is timid and reluctant to appear.

There is criticism of the Indian government both by Indian and American capital. The socialist program of the government—specifically its nationalization of the railroads and its announcement that certain other basic industries such as steel would eventually be nationalized—is blamed. But the problem is not so simple as that. India is willing to make an *ad hoc* arrangement with any investment group, agreeing to provide foreign exchange for the conversion of profits into dollars and guaranteeing immunity from nationalization for, say thirty years. India wants some participation with foreign capital; it wants to share in the profits of these new and vast undertakings, though it is content with a minority position. But foreign private capital is shy and timid. It may be necessary for foreign governmental capital to do service for private capital. Certain it is that new capital is basic and essential to India's emancipation from poverty and squalor and to the full realization of her new independence.

Land ownership has been a scourge to India for centuries. Maharajahs owned many square miles and leased land to the peasants, who, as in the Middle East, were no more than serfs. They paid as high as 75 per cent of the crop for rent. Rabindranath Tagore once described them as "eternal tenants in an extortionate world having nothing of their own."

This feudal system was not universal in India, but it was sufficiently prevalent to cast a plague across the land. The rich got richer, and the poor got poorer. There was no sound base on which a democratic society could be built. Talk of social justice to people who have a bare subsistence and no avenue of escape from their squalor is no more than words lost in the mounting fury of a storm. The feudal land system is, indeed, the main leverage of Communist propaganda in the whole reach of country from the Mediterranean to the Pacific.

This advantage was sought to be taken from the Communists in India, where the Congress party made the distribution of land to the peasants one of its main tenets. The execution of that program rests largely with the provinces or states, and is now in various stages. Some states—Bengal for one—have not yet launched it. They give as an excuse in Calcutta the influx of four million refugees from East Pakistan that drained the resources of the province and temporarily postponed any land distribution. It is farthest along in Uttar Pradesh. There the landlord is left with his land provided he cultivates it directly, not through tenants. The rest goes to the tenants. They pay the government the value of the land, as determined by the government, over a period of years. The government pays the landlord over a term. Future acquisitions of land are limited so that hereafter no person may acquire more than fifty acres.

Some Indian courts have enjoined the land distribution programs on the ground that the payments to the landowners were insufficient by constitutional standards. It took a constitutional amendment in 1951 to rid the program of that obstacle.

I talked with landlords who were convinced that evil times have come to India; that the curse of a Socialist philosophy has blighted the nation. But this land program has had an electrifying effect in the villages. At the outset it did more than any other single thing to weld the masses to Nehru's leadership.

How secure that leadership will be depends in large measure on the speed with which the land-distribution program is carried out. In that connection the Communists are causing considerable political trouble. The Communists took more direct action than the Congress party. Though small in number they are well organized; and they move with unity and vigor. India's independence had hardly been proclaimed in 1947 when they undertook land reform in Hyderabad, a province of seventeen million people in south central India. Perhaps Hyderabad was chosen because it represented the worst in the vicious tenancy system in all of India. In hundreds of villages the Communists aroused the peasants, armed them, drove out the landlords and the feudal lords' representatives, and distributed the land to the peasants. The central government moved in and restored order. But the idea of land reform which the Communists dramatically put into practice has become a powerful revolutionary force that will harass any recalcitrant government. The Socialist party these days is clamoring for speedier action.

Another generating force that is beginning to appear in some of the villages of India is the panchayat, a form of local government, ancient in Indian history but not used for some centuries. Nehru's government has revived it. It has a special place in the new constitution. A group of villages—depending on their size—elect a council and a court to handle their local affairs. This is the town hall come to India, democracy at the village level. It has to date been used only in Uttar Pradesh, but its operation there has met the highest expectations of its sponsors. India is being returned to the Indians.

People in the faraway hill country are getting a new sense of citizenship, of belonging to a dynamic movement. As one villager said to me with pride, "Now we can have our own school."

Still another force working toward a feeling of equality in Indian society and a sense of joint adventure is the abolition of the caste system. The constitution outlaws it. Discrimination against "an Untouchable" carries a heavy penalty.

Dr. B. A. Ambedkar, brilliant Minister of Law in the central government, is an "Untouchable." He married a Brahmin and is in all of India a shining example of Gandhi's preachings that all caste distinctions must be abolished.

The intellectual group in India accepts this law in its full spirit. The government is behind it wholeheartedly. But that does not mean that the caste system is abolished. Like racial discrimination in this country, it has deep roots. It still prevails in the villages, though even there it is beginning to break. In one small town I was talking with a young high school student, bright-eyed and alert, on his way home from school with an English book containing

Gandhi's writings under his arm. I pointed to a man on the street (who I later learned was an Untouchable) and asked the boy, "Is that man an Untouchable?"

The boy turned to me, wide-eyed at my inquiry, and said in full sincerity, "There is no such person in all of India anymore."

Thus are Gandhi's teachings and India's law beginning to take hold even in the back country.

These are the main foundations of Nehru's program. It has other and manifold aspects—adequate schools in each of the 500,000 villages; ambitious plans for vocational and professional education; public works; and many other social programs which in India are known in the aggregate as the blueprint for a "welfare state." Some parts of the program are well advanced, others have just started. Some will be shortly realized; others will take perhaps generations to realize. But the program in its totality is real, alive, and dynamic. It has captured the enthusiasm of the masses.

This does not mean that its success is assured. It has its opponents. Some thought that when Purshottamdas Tandon was recently elected president of the Congress party the tide against Nehru's policies had turned. But the Nasik meeting of the Congress in September, 1950, endorsed all of Nehru's policies. There is no complete agreement in the party on how the program will be implemented, and it is possible that elements in the party may succeed in mutilating parts of it. But as long as the philosophy of men such as Nehru, Prasad, and the rising young Socialists dominate Indian politics this program will in the main move forward.

The political alternative to Nehru and the Socialists in India is not communism. It is the reactionary, right-wing party, the Mahasabah, which has as its goal the establishment of a Hindu state. Reactionaries in India, as in other parts of southeast Asia, may produce communism. The masses in that part of the world have decided to throw off the yoke of permanent poverty. Gandhi and Nehru have shown them how to do it in the democratic way. If Nehru's welfare state lives, communism will gain no political victory in India.

44. Jai Hind

I WAS IN Almora during the festival of Nanda Devi. This town is located on a ridge facing snowy sentinels of the Himalayas that mount higher in the sky than any peak on the North American continent. Legend has it that the town was founded there because at that point a king who was chasing a rabbit saw the rabbit turn into a tiger. His seers said that was a good omen; hence the selection of the spot for a village. But the view which the town commands of the Himalayas—the Snows as the natives call them—is reason enough for the choice. The Snows dominate the scene; and while I was there they dominated my thinking. They seem to belong to another firmament—a world where gay colors streak as far as the eye can see across glacial ice and then fickly change.

Indians have for centuries associated the Snows with the other world. They are indeed a place of magic and mystery, wrapped in the mists of superstition and legend. Throughout the ages men on distant ridges or in deep valleys have looked heavenward to the Himalayas in worship. In those high peaks they have found comfort and inspiration. The reverence in which the Snows have been held was summed up by an ancient sage of India, "As the dew is dried up by the morning sun, so are the sins of mankind by the sight of the Himachal."

India's most sacred rivers—the Ganges and the Jumna—rise in the Himalayas. The Snows are also the home of many spirits. One of the highest peaks (25,660 feet) is named for Nanda Devi, a goddess. She is a Blessed Goddess. Her high and remote sanctuary is said to bring a lasting peace, though few have ever reached the top.

Nanda Devi is a goddess of many moods. At Naini Tal, where there is a crater lake nestling under high peaks, she exacts an annual toll. Legend says that someone must drown there each year to appease the goddess. The more superstitious are reluctant to go near the water until a drowning has taken place. In fact, one man recently was urged by a native not to go to the rescue of his wife who was attempting suicide, since rescue would offend the goddess. When I was there many boats were on the lake, for a swimmer had drowned that spring.

In Naini Tal the Nanda Devi festival starts with the sacrifice of a buffalo. The town has an executioner who usually is able to sever the head with one swift stroke. If he fails, the goddess is offended and another buffalo must be sacrificed. And so it goes until one stroke accomplishes the beheading. When I was in Naini Tal, the Nanda Devi festival was just starting. The executioner was sick; a less competent man had to take his place. And so the villagers were searching for a buffalo with a skinny neck—a one-stroke animal for a second-rate executioner.

Everywhere a sacrifice is made to the goddess during this annual festival. In Almora a sheep had been killed. Apart from the sacrifice, there was a service in the temple followed by a procession in which a symbolic representation of the goddess was carried. But apart from these rituals the festival was gay. There was a carnival that moved from village to village—a carnival with a ferris wheel and side shows.

The day I was in Almora there was dancing in the streets. Men and boys with flutes and bagpipes gathered crowds in the courtyard of the temple and on street corners, where they played wild, exotic tunes. Everyone was happy. Thousands filled the town; they were packed in the streets and the bazaars; they sat on roofs in bright-colored clothes waiting for the procession. It was a joyful, milling crowd out on a holiday, such as we find in our county fairs. It, indeed, looked like a county fair. There was an excellent display of local products. Government experimental stations had exhibits, showing new fruits and vegetables. Boshi Sen—a noted Indian scientist who is searching out the secrets of protoplasm—had hybrid corn and new types of potatoes (which would challenge both Idaho and Maine) on display. Vocational schools showed woodwork, needlework, weaving; villagers brought in beautiful hand-woven shawls and cloth. A young Indian veterinarian had a stall showing the scientific way to prevent and treat the dread liver fluke among cattle.

All the work of the district and the skills and inventive genius of the people were on display. There was pride in this offering to the goddess; and everyone reveled in it. It was an enthusiastic community outpouring. It was as if the crowd were saying, "Look what we have done." It was somehow the spirit of a new India—the tireless energy of millions dedicated to a challenging and vast undertaking. Ancient hand skills, new technology, and modern science were combined to make public an interesting progress report. And yet it was all done under the auspices of Nanda Devi, a goddess born of myth and integrated into the Hindu religious system of thought.

When my party returned to Boshi Sen's cottage for luncheon the conversation turned to this combination of science and mysticism and the place of religion in the life of the Hindu.

We started with the problem of food; and someone suggested that if America underwrote India's deficiency in food for a few years it would be the greatest contribution that could be made to the problems of southeast Asia. We went from the subject of food to the curing of the sick. Then we discussed the importance of education—education that would enable people to grow more food, to prevent illness, to face their problems with insight as well as with courage.

Boshi Sen interrupted to say that these were all worthy aims. Feeding the hungry is the least enduring, he said. Curing the sick is more enduring. Education is more desirable than the other two. And then he added, "But the most enduring gift of all is spiritual. It is to help one realize God. That is the highest gift, the gift of eternal duration."

Hinduism is not a fanatic faith; it has a charity that is comprehensive. It acknowledges the validity of the gods of the most superstitious as well as the highest conception of the unity of God. It teaches that God's scheme embraces the whole human race. An Indian song expresses this religious tolerance:

> Into the bosom of one great sea
> Flow streams that come from hills on every side,
> Their names are various as their springs,
> And thus in every land do men bow down
> To one great God, though known by many names.

But Hinduism requires of each man's God requisites of the Supreme Being.

Hinduism sees in each man a divine potential. It is the role of great souls to awaken in common folks this spark of divinity. "They who worship Me with devotion are in Me, and so am I in them," says the Bhagavad Gita. By devotion, discipline, and rectitude in conduct man can himself become like God. It is the spirit, not bread alone, that sustains man. The fulfillment of the spirit is the aim of life. Spiritual realization is self-emancipation, freedom; perfection of every type of activity is an expression of divinity. "Whatsoever is glorious, good, beautiful and mighty, understand that it goes forth from out of a fragment of my splendour."

We talked of these things with Boshi Sen and his wife Gertrude Emerson Sen.

There was a long silence broken only by the pitapat of goats' feet below the garden wall—goats driven by a scraggy Tibetan. Then Boshi Sen spoke up and said with deep emotion, "There is no power on earth that can destroy India. At no time in history has India been without her great spiritual giants; it is from them that she derives her enduring strength."

Later I drove down from the hill country to the Ganges plain in an open car. It was early morning. The Snows disappeared behind an intervening ridge. The excellent asphalt road—built by the British—twisted corkscrew fashion down ravines whose slopes were covered with oak, deodars, and a long-leaf pine called the chir. Below us the Kosi River poured like a cataract through deep gorges. We were nearing a village. As we made a sharp horseshoe turn we came upon a group of school boys—ten to twelve years old—with books under their arms. They were dressed like ragamuffins—barefooted, torn and patched trousers, coarse shirts. As the car passed they shouted at the top of their lungs, "Jai Hind [Glory to India]."

Gandhi's teachings, Nehru's example, the spiritual strength that Boshi Sen spoke of had somehow reached down to the boys of a remote Indian village. In the fleeting second of my contact with them I felt the spirit that is carrying India through valleys of poverty, squalor, and suffering to her tryst with destiny.

PART VII

In Summary

One who loses himself in the villages of Asia for weeks on end returns to America profoundly disturbed. The America he loves is not the America the people of Asia see. The attitudes we express, the words we use, the policies we pursue too often injure rather than help the cause of freedom-loving people. The reason is that we live in one world, the people of Asia in a different world. They do not understand us nor we them. To most Americans Asia is a continent of strange lands and strange people. The attitudes and viewpoints of Arabs, Persians, and Indians often puzzle us. They react in ways that frequently fill us with doubt and alarm. At times they seem to be mere instruments of Russian policy, venting their spleen on us. They seem remote and aloof, even unwilling to understand us. Our doubts and suspicions grow until we wonder if they are not in truth aligned with Russia for our ultimate destruction. Being filled with confusion we lose our power and strength. As the Bhagavad Gita says, "Confusion is not the nature of a leader."

The world is different than we in America have thought. Asia is in revolution. There are rumblings in every village from the Mediterranean to the Pacific. A force is gathering for a mighty effort. We think of that force as communistic. Communists exploit the situation, stirring every discontent and making the pot boil. The revolutions which are brewing are not, however, Communist in origin nor will they end even if Soviet Russia is crushed through war. *The revolutionaries are hungry men who have been exploited from time out of mind. This is the century of their awakening and mobilization.*

What I saw and heard as I traveled this vast territory that lies under the southern rim of Russia reminded me very much of what I had read about other revolutions. The spirit that motivates these people is pretty much the same as the spirit that inspired the French and the American Revolutions. The abuses against which our American forebears protested in 1776 were piled high. They are listed in our Declaration of Independence: dissolution of legislative bodies by the King; corruption of judges; maintenance of a standing army and quartering of troops among the people; imposition of taxes without the consent of the colonies; transporting citizens beyond the seas for trial of offenses committed here. These and other practices of the King brought our people to a boiling point; and we declared ourselves free.

The complaints of the peasants of Asia are just as specific as those in our own Declaration of Independence; and to them they are just as important. The absence of medical care always comes first. The absence of schools is always second. Then comes land reform. These people have a passion for land ownership that we Americans can understand. We expressed it in our homestead laws and in the great westward movement that built a nation out of the wilderness. Next comes the desire to learn how to farm the modern way. The right to vote, the right to elect a representative government, the power to expel and punish corrupt officials—these too are important claims. Finally, the people of this area have a new sense of nationalism. It reflects itself in many ways—the growing tendency in underdeveloped and exploited countries to nationalize their natural resources and keep the profits for themselves; the desire to have local capital a partner with foreign capital in developing the nation; an exultant feeling of independence and resentment against intermeddling by outside powers. Perhaps the best example is Persia.

For centuries Asia has been under the domination of the foreigner. The Arab world has been dominated by the Turks for the last four hundred years; Persia by the Russians and British for the last one hundred fifty; India by the British for three hundred years; the Philippines by Spaniards and by Americans; Indonesia by the Dutch; China by the Boxer powers; and so on. Those were mostly forms of imperialism that exploited the nations and left nothing for the peasants. That day is over and done with. Asia is united in one cause—to be rid of the foreigners' domination. In southeast Asia that unity receives powerful impetus from a race and color consciousness that is a dominant and often overriding factor in basic policy issues.

There are professional agitators who stir this brew of discontent; but the rebellious drive comes from the masses. I have not seen a village between the Mediterranean and the Pacific that was not stirring uneasily.

The faces of these people and their words keep coming back to me. Some of their words sting.

A peasant of India pointing to dead bodies of those who had died of starvation and asking me, "Is America the good nation we were told when it destroys its surplus potatoes and lets people die?"

The peasant at a thrashing floor in Bashan, south of Damascus, shaking a pitchfork as he asked me, "Why should a few men own all the land and make us work for nothing?"

The searching eyes and the imploring voice of an Iraqi villager near Basra who said, "I would be glad to live like a dog if only there was hope for my children."

A peasant in a dusty village in Persia on the road between Tehran and Tabriz presented the complaints of his people with the vigor of a Thomas Paine, "When Russian influence was strong in Persia and the Tudeh party flourished, our rent dropped to one-third of the crop. Now American influence runs Persia and our rents are up to 50 per cent and more."

American foreign policy has never been addressed to the conditions under which these revolutions flourish. Democracy, peace, aggression are important words to us; but to those in the hinterland they are apt to be hollow and meaningless. America's voice when heard in this poverty and disease-ridden belt often sounds coarse and cheap—not because we intend it but because we do not know the world in which we live.

We tell about our high standard of living, how well our workers eat, the fine houses they live in. And it sounds like boasting and bragging.

We finance agrarian projects for the benefit of the landlords instead of requiring, as we do in our domestic projects, that the beneficiaries be the men who work the land.

We send technical experts abroad to help in seed selection, soil conservation, malaria control and the like. But we never raise our voice for reform of the vicious tenancy system of Asia under which increased production inures to the benefit of a few. We seem to forget that health programs unrelated to land distribution projects, minimum wages, maximum hours of work and the like merely increase the number of people among whom the existing poverty must be rationed.

We talk about democracy and justice; and at the same time we support regimes merely because they are anti-Communist—regimes whose object is to keep democracy and justice out of reach of the peasants for all time, so as to protect their own vested interests.

We put billions of dollars behind corrupt and reactionary governments which exempt the rich from income taxes and fasten the hold of an oligarchy tighter and tighter on the nation. At the same time we fail to support to the hilt men who back reforms that would stem the tide of communism.

The matter was best summed up by Musa Bey Alami of Jericho. He came up to Jerusalem to see me; and a small group of us sat under a pepper tree in an ancient and lovely garden talking about this problem. Across the Valley of Judgment to the east was the Mount of Olives—crowned with dark-green conifers and somber in the afternoon sun. Below was Gethsemane where giant olive trees— perhaps the very ones that sheltered Christ in His sorrow—spread their light-green leaves. Across from it were the walls of Jerusalem and the Golden Gate sealed tight against the Day of Judgment. A breeze swept across the mountains of Judea and touched the Old City with a cool breath. Talk turned to the Western powers. The group expressed the view that the United States, Great Britain, and France were following policies that were certain to be destructive of democratic standards and would lead to the seizure of control over the area by the Communists. Musa Bey Alami spoke with intensity of feeling. His words tumbled in a torrent as if they had been pent up too long:

"America talks about individual freedom and preaches it to the Arab people. That is idle talk, for we Arabs well know that in the countries of the Middle East the rights of free press, freedom of assembly, and other individual rights exist to no greater extent than they do in the Soviet satellites of Europe. Those rights are denied to all in the Middle East except supporters of the regimes in power. And yet the Western powers support and control these regimes."

These Arabs discussed how it was that no government in the Middle East would long endure if the weight of the Western powers was against it. Neither these governments nor the people want to join the Soviet axis; it is to the West that they look for leadership and guidance; it is with the West that they want to keep their partnerships in oil, in irrigation, and in industry. The West therefore has leverage which it should use.

Musa Bey Alami made a special plea, "Please tell the people of America not to lecture us about democracy. Don't tell our people that they must choose between democracy and communism. The people of this region are not free to make the choice. They are slaves. They are illiterate. They have no present escape from their misery. There is for them no such thing as liberty."

A young Arab turned to Musa Bey Alami and said: "Say what we think America should do."

"America should help us get rid in a peaceful way of the feudal system that holds us in its grip. America should throw its weight on the side of the honest, liberal elements which can be found in every country. If, for example, America had done that in China —if America had demanded a real liberal program as a condition of financial help—China would not be Communist today."

"Would not that be intervention?" someone asked.

"Call it intervention if you like," said Musa Bey Alami. "But when American influence is used to prop up or to strengthen a corrupt or reactionary political regime, that is also intervention."

I learned on my journeys that what Musa Bey Alami said expressed the views of the young, liberal, idealistic leaders who are to be found in every country across this vast stretch of land.

There are liberal forces in practically all of the Asian countries. At times they are either in a minority position in the cabinet or outside the government completely. But each of these nations has men who have the dream of a new freedom for their people, who have the character and ability to rid the nation of the feudal system that is as old as Asia. In other words, there is both the leadership and the energy within these countries to accomplish the necessary programs of social reconstruction. Yet to date our weight has been with the opposing forces.

Our great weakness has been our negative attitude. We have been anti-Communist. We have been pledged to root it out and expose it for all its ugliness. We have taken up the hunt inside our country for every human being who was, is, or may be a Communist. Yet no matter how feverish our efforts, the red tide of communism seems to spread abroad. We are seized with panic as the waters lap at feeble dikes. So we rush to the support of every group that opposes Soviet communism. That puts us in partnership with the corrupt and reactionary groups whose policies breed the discontent on which Soviet communism feeds and prospers.

The second basic reason for our default is that we have relied more and more on our military to do our thinking and planning for us. Beginning in 1945 with the fall of Japan and continuing until the removal of General Douglas MacArthur by President Truman on April 10, 1951, we entrusted the management of our policy toward Asia largely to the Army. The military, rather than the diplomats, in fact made policy for us. It is no reflection on the military to deplore that fact. The situation in Asia is delicate and complex. It requires astute handling at the political level—the best that we can muster in skill and understanding. As a consequence of our negative attitude and military approach to problems, the tide of Soviet communism has picked up momentum.

Our third grave mistake has been our subservience to British policy in the Middle East. Britain has long treated Persia, as it has other countries in this area, as a colony. We have largely backstopped the British throughout this region. The British oil concession in Persia is a good example. It is a concession obtained years ago by the British in a corrupt and unconscionable way. Millions of pounds were spent in bribing officials. The concession was extremely favorable to the British, extremely unfair to the Persians. We were silent when England during recent years tried to force the concession on rebellious Persian governments. The British are thoroughly hated in the Middle East; and we, by supporting British policy there, have had some of that hate directed to us.

Our fourth major error has been our belief that we could save the world from communism by dollars. We have wasted billions in that way and have little to show for it. Our vast expenditures in Asia have ended up largely in the hands of corrupt people. We have financed the causes of those who want to hold the people in serfdom. In doing so we have alienated the support of the masses. The depreciation of our prestige abroad has about kept pace with the depreciation of the dollar at home.

It is ideas that will win, not dollars. Dollars are secondary. We have planned things pretty much in reverse. Our reports and projects call for vast industrial undertakings—the installation of factories and plants in Asia and the development of its natural resources. We seem bent on trying to remake the East in our own image, to transform it from an agricultural to an industrial economy. That will eventually happen; but the process must be slow. Many other things must be done too. While industrialization should move ahead, it must be done cautiously and on a small, selective scale. There will be tragedy in the other course. For example, Asia has the cheapest labor market in the world. Trade unionism there is in its infancy. Skilled labor will not receive more than ninety cents or a dollar a day. The labor supply is almost unlimited. Factories built in these cheap labor markets, where no real trade unions are known, could easily be the greatest sweatshops in the world. They would tend to drag down the free workers of the world by cheap competition. Resulting tariff barriers would only increase the friction between East and West. The vast industrial projects for Asia which one hears discussed in Washington, D.C., would merely quicken the tempo of exploitation of the masses and hasten the day when the Communists take over.

It is frequently said that even if industrialization cannot be hurried, modernization of farms can be. And so great efforts are made to introduce mechanized farming in Asia. Even that is not so simple as it sounds. The introduction of modern methods of agriculture to Asia has been too fast. It already has become a project wasteful both of American dollars and of the expectation of the peasants.

In August, 1950, I found in Kurdistan (northwest Persia) $500,000 worth of farm machinery owned by one large operator that was idle for lack of spare parts; and even if the spare parts had been available there were no mechanics to do the repair work. No spare parts could be obtained, because there was no foreign exchange to buy them. Near Kermanshah, Persia, I saw dozens of water pumps, used for irrigating sugar beets, that were out of commission because some simple part had worn out. Since no parts were available, the crops were jeopardized. At Bareilly in Uttar Pradesh, India, as previously noted, I saw 500 tractors, 375 of which were laid up for repairs and spare parts. When farm machinery is sold in this part of the world, trade schools for mechanics to service the machines must also be established; and plants to manufacture parts must often be built.

The place to start reform in Asia is with the land. The basic illness there is the vicious tenancy system. All other ills stem from that. No other project will be worthy of American aid unless it is tied to that. Land reform above all else is the starting point for launching the counterrevolution against communism. No program of reform can long succeed unless land reform is first carried through. That is the philosophy of the present Shah of Persia who recently distributed Royal Lands to the peasants in 4,000 villages. As the Shah told me, "The pride of land ownership inculcated and the incentive given to increased production will raise the standard of life of the people and prove a bulwark against any political infiltration."

American dollars can help on a small scale in some phases of the land reform problem. American capital obviously cannot finance the redistribution of the land. That must be done by each country, either on the installment basis as India is doing it, or as Ireland did it. The plight of Ireland's tenants was perhaps as severe as anything one sees in Asia. At least Jonathan Swift over two hundred years ago painted a dismal picture in *A Modest Proposal.* I stopped in Ireland in 1949 to see what had been done, and learned that the Irish had solved the heart of the problem without the use of much cash. Under the Land Act of 1923 the tenant got the land through the agency of a Land Commission and the landlords got Land Bonds (later guaranteed as to principal and interest by the British government). They turned out to be one of the best investments in Ireland, the bonds going to a premium.

There is one clear way in which our dollars can be put to a constructive use in Asia. We would, for example, revolutionize much of the Middle East if we threw our weight behind the right kind of TVA along the Tigris and Euphrates. If we insisted, as a condition of our financial help, that every farm that is watered by the project be owned by the man who works it and that no man own more than, say, thirty acres, there would be the start of a peaceful but powerful revolution in the Middle East. A basis would have been laid for public health projects, modern villages, good schools, and all the other things that raise the standard of living of people. Iraq, which has a population of three and a half million, could on this principle support forty million; Persia, which has sixteen million people, could support one hundred million.

It is ideas and projects such as the TVA that will start Asia on the road to freedom. A TVA that is the instrument for making every farmer a landowner will be remembered throughout all time and identify America with the force that would influence Asia in the democratic way of life.

America is fitted by tradition for directing and guiding revolutions. We won our freedom by revolution and set the example which today inspires the peasants of Asia. We cannot remake the world in our image; but we can help those who are seeking an escape from squalor to find alternatives to communism. We cannot do it by talking democracy and peace. We can do it only by making our foreign policy understandable in terms of the aspirations of these people. Our foreign policy must be specifically related to the land problem. We should be behind those who sincerely have as their motto—"the man who works the land should own it." If that were our announced policy, if that were the word that went out from all our embassies and legations, the masses of Asia would soon be on a basis of understanding with us.

This would not be a new form of imperialism. America would not be dictating policies to governments. But every government would know where the weight of America's influence would be and the kind of projects that would enlist American support. They would know that if American dollars were to be obtained for the financing of any projects, those projects would have to serve the interests of the masses. The implementation of that kind of political program would be relatively easy. The Philippines, already the showcase of Asia, could be transformed into a healthy, prosperous democratic community.

This kind of foreign policy would have far-reaching consequences. It would mean that in every capital of Asia American sympathy and understanding would be behind the liberal, progressive groups, whose mission it is to break the hold of the feudal system. Groups who enjoyed the prestige of that kind of American support would be in a strong political position. Asians do not want any foreign domination—American, British, or Russian. They do not want any form of imperialism. They are passionately opposed to becoming colonies either of the West or of Russia. But by and large they do want friendship and co-operation with the western world. They want the West as a partner in many of their undertakings. They want the help of the West as an ally. They have a fear of any dependency on Soviet Russia, whose imperialistic designs on Asia are more ominous than those of any foreign power in history.

A foreign policy of a positive political character for Asia would have tremendous military value. We cannot possibly defend with our armies the wide perimeter stretching from Japan to Morocco. We have not the men to do it. Anyone who has seen the jungles of Malaya and the swamps of Indo-China knows we could easily lose our armies in them. Soviet Russia's military strategy takes this into account. She does not plan to dissipate her own strength in that way. Behind her military strategy is a program of political action. Her aim is to get native Communists in control of every country. Then these countries will become neutral in a pro-Soviet sense or raise local armies (Korean style) to fight her battles for her. We cannot defeat those tactics by military action, for we are too small and the military theaters are too scattered. We can counter that military strategy only by a program of political action of our own.

An Asian foreign policy of the character I have described will require faith and courage—courage born of reason, not of hysteria, not of fear.

1. It means that we must give up the idea that the world can or ought to be standardized to American specifications. Bullets will not kill communism. The world will for a long time have great numbers of Communists in it. Moreover, the new world that the Asians desire to create and which fits them best is not of the architectural design that we would choose for ourselves. The new world of Asia will be different from ours; it will have a large element of socialism which we would not want for ourselves. We must learn tolerance of new ideas. We must remember that a distinctive characteristic of the universe is diversity. The world will not be remade in the image of the West. All the legions of the empires failed and their failure is today's problem.

2. There are tremendous tensions inside Asia—tensions of religion,

traditions, political ambitions, nationalism. Those tensions will survive even if communism sweeps nation after nation into its orbit. Many of the tensions are in fact created by the perilous propinquity of Russia—by the nearness of Russian armies and planes, by the appetite of the Soviets for power. Soviet expansion does not necessarily mean Soviet supremacy. The Asian imperialism which the Soviets are building can be made the source of Soviet weakness, rather than Soviet strength. Asia needs the West if she is to escape the tyranny of the Soviets and a complete dependency on the Soviet economy. The conflicts between what Asians want and what the Soviets are trying to get from them are so great that statesmanlike management can make Soviet expansion in Asia Russia's greatest menace.

3. America, the nation of surplus food, must find ways and means of sharing her surplus with the world. Gandhi said, "It is the fundamental law of nature, without exception, that nature produces enough for our wants from day to day; and if only everybody took enough for himself and nothing more there would be no pauperism in this world; there would be no man dying of starvation." That idea will not be denied. It presses for acceptance in Asia where millions have died from starvation since World War II ended. We must enter the Asian markets (particularly India) with our food and expend our surplus there, obtaining in return where possible raw materials which we need. But the important thing is to send our surplus food into these deficit areas, expecting primary payment in the good will which we sorely need in that part of the world.

Our aim should be the development of partners for world peace rather than customers for our surplus goods. If we take the contrary course we will deny the American ideal and harm ourselves far more than Soviet propaganda can ever do.

4. The greatest heritage that America has in the East comes from our teachers and missionaries. Through our educational emissaries the people of Asia came to know the warm and understanding heart of America. We have had no more important ambassadors of good will in the Arab world than Dr. Bayard Dodge and Dr. S. B. L. Penrose of American University in Beirut. None did America higher service in Persia than Dr. Samuel M. Jordan, who taught for about forty years in Tehran. The primary political task of Soviet Russia in China after the fall of the Nationalist government

was to liquidate one hundred years of American friendship and good will, built largely through our cultural ties, including our missions.

If we are to save Asia from communism, we must by deed as well as by word show her people our true Christian attitude. We must emulate the teacher and missionary, identify ourselves with the aspirations of the peasants, and help them by kindness and understanding achieve a fuller life. We must go to the East with humility not condescension, mindful of our debt for the great cultures which the East has given us.

5. We Americans have been used to quick, clean-up jobs of critical situations. By temperament we want things accomplished in a hurry and to have a project over and done with. The political program of which I speak is long term; it cannot be done quickly. We need patience to see it through; the wisdom to nurture it in our time and to make another generation the stewards of it.

6. Security for the United States and the other democracies will be found not in the balance of armed might but in the balance of political power. We will be secure only when the bulk of the world is aligned on the democratic front. That is the reason for the tremendous urgency of a *political* rather than a *military* program in Asia.

Such a program to be successful must be geared to the hopes and aspirations of the masses of the people. Dollars and guns cannot build these alliances. Only faith and understanding and ideas that are liberal in their reach will create the conditions under which democratic influence will flourish. Neither wealth nor might will determine the outcome of the struggles in Asia. They will turn on emotional factors too subtle to measure. *Political alliances of an enduring nature will be built not on the power of guns or dollars, but on affection.* The ties that will hold the people of Asia close to each other and close to us will be of that character. We must work at that level, if we want to be partners in the exciting Asian history that is about to be written. We must, in other words, go to the East with warmth and understanding. The rewards will be bitter if we continue to go the other way. It is clear to one who travels the villages of Asia that if we continue to play the role we have played in the last five years, these people will become united in one great crusade—a crusade against America. Nothing would be more needless, nothing more tragic. Yet the anti-American attitude in Asia continues to mount—*for to Asians America is too powerful to cooperate with them and too rich to understand them.*

7. We Americans tend to judge people by their *standard of living* and to consider "backward" all who do not know our conveniences, such as plumbing, refrigerators, window screens, and electricity. Those are false yardsticks. The important criterion is not the rate of progress of a people but the *standard of life* which its leaders espouse and to which they aspire. Yet even then it is easy to judge harshly. Democracy as we know it will take generations to develop in Asia. After all, we ourselves are not yet perfect. Democracy cannot be imposed from without or from above; it comes from within a people as a result of education and experience. We must learn tolerance of crude beginnings and not be harsh in our judgments.

The people of Asia want the good things of life; but they also want freedom and justice. The desire for freedom and justice is indeed the powerful motive force behind the revolutions that sweep Asia. Communism does not offer that *standard of life*. We of the West have it for ourselves and can help Asia attain it. Freedom and justice are indeed our missions in life. If we forget that, we will never receive the verdict for civilization.

Index

Abana River (*see* Barada River)
Abdullah of Trans-Jordan, 240, 251-253
Abol Qasim Samsam, 135
Abou Shanab, 191
Acropolis, 166
Adonis, River of, 236
Afcheh, 88, 89, 92
Afka, 236
Afshar, General, 135
Agha Mohammed, 107
Ahmad Gholi, 114
Ahmad Khan, 100, 101
Ahwaz, 136
Akoura, 178, 181, 183
Al-Hakim, 198-199
Albania, proximity of, to Greece, 7
Ali-Goudarz district of southern Persia, 37
All India Trade Union Congress, 297
Allen, George, 73
Almora, 310, 311
Amar Khan, 58, 59, 73-83, 86, 130
   children of, 74-75
Ambedkar, B. A., 308
American University at Beirut, 167-169, 251, 325
Amir Ahmadi, 106-109
Amir Bahman, 114
Amman, 196, 205, 248, 252, 253
Andimeshk, 124
Anti-Lebanon Mountains, 164, 180, 193, 226, 227, 229
   limestone of, 165
Anti-Zionists, 195
Antioch, 162
Arab civilization, 162

Arab world, Soviet propaganda in, 191-192, 195
Arabia, 216
Arabs and Jews, 253, 266
Ararat, Little, 67
Ararat, Mount, 38, 56, 66-68, 77
Aras River, 33, 37, 38, 68
Araxes River (*see* Aras River)
Ardalan Kurds, 86
Argob, 196
Aristotle, 16
Armenia, 30-37
   history of, 31-32
   and Persia, contrasts of, 33
   Soviet, 32-37, 65
Armenians in Persia, 33-37
Aronson, Jacob, 277
Arslan, May (*see* Djumblatt, May)
Arslan family, 212
Arz-ar-Rubb, 185
Ashdot Yacov, 282
Askar Abad, 70
Athens, 166
   Communist underground in, 8-10
Atrashes, 203, 204
Attica, 7-10
Ayios Epiktetos, Cyprus, 23
Azerbaijan, 30-31, 38-50
   history of, 39
   landlords of, 45-47
   people of, 39-40
   Persian Army in, 43, 45
   Russian, 31
   Russian invasion of, 40-42
   Russian political measures in, 42-50
   winters in, 46, 47

Azm, palace of, gardens in, 193
Azna, 95

Baalbek, 226
Babbila, 234
Babylon, 164
Baghcheh Jough, 67
Baghdad, 161, 162, 164, 223
Bahador, Rustam, 100
Bahai faith, 51
Baharvand Lurs, 100
Bahman Khan, 126, 127, 149
Bakhtiari, 34, 52, 54, 55, 114-129, 136,
    151, 156
  faith of, 122-123
  horses of, 126
  migrations of, 124-125
    stopping of, by Reza Shah, 125,
    126
  needs of, 127-128
Baku, 43, 58
Barada River, 226, 227, 229
Barazi, Muhsin, 194, 195
Barzani, Mulla Mustafa, 59, 60, 65, 66,
    70, 71, 77
Bashan, plains of, 186, 196, 197, 200
Basra, 161, 164, 242
Bazaars in Damascus, 230
Bedouins, 197, 223-227, 254-255
Beersheba, 280, 286
Behbehan, 152
Beirut, 161, 166-169, 207, 226
Beit-ed-Dine, 210, 211
Beit Yitzhak, 283, 284
Ben-Gurion, David, 267
Bhatnagar, S. S., 306
Biranavand Lurs, 100
Bishara, Yacoub, 176-178, 187
Biskinta, 169, 170, 173-175
Boar hunt, 150
Boqaa Valley, 163-164, 188
Boshi Sen, 311-313
Bozorg, Agha, 139
Bsharreh, cedars of, 185, 186
Btekhnay, 210
Bukan, 84-86
Bulgaria, 14
  proximity of, to Greece, 7
Bushire, 135, 136, 144

Caller, Yetta, 281
Cardozo, Justice Benjamin, 200, 267
Carrol, Father, 264, 265

Cascade Mountains, 181
Caspian Sea, 87
Cedars of Lebanon, 185-187
  and Solomon, 183-184, 186
Christ, Jesus, 232-233, 256-258
Clerides, John, 28, 29
Cohn, Herman, 266
Committee of Kurdish Youth (*see*
    Kumela)
Communist Manifesto, 1
Communist tactics, in Azerbaijan, 42
  among Kurds, 56-60
  in Persia, 3-4
Communists, in Cyprus, 23-29
  in Greece, granting of equality to
    women by, 12-13
  political program of, in Middle
    East, 2-5
  (*See also* Soviet propaganda)
Conrad Creek Trail, Washington, 181
Conservation, soil, 181-183
Constantinople, 163
Cooper, Merian C., 124
Crusades, 219-222
Cypriots, political grievances of, 22
Cyprus, 19-29, 166
  British reforms in, 21-22
  fellow travelers in, 28-29
  Mule Pack Transport Regiment of,
    in British Army, 23
  Ottoman law on tenures in, 20-21
  Party Central Committee of, 23
  politics in, 25-26
  Socialist party of, 29
Cyprus Mining Corporation, 23
Cyrus, 51

Dalvand Lurs, 100
Damascus, 37, 161, 164, 191, 193, 194,
    197, 200, 216, 223, 225-228, 234
  bazaars in, 230
  public health and education in, 234-
    235
  St. Paul in, 230-231
Dan, 280
Darashori tribe, 138
  horses of, 145
Darazi, 199
Darius, 51
Dashtistan, 152
Dayan, Col. Moshe, 262-264, 283
Dayan, Ruth, 262, 283, 284
Dead Sea, 233, 280

Death and torture, Asian ways of, 106-107
Debukri Kurds, 84, 85
Demavend, 87, 89
Democrat party of Kurdistan, 58-59
Dimitros, 16-17
Direkvan Lurs, 100
Divan Darreh, 56, 57, 59
Djehanbani, Gen. A. M., 88-91
Djumblatt, Kemal, 207-215, 242
Djumblatt, May, 207, 208, 210, 243
Djumblatt, Nazira, 212, 242-243
Djumblatt family, 207, 212, 213
Dodge, Bayard, 325
Dog River, 163
Doueihy, Saliba, 165
Douglas, Bill, 169, 177, 200, 201, 205, 210, 220, 221, 252, 256
Druzes, 197-212
  history of, 198-200
  Populist movement of, 203-204
  religion of, 199
Dugh, 132

Edessa, 162
Egypt, land in, 188
Ein Karem, 264-266
El Moukhtara, 207, 208, 210-212
Elburz Mountains, 38, 87-91
Emir Bachir Shahab, 211
Engels, Friedrich, 1
Enosis, 22
  Greek Orthodox church vs. Communists on, 22
Enzeli, 118
Epic of Kings, 51
Erosion, 98, 179-184, 190
Euphrates River, 164, 190

Fard, Sol, 174, 178
Faris Usuf Hajj, 169
Farmers Federation in Israel, 273
Farming, methods of, in Middle East, 189-190
Fars, 133, 134
Feili Lurs (*see* Lurs)
Fellow travelers in Cyprus, 28-29
Fereydoom, 114
Fertile Crescent, 253
Firdausi, 51
Foreign policy for Asia, 315-327
Foundations of Leninism, 2
Franks, Sir Oliver, 192

Free French, 161
Freedom, 28
French Foreign Legion, 204

Galilee, Sea of, 220, 282, 283
Gandhi, Mohandas, 218, 295, 298, 299, 305, 309, 325
Ganges River, 291, 310
Gardens of Middle East, 193
Gazelle hunt, 148-149
Gelich, Batman, 87
George VI, Supreme Patriarch Catholicos of Armenian church in Russia, 32-33
Geshur, 196
Ghashghais, 52, 54, 55, 114, 117, 133-159
  agriculture of, 151-152
  culture of, 155-159
  five classes of, 143
  horses of, 145-150
  migrations of, 138, 152-153
  nomads, 138-139
  rebellion of, 133-137
  women of, 155, 158, 159
Ghazanfari, Ali Mohammed, 111, 113
Ghazanfari, Mohammed Hossein, 111
Ghorban, Dr. Sabih, 128
Gibran, Kahlil, 174
Gilbert, Elon, 212, 232
Goats, 179-181
Goren, Ahron, 286
Grady, Henry, 3, 8
Grady, Mrs. Henry, 10
Grammos area of West Macedonia, 10-11
Grass, 124
Greece, 6-18
  coffee shops in, 16
  new, dream of, 11
  Union with (*see* Enosis)
  women of, 12-15, 23
Greek Army, 7-8, 11
Greeks as enthusiastic vacationists, 8
Guerrillas, Greek, 6-8, 11-17
  tactics of, 6
  women, 12-15
Guyum, 152

Habbaniya, 164
Hadeth, 169-171
  cedars of, 185
Hafiz, 51

Haifa, 283
Hamdans, 199
Hamzi el Darwishe, 203, 204
Harsin, 95
Hattin, 220-222
Hayat Davudi tribe, 135
Hazhar, 61
Hedavand Kurds, 91-94
Helena, Queen, 162
Hermon, Mount, 164, 198, 220, 228, 280
Hieman, 61
Himalayas, 310-311, 313
Hinduism, 312-313
Histadrut, 276-279
    Workers Bank of, 278-279
Horses, of Bakhtiari, 126
    of Darashori tribe, 145
    of Ghashghais, 145-150
        shooting contests on, 149-150
    of Persia, 126
Hyderabad, land reform in, 307

Ibex, hunting of, 130-131, 147-148
Ilkhanizadeh, Abdollah, 84-86
Ilkhans, 54, 55, 120, 133, 134, 143
India, 293-313
    and China, 295-297
    color consciousness in, 295-296
    food problem in, 302-304
    health problem in, 304-305
    land ownership in, 306-308
    natural resources of, 305
    neutrality of, 295
    and Pakistan, 292, 309
    passion for independence in, 294
Indian Administrative Service, 301-302
Iran (see Persia)
Iranian-Soviet Cultural Relations Societies, 58
Iraq, 161, 164
    land in, 188
Isfahan, 35, 115, 124, 135, 144, 241, 246
Islam, Brotherhood of, 216-218, 245, 246
Israel, 266, 267, 269-289
    co-operative villages of, 283-284
    economic organizations of, 273-279
    Farmers Federation in, 273

Jahanshah, 114, 135
Jalali Kurds, 70

Jami, 51
Jamil Abou Assali, 204
Javanrudis Kurds, 85
Jebel el Druze, 196, 197, 199, 200, 203, 204, 208
    (See also Druzes)
Jenkins, Gen. Reuben E., 8
Jericho, 233
Jerusalem, 162, 196, 219, 221, 222, 266, 267, 270
    historic spots of, 256-261
Jewish National Fund, 275-276, 278
Jews, and Arabs, 253, 266
    in Palestine, 262-263
    (See also Israel)
Jordan, Samuel M., 325
Jordan Valley, 220, 232
Judea, Mountains of, 270, 280
Jumna River, 310

Kaber Essit, 234
Kadkhodas, 55, 120, 127
Kaftar, 158
Kajar dynasty, 52, 54, 85, 95
Kalantars, 55, 120, 127, 129, 136, 137, 141, 156, 157
Kalar, Mount, 130-132
Kamen, Mount, 11
Kamyaran, 46
Kashgan River, 105, 110, 113
Kaur, Rajkumari Amrit, 304
Kazerun, 135
Kazi, 74, 76
Kefar Giladi, 281, 282
Kefar Monash, 285
Kefar Warburg, 283, 284
Kermanshah, 56, 95, 98, 100, 114
Khadejeh Bibi, 155
Khalil Yusuf, 169
Khan, Genghis, 52
Khans, 55, 79, 97, 120-122, 138, 139, 142, 143, 152, 156
Khayyám, Omar, 51
Khersan, 145
Khorram-shahr, 118
Khorramabad, 95, 96, 99, 101, 103-105, 110, 111, 113
Khosrov, 134
Khoy, 4, 38, 41, 46
Khuzistan, 124, 127, 145
Kibbutz, 274-275, 281-286
Komisarov, Daniel, 43

Koran, 1-2, 62, 63, 80, 82, 135, 216,
218, 239, 248, 249
Kozani on Florina Plain, prison camp
at, 11-15
women in, 12-15
Krai, 204, 205
Kroll, Elizer, 281
Kuhdasht, 110-113
Kuh-i-Dina range of Zagros Moun-
tains, 151
Kumela, 57, 58, 73, 76
Kurdish People's Government, 59
Kurdistan, 46, 56-64, 86, 98, 164
Democrat party of, 58-59
and Treaty of Sèvres, 56
Kurdistan-Soviet Cultural Relations
Society, 58
Kurds, 52, 54, 55, 60-64, 121, 136
adultery among, 80
Ardalan, 86
and Communist tactics, 56-60
dances of, 77-78
Debukri, 84, 85
Hedavand, 91-94
Jalali, 70
Javanrudis, 85
Milani, 70
nationalism of, 70-71
radios of, 75-76
Shakkak, 78-79
and Soviet Russia, 65-66, 70
welcoming ceremony of, 72
Kvutsat Saad, 286, 287
Kyrenia, 25

Land ownership, in India, 306-308
system of, in Middle East, 188-191,
193-194, 203
Landlords, 269-270
of Azerbaijan, 45-47
of Maku, 68-70
Landu, Leah, 284-285
Laqlouq, 169, 171, 175-177
Lar, 112, 113
Lar Valley, 89-92
Larissa on Thessaly Plain, prison
camp at, 15-18
Laristan, 152
Lavrion, lead mines at, 9
Lebanon, 161-189, 195, 197, 198, 207,
218
cedars of (see Cedars of Lebanon)
corruption in, 173

Lebanon—*Continued*
land in, 188, 189
Progressive Socialist party in, 208-
209, 244
Lebanon Mountains, 164, 165, 168, 180,
207, 226
limestone of, 165
Lenin, Nikolai, 30
Limassol, 25
Lipsitz, M. D., 284
Luban, Abu, 273
Luristan, 95, 98, 104, 124
Butcher of (see Amir Ahmadi)
paved highway through, trouble
about, 104-106
Lurs, 52, 54, 55, 95-103, 113, 121, 124,
127, 136
adultery among, 80
Baharvand, 100
Biranavand, 100
Dalvand, 100
Direkvan, 100
Greater (see Bakhtiari)
Mir Baharvand, 100
Papi, 100, 101, 110
poverty of, 97, 98, 100, 102-105
Sagavand, 98-99
Tarhan, 110-113
Tulabi, 96, 100

MacArthur, Douglas, 320
Macedonia, 7, 8, 11
West, 10-11
Macronisos Island, 11
McSoud, Clovis, 30
Mahabad, 57-61, 63, 65, 73, 84
Kurdish Republic at, Russian-spon-
sored, 134
Majid, 114
Majlis, 117, 118
Maku, 63, 66-71, 85
landlords of, 68-70
Maku River, 66
Malayer, 95
Malek Mansour, 133, 136, 137, 144,
147, 149, 150, 159
Mand River, 152
Maragheh, 39
Marx, Karl, 1
Mast, 92, 93
Medes, 39
Medical program at Shiraz, 128

Messoria plain, Cyprus, 20
Middle East, land in, 179
  squalor in, 232-233
Migrations, of Bakhtiari, 124-125
  bribery of Persian Army in, 139-141
  of Ghashghais, 138, 152-153
Milani Kurds, 70
Miner, Mr. and Mrs. Robert G., 8
Mir Baharvand Lurs, 100
Mirdad, 174
Moab, land of, 186, 247-248, 269
Moghan steppe, 45
Mohammed, 216, 260, 261
Mohammed Ali Shah, 117, 118
Mohammed Hossein, 133, 143, 144, 147
Mohammed Mossadegh, 119
Monk's Spring, 175
Morteza Gholi Khan, 114-123, 126, 130, 135
  constitution for Persia saved by, 117-119
Moses, 186
Moslems, 62, 218, 227-229
  vs. Christians, 227-229
  in Russia, 245-246
  Shiah, 52, 96, 156
  women, 227, 237-246
Mosul, 161
Mullah, 79, 97, 121, 156
Mullah Nasr-ed-Din, 91, 154
Murphy, Justice Frank, 267
Musa Bey Alami, 233, 234, 318-319
Musa Bey Nasser, 253
Muzaffar-ed-Din, 117

Naaman, 226
Nadir Shah, 133
Nahalal, 283
Naimy, Mikhail, 174, 175, 178
Naini Tal, 310, 311
Najaf Gholi Khan Samsam-Os-Sal-taneh, 117, 118, 143, 144
Namdan Plain, 147, 148, 150
Nanda Devi, 310-312
Narayan, Jiaprakash, 301
Naroon, 88
Nasser Khan, 133-137, 152
Nathanya, 284
Navaii, 46
Nazareth, 283
Near East Foundation, 234
Neba Leben River, 179, 180, 186

Nehru, Pandit Jawaharlal, 215, 293, 295-297, 299-301, 305, 307, 308
  government program of, 299-309
  on food problem, 303-304
Nelson, Jack, 116
Nicosia, 25-28, 166
Nile River, 190
Nira, 284
Nizami, 51
Noozhian, 101
Nour-Abad, 47, 48, 96

Omoei, Omar Agha, 70
Onim, youth center at, 277
Oregon, Persia, 34, 120, 125-128, 130, 158
Ottoman Empire, 161

Pahlavi, Reza Shah (*see* Reza Shah)
Pakistan, 218
  and India, 292, 309
Palmyra, 226
Papagos, Gen. Alexander, 8
Papi Lurs, 100, 101, 110
Partassides, Costas, 25-26
Parthenon, 166
Pasha Atrash, Sultan, 197
Patel, Sardar Vallabhbhai, 300
Paul of Greece, 8
Peacock Throne, 133
Peloponnesus, 7
Penrose, S. B. L., 167-169, 325
Pericles, 16
Persepolis, 51
Persia, 51-55
  and Armenia, contrasts of, 33
  Communist policy in, 3-4
  contributions of, to Western civili-zation, 130
  elections in, 111-112
  history of, 52-53
  tribes of, 52-55
Persian Army, bribery of, in migra-tions, 139-141
Persian Communist party (*see* Tudeh party)
Persian Gulf Command of American Army, 40, 105
Persians, characteristics of, 53
Pharpar River, 226
Pishevari, Jafar, 43-45, 50, 57, 134
  reform program of, 44-45, 50
Plato, 16

Platres, 20
Plour, 88
Polo, Marco, 95
Porsartib, 99
Poseidon, ancient temple of, 9
Poverty, in Arab world, 188-192
  (*See also* Lurs, poverty of)
Prasad, Rajendra, 300, 303, 309
Preventive Detention Act, 298
Prison camp, at Kozani on Florina
    Plain, 11-15
  at Larissa on Thessaly Plain, 15-18
Problems of Leninism, The, 2
Prodromos, 20
Progressive Socialist party in Leba-
    non, 208-209, 244
Propaganda (*see* Soviet propaganda)
Prophet, The, 174

Qadisha Canyon, 185
Qanat, 115
Qashquais (*see* Ghashghais)
Qavam-os-Saltaneh, 134-136
Qazi Mohammed, 57-64, 73
  grave of, 63-64
  reform program of, 61-63
Qishlaq, 139

Raji Tannus Tannouri, 169-171, 173
Ramadan, 252, 261
Ramataim, 276
Ramiz Abi-Suab, 208
Ramot Hashavim, 283, 284
Ramsar, 104
Ratner, Col. Yochana, 220
Razmara, Ali, 69
  assassination of, 3
Red Cross, 247-250, 254, 255
Refugee camp, at Shaieba, 251
  at Soueida, 201
  at Sukhneh, 247-255, 264
Rehovoth, 270, 271
Reiser, Karl, 248, 249, 251, 254, 255
Religion, of Druzes, 199
  in Middle East, 218, 227-229
Resht, 43, 118
Revivim, 286-287
Reza Shah, 43, 52, 55, 59, 61, 67, 70,
    85, 95, 104-106, 125, 130, 133, 134,
    138, 141, 142, 152, 244
Rezaieh, 39, 41, 58, 75, 78
Rhazes, 162
Rhodes, 166

Richard the Lion Hearted, 222
Richon Le Zion, 283
Rish-safids, 55, 120, 127
Robinson, Rev. William, 200
Roosevelt, Franklin D., 121
Rosenblum, Sonia, 284
Royal Society, 86
Russia, Moslems in, 245-246
Russian Orthodox church and Com-
    munism, 30

Saadi, 51
Safad, 283
Sagavand Lurs, 98-99
St. Stephen's Gate, 256, 260
Saladin, 162, 221-222
Sampson, Edith, 296
Samsam, Morteza Gholi Khan (*see*
    Morteza Gholi Khan)
Sanandaj, 86
Sannine, Mount, 174, 175, 179, 180
Saudi Arabia, 136
Schur, Jacob, 282, 283
Semirum, 143
Sen, Boshi, 311-313
Sen, Gertrude Emerson, 313
Servas, Ploutis, 26
Sèvres, Treaty of, and Kurdistan, 56
Shah Namah, 51
Shahabad, 118
Shahbaz, 102, 113
Shaieba Refugee Camp, 251
Shakkak Kurds, 78-79
Shalamzar, 34, 115-118, 120, 122, 125
Sharifi, Amar Khan (*see* Amar Khan)
Sheikh Meskine, 196
Sheikh Saleem el Hashem, 171
Shiah Moslems, 52, 96, 156
Shiraz, 112, 128, 135, 139, 140, 152,
    154
  medical program at, 128
Siblene, private ownership of land
    in, 212-215
Sidon, 207, 212
Skouridiossa, copper deposit at, 23
Smoira, Moshe, 267
Solat-ud-Dowleh, 133, 134
Solomon, and cedars of Lebanon,
    183-184, 186
  on goats, 180
  Throne of, 89
Soueida, 30, 196, 197, 200, 204, 205
  refugee camp at, 201

Sounion, Attica, 8
South Persia Rifles, 133
Soviet propaganda, in Arab world, 191-192, 195
  in Cyprus, 22-23
  in Jebel el Druze, 200
  in Middle East, 1-2, 4, 30, 33
  radio, 4
Squalor in Middle East, 232-233
Stabler, Wells, 253, 254
Stalin, Joseph, 2, 61, 191
Stavrinides, Demosthenes, 28
Stavrinides, Militza, 27, 28
Stern, William, 284
Stern Gang at Deir Yassin, 265
Sufism, 51
Sukhneh, 247, 248, 251, 266
  education in, 248-249
  refugee camp at, 247-255, 264
  undernourishment and dysentery in, 250
Sultan Pasha el Atrash, 203-205
Sunni creed, 52
Syria, 161, 198
  French rule in, 203, 204, 245
  land in, 188, 189
  and Russia, 194, 195

Tabriz, 39, 42-46, 48-50, 57
  Russian-sponsored government at, 134
  University of, 44
Tagore, Rabindranath, 306
Taky Deen, Said, 197, 200, 202, 203
Tandon, Purshottamdas, 309
Tarhan Lurs, 110-113
Tavakoli, Abdol Hossein, 100
Tehran, 42, 43, 71, 87, 91, 92, 100, 105, 108, 109, 117, 118, 125, 134, 135, 137
  capture of, by Bakhtiaris, 118
Tel Aviv, 270
Thessaly, 7
Thomas, Lowell, Jr., 157
Throne of Solomon, 89
Tigris River, 164, 190
Tito, 7
Torture and death, Asian ways of, 106-107
Transcaucasian Railroad, 39, 46
Trans-Caucasian S. S. Federative Republic, 31
Trans-Jordan, 161, 205, 248

Tripoli, 162, 163, 169
Troodos, 20, 27
Trott, Alan C., 136
Tsaldaris, Constantin, 8, 10
Tsaldaris, Mrs. Constantin, 10
Tudeh party, 3-4, 43, 58, 93, 134-136, 246
Tulabi Lurs, 96, 100

United States Agricultural Mission, 190, 205
Urban II, Pope, 219
Urmia, Lake, 38, 60, 75, 78, 84

Vakili, Mostafa, 68-69
Valley of the Skull (Wadi Jmej), 174
Van Fleet, Gen. James A., 8
Varamin Plain, 91
Venizelos, 16
Vitsi area of West Macedonia, 10-11

Wadi Jmej (Valley of the Skull), 174
Weizmann Institute, 270-271
West, Dave, 178
West, William, 169-172, 180, 238
White Valley, 90-92
William, Father, 254-255
Women, in Cyprus, 23
  Druze, 208, 242-244
  Ghashghai, 155, 158, 159
  of Greece, 12-15, 23
  Kurdish, 61
  Moslem, 227, 237-246
World Peace Congress, Permanent Committee of, Stockholm session of, 32-33

Xenophon, 71
Xerxes, 51

Yarmuk, 216
Yugoslavia, proximity of, to Greece, 7

Zafari, Sanyieh, 234-235
Zagros Mountains, 38, 52, 56, 60, 95, 101, 151, 154
Zayim, Husni, 194, 195, 253
Zia-Ed-Din, Seyid, 100
Ziad Khan, 145, 149
Zindasht, 85
  economic problems of, 81-82
  stay at, 73, 75-83
Zoroaster, 39, 51, 91, 96, 157
Zurayk, Costi K., 168

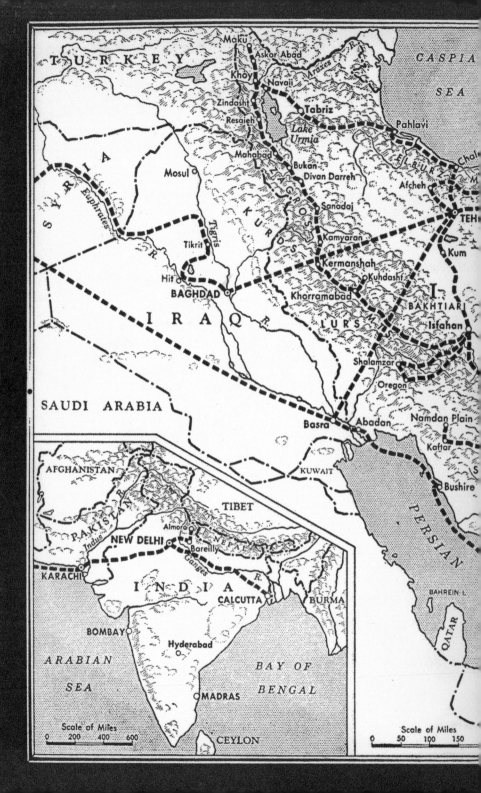